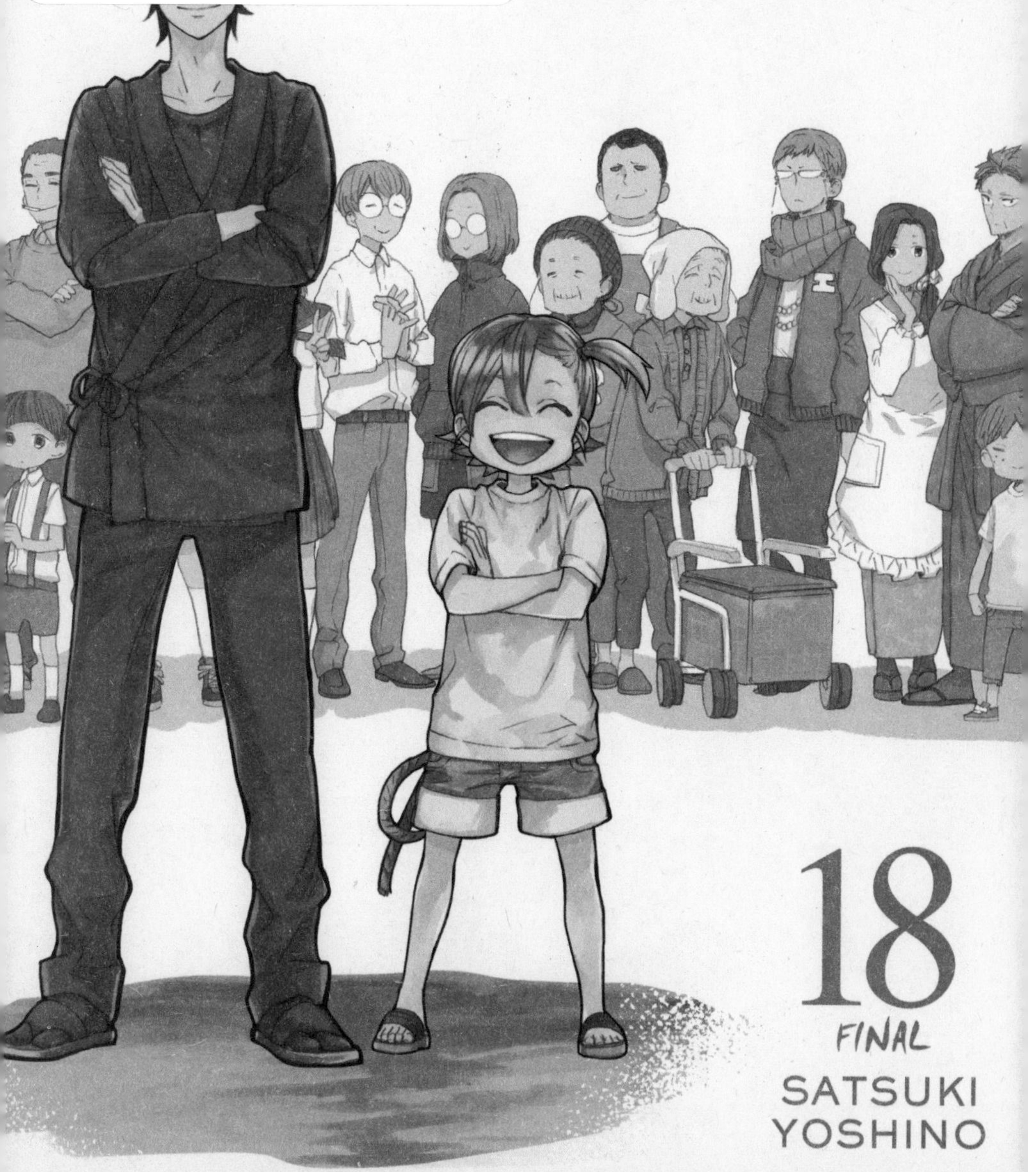

18

FINAL

SATSUKI
YOSHINO

Contents

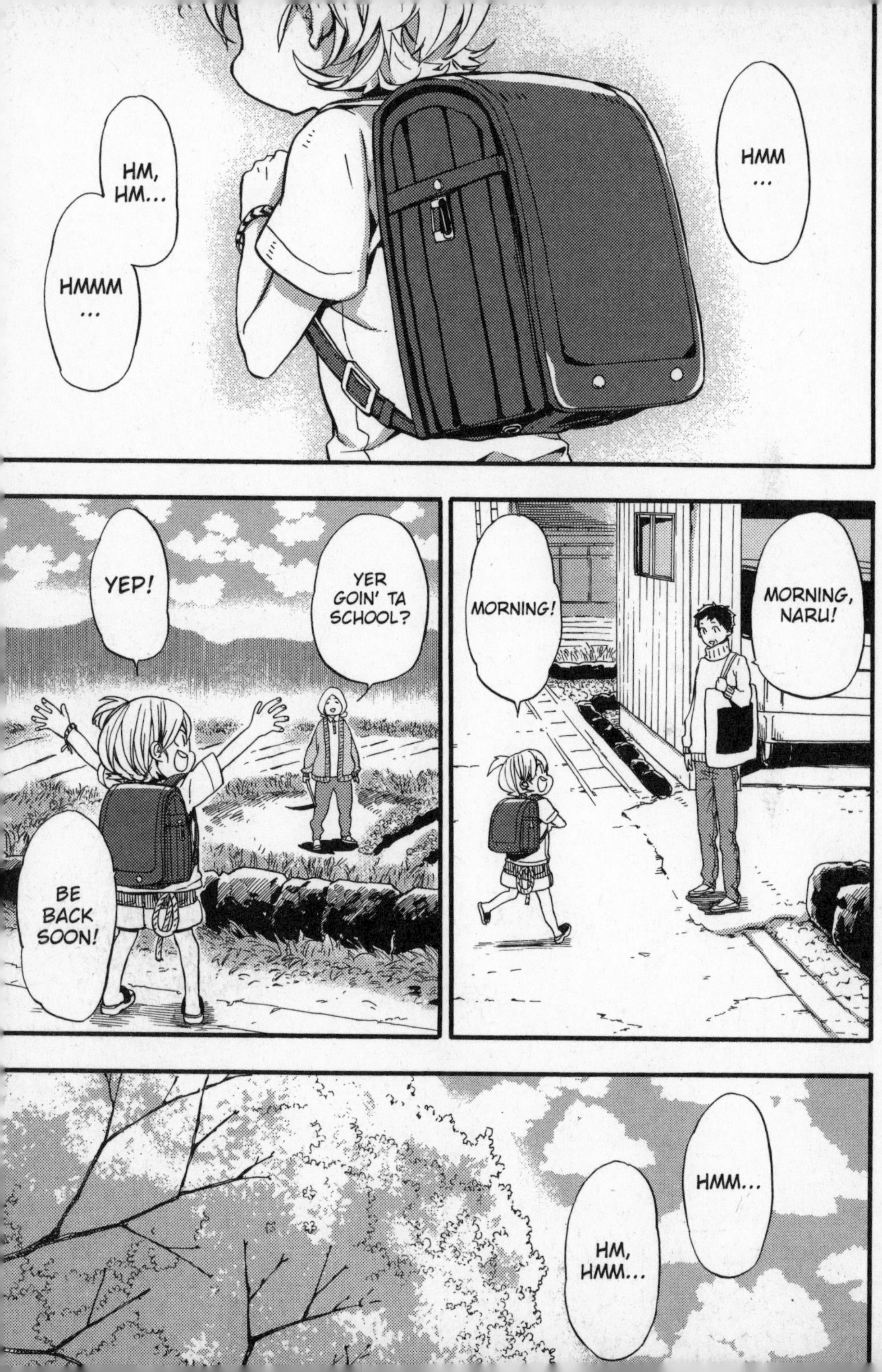
HMM ...
HM, HM...
HMMM ...
MORNING, NARU!
MORNING!
YER GOIN' TA SCHOOL?
YEP!
BE BACK SOON!
HMM...
HM, HMM...

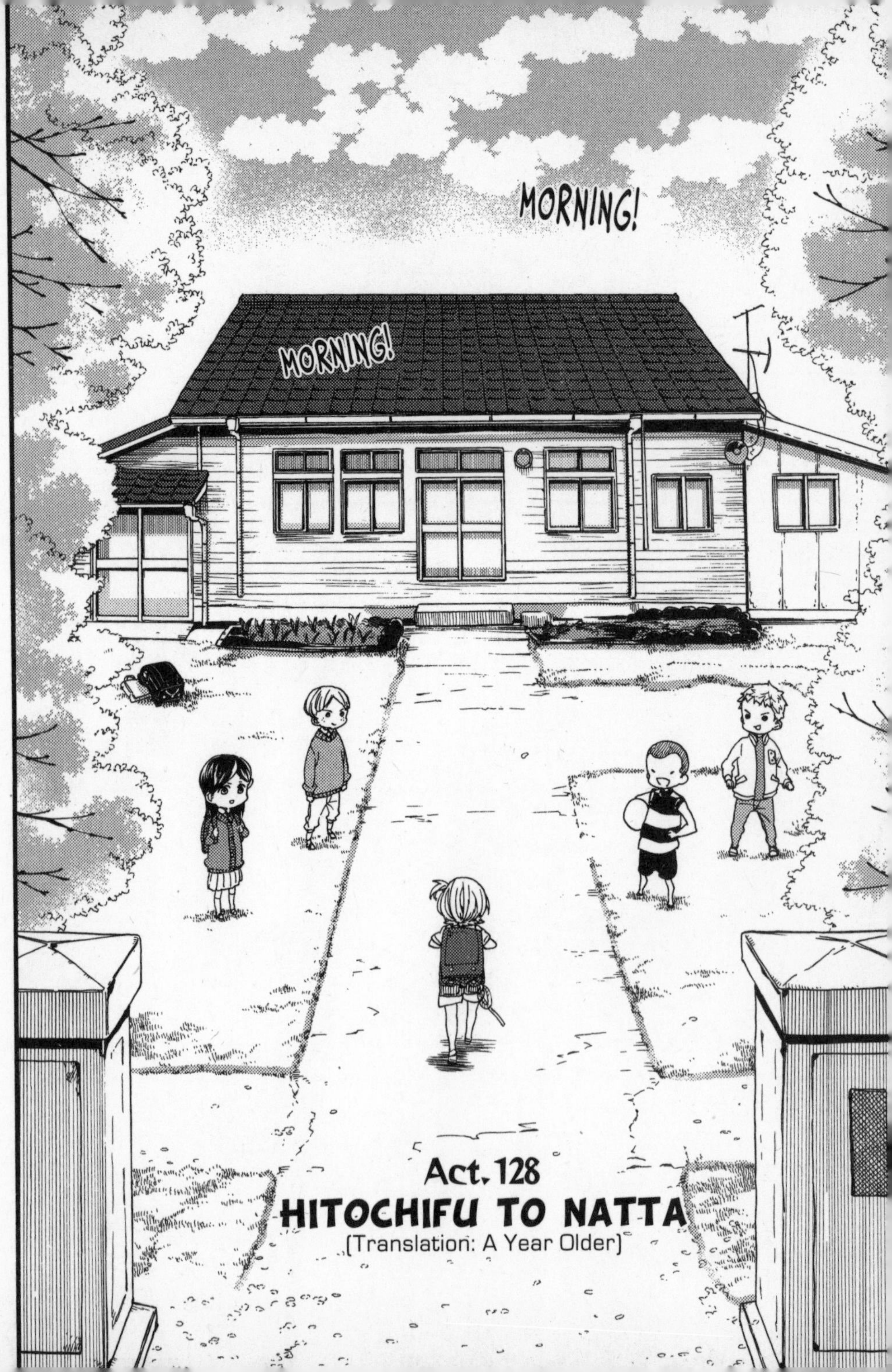
MORNING!
MORNING!
Act. 128
HITOCHIFU TO NATTA
(Translation: A Year Older)

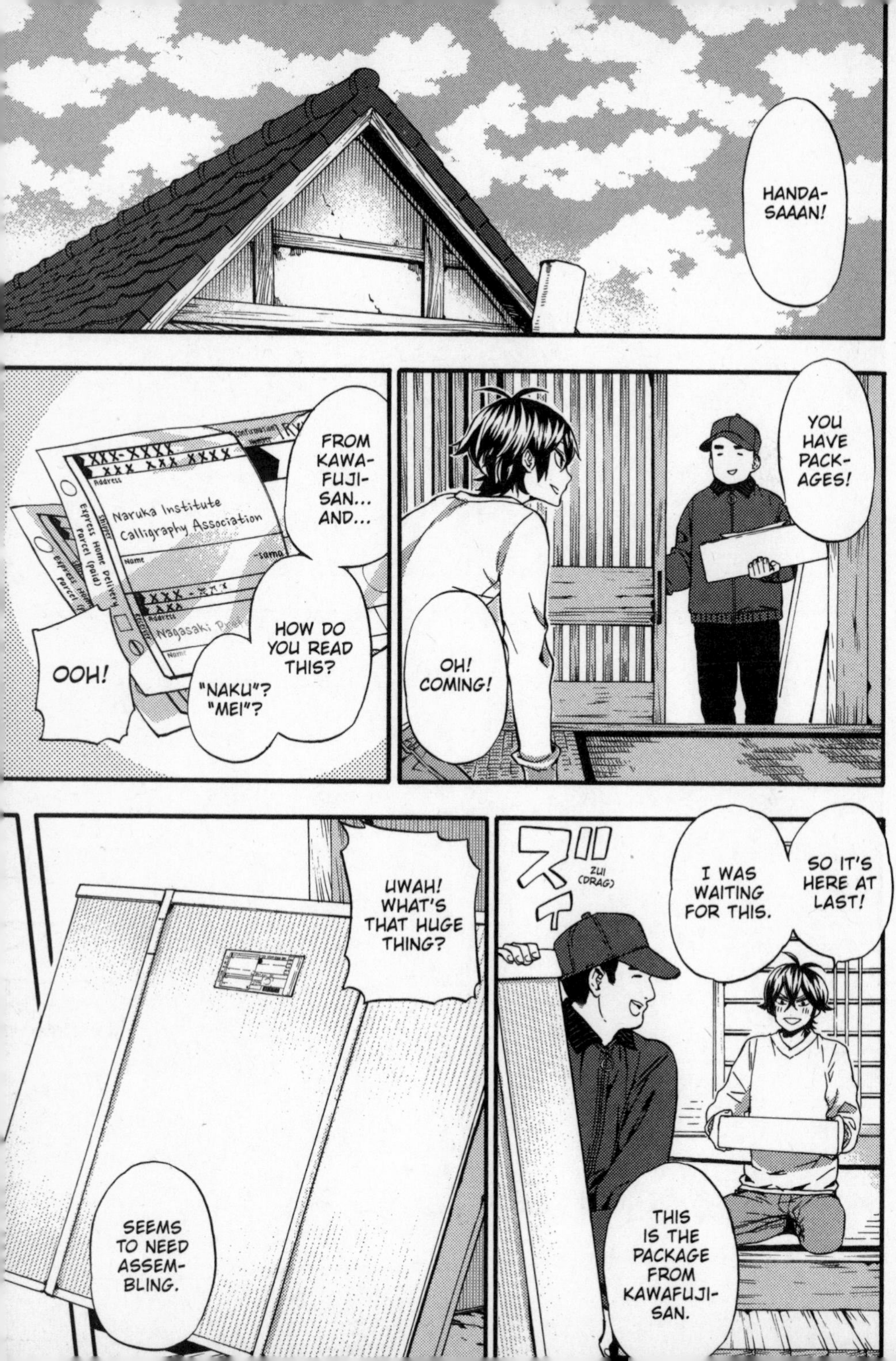
HANDA-SAAAN!
YOU HAVE PACK-AGES!
OH! COMING!
FROM KAWA-FUJI-SAN... AND...
Address
Shipper
Naruka Institute Calligraphy Association
-sama
Name
Express Home Delivery Parcel (paid)
HOW DO YOU READ THIS?
"NAKU"? "MEI"?
OOH!
SO IT'S HERE AT LAST!
I WAS WAITING FOR THIS.
ZUI (DRAG)
THIS IS THE PACKAGE FROM KAWAFUJI-SAN.
UWAH! WHAT'S THAT HUGE THING?
SEEMS TO NEED ASSEM-BLING.

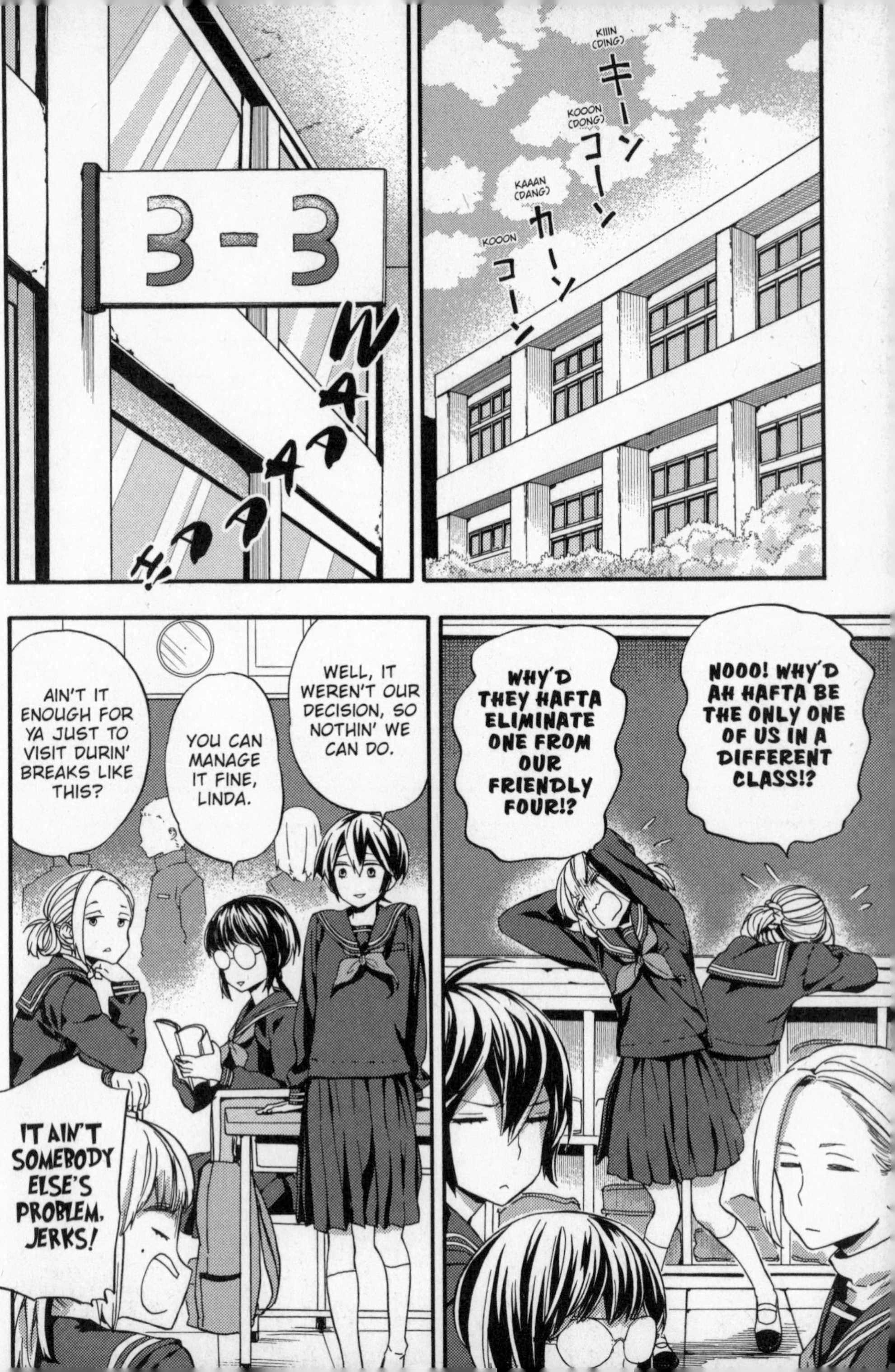
KIIN (DING)
キーン
KOOON (DONG)
コーン
KAAAN (DANG)
カーン
KOOON
コーン
3-3
WAAAAH!
NOOO! WHY'D AH HAFTA BE THE ONLY ONE OF US IN A DIFFERENT CLASS!?
WHY'D THEY HAFTA ELIMINATE ONE FROM OUR FRIENDLY FOUR!?
WELL, IT WEREN'T OUR DECISION, SO NOTHIN' WE CAN DO.
YOU CAN MANAGE IT FINE, LINDA.
AIN'T IT ENOUGH FOR YA JUST TO VISIT DURIN' BREAKS LIKE THIS?
IT AIN'T SOMEBODY ELSE'S PROBLEM. JERKS!

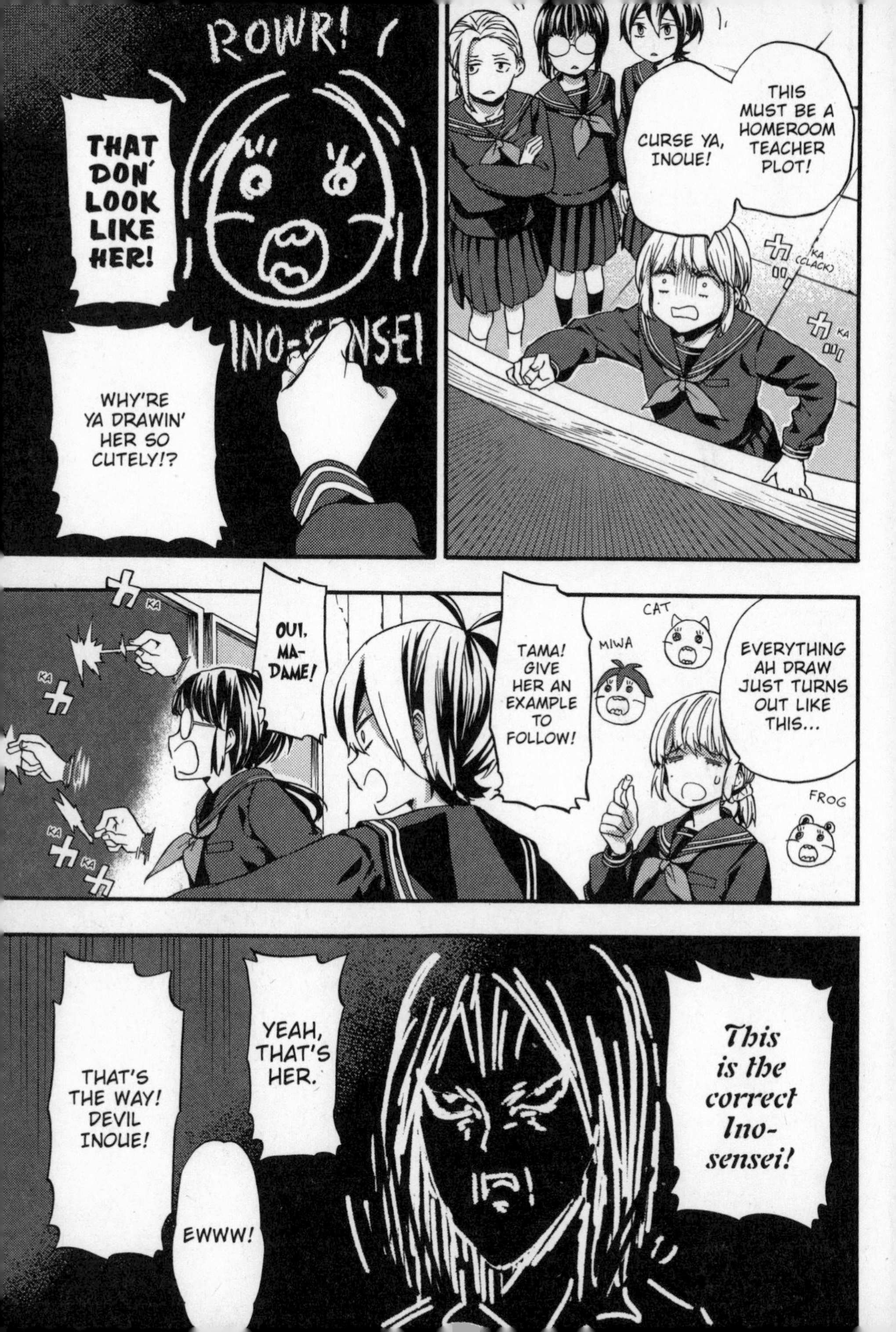
THIS MUST BE A HOMEROOM TEACHER PLOT!
CURSE YA, INOUE!
KA (CLACK)
KA
ROWR!
INO-SENSEI
THAT DON' LOOK LIKE HER!
WHY'RE YA DRAWIN' HER SO CUTELY!?
EVERYTHING AH DRAW JUST TURNS OUT LIKE THIS...
CAT
MIWA
FROG
TAMA! GIVE HER AN EXAMPLE TO FOLLOW!
OUI, MA-DAME!
KA
KA
KA
KA
This is the correct Ino-sensei!
YEAH, THAT'S HER.
THAT'S THE WAY! DEVIL INOUE!
EWWW!

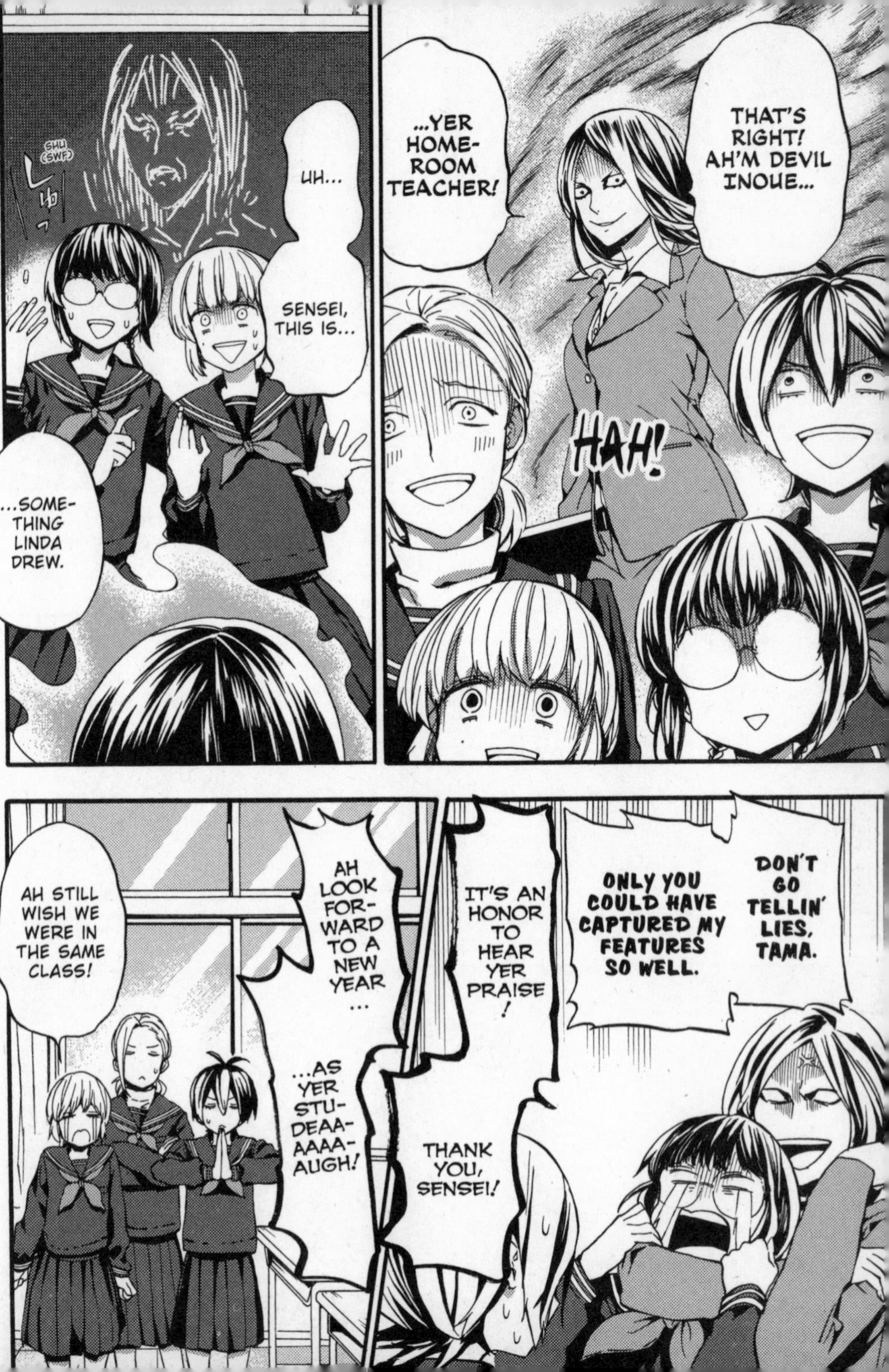
THAT'S RIGHT! AH'M DEVIL INOUE...
...YER HOME-ROOM TEACHER!
HAH!
SHU (SWF)
UH...
SENSEI, THIS IS...
...SOME-THING LINDA DREW.
DON'T GO TELLIN' LIES, TAMA.
ONLY YOU COULD HAVE CAPTURED MY FEATURES SO WELL.
IT'S AN HONOR TO HEAR YER PRAISE!
THANK YOU, SENSEI!
AH LOOK FOR-WARD TO A NEW YEAR...
...AS YER STU-DEAAA-AAAA-AUGH!
AH STILL WISH WE WERE IN THE SAME CLASS!

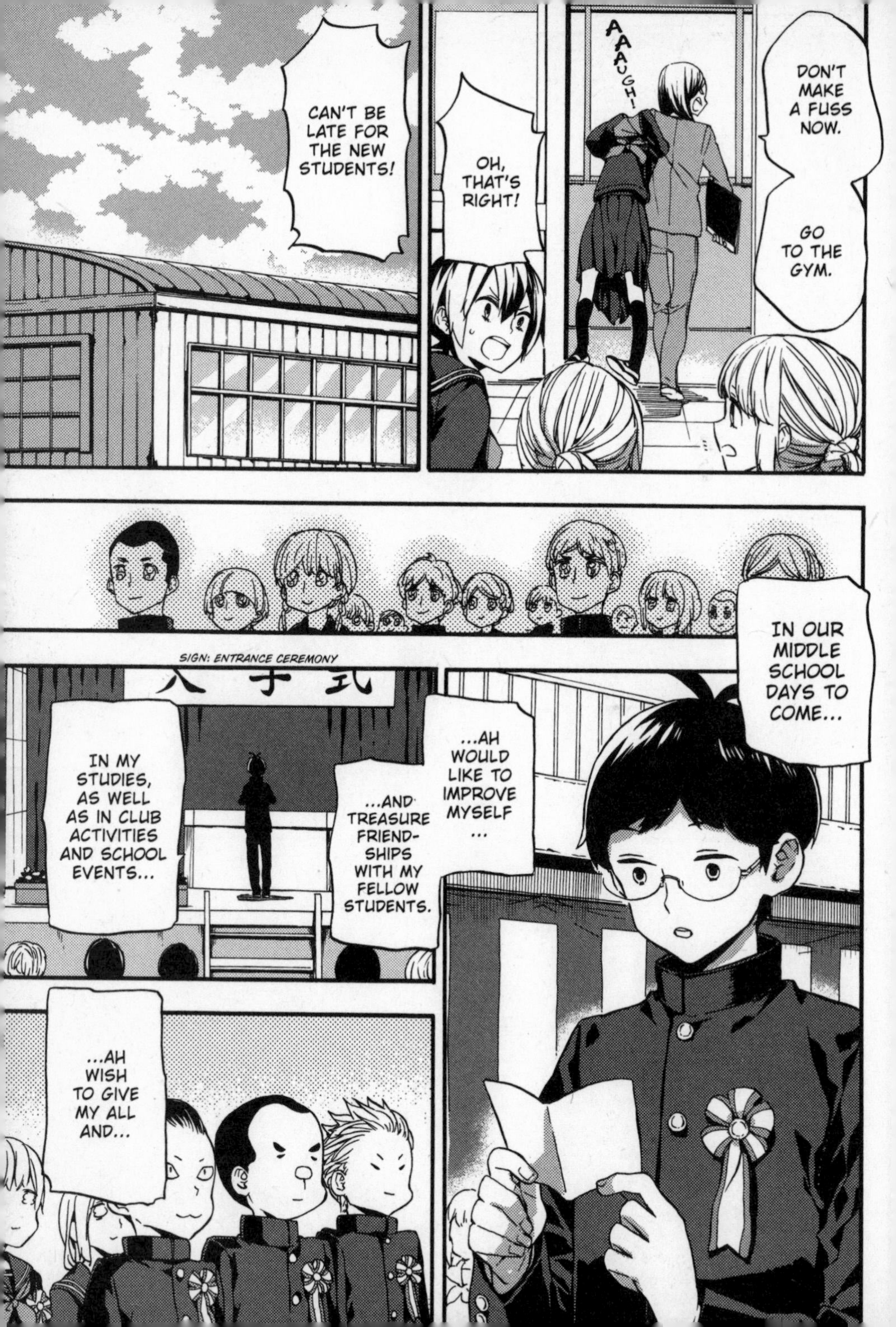
DON'T MAKE A FUSS NOW.
GO TO THE GYM.
AAAUGH!
OH, THAT'S RIGHT!
CAN'T BE LATE FOR THE NEW STUDENTS!
IN OUR MIDDLE SCHOOL DAYS TO COME...
SIGN: ENTRANCE CEREMONY
IN MY STUDIES, AS WELL AS IN CLUB ACTIVITIES AND SCHOOL EVENTS...
...AH WISH TO GIVE MY ALL AND...
...AND TREASURE FRIEND-SHIPS WITH MY FELLOW STUDENTS.
...AH WOULD LIKE TO IMPROVE MYSELF...

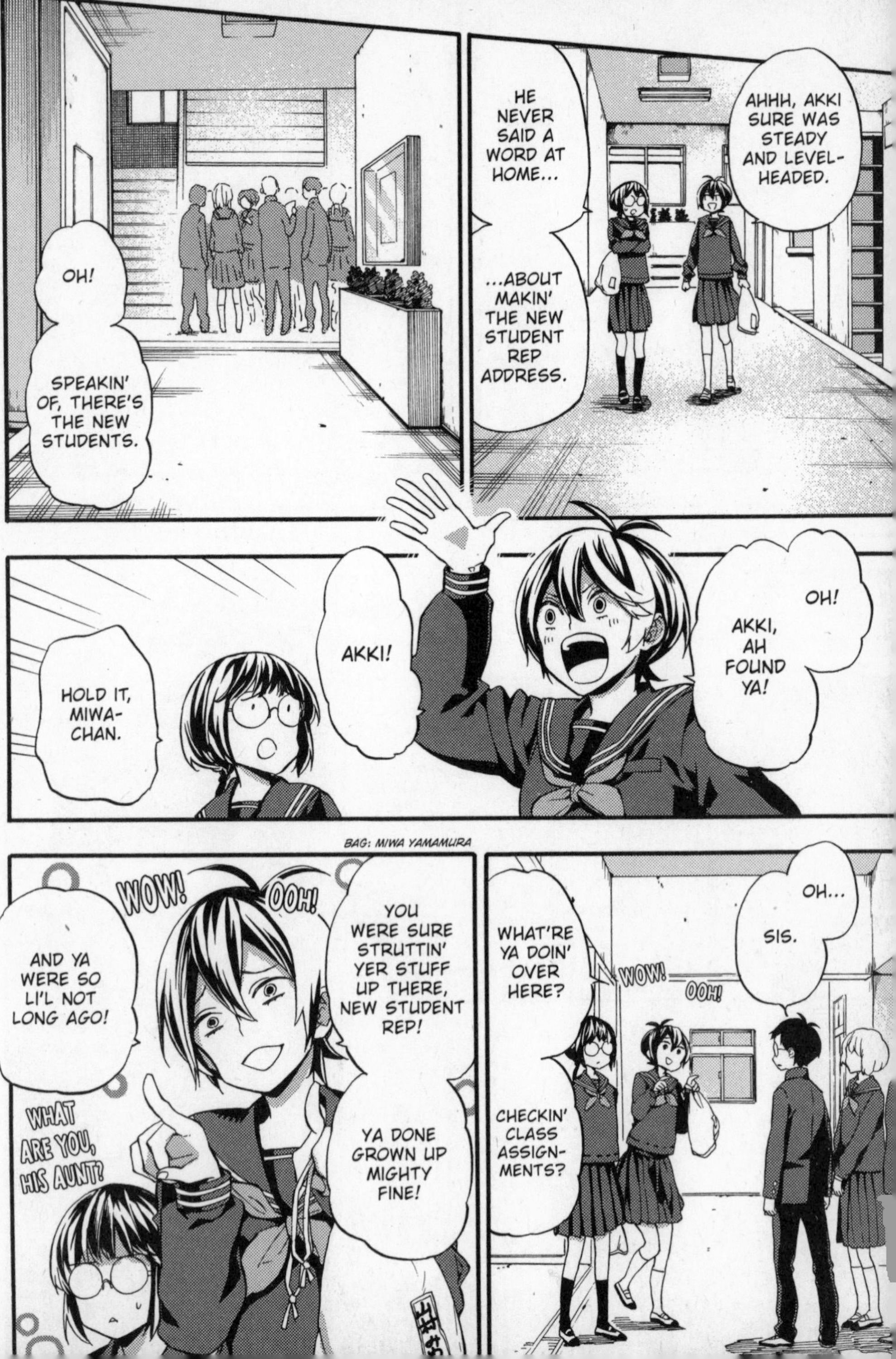
AHHH, AKKI SURE WAS STEADY AND LEVEL-HEADED.
HE NEVER SAID A WORD AT HOME...
...ABOUT MAKIN' THE NEW STUDENT REP ADDRESS.
OH!
SPEAKIN' OF, THERE'S THE NEW STUDENTS.
OH!
AKKI, AH FOUND YA!
AKKI!
HOLD IT, MIWA-CHAN.
BAG: MIWA YAMAMURA
OH...
SIS.
WHAT'RE YA DOIN' OVER HERE?
CHECKIN' CLASS ASSIGNMENTS?
WOW!
OOH!
WOW!
OOH!
YOU WERE SURE STRUTTIN' YER STUFF UP THERE, NEW STUDENT REP!
YA DONE GROWN UP MIGHTY FINE!
AND YA WERE SO LI'L NOT LONG AGO!
WHAT ARE YOU, HIS AUNT?

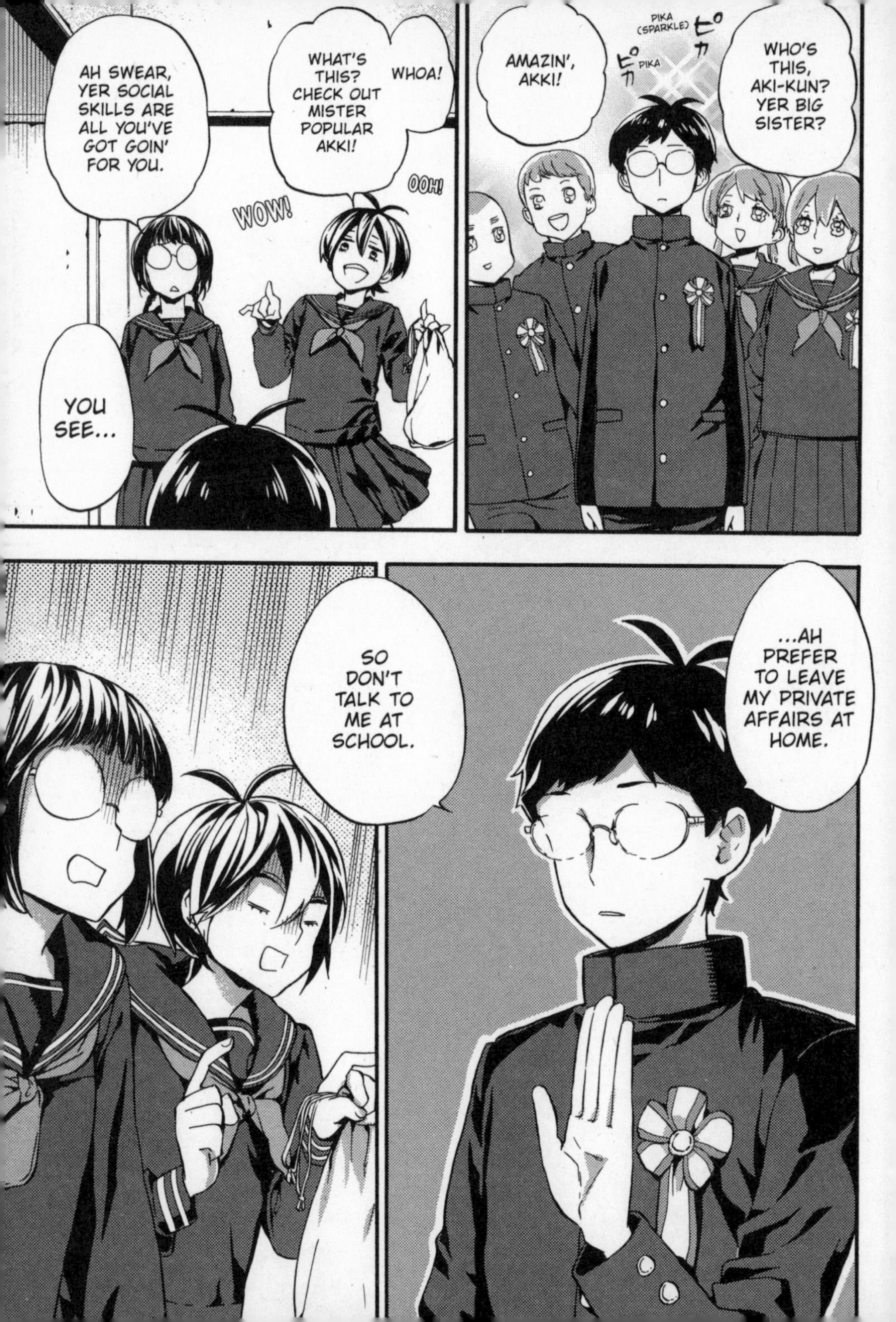
WHO'S THIS, AKI-KUN? YER BIG SISTER?
PIKA (SPARKLE)
PIKA
AMAZIN', AKKI!
WHOA!
WHAT'S THIS? CHECK OUT MISTER POPULAR AKKI!
OOH!
WOW!
AH SWEAR, YER SOCIAL SKILLS ARE ALL YOU'VE GOT GOIN' FOR YOU.
YOU SEE...
...AH PREFER TO LEAVE MY PRIVATE AFFAIRS AT HOME.
SO DON'T TALK TO ME AT SCHOOL.

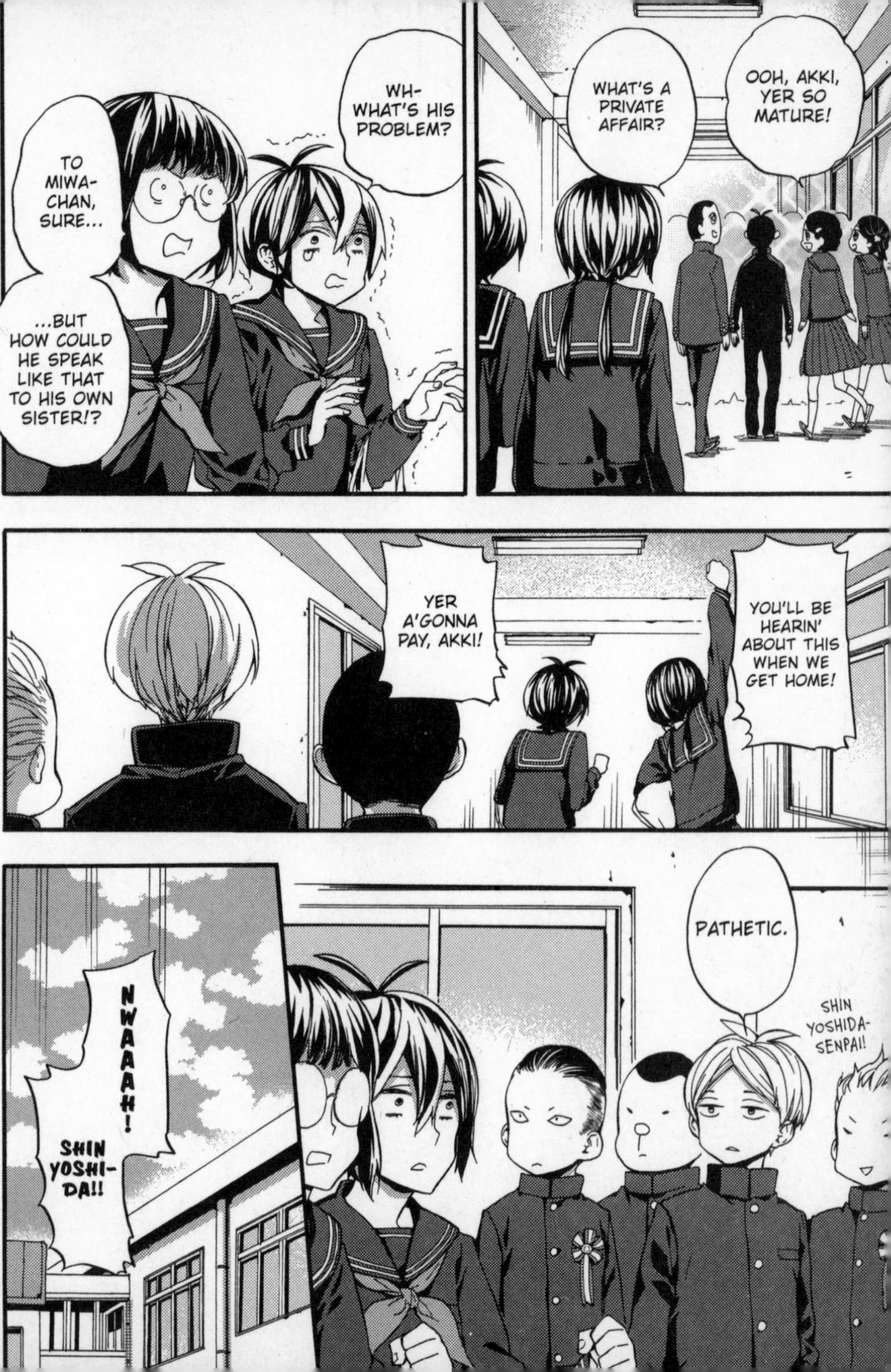
OOH, AKKI, YER SO MATURE!
WHAT'S A PRIVATE AFFAIR?
WH- WHAT'S HIS PROBLEM?
TO MIWA-CHAN, SURE...
...BUT HOW COULD HE SPEAK LIKE THAT TO HIS OWN SISTER!?
YOU'LL BE HEARIN' ABOUT THIS WHEN WE GET HOME!
YER A'GONNA PAY, AKKI!
SHIN YOSHIDA-SENPAI!
PATHETIC.
NWAAAAH!
SHIN YOSHIDA!!

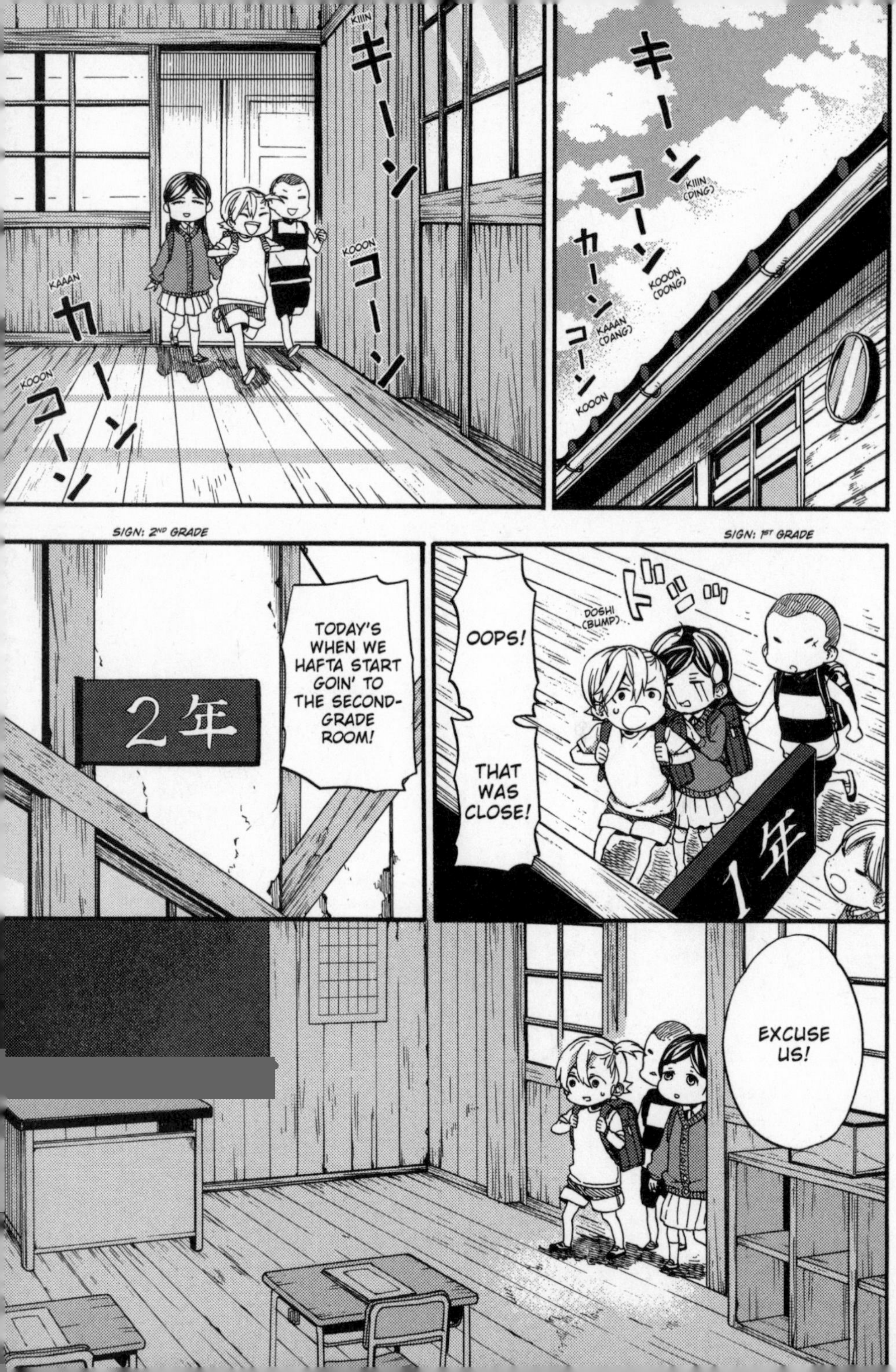
キーン
KIIIN (DING)
コーン
KOOON (DONG)
カーン
KAAAN (DANG)
コーン
KOOON
KIIIN
キーン
KOOON
コーン
KAAAN
カーン
KOOON
コーン
SIGN: 1ST GRADE
ドシッ
DOSHI (BUMP)
OOPS!
THAT WAS CLOSE!
1年
SIGN: 2ND GRADE
2年
TODAY'S WHEN WE HAFTA START GOIN' TO THE SECOND-GRADE ROOM!
EXCUSE US!

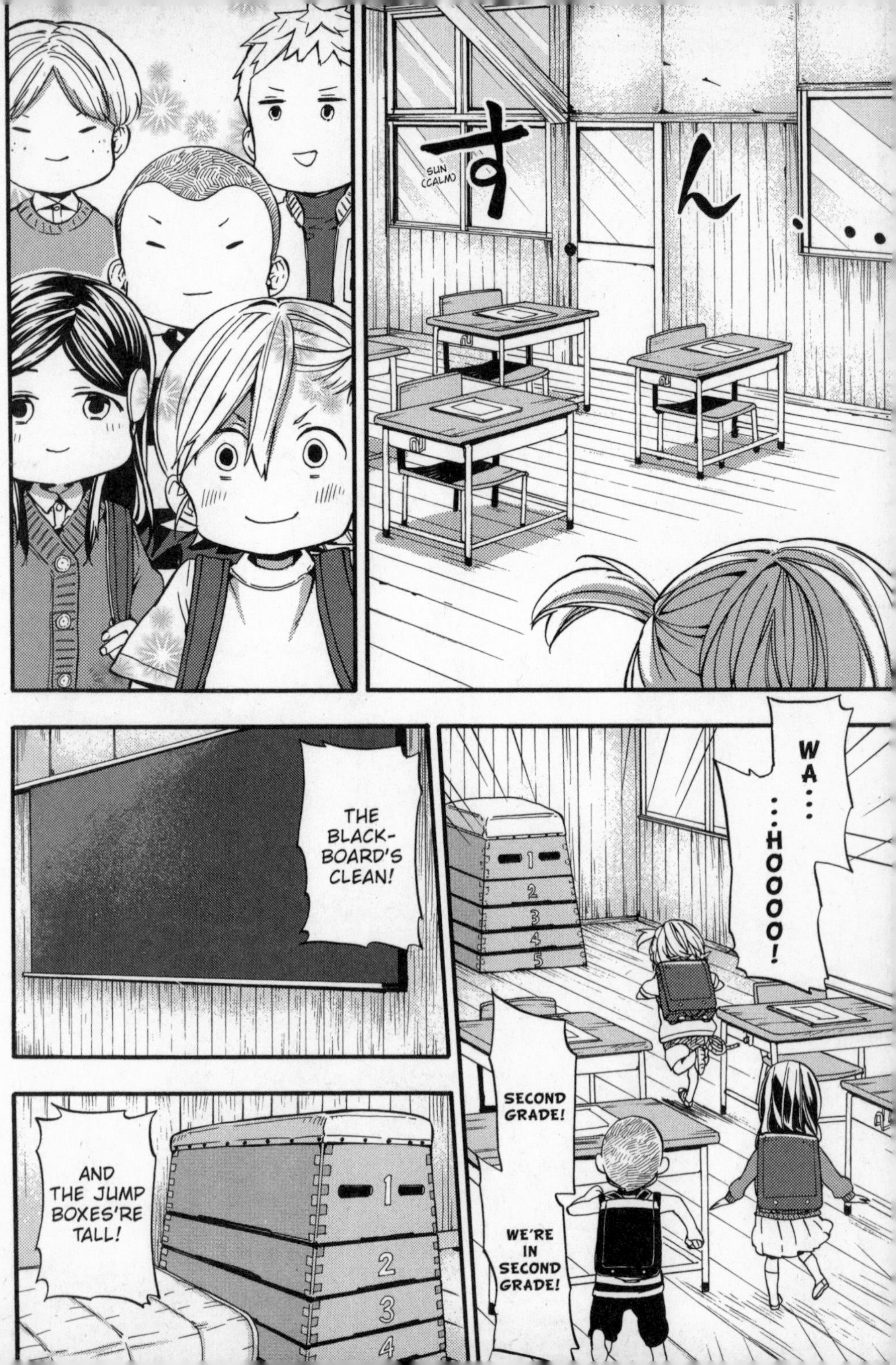
すん……
SUN (CALM)
WA… …HOOOOO!
SECOND GRADE!
WE'RE IN SECOND GRADE!
THE BLACK-BOARD'S CLEAN!
AND THE JUMP BOXES'RE TALL!

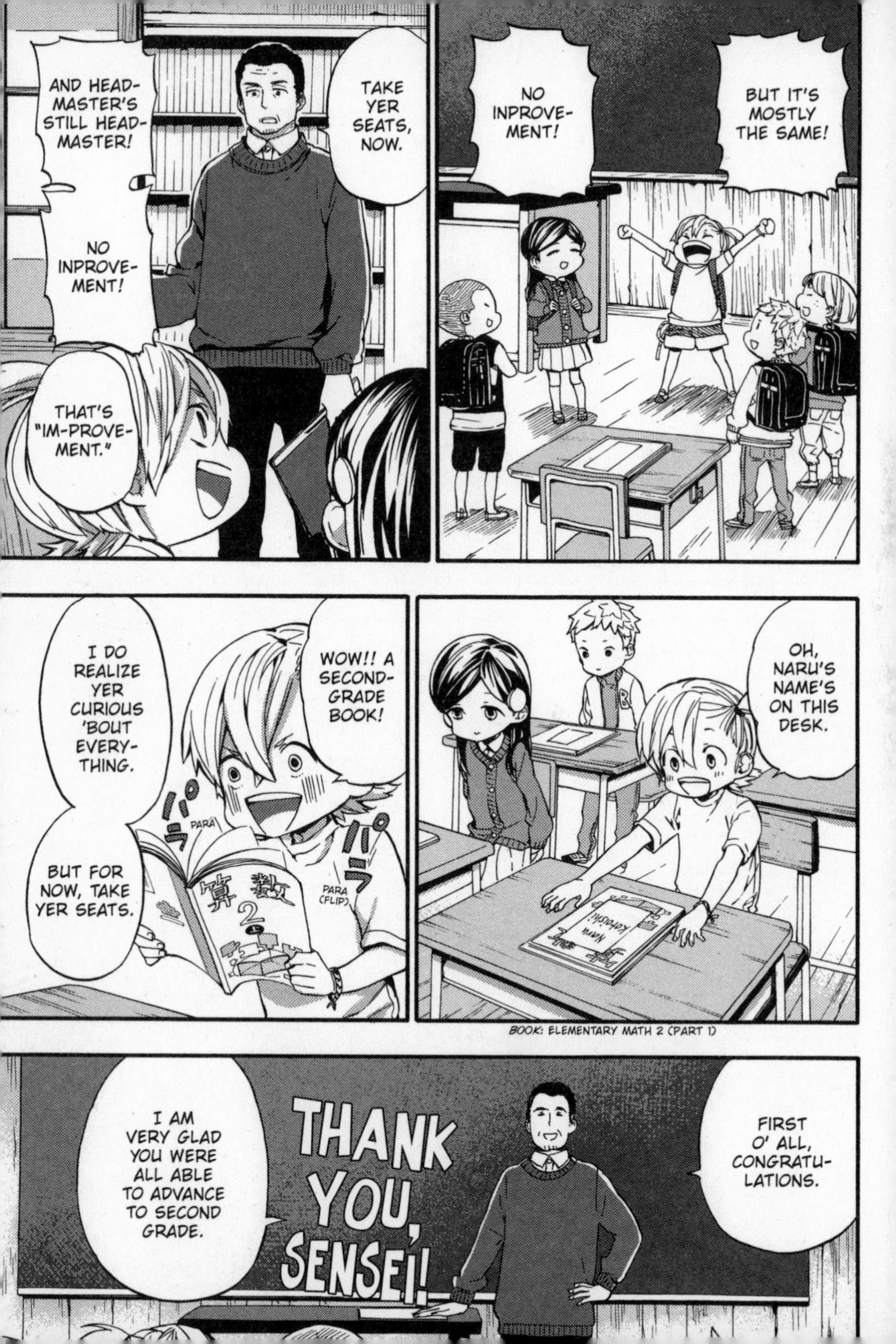
BUT IT'S MOSTLY THE SAME!
NO INPROVEMENT!
TAKE YER SEATS, NOW.
AND HEADMASTER'S STILL HEADMASTER!
NO INPROVEMENT!
THAT'S "IM-PROVEMENT."
OH, NARU'S NAME'S ON THIS DESK.
Naru Kotoishi
WOW!! A SECOND-GRADE BOOK!
I DO REALIZE YER CURIOUS 'BOUT EVERYTHING.
PARA
PARA (FLIP)
算数 2
BUT FOR NOW, TAKE YER SEATS.
BOOK: ELEMENTARY MATH 2 (PART 1)
FIRST O' ALL, CONGRATULATIONS.
THANK YOU, SENSEI!
I AM VERY GLAD YOU WERE ALL ABLE TO ADVANCE TO SECOND GRADE.

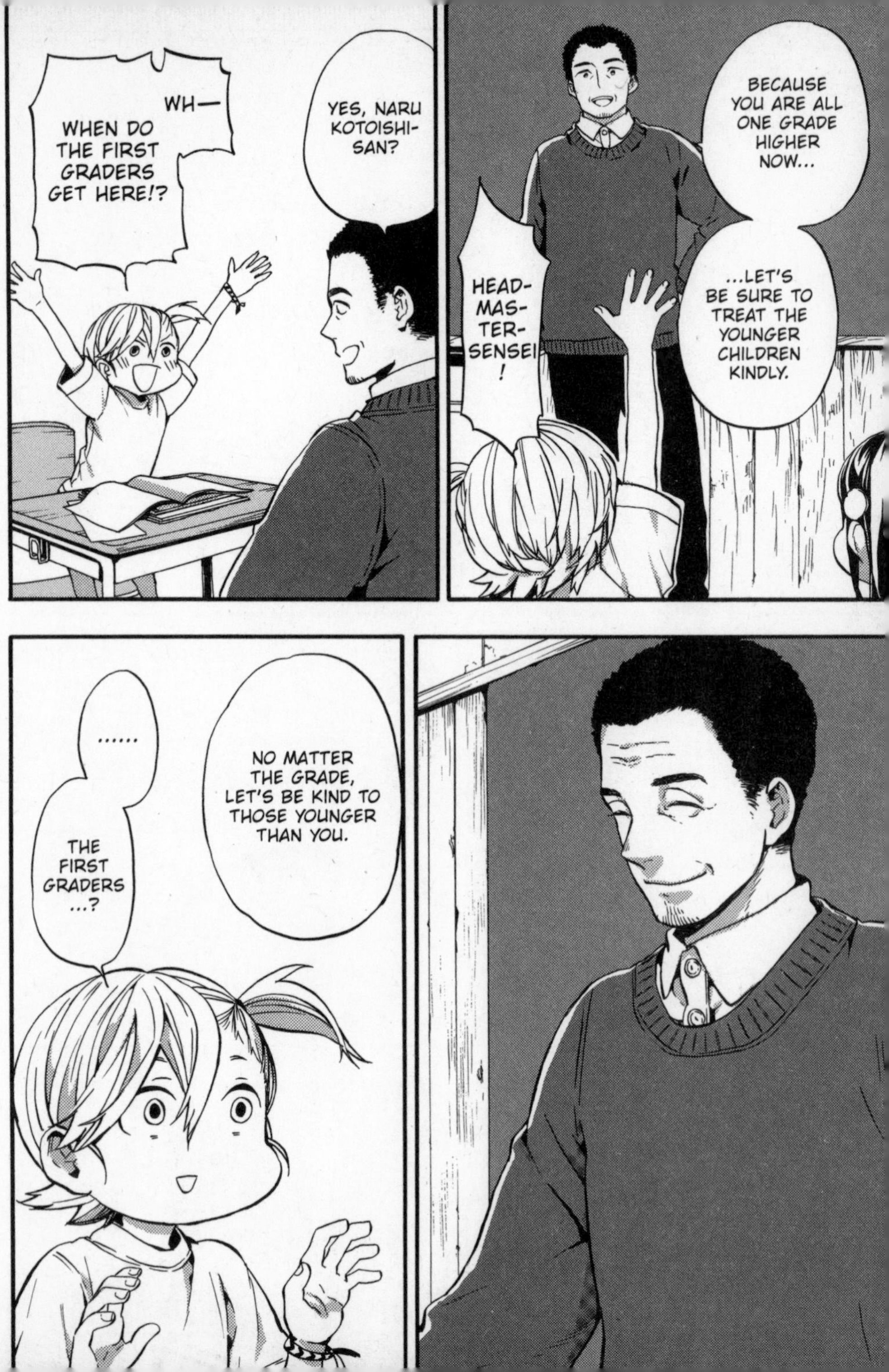
BECAUSE YOU ARE ALL ONE GRADE HIGHER NOW...
...LET'S BE SURE TO TREAT THE YOUNGER CHILDREN KINDLY.
HEAD-MAS-TER-SENSEI!
YES, NARU KOTOISHI-SAN?
WH— WHEN DO THE FIRST GRADERS GET HERE!?
NO MATTER THE GRADE, LET'S BE KIND TO THOSE YOUNGER THAN YOU.
......
THE FIRST GRADERS ...?

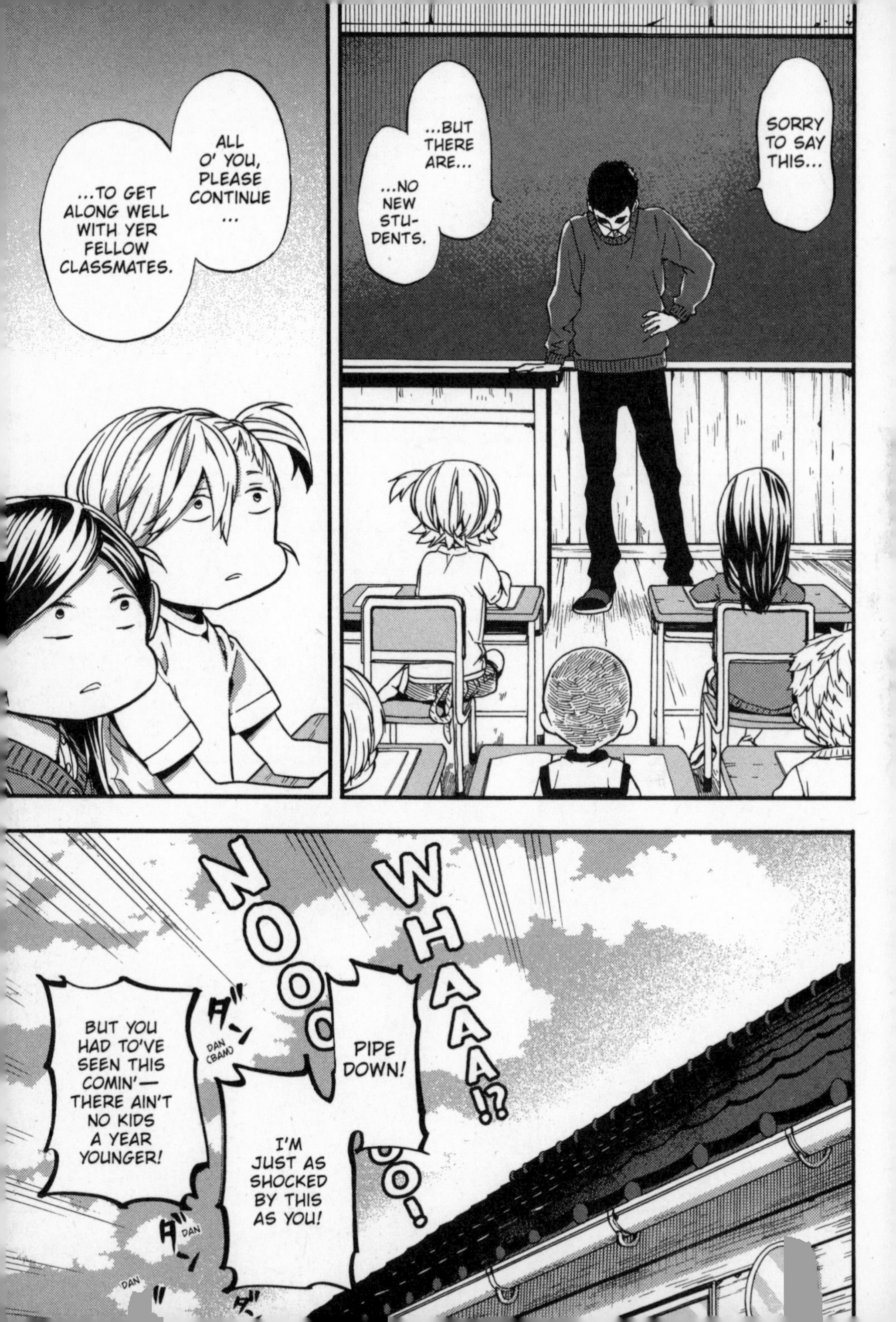
SORRY TO SAY THIS...
...BUT THERE ARE...
...NO NEW STUDENTS.
ALL O' YOU, PLEASE CONTINUE ...
...TO GET ALONG WELL WITH YER FELLOW CLASSMATES.
WHAAAA!?
NOOOOO!
PIPE DOWN!
I'M JUST AS SHOCKED BY THIS AS YOU!
DAN (BAM)
BUT YOU HAD TO'VE SEEN THIS COMIN'— THERE AIN'T NO KIDS A YEAR YOUNGER!
DAN
DAN

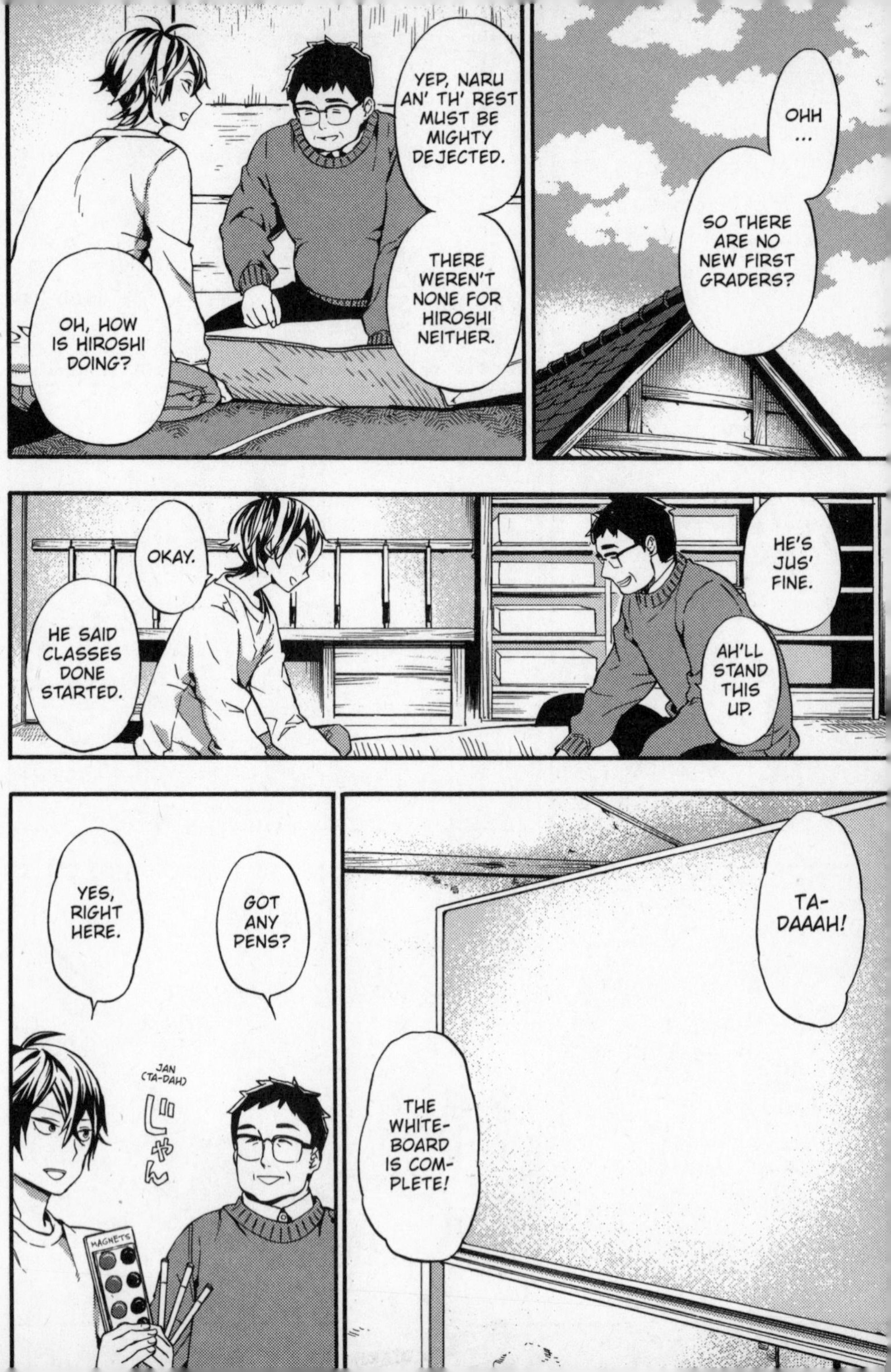
OHH ...
SO THERE ARE NO NEW FIRST GRADERS?
YEP, NARU AN' TH' REST MUST BE MIGHTY DEJECTED.
THERE WEREN'T NONE FOR HIROSHI NEITHER.
OH, HOW IS HIROSHI DOING?
HE'S JUS' FINE.
AH'LL STAND THIS UP.
OKAY.
HE SAID CLASSES DONE STARTED.
TA-DAAAH!
THE WHITE-BOARD IS COM-PLETE!
GOT ANY PENS?
YES, RIGHT HERE.
JAN (TA-DAH)
じゃん
MAGNETS

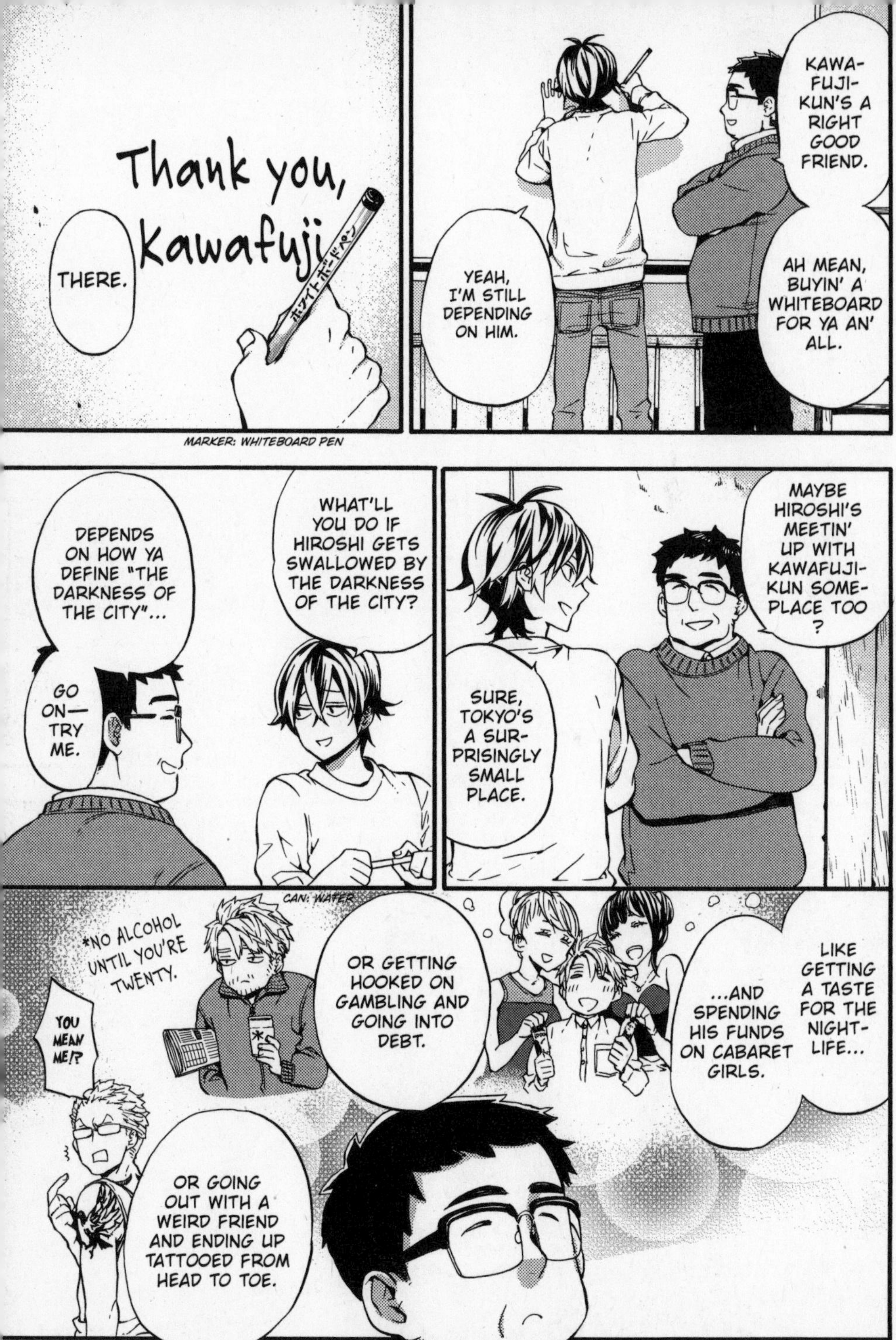
KAWA-FUJI-KUN'S A RIGHT GOOD FRIEND.
AH MEAN, BUYIN' A WHITEBOARD FOR YA AN' ALL.
YEAH, I'M STILL DEPENDING ON HIM.
Thank you, Kawafuji
ホワイトボードペン
THERE.
MARKER: WHITEBOARD PEN
MAYBE HIROSHI'S MEETIN' UP WITH KAWAFUJI-KUN SOME-PLACE TOO?
SURE, TOKYO'S A SUR-PRISINGLY SMALL PLACE.
WHAT'LL YOU DO IF HIROSHI GETS SWALLOWED BY THE DARKNESS OF THE CITY?
DEPENDS ON HOW YA DEFINE "THE DARKNESS OF THE CITY"...
GO ON— TRY ME.
LIKE GETTING A TASTE FOR THE NIGHT-LIFE...
...AND SPENDING HIS FUNDS ON CABARET GIRLS.
OR GETTING HOOKED ON GAMBLING AND GOING INTO DEBT.
CAN: WATER
*NO ALCOHOL UNTIL YOU'RE TWENTY.
YOU MEAN ME!?
OR GOING OUT WITH A WEIRD FRIEND AND ENDING UP TATTOOED FROM HEAD TO TOE.

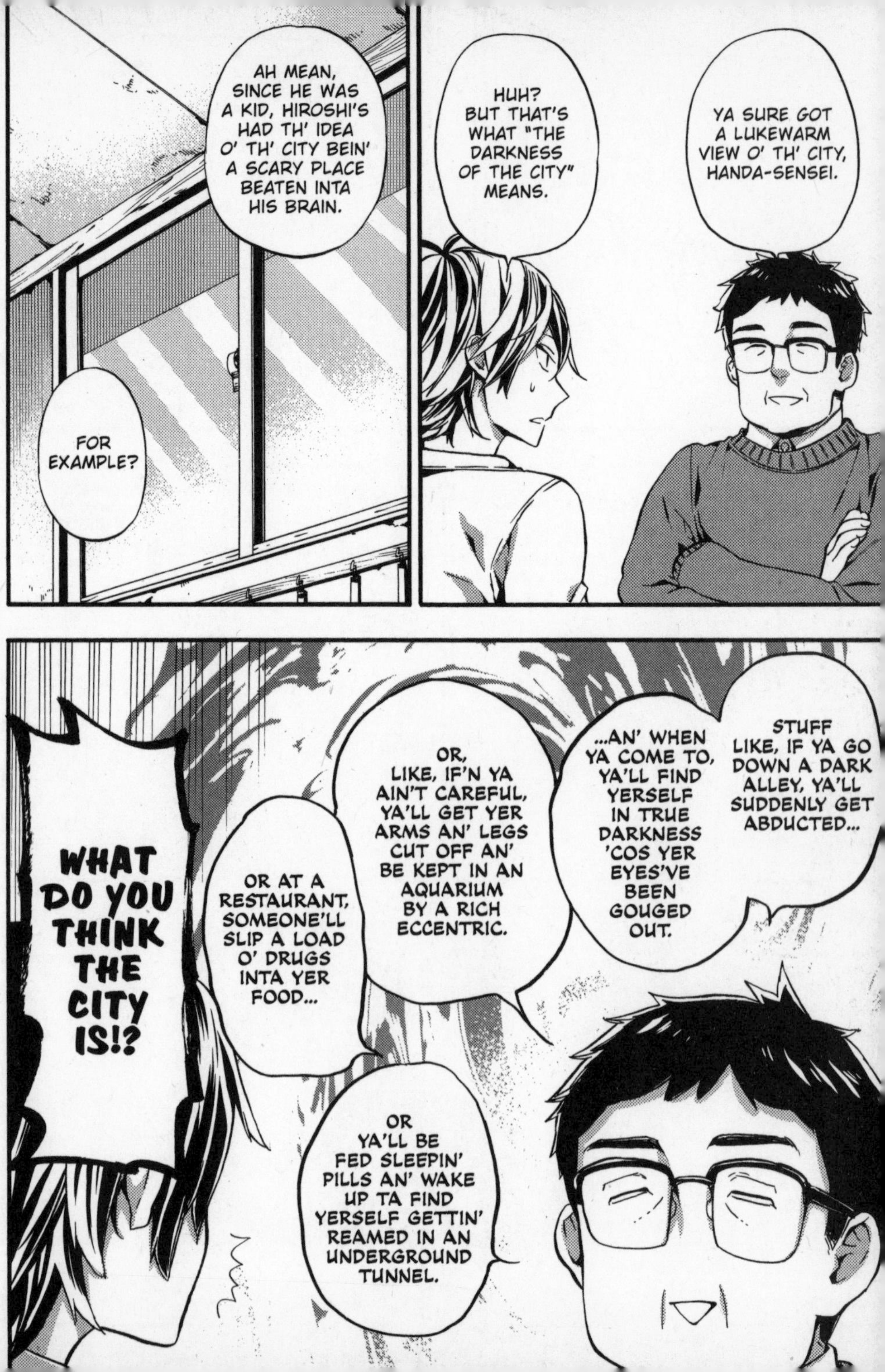
YA SURE GOT A LUKEWARM VIEW O' TH' CITY, HANDA-SENSEI.
HUH? BUT THAT'S WHAT "THE DARKNESS OF THE CITY" MEANS.
AH MEAN, SINCE HE WAS A KID, HIROSHI'S HAD TH' IDEA O' TH' CITY BEIN' A SCARY PLACE BEATEN INTA HIS BRAIN.
FOR EXAMPLE?
STUFF LIKE, IF YA GO DOWN A DARK ALLEY, YA'LL SUDDENLY GET ABDUCTED...
...AN' WHEN YA COME TO, YA'LL FIND YERSELF IN TRUE DARKNESS 'COS YER EYES'VE BEEN GOUGED OUT.
OR, LIKE, IF'N YA AIN'T CAREFUL, YA'LL GET YER ARMS AN' LEGS CUT OFF AN' BE KEPT IN AN AQUARIUM BY A RICH ECCENTRIC.
OR AT A RESTAURANT, SOMEONE'LL SLIP A LOAD O' DRUGS INTA YER FOOD...
OR YA'LL BE FED SLEEPIN' PILLS AN' WAKE UP TA FIND YERSELF GETTIN' REAMED IN AN UNDERGROUND TUNNEL.
WHAT DO YOU THINK THE CITY IS!?

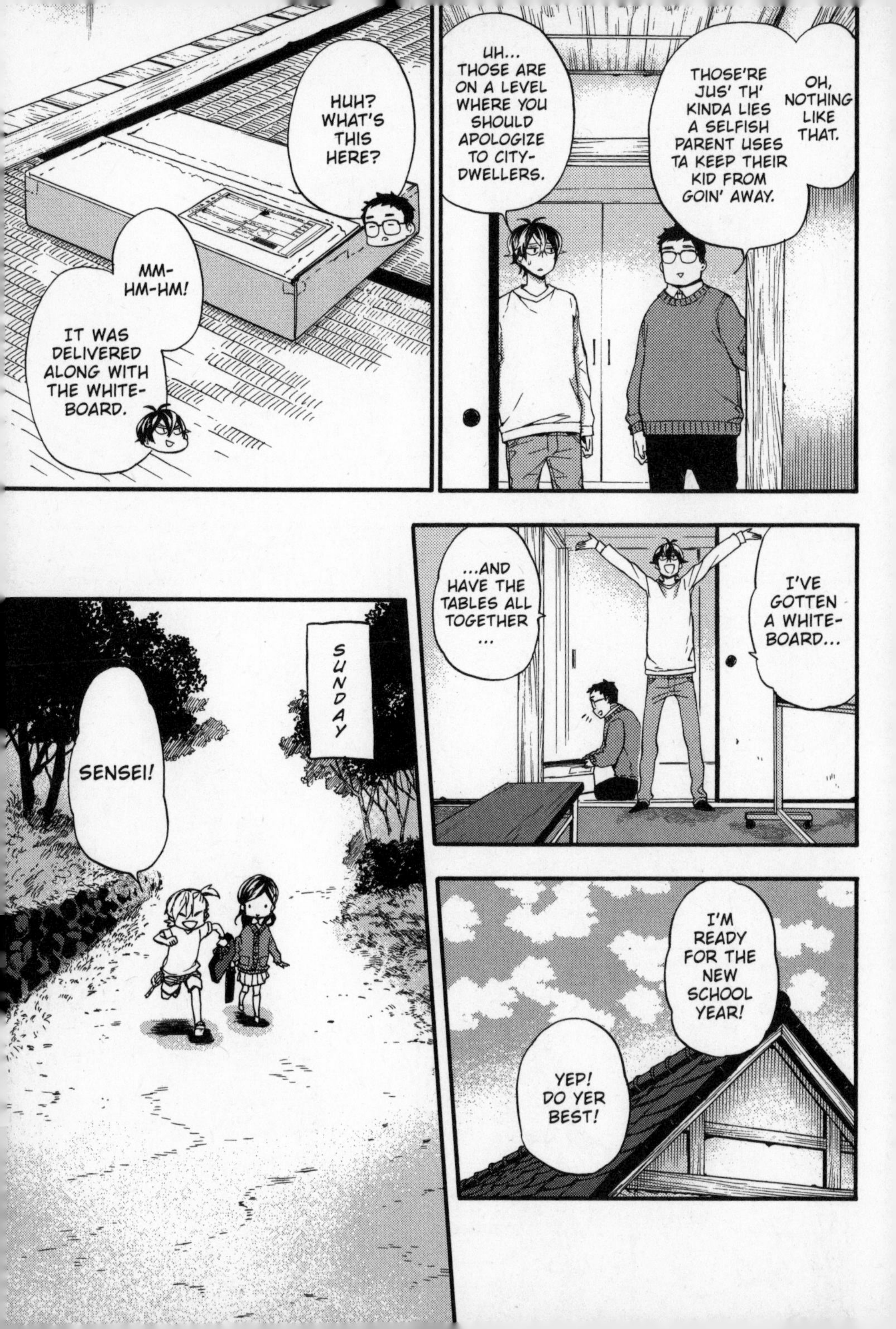
OH, NOTHING LIKE THAT.
THOSE'RE JUS' TH' KINDA LIES A SELFISH PARENT USES TA KEEP THEIR KID FROM GOIN' AWAY.
UH... THOSE ARE ON A LEVEL WHERE YOU SHOULD APOLOGIZE TO CITY-DWELLERS.
HUH? WHAT'S THIS HERE?
MM-HM-HM!
IT WAS DELIVERED ALONG WITH THE WHITE-BOARD.
I'VE GOTTEN A WHITE-BOARD...
...AND HAVE THE TABLES ALL TOGETHER...
I'M READY FOR THE NEW SCHOOL YEAR!
YEP! DO YER BEST!
SUNDAY
SENSEI!

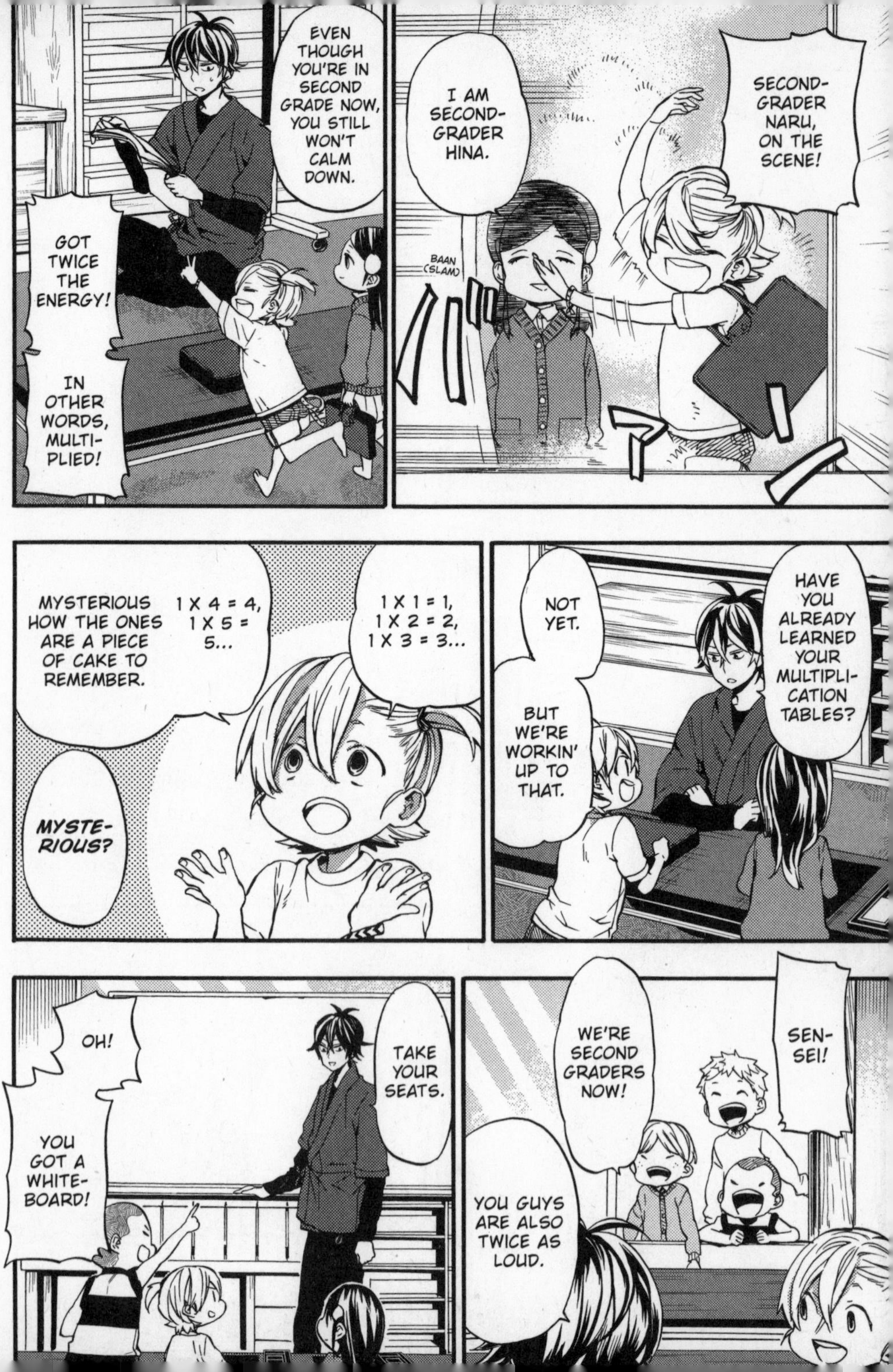
SECOND-GRADER NARU, ON THE SCENE!
I AM SECOND-GRADER HINA.
BAAN (SLAM)
EVEN THOUGH YOU'RE IN SECOND GRADE NOW, YOU STILL WON'T CALM DOWN.
GOT TWICE THE ENERGY!
IN OTHER WORDS, MULTIPLIED!
HAVE YOU ALREADY LEARNED YOUR MULTIPLICATION TABLES?
NOT YET.
BUT WE'RE WORKIN' UP TO THAT.
1 X 1 = 1, 1 X 2 = 2, 1 X 3 = 3...
1 X 4 = 4, 1 X 5 = 5...
MYSTERIOUS HOW THE ONES ARE A PIECE OF CAKE TO REMEMBER.
MYSTERIOUS?
SENSEI!
WE'RE SECOND GRADERS NOW!
YOU GUYS ARE ALSO TWICE AS LOUD.
TAKE YOUR SEATS.
OH!
YOU GOT A WHITEBOARD!

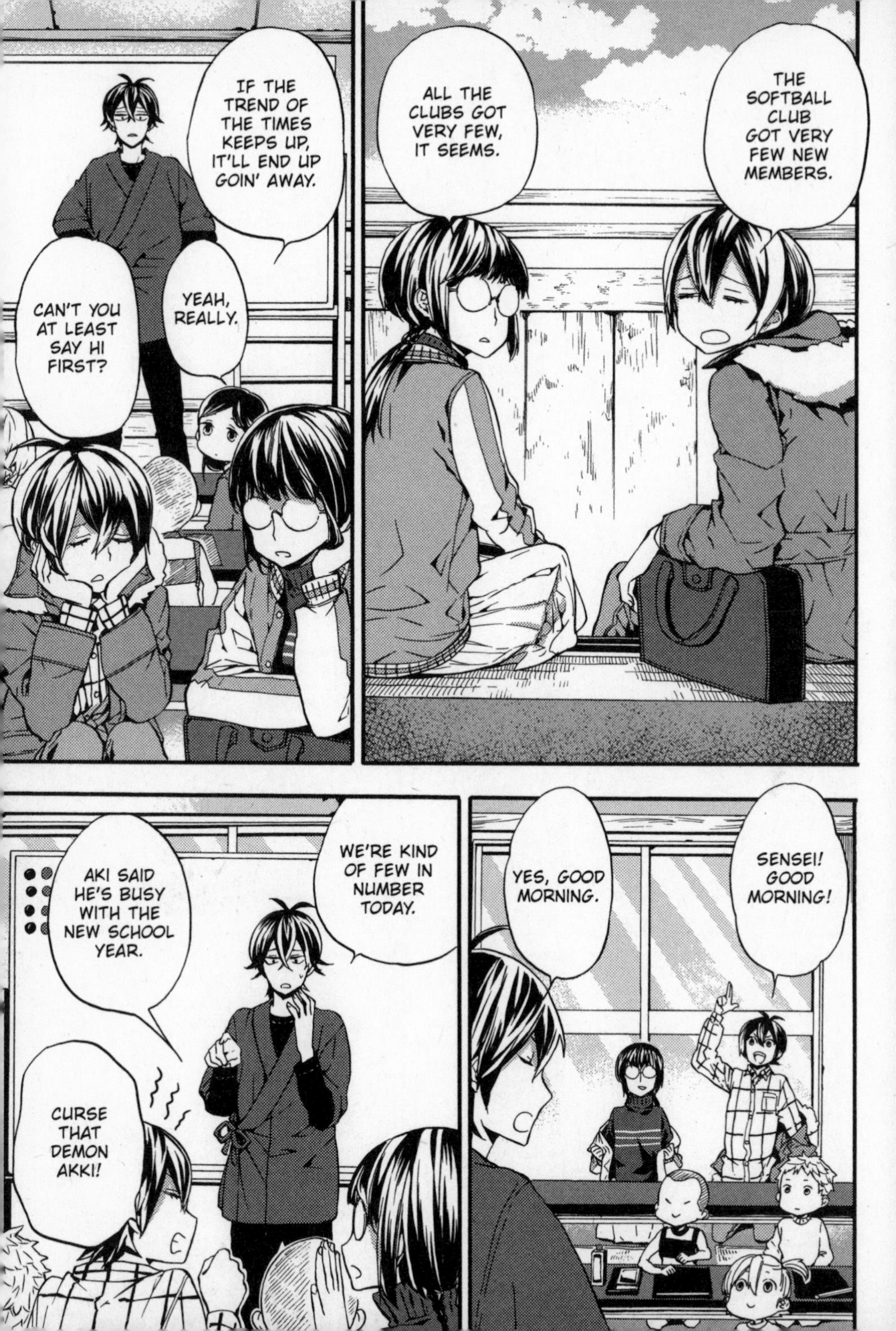
THE SOFTBALL CLUB GOT VERY FEW NEW MEMBERS.
ALL THE CLUBS GOT VERY FEW, IT SEEMS.
IF THE TREND OF THE TIMES KEEPS UP, IT'LL END UP GOIN' AWAY.
YEAH, REALLY.
CAN'T YOU AT LEAST SAY HI FIRST?
SENSEI! GOOD MORNING!
YES, GOOD MORNING.
WE'RE KIND OF FEW IN NUMBER TODAY.
AKI SAID HE'S BUSY WITH THE NEW SCHOOL YEAR.
CURSE THAT DEMON AKKI!

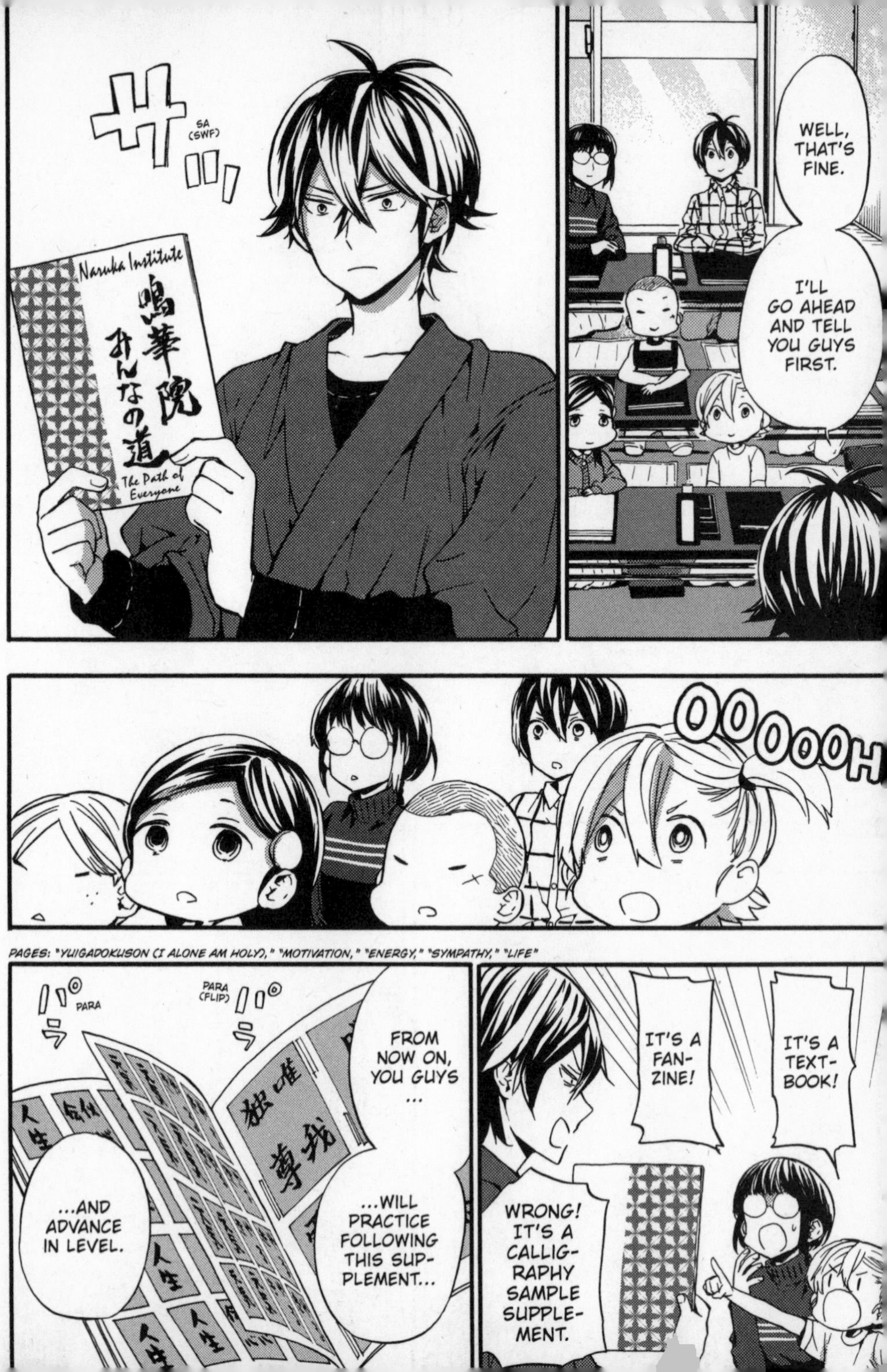
WELL, THAT'S FINE.
I'LL GO AHEAD AND TELL YOU GUYS FIRST.
SA (SWF)
Naruka Institute
鳴華院 みんなの道
The Path of Everyone
OOOOOH
PAGES: "YUIGADOKUSON (I ALONE AM HOLY)," "MOTIVATION," "ENERGY," "SYMPATHY," "LIFE"
IT'S A TEXT-BOOK!
IT'S A FAN-ZINE!
WRONG! IT'S A CALLIG-RAPHY SAMPLE SUPPLE-MENT.
PARA (FLIP)
PARA
FROM NOW ON, YOU GUYS ...
...WILL PRACTICE FOLLOWING THIS SUP-PLEMENT...
...AND ADVANCE IN LEVEL.

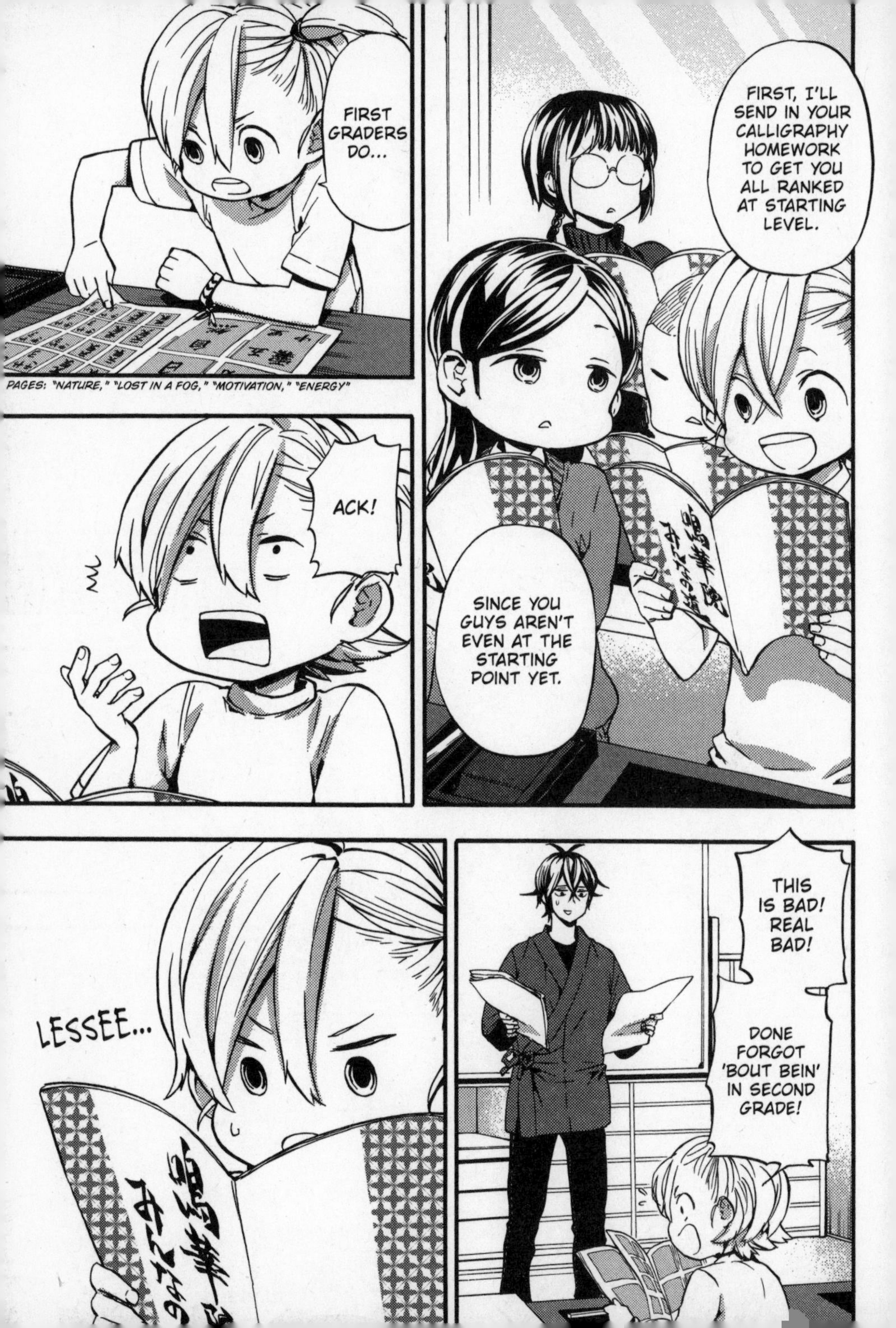
FIRST, I'LL SEND IN YOUR CALLIGRAPHY HOMEWORK TO GET YOU ALL RANKED AT STARTING LEVEL.
SINCE YOU GUYS AREN'T EVEN AT THE STARTING POINT YET.
FIRST GRADERS DO...
PAGES: "NATURE," "LOST IN A FOG," "MOTIVATION," "ENERGY"
ACK!
THIS IS BAD! REAL BAD!
DONE FORGOT 'BOUT BEIN' IN SECOND GRADE!
LESSEE...

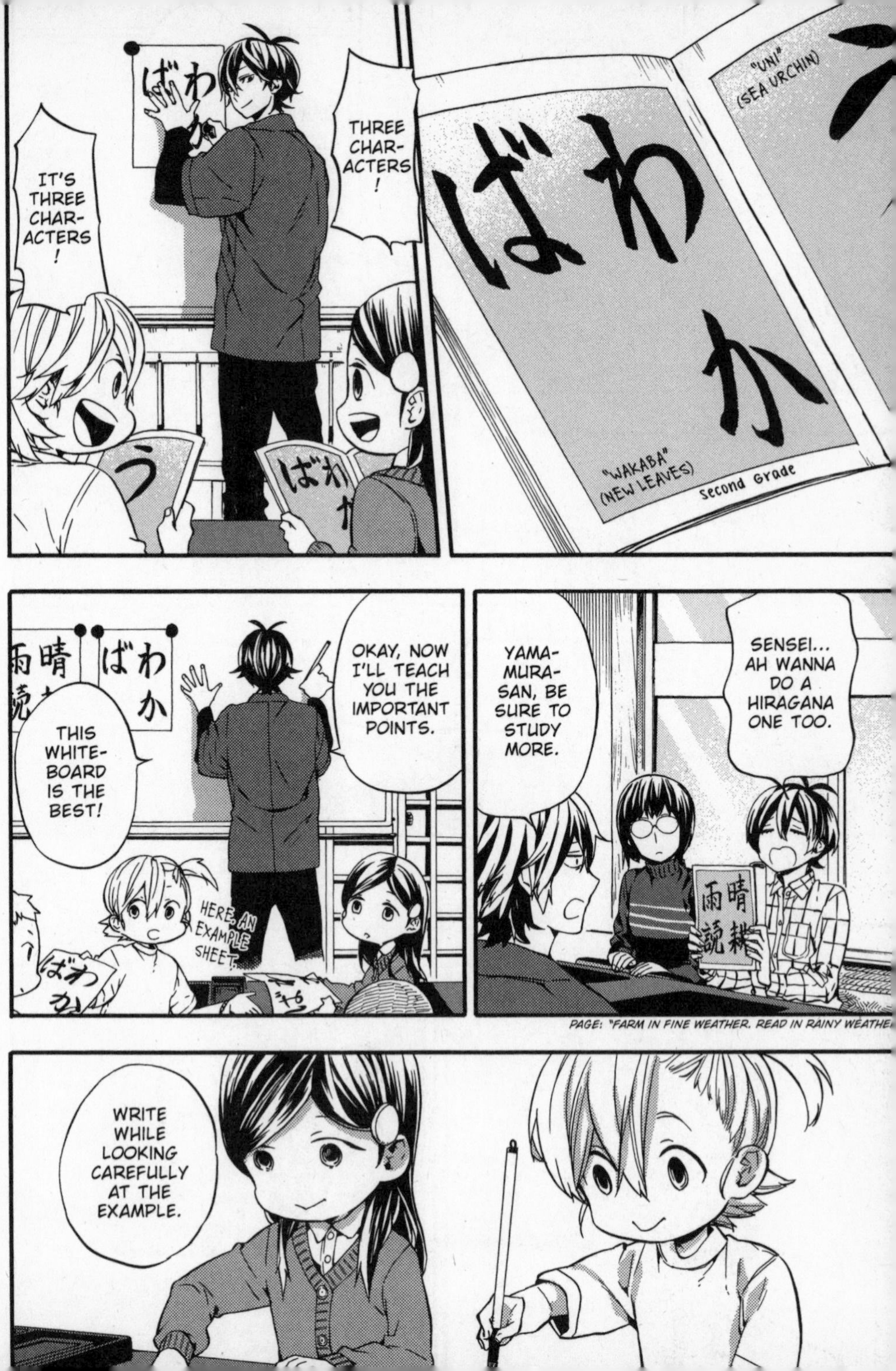
"UNI" (SEA URCHIN)
"WAKABA" (NEW LEAVES)
Second Grade
THREE CHARACTERS!
IT'S THREE CHARACTERS!
SENSEI... AH WANNA DO A HIRAGANA ONE TOO.
YAMAMURA-SAN, BE SURE TO STUDY MORE.
PAGE: "FARM IN FINE WEATHER. READ IN RAINY WEATHE
OKAY, NOW I'LL TEACH YOU THE IMPORTANT POINTS.
THIS WHITEBOARD IS THE BEST!
HERE, AN EXAMPLE SHEET.
WRITE WHILE LOOKING CAREFULLY AT THE EXAMPLE.

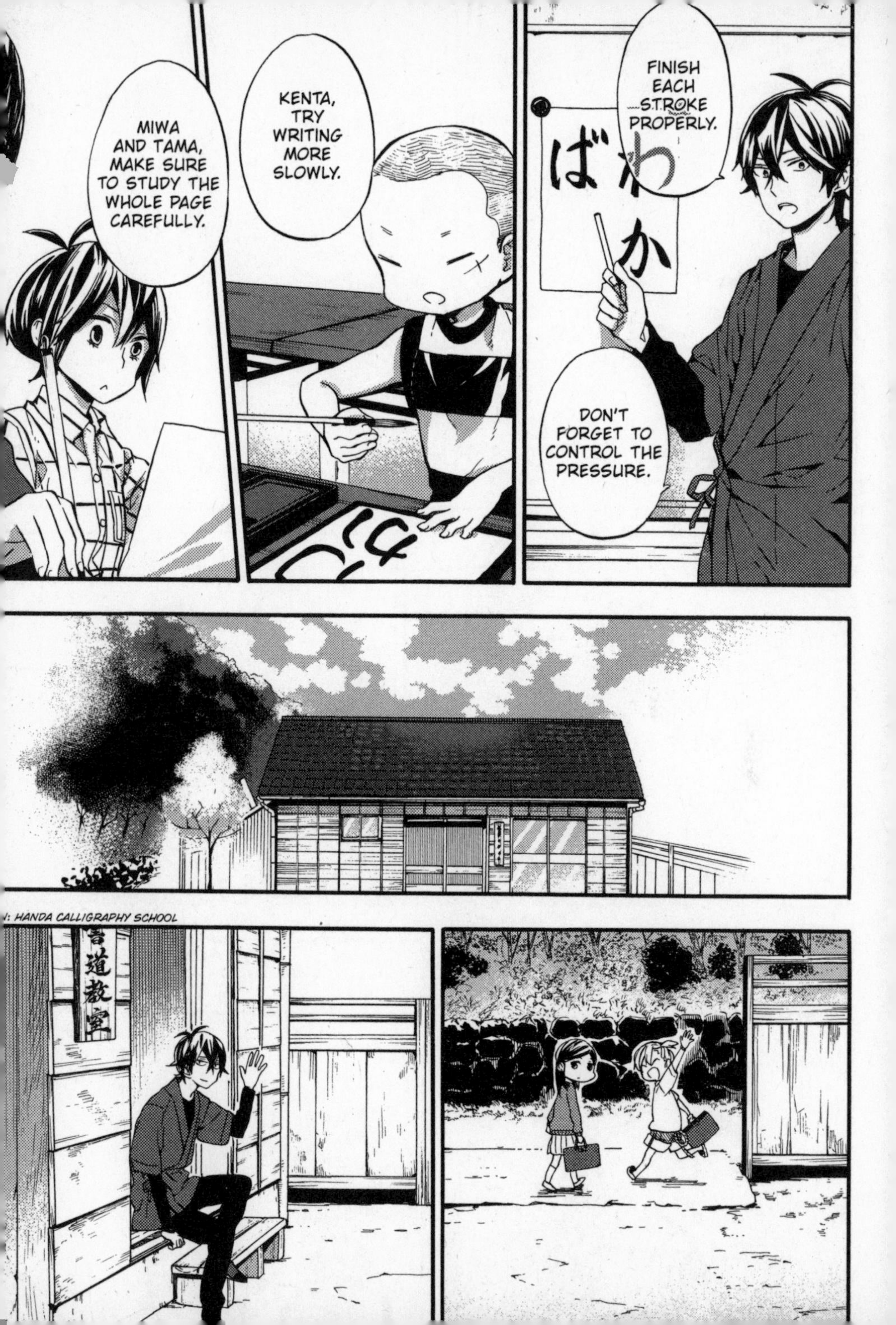
FINISH EACH STROKE PROPERLY.
DON'T FORGET TO CONTROL THE PRESSURE.
KENTA, TRY WRITING MORE SLOWLY.
MIWA AND TAMA, MAKE SURE TO STUDY THE WHOLE PAGE CAREFULLY.
HANDA CALLIGRAPHY SCHOOL

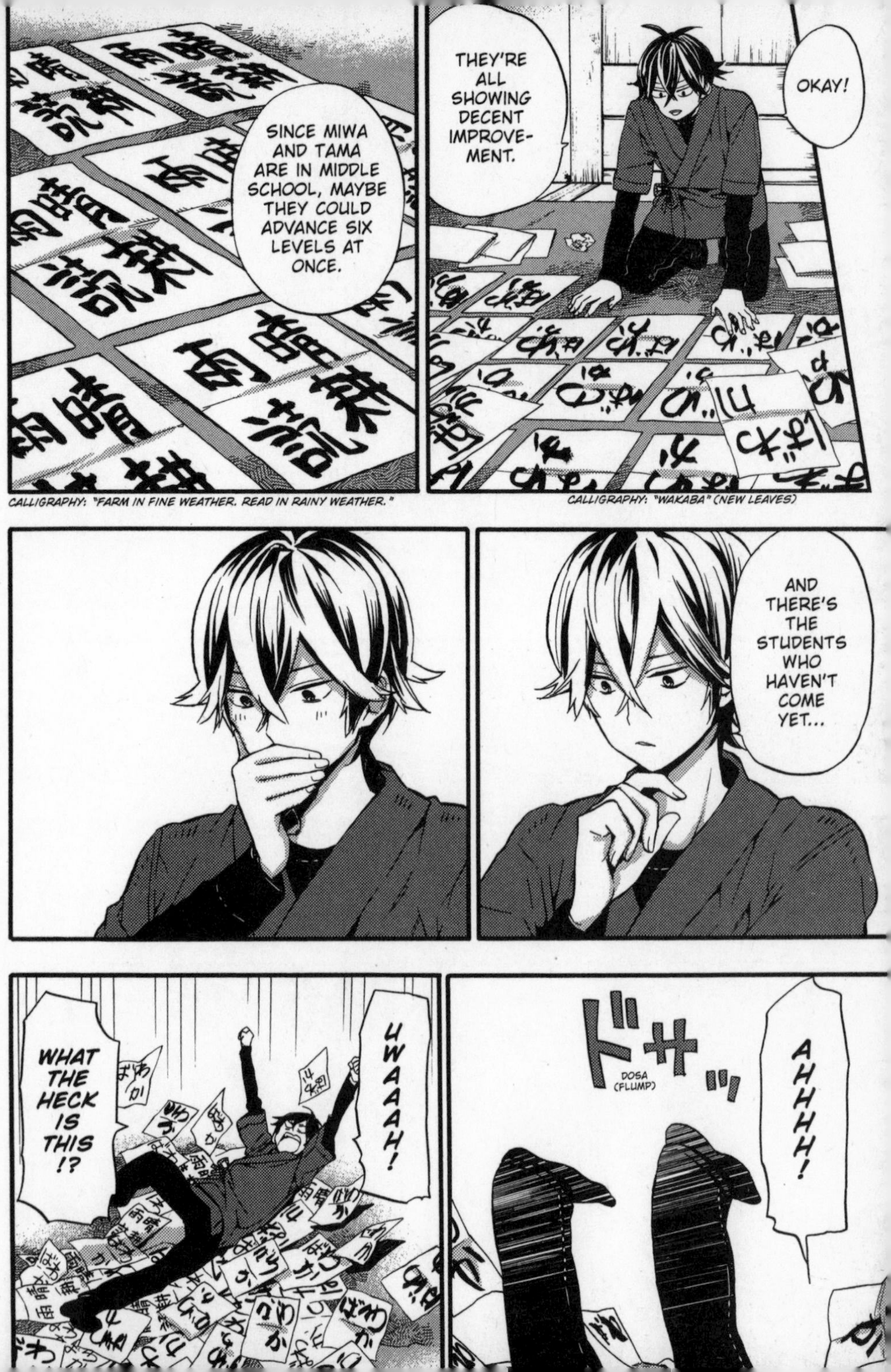
OKAY!
THEY'RE ALL SHOWING DECENT IMPROVEMENT.
CALLIGRAPHY: "WAKABA" (NEW LEAVES)
SINCE MIWA AND TAMA ARE IN MIDDLE SCHOOL, MAYBE THEY COULD ADVANCE SIX LEVELS AT ONCE.
CALLIGRAPHY: "FARM IN FINE WEATHER. READ IN RAINY WEATHER."
AND THERE'S THE STUDENTS WHO HAVEN'T COME YET...
AHHHH!
ドサッ
DOSA (FLUMP)
UWAAAAH!
WHAT THE HECK IS THIS!?

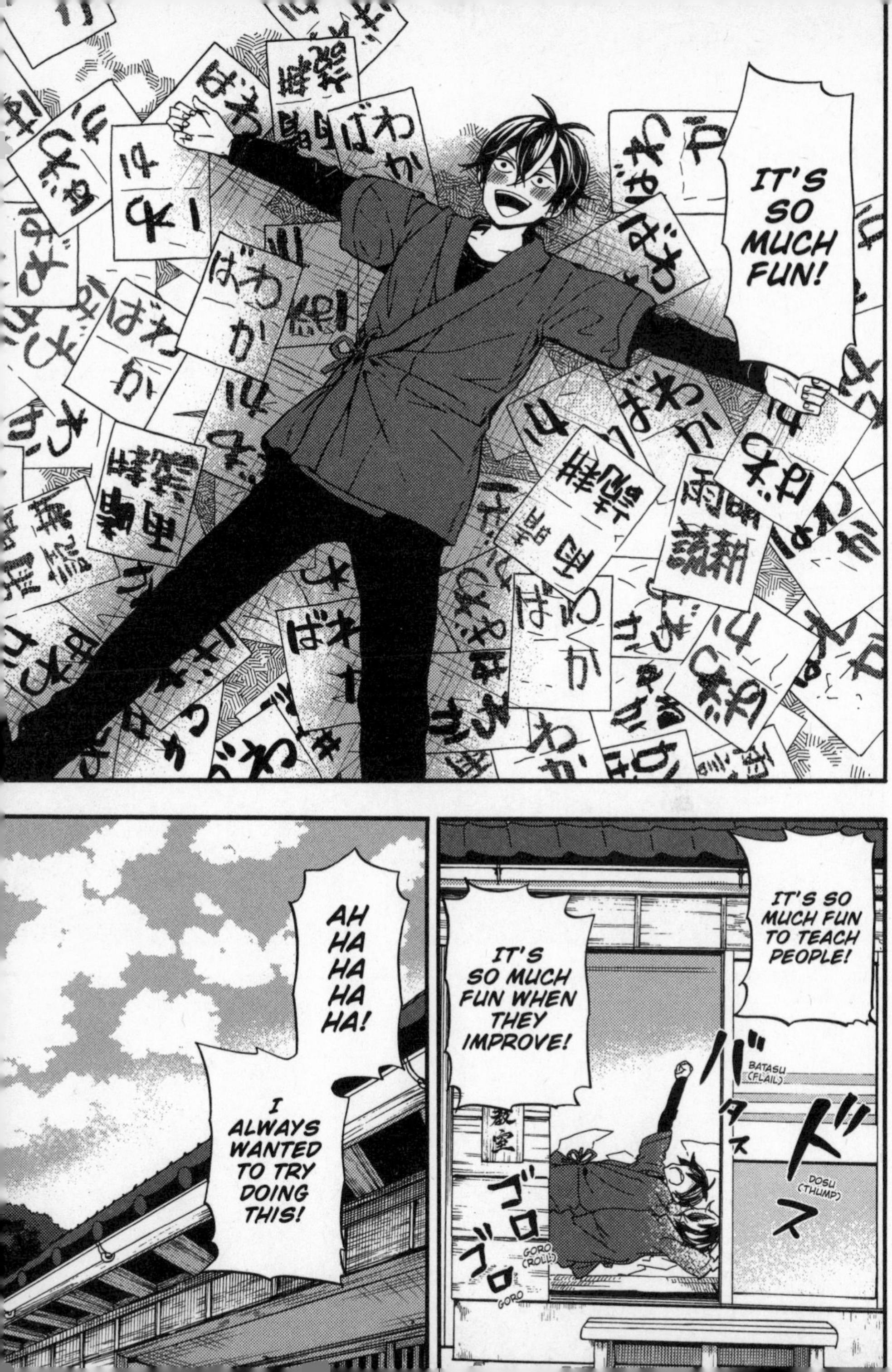
IT'S SO MUCH FUN!
IT'S SO MUCH FUN TO TEACH PEOPLE!
IT'S SO MUCH FUN WHEN THEY IMPROVE!
BATASU (FLAIL)
DOSU (THUMP)
GORO (ROLL) GORO
AH HA HA HA HA HA!
I ALWAYS WANTED TO TRY DOING THIS!

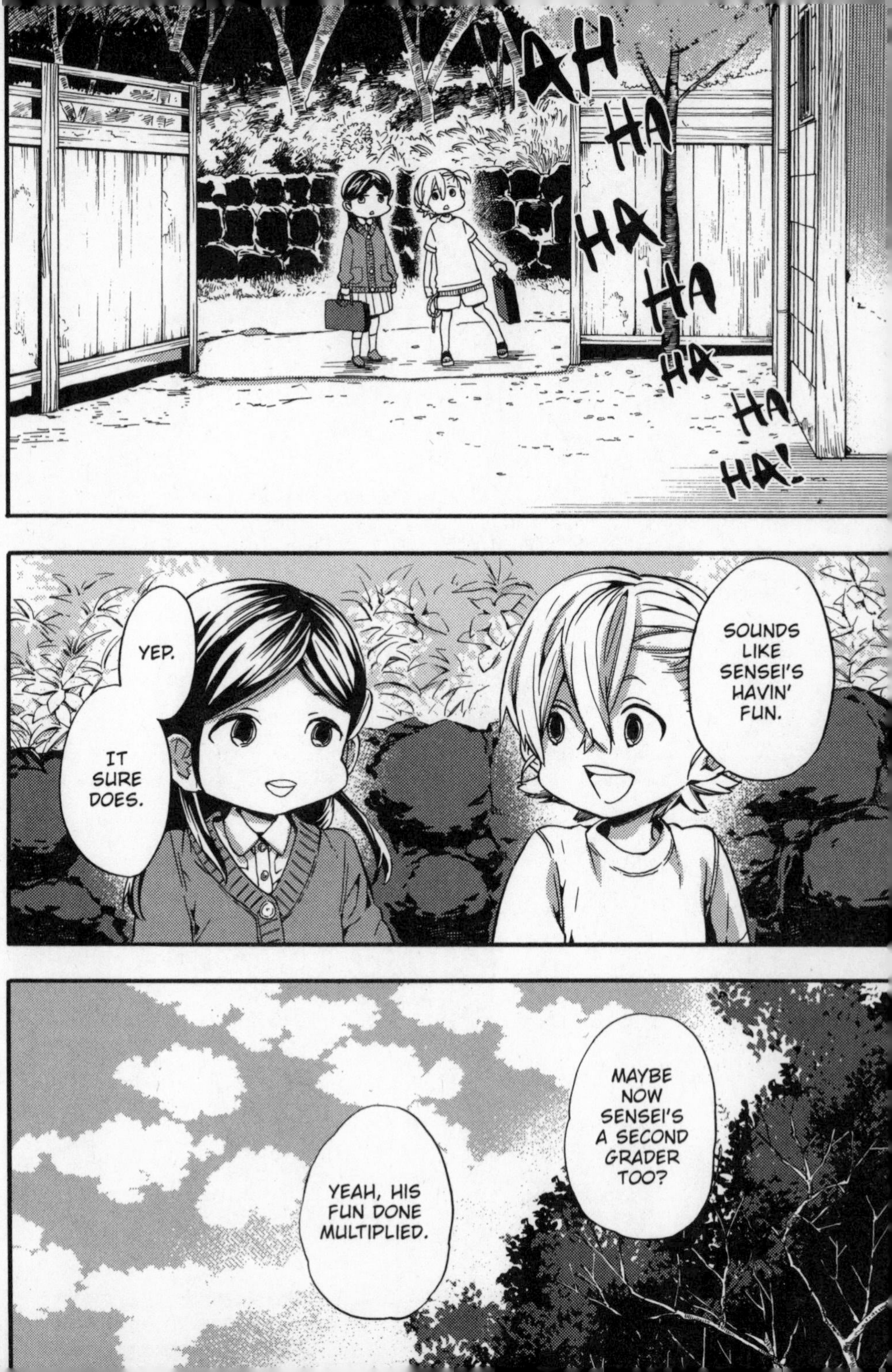
AH HA HA HA HA HA HA!
SOUNDS LIKE SENSEI'S HAVIN' FUN.
YEP.
IT SURE DOES.
MAYBE NOW SENSEI'S A SECOND GRADER TOO?
YEAH, HIS FUN DONE MULTIPLIED.

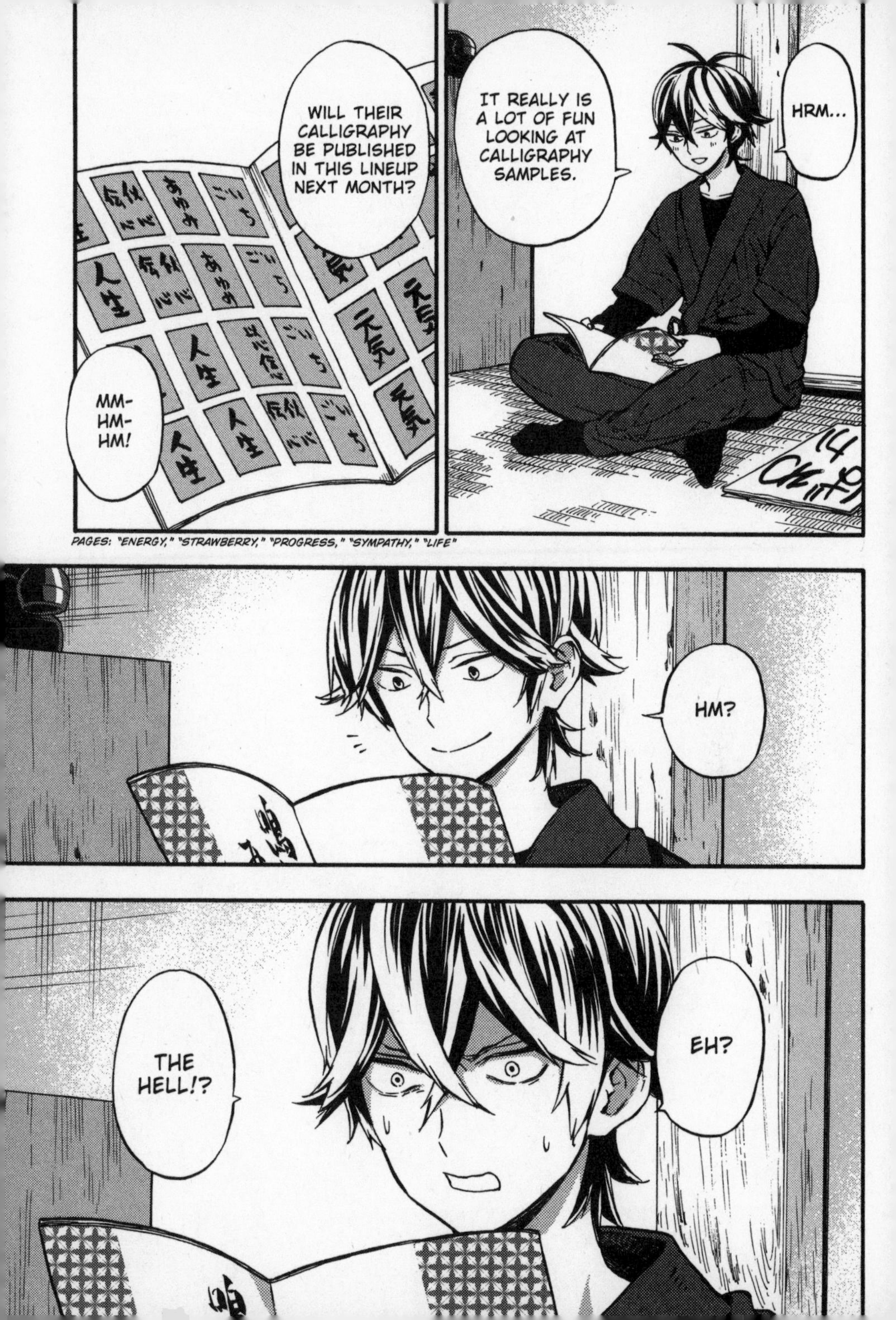
HRM...
IT REALLY IS A LOT OF FUN LOOKING AT CALLIGRAPHY SAMPLES.
WILL THEIR CALLIGRAPHY BE PUBLISHED IN THIS LINEUP NEXT MONTH?
MM-HM-HM!
PAGES: "ENERGY," "STRAWBERRY," "PROGRESS," "SYMPATHY," "LIFE"
HM?
EH?
THE HELL!?

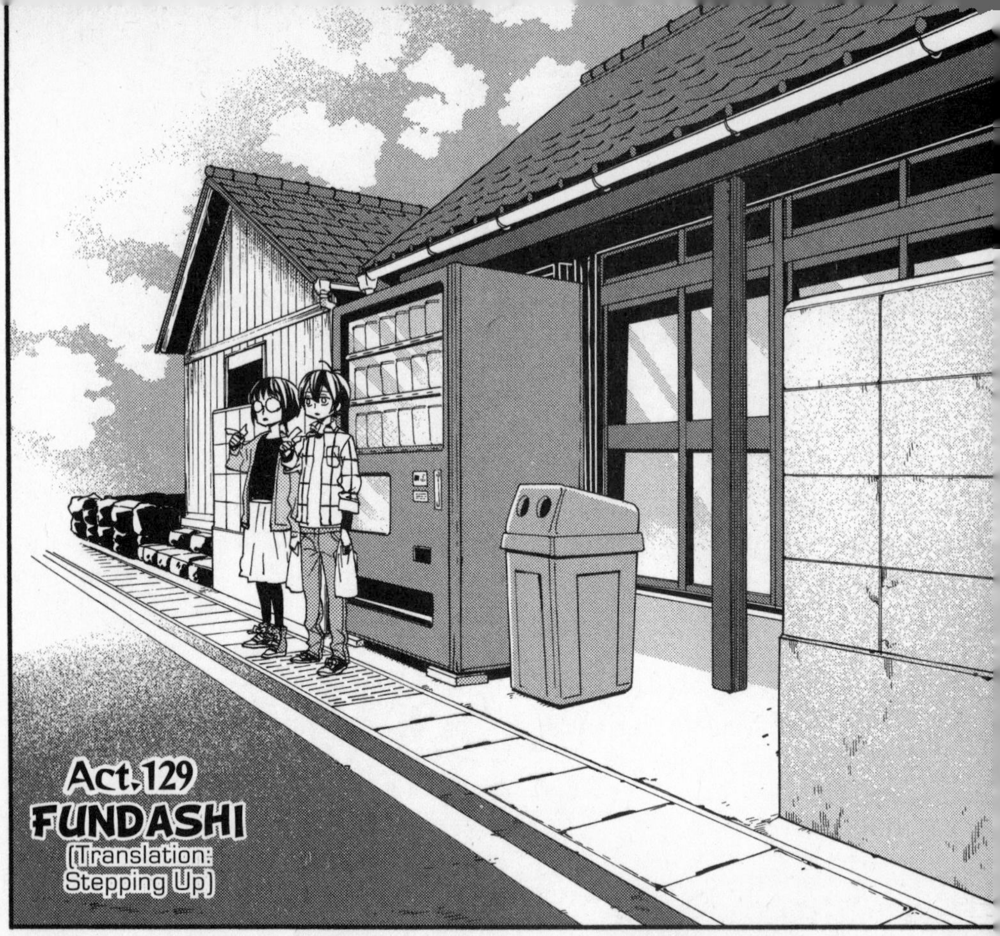
Act.129
FUNDASHI
(Translation: Stepping Up)

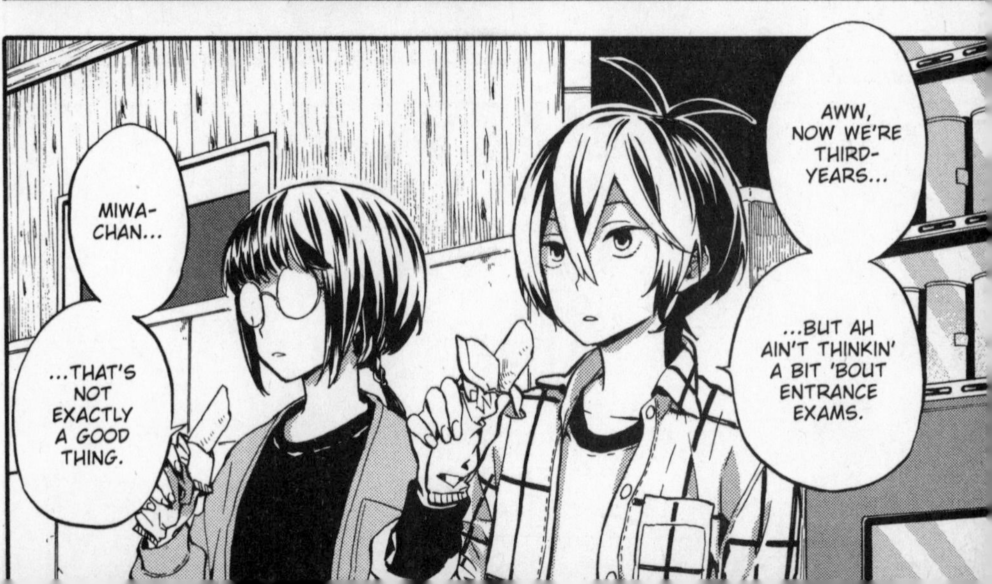
AWW, NOW WE'RE THIRD-YEARS...
...BUT AH AIN'T THINKIN' A BIT 'BOUT ENTRANCE EXAMS.
MIWA-CHAN...
...THAT'S NOT EXACTLY A GOOD THING.

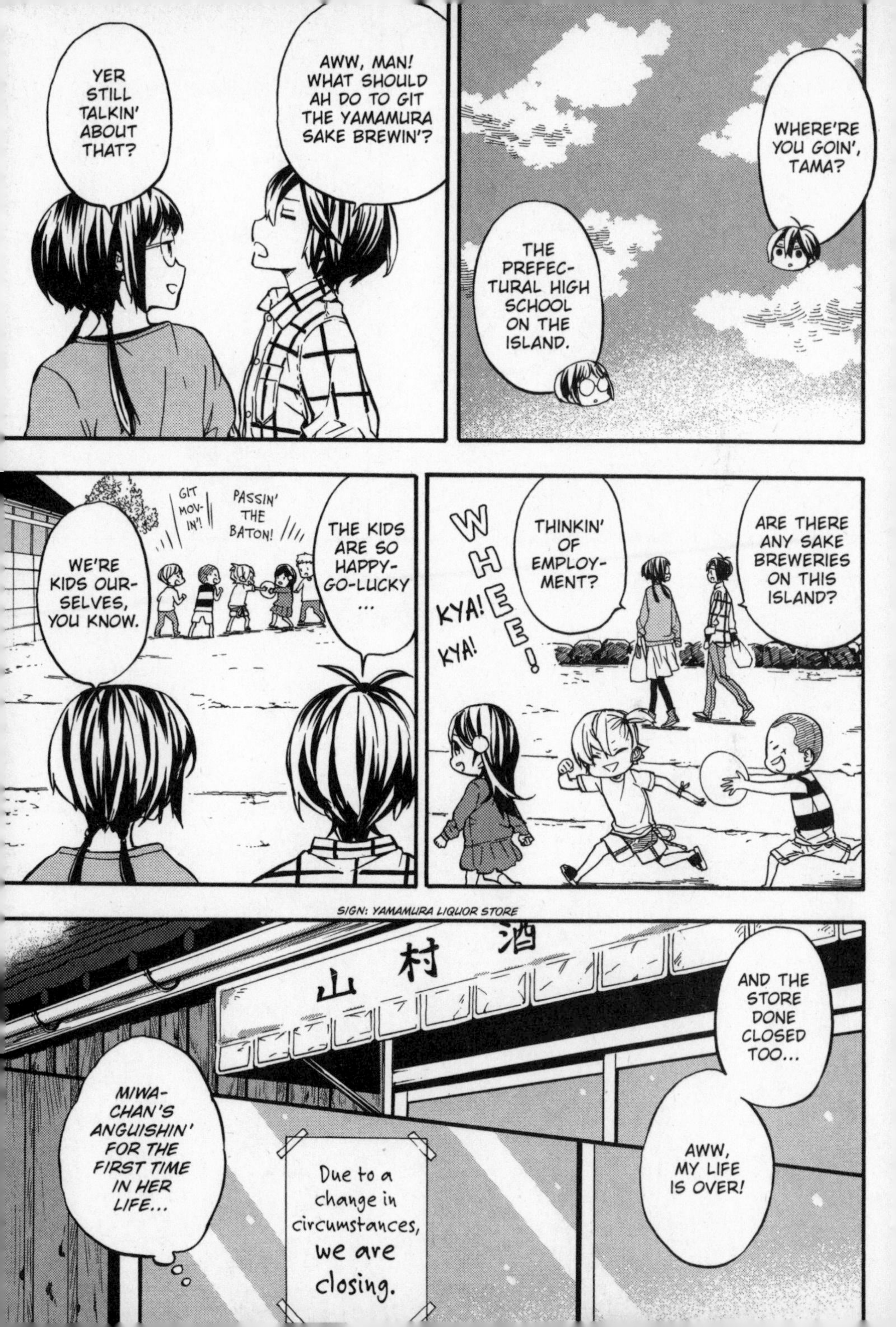
WHERE'RE YOU GOIN', TAMA?
THE PREFECTURAL HIGH SCHOOL ON THE ISLAND.
AWW, MAN! WHAT SHOULD AH DO TO GIT THE YAMAMURA SAKE BREWIN'?
YER STILL TALKIN' ABOUT THAT?
ARE THERE ANY SAKE BREWERIES ON THIS ISLAND?
THINKIN' OF EMPLOYMENT?
WHEE!
KYA!
KYA!
THE KIDS ARE SO HAPPY-GO-LUCKY...
PASSIN' THE BATON!
GIT MOVIN'!
WE'RE KIDS OURSELVES, YOU KNOW.
SIGN: YAMAMURA LIQUOR STORE
山村酒
AND THE STORE DONE CLOSED TOO...
AWW, MY LIFE IS OVER!
Due to a change in circumstances, we are closing.
MIWA-CHAN'S ANGUISHIN' FOR THE FIRST TIME IN HER LIFE...

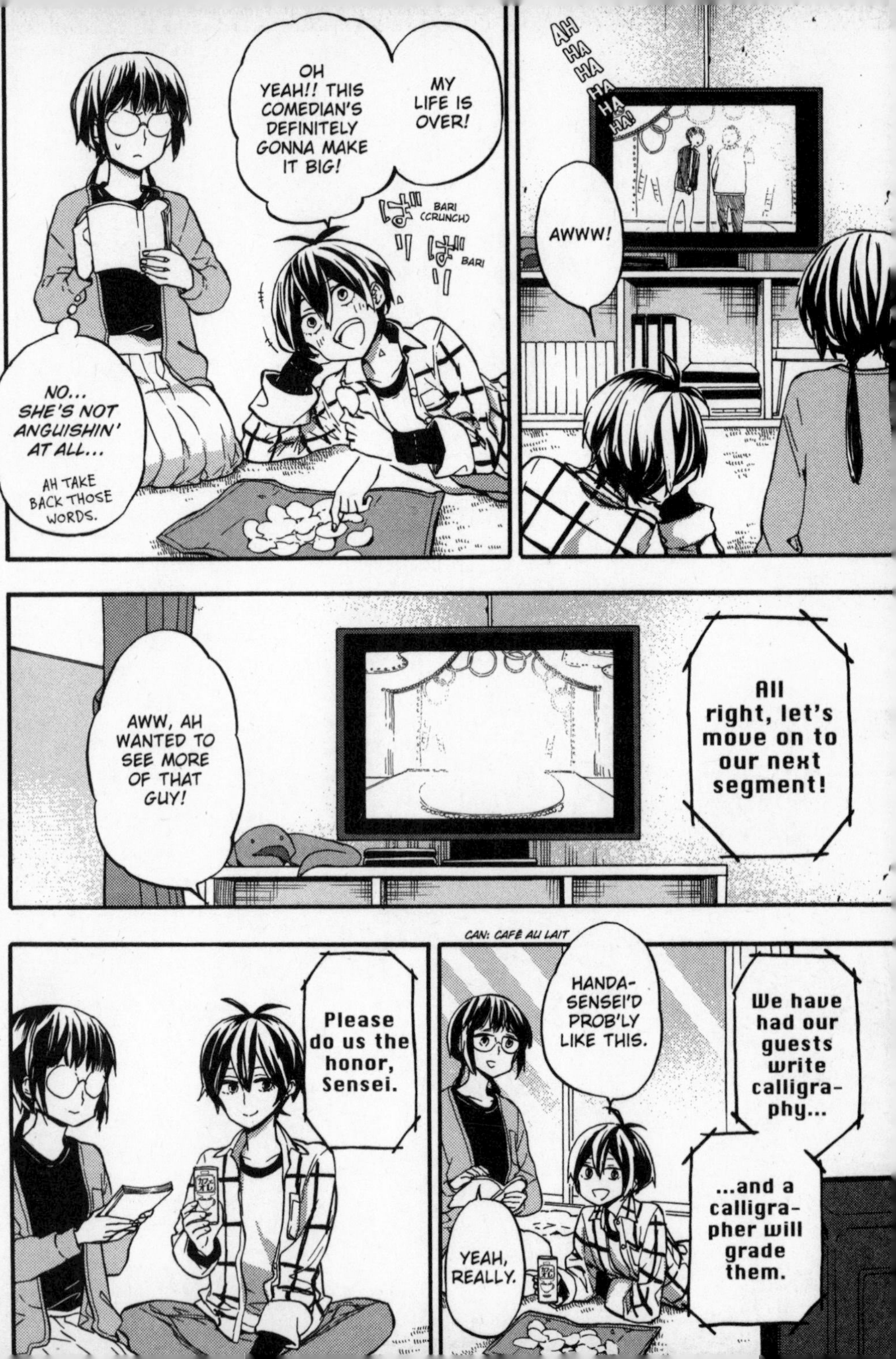
AH HA HA HA HA HA!
AWWW!
MY LIFE IS OVER!
OH YEAH!! THIS COMEDIAN'S DEFINITELY GONNA MAKE IT BIG!
ばり BARI (CRUNCH)
ばり BARI
NO... SHE'S NOT ANGUISHIN' AT ALL...
AH TAKE BACK THOSE WORDS.
All right, let's move on to our next segment!
AWW, AH WANTED TO SEE MORE OF THAT GUY!
CAN: CAFÉ AU LAIT
We have had our guests write calligraphy...
HANDA-SENSEI'D PROB'LY LIKE THIS.
...and a calligrapher will grade them.
YEAH, REALLY.
Please do us the honor, Sensei.

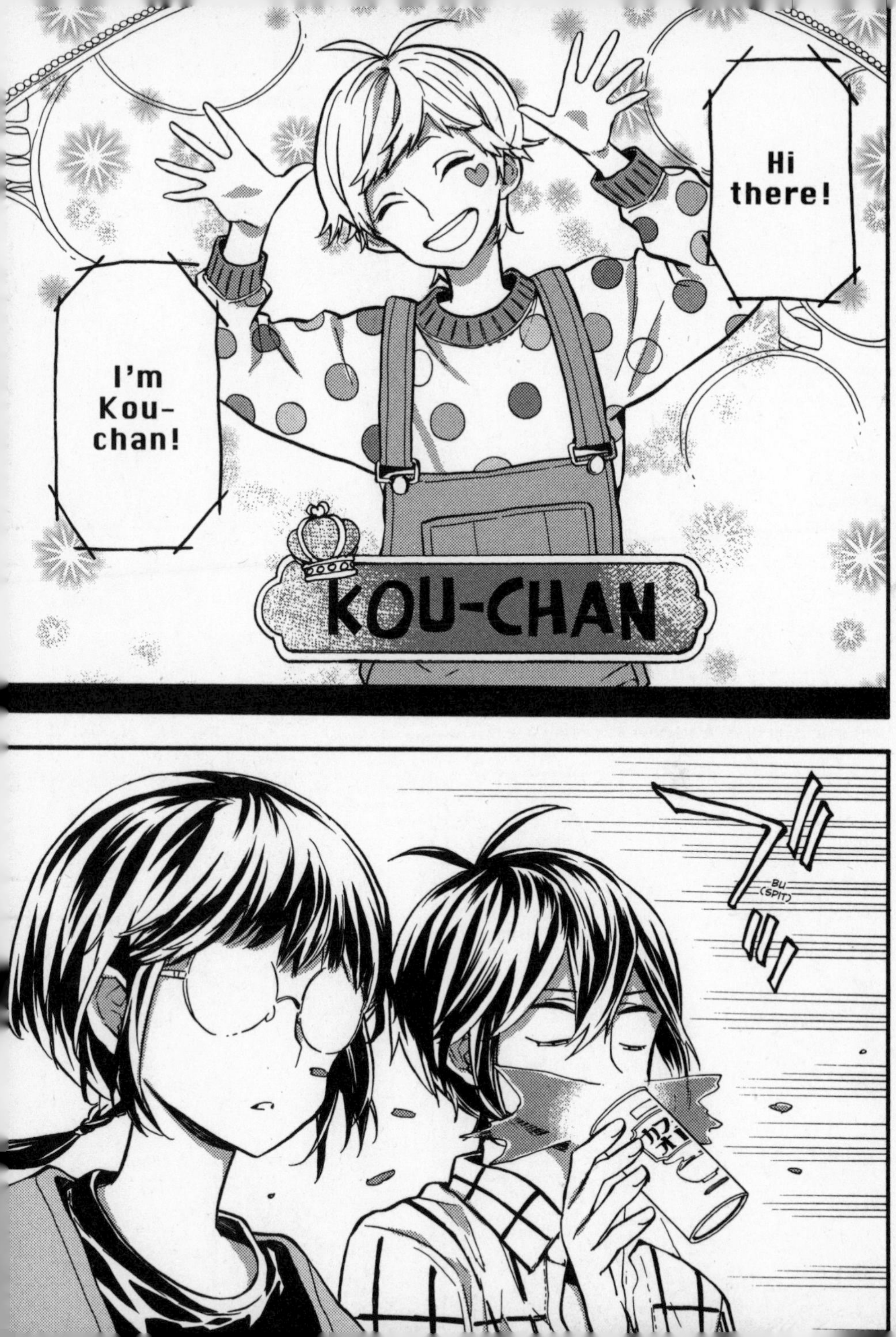
Hi there!
I'm Kou-chan!
KOU-CHAN
BU (SPIT)

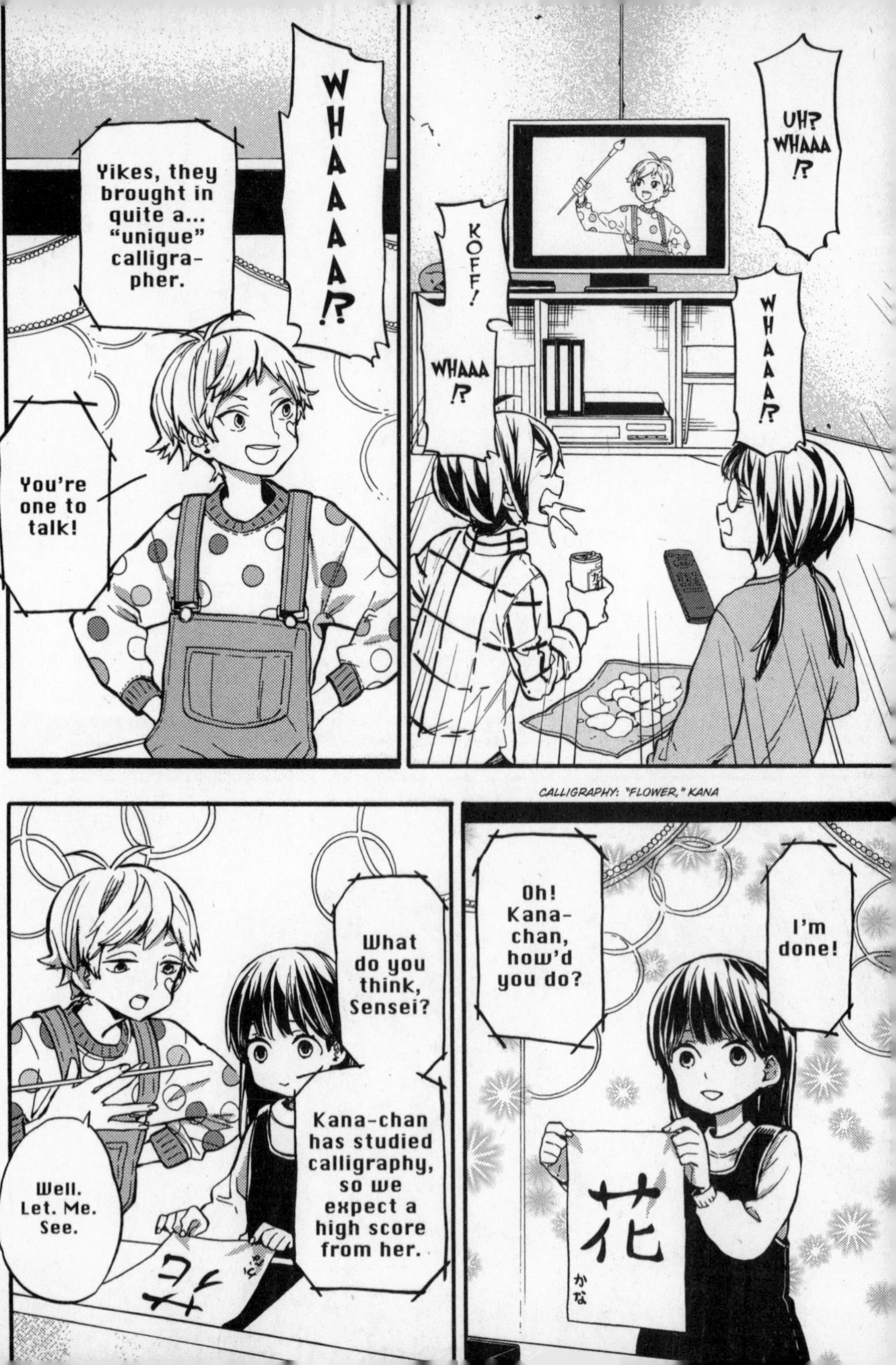
UH? WHAAA⁉
KOFF!
WHAAA⁉
WHAAA⁉
WHAAAA⁉
Yikes, they brought in quite a... "unique" calligrapher.
You're one to talk!
CALLIGRAPHY: "FLOWER," KANA
I'm done!
Oh! Kana-chan, how'd you do?
花
かな
What do you think, Sensei?
Kana-chan has studied calligraphy, so we expect a high score from her.
Well. Let. Me. See.

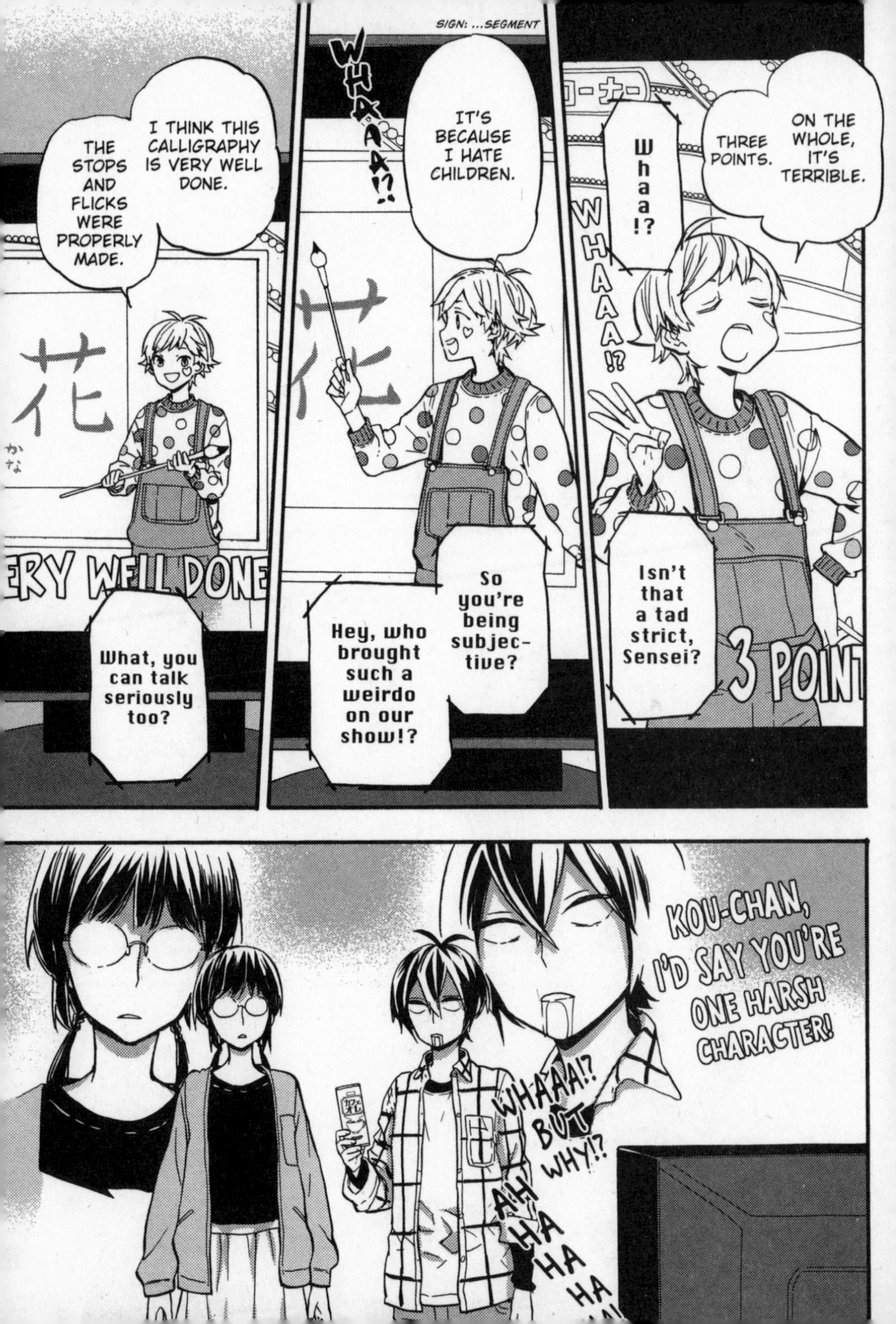
ON THE WHOLE, IT'S TERRIBLE.
THREE POINTS.
Whaa!?
WHAAAA!?
Isn't that a tad strict, Sensei?
3 POINT
SIGN: ...SEGMENT
WHAAA!?
IT'S BECAUSE I HATE CHILDREN.
So you're being subjective?
Hey, who brought such a weirdo on our show!?
I THINK THIS CALLIGRAPHY IS VERY WELL DONE.
THE STOPS AND FLICKS WERE PROPERLY MADE.
花
かな
ERY WELL DONE
What, you can talk seriously too?
KOU-CHAN, I'D SAY YOU'RE ONE HARSH CHARACTER!
WHAAAA!? BUT WHY!?
AH HA HA HA HA

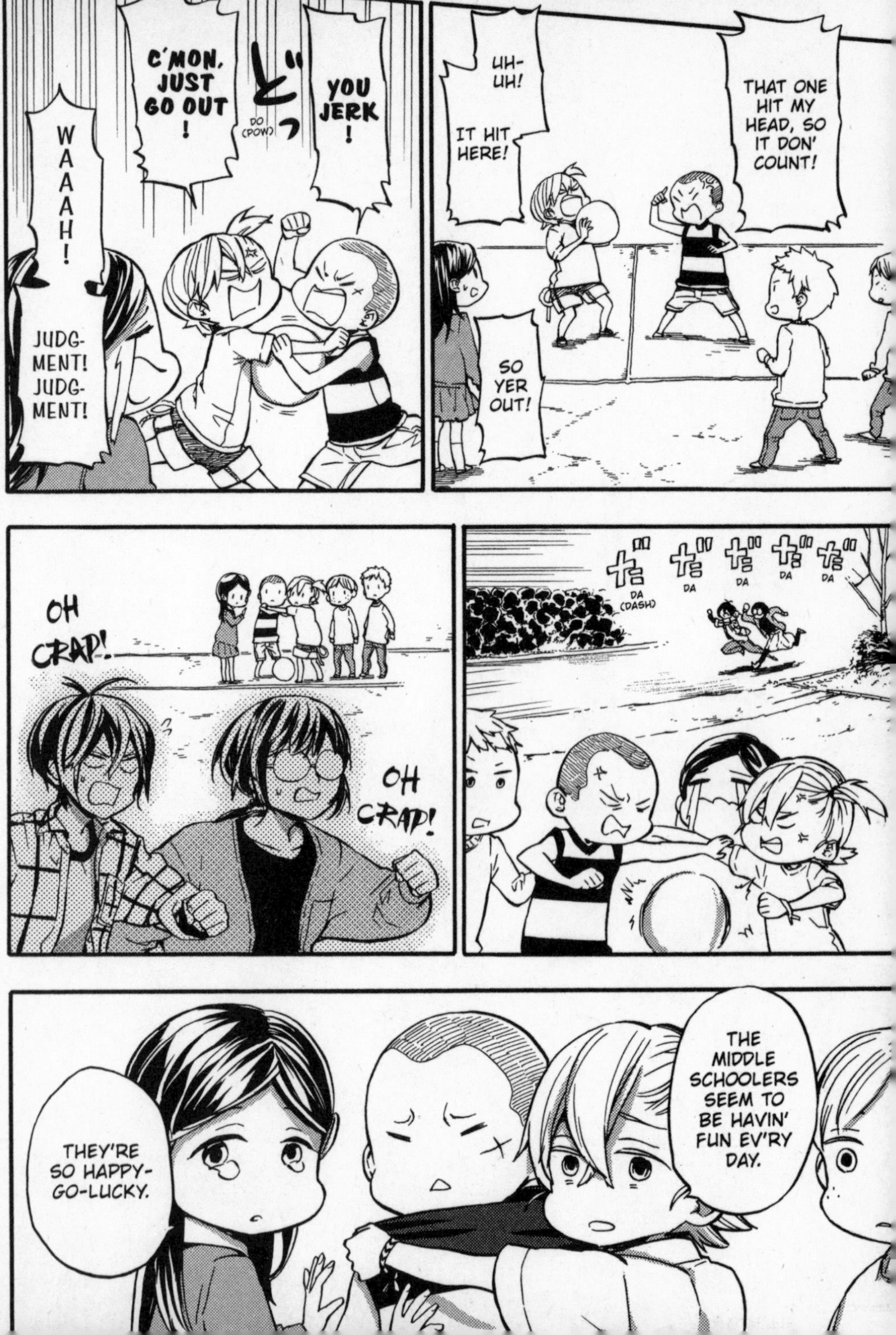
THAT ONE HIT MY HEAD, SO IT DON' COUNT!
UH-UH! IT HIT HERE!
SO YER OUT!
YOU JERK!
どっ
DO (POW)
C'MON, JUST GO OUT!
WAAAAH!
JUDGMENT! JUDGMENT!
ダダダダダ
DA (DASH) DA DA DA DA
OH CRAP!
OH CRAP!
THE MIDDLE SCHOOLERS SEEM TO BE HAVIN' FUN EV'RY DAY.
THEY'RE SO HAPPY-GO-LUCKY.

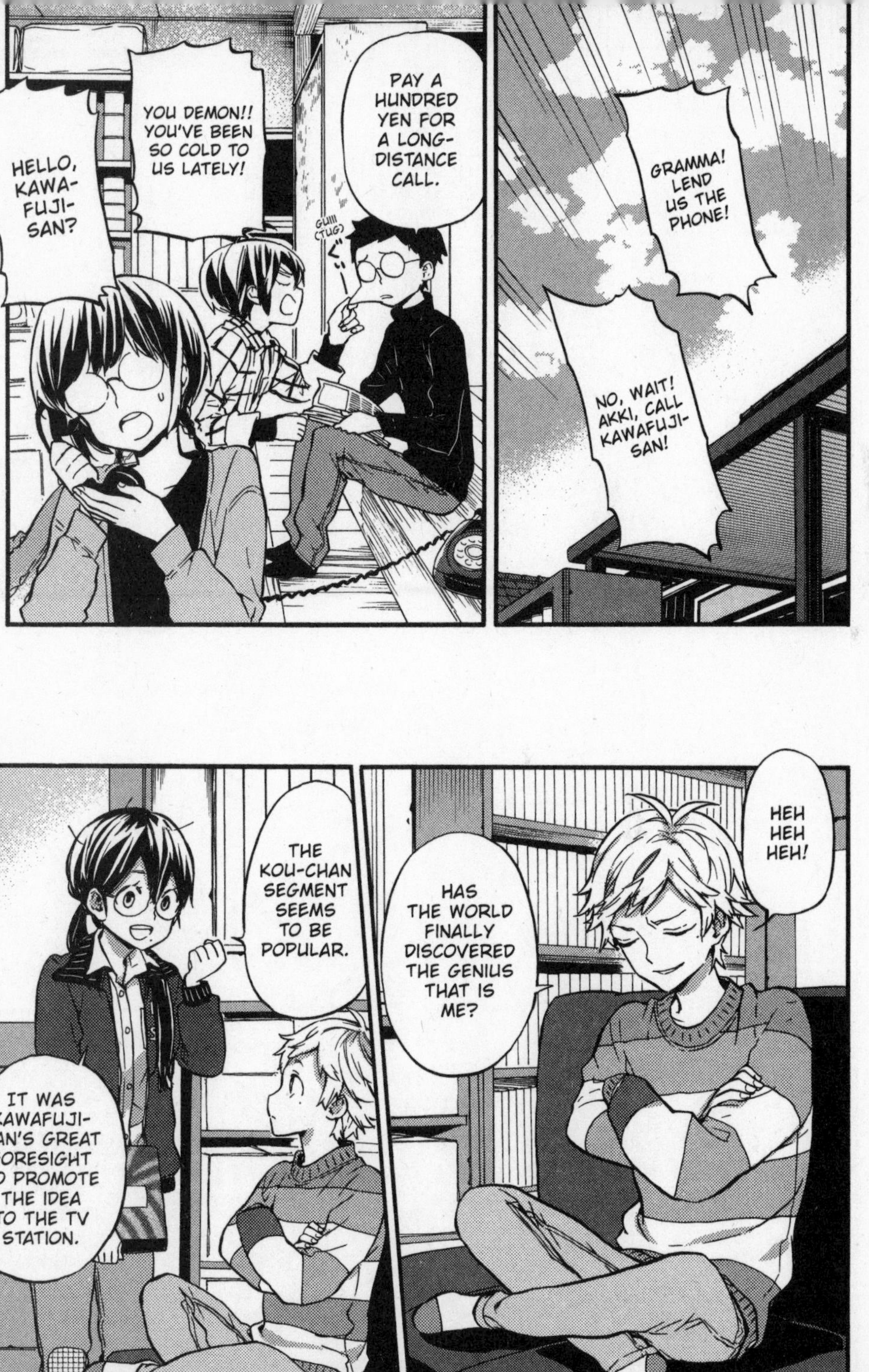
GRAMMA! LEND US THE PHONE!
NO, WAIT! AKKI, CALL KAWAFUJI-SAN!
PAY A HUNDRED YEN FOR A LONG-DISTANCE CALL.
GUIII (TUG)
YOU DEMON!! YOU'VE BEEN SO COLD TO US LATELY!
HELLO, KAWAFUJI-SAN?
HEH HEH HEH!
HAS THE WORLD FINALLY DISCOVERED THE GENIUS THAT IS ME?
THE KOU-CHAN SEGMENT SEEMS TO BE POPULAR.
IT WAS KAWAFUJI-SAN'S GREAT FORESIGHT TO PROMOTE THE IDEA TO THE TV STATION.

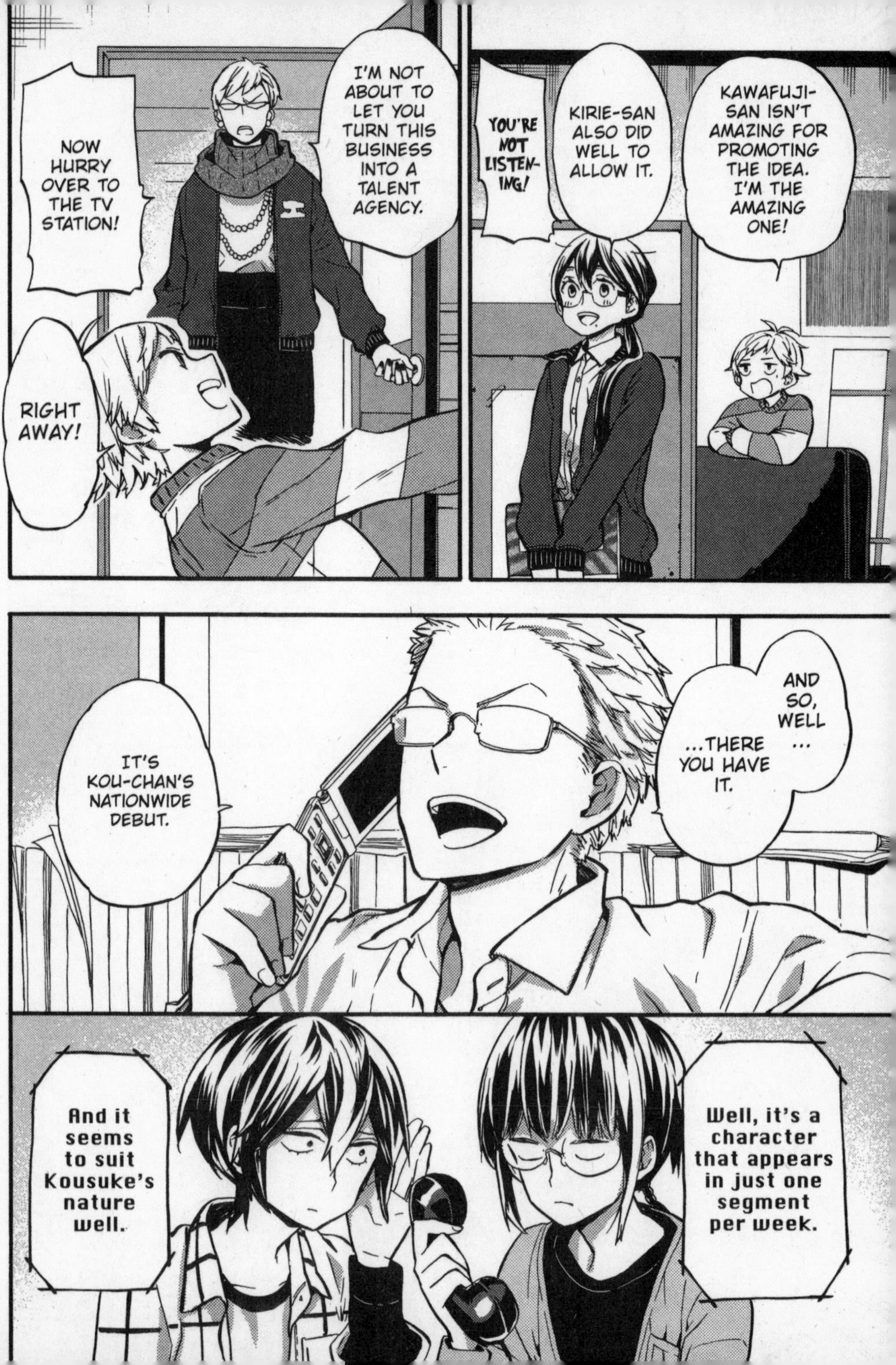
KAWAFUJI-SAN ISN'T AMAZING FOR PROMOTING THE IDEA. I'M THE AMAZING ONE!
KIRIE-SAN ALSO DID WELL TO ALLOW IT.
YOU'RE NOT LISTENING!
I'M NOT ABOUT TO LET YOU TURN THIS BUSINESS INTO A TALENT AGENCY.
NOW HURRY OVER TO THE TV STATION!
RIGHT AWAY!
AND SO, WELL...
...THERE YOU HAVE IT.
IT'S KOU-CHAN'S NATIONWIDE DEBUT.
Well, it's a character that appears in just one segment per week.
And it seems to suit Kousuke's nature well.

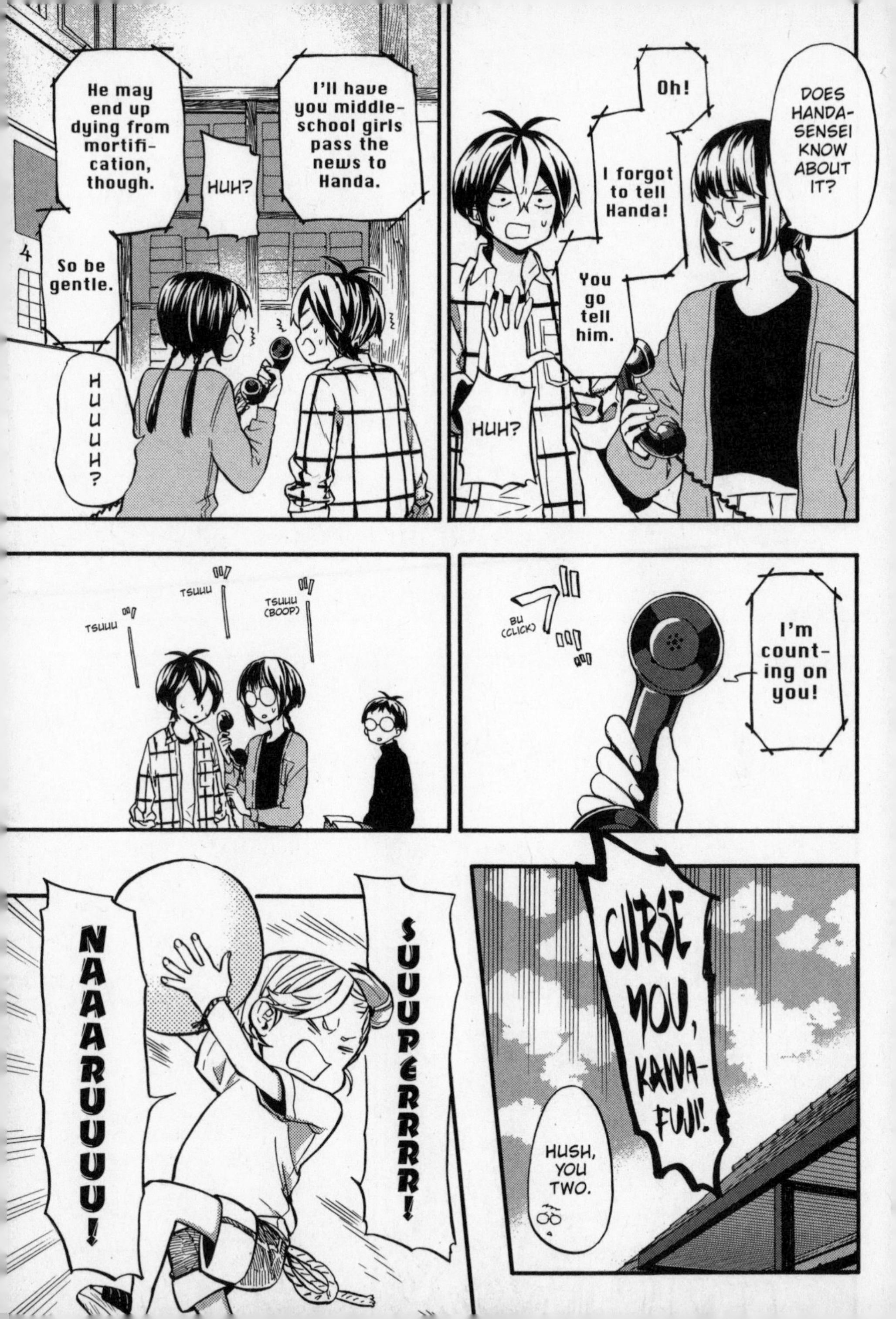
DOES HANDA-SENSEI KNOW ABOUT IT?
Oh!
I forgot to tell Handa!
You go tell him.
HUH?
I'll have you middle-school girls pass the news to Handa.
HUH?
He may end up dying from mortification, though.
So be gentle.
HUUUUH?
BU (CLICK)
I'm counting on you!
TSUUU (BOOP)
TSUUU
TSUUU
CURSE YOU, KAWAFUJI!
HUSH, YOU TWO.
SUUUPERRRR!
NAAARUUUUU!

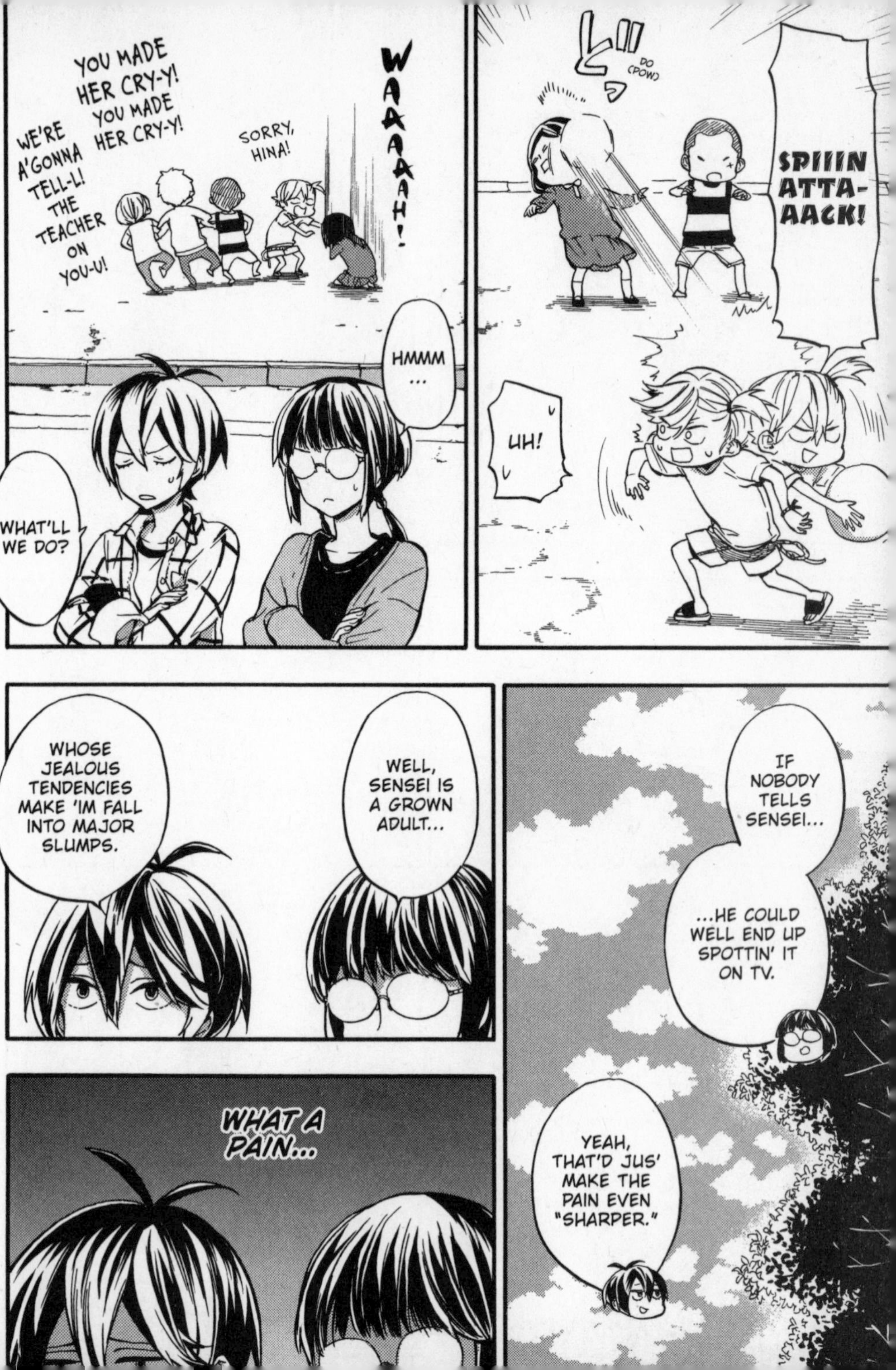

SPIIIN ATTA-AACK!
DO (POW)
UH!
WAAAAAAH!
SORRY, HINA!
YOU MADE HER CRY-Y! YOU MADE HER CRY-Y!
WE'RE A'GONNA TELL-L! THE TEACHER ON YOU-U!
HMMM...
WHAT'LL WE DO?
IF NOBODY TELLS SENSEI...
...HE COULD WELL END UP SPOTTIN' IT ON TV.
YEAH, THAT'D JUS' MAKE THE PAIN EVEN "SHARPER."
WELL, SENSEI IS A GROWN ADULT...
WHOSE JEALOUS TENDENCIES MAKE 'IM FALL INTO MAJOR SLUMPS.
WHAT A PAIN...

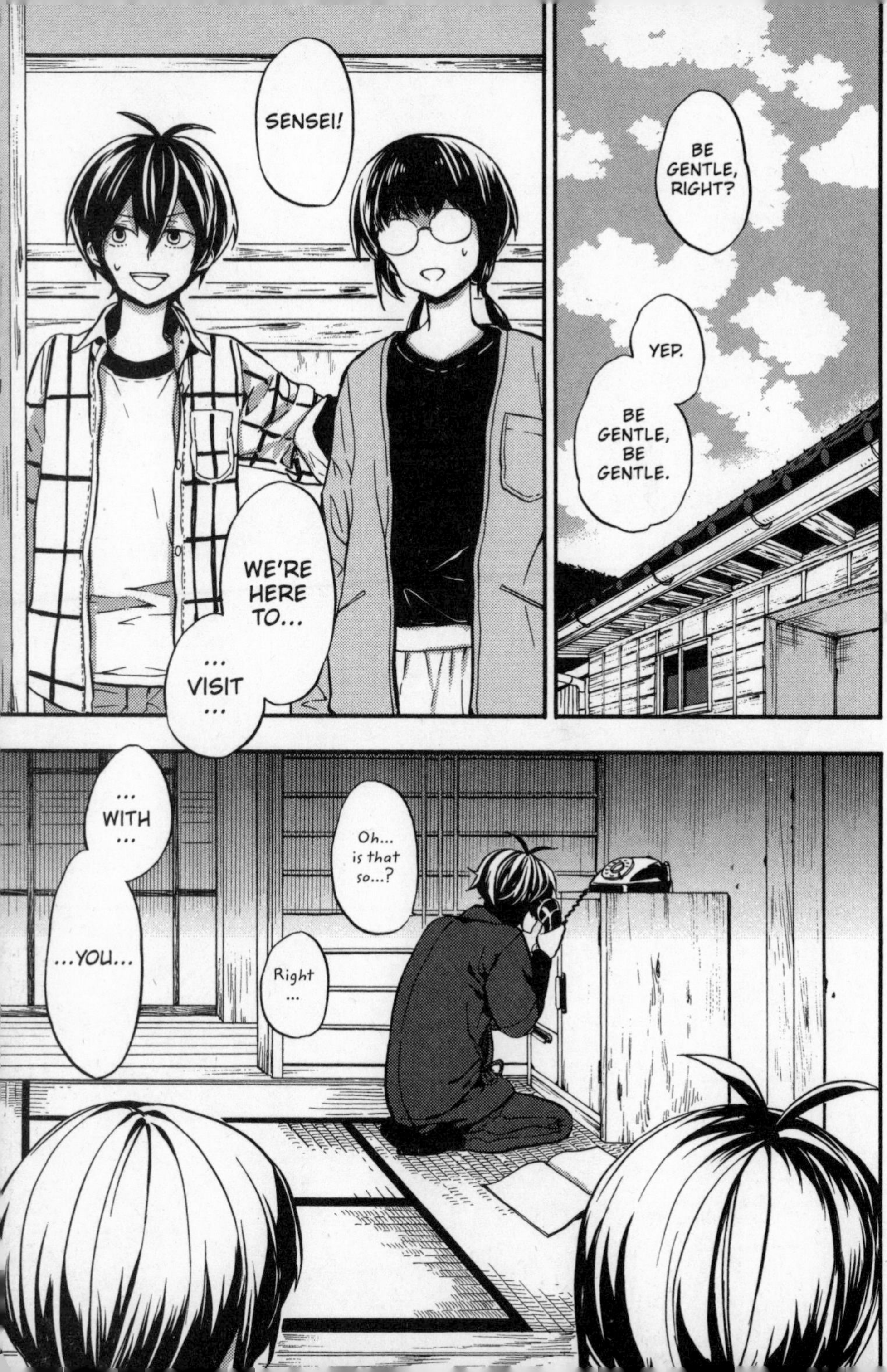
BE GENTLE, RIGHT?
YEP.
BE GENTLE, BE GENTLE.
SENSEI!
WE'RE HERE TO...
...VISIT...
Oh... is that so...?
Right...
...WITH...
...YOU...

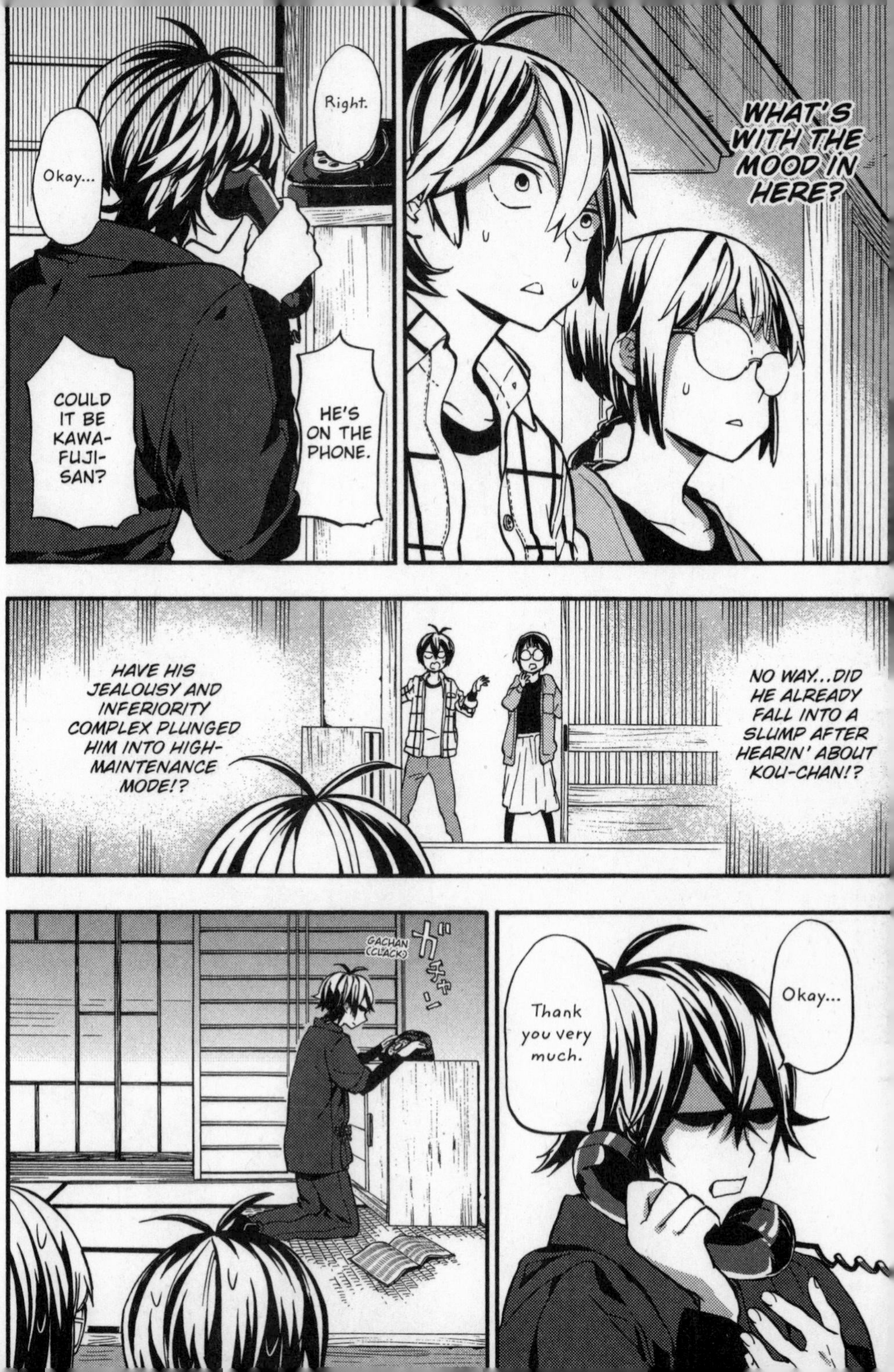
WHAT'S WITH THE MOOD IN HERE?
Right.
Okay...
HE'S ON THE PHONE.
COULD IT BE KAWA-FUJI-SAN?
NO WAY...DID HE ALREADY FALL INTO A SLUMP AFTER HEARIN' ABOUT KOU-CHAN!?
HAVE HIS JEALOUSY AND INFERIORITY COMPLEX PLUNGED HIM INTO HIGH-MAINTENANCE MODE!?
Okay...
Thank you very much.
ガチャ！
GACHAN (CLACK)

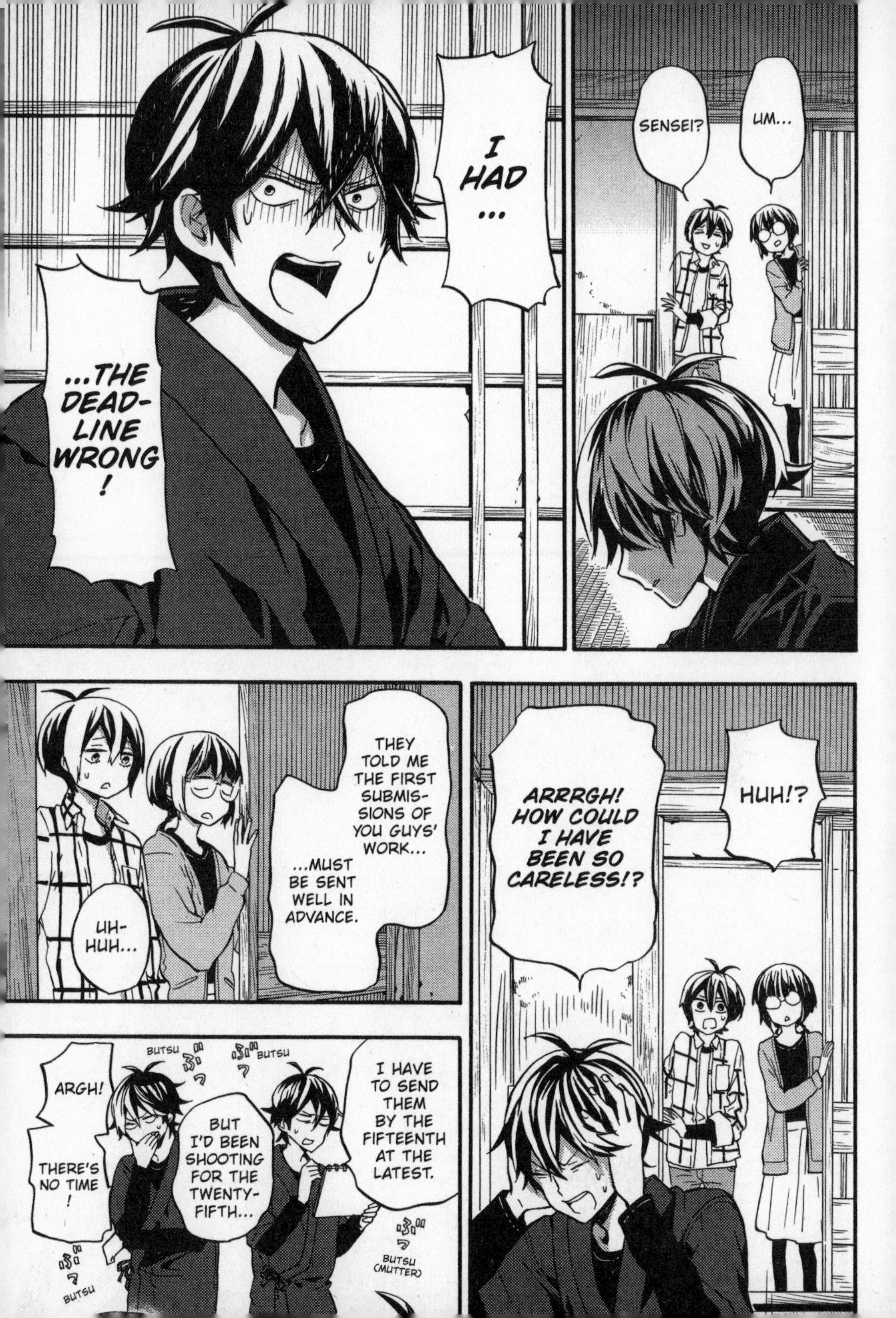
UM...
SENSEI?
I HAD...
...THE DEAD-LINE WRONG!
HUH!?
ARRRGH! HOW COULD I HAVE BEEN SO CARELESS!?
THEY TOLD ME THE FIRST SUBMIS-SIONS OF YOU GUYS' WORK...
...MUST BE SENT WELL IN ADVANCE.
UH-HUH...
BUTSU
I HAVE TO SEND THEM BY THE FIFTEENTH AT THE LATEST.
BUTSU (MUTTER)
BUT I'D BEEN SHOOTING FOR THE TWENTY-FIFTH...
BUTSU
ARGH!
THERE'S NO TIME!
BUTSU

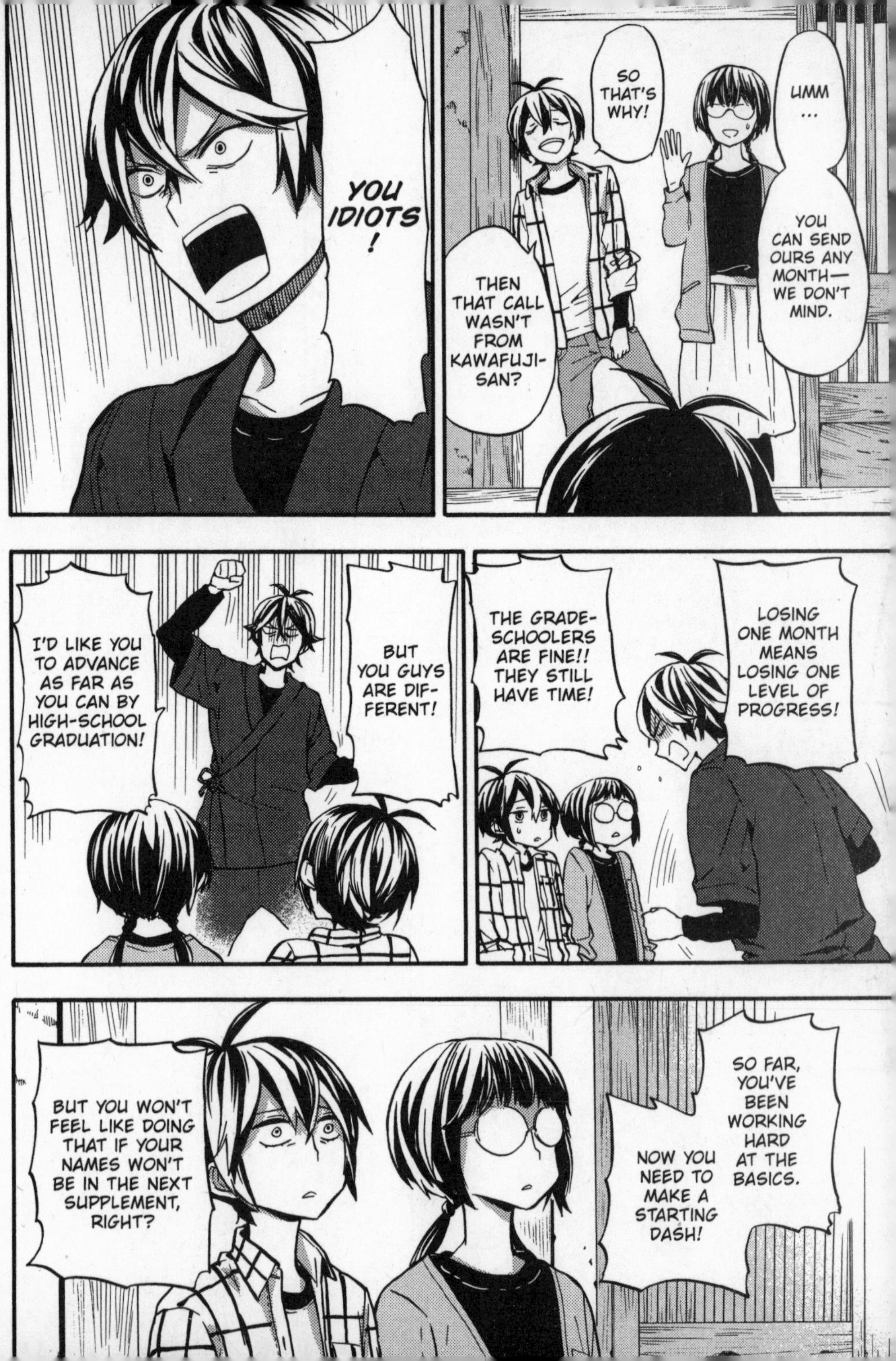
UMM ...
SO THAT'S WHY!
YOU CAN SEND OURS ANY MONTH— WE DON'T MIND.
THEN THAT CALL WASN'T FROM KAWAFUJI-SAN?
YOU IDIOTS!
LOSING ONE MONTH MEANS LOSING ONE LEVEL OF PROGRESS!
THE GRADE-SCHOOLERS ARE FINE!! THEY STILL HAVE TIME!
BUT YOU GUYS ARE DIF-FERENT!
I'D LIKE YOU TO ADVANCE AS FAR AS YOU CAN BY HIGH-SCHOOL GRADUATION!
SO FAR, YOU'VE BEEN WORKING HARD AT THE BASICS.
NOW YOU NEED TO MAKE A STARTING DASH!
BUT YOU WON'T FEEL LIKE DOING THAT IF YOUR NAMES WON'T BE IN THE NEXT SUPPLEMENT, RIGHT?

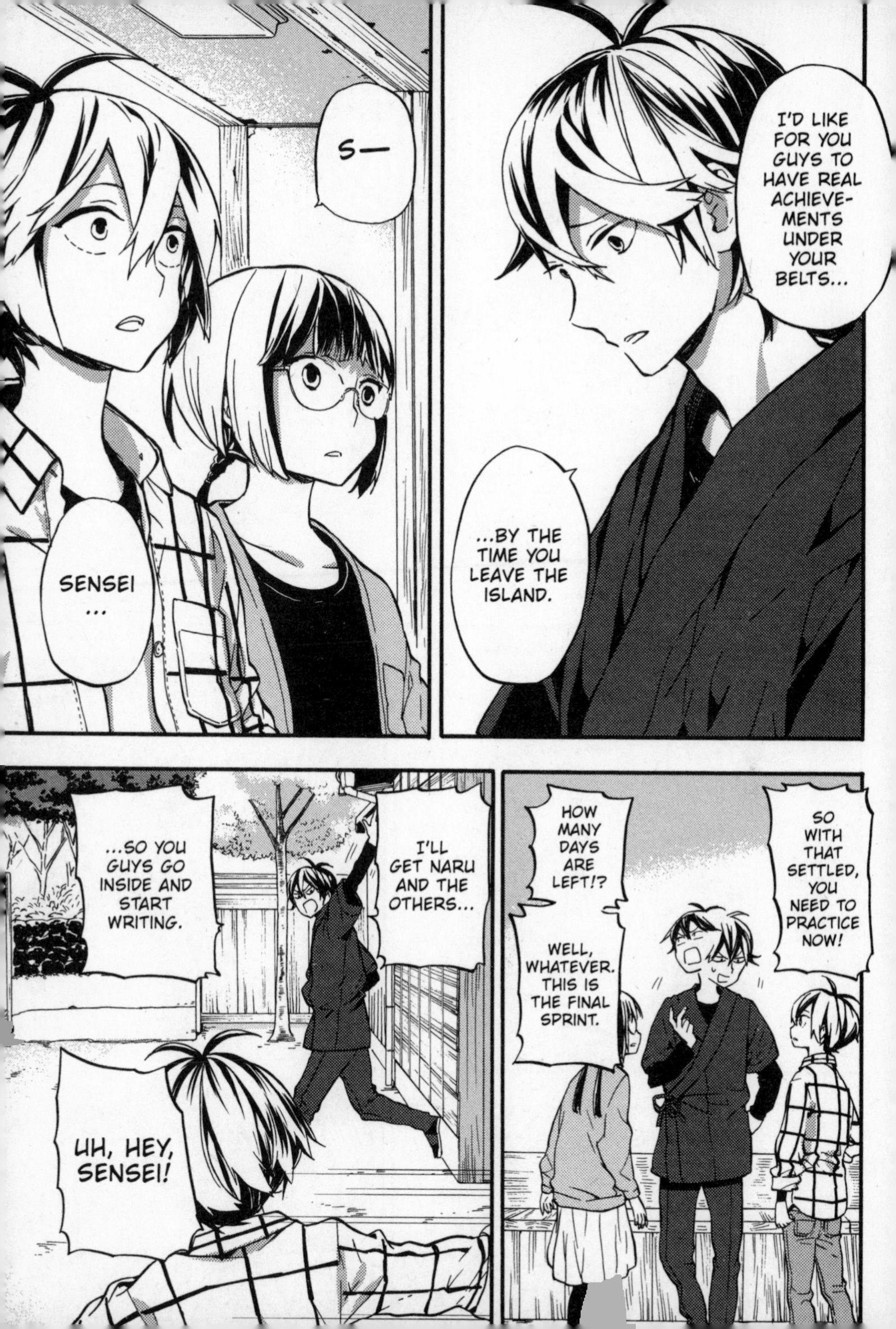
I'D LIKE FOR YOU GUYS TO HAVE REAL ACHIEVE-MENTS UNDER YOUR BELTS...
...BY THE TIME YOU LEAVE THE ISLAND.
S—
SENSEI ...
SO WITH THAT SETTLED, YOU NEED TO PRACTICE NOW!
HOW MANY DAYS ARE LEFT!?
WELL, WHATEVER. THIS IS THE FINAL SPRINT.
I'LL GET NARU AND THE OTHERS...
...SO YOU GUYS GO INSIDE AND START WRITING.
UH, HEY, SENSEI!

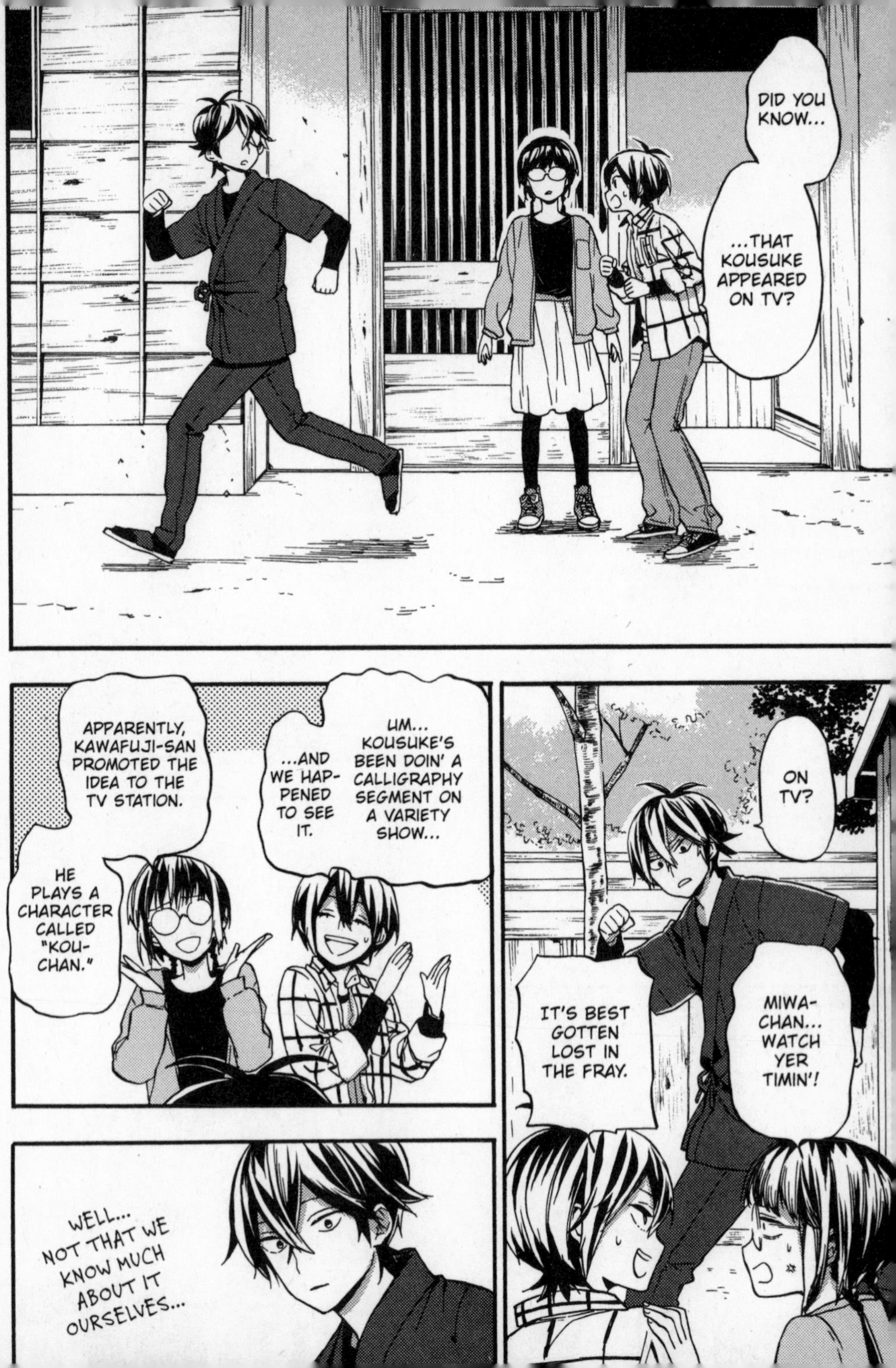
DID YOU KNOW...
...THAT KOUSUKE APPEARED ON TV?
ON TV?
MIWA-CHAN... WATCH YER TIMIN'!
IT'S BEST GOTTEN LOST IN THE FRAY.
UM... KOUSUKE'S BEEN DOIN' A CALLIGRAPHY SEGMENT ON A VARIETY SHOW...
...AND WE HAP-PENED TO SEE IT.
APPARENTLY, KAWAFUJI-SAN PROMOTED THE IDEA TO THE TV STATION.
HE PLAYS A CHARACTER CALLED "KOU-CHAN."
WELL... NOT THAT WE KNOW MUCH ABOUT IT OURSELVES...

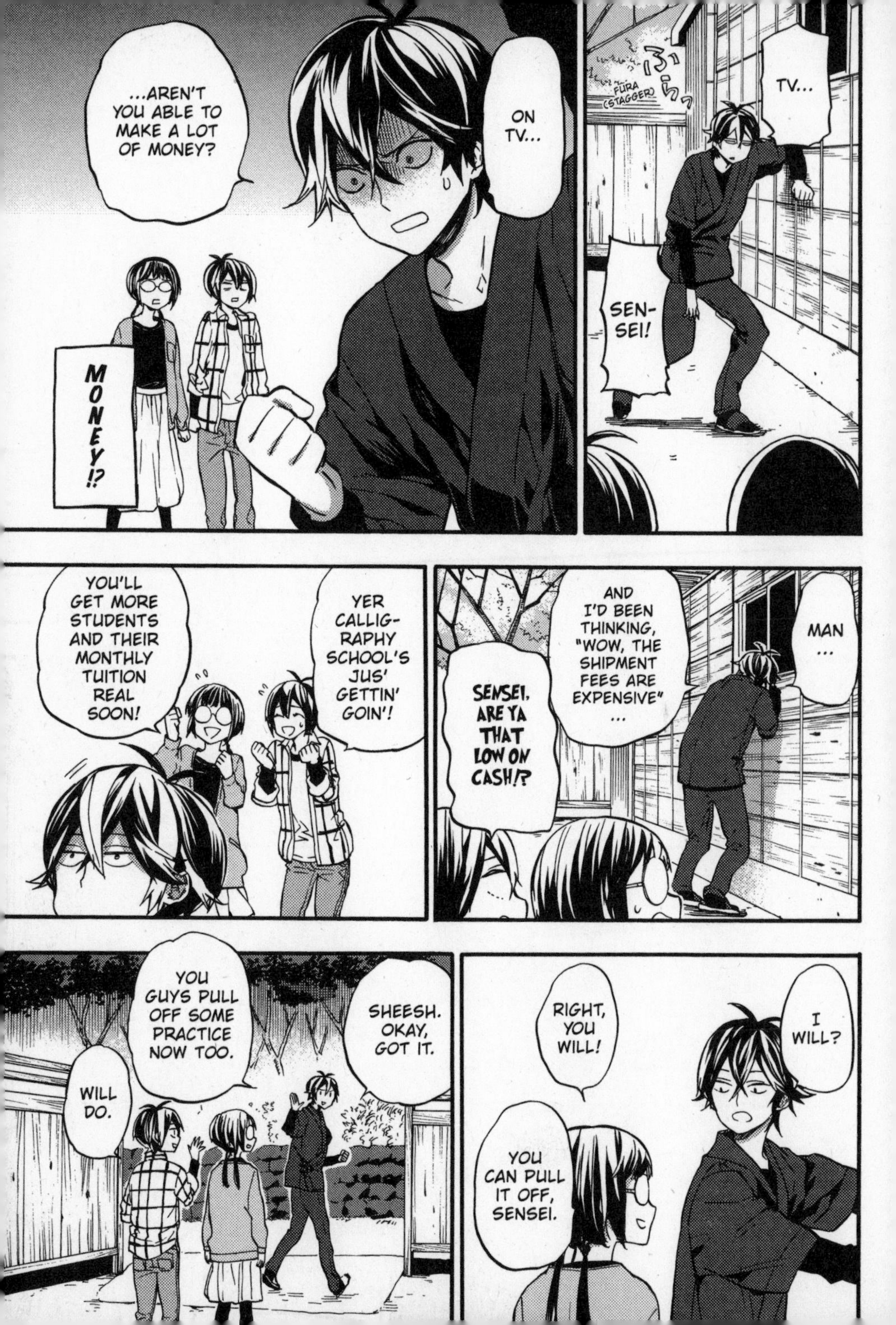
TV...
ふらっ
FURA (STAGGER)
SEN-SEI!
ON TV...
...AREN'T YOU ABLE TO MAKE A LOT OF MONEY?
MONEY!?
MAN ...
AND I'D BEEN THINKING, "WOW, THE SHIPMENT FEES ARE EXPENSIVE" ...
SENSEI, ARE YA THAT LOW ON CASH!?
YER CALLIG-RAPHY SCHOOL'S JUS' GETTIN' GOIN'!
YOU'LL GET MORE STUDENTS AND THEIR MONTHLY TUITION REAL SOON!
I WILL?
RIGHT, YOU WILL!
YOU CAN PULL IT OFF, SENSEI.
SHEESH. OKAY, GOT IT.
YOU GUYS PULL OFF SOME PRACTICE NOW TOO.
WILL DO.

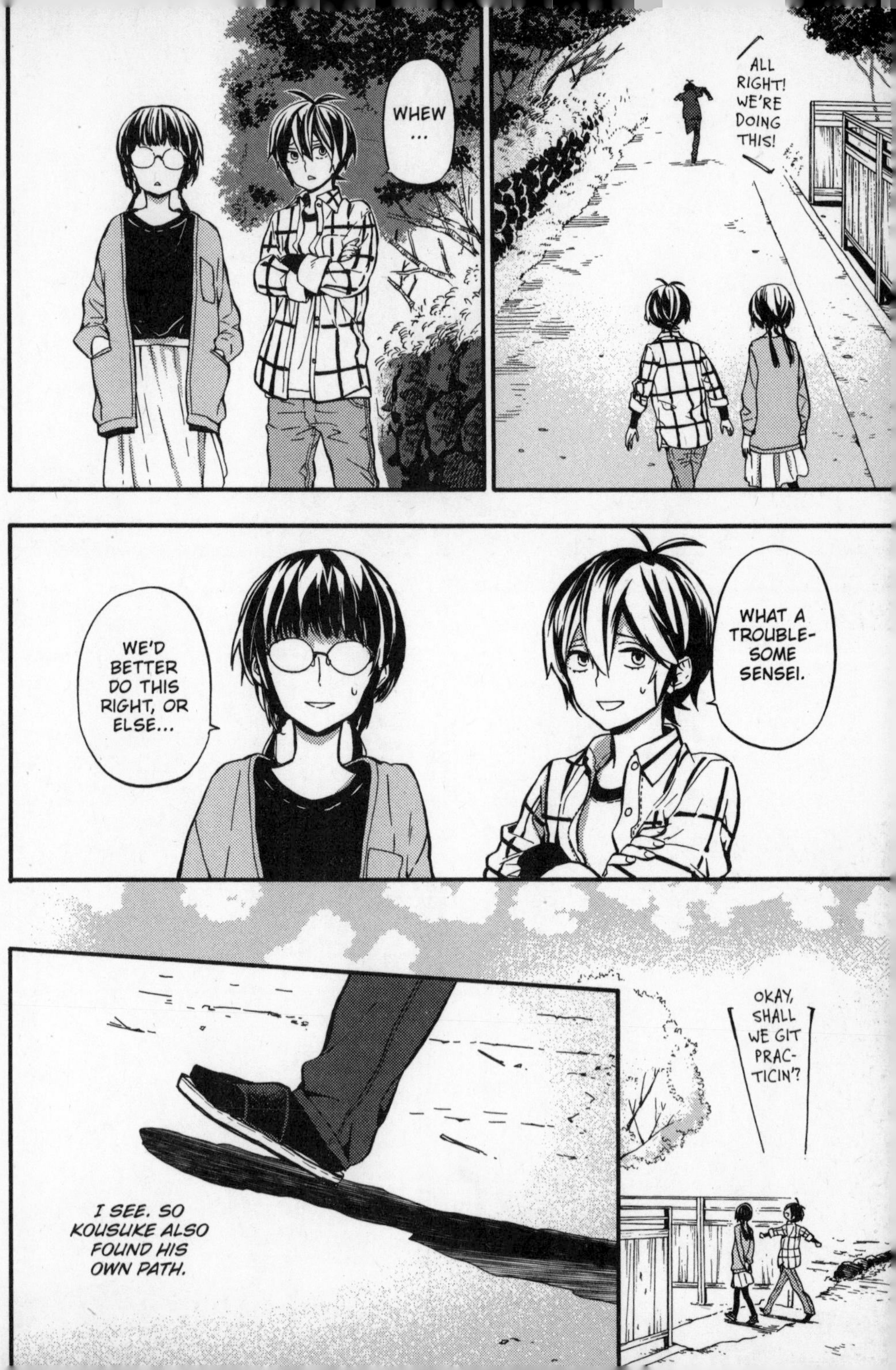
ALL RIGHT! WE'RE DOING THIS!
WHEW...
WHAT A TROUBLE-SOME SENSEI.
WE'D BETTER DO THIS RIGHT, OR ELSE...
OKAY, SHALL WE GIT PRAC-TICIN'?
I SEE. SO KOUSUKE ALSO FOUND HIS OWN PATH.

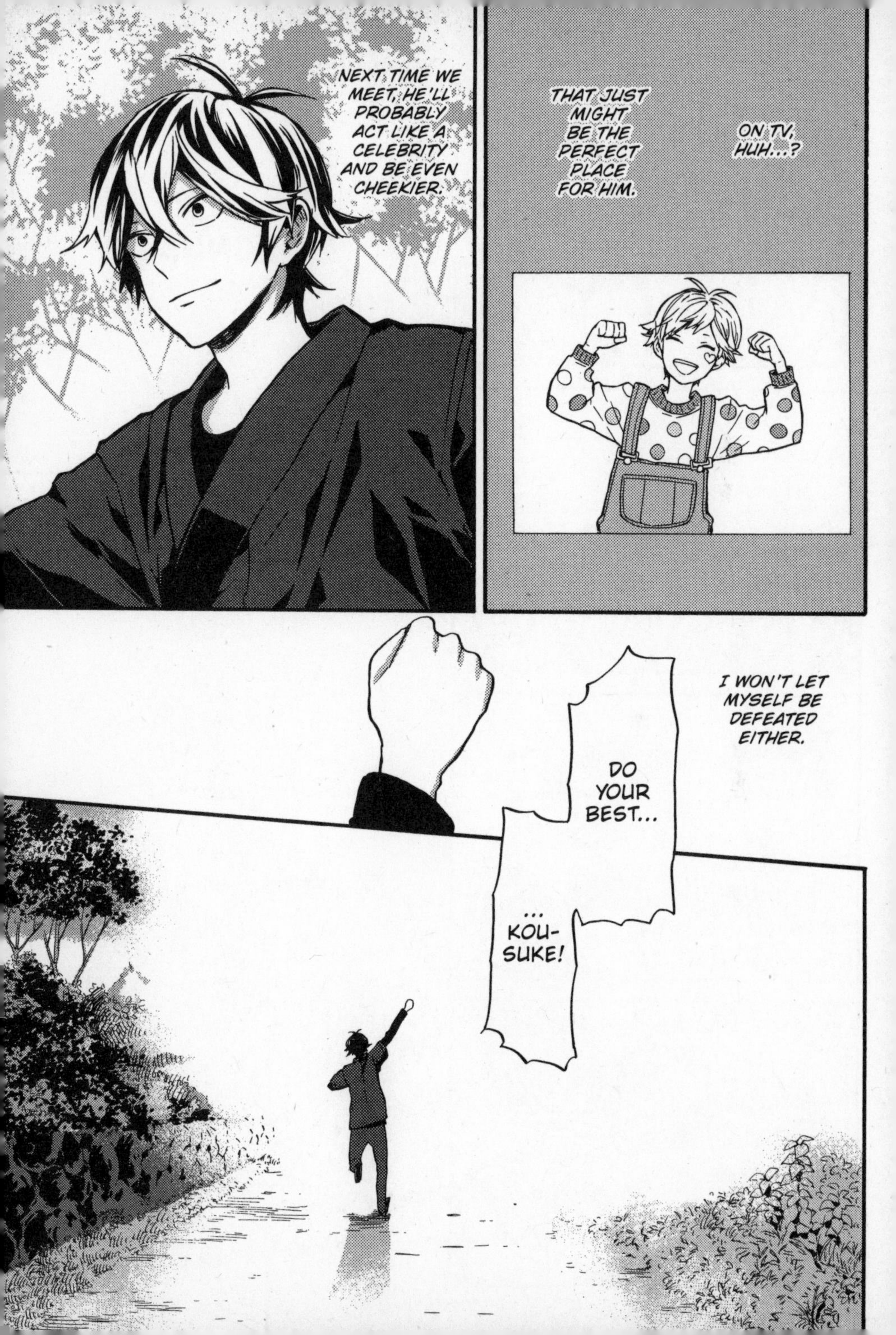
ON TV, HUH...?
THAT JUST MIGHT BE THE PERFECT PLACE FOR HIM.
NEXT TIME WE MEET, HE'LL PROBABLY ACT LIKE A CELEBRITY AND BE EVEN CHEEKIER.
I WON'T LET MYSELF BE DEFEATED EITHER.
DO YOUR BEST...
...KOU-SUKE!

BONUS

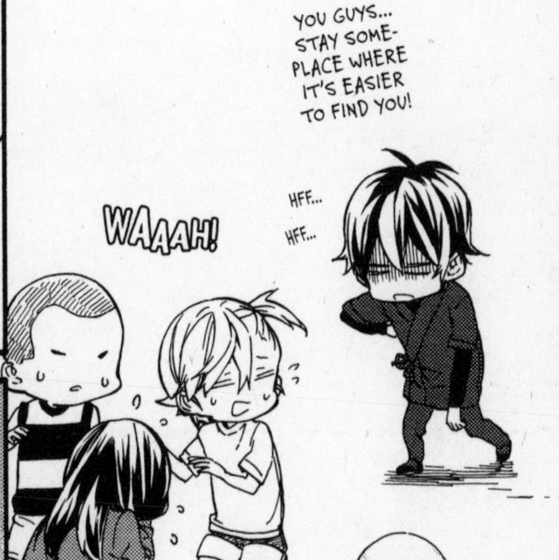
YOU GUYS... STAY SOME-PLACE WHERE IT'S EASIER TO FIND YOU!
HFF... HFF...
WAAAH!

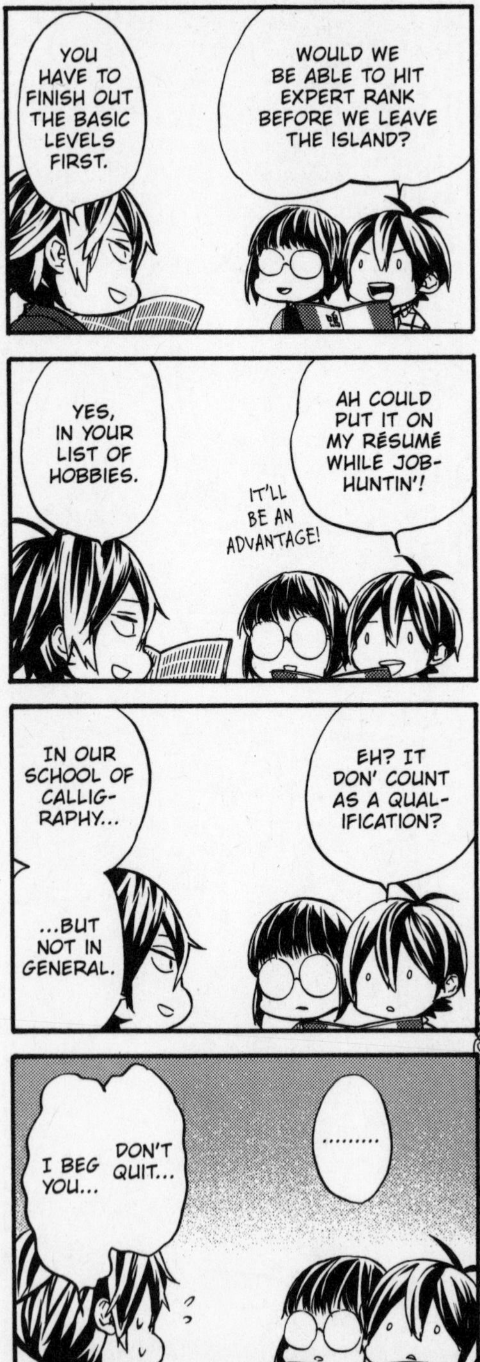
WOULD WE BE ABLE TO HIT EXPERT RANK BEFORE WE LEAVE THE ISLAND?
YOU HAVE TO FINISH OUT THE BASIC LEVELS FIRST.
AH COULD PUT IT ON MY RÉSUMÉ WHILE JOB-HUNTIN'!
IT'LL BE AN ADVANTAGE!
YES, IN YOUR LIST OF HOBBIES.
EH? IT DON' COUNT AS A QUAL-IFICATION?
IN OUR SCHOOL OF CALLIG-RAPHY...
...BUT NOT IN GENERAL.
....
DON'T QUIT...
I BEG YOU...

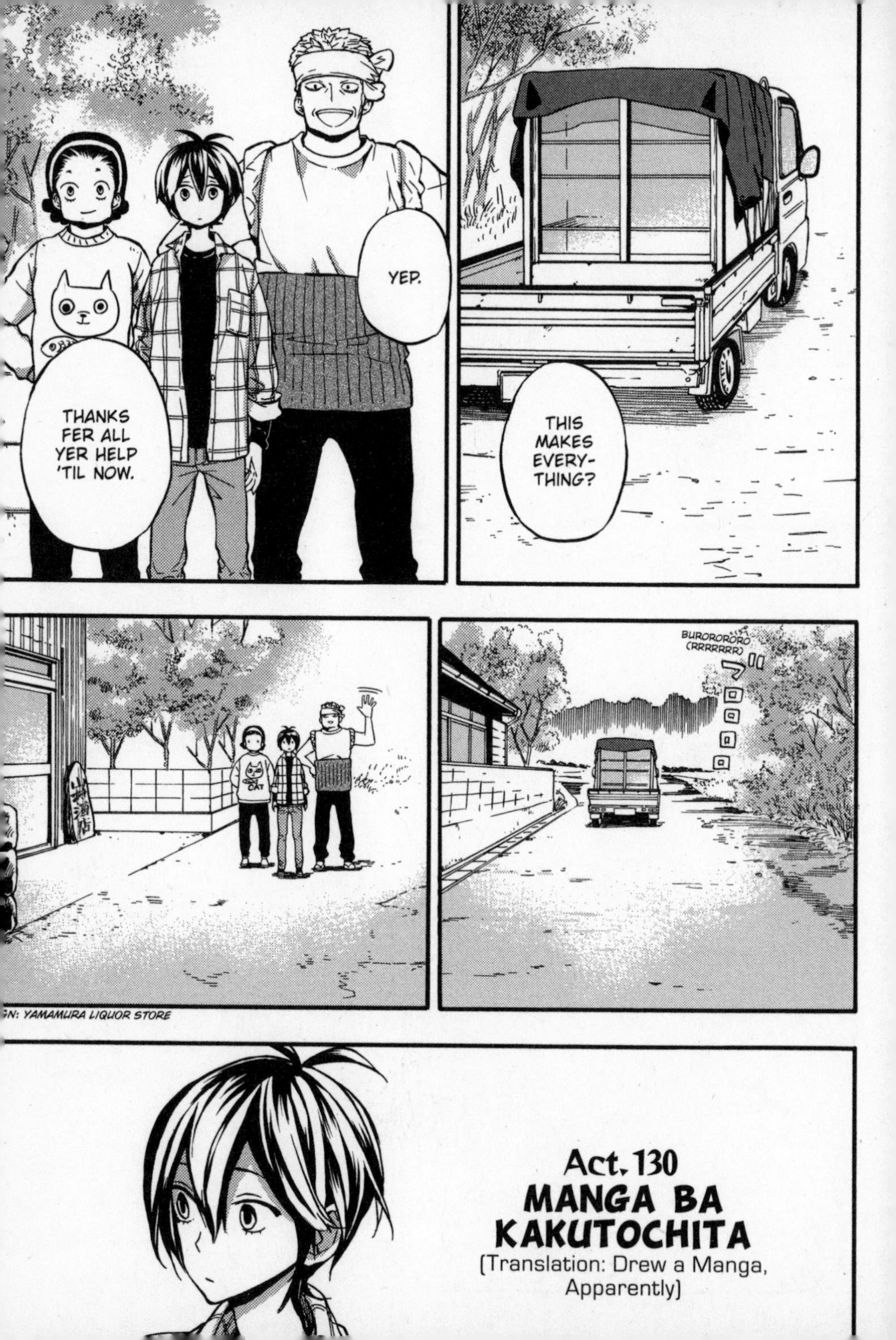
THIS MAKES EVERYTHING?
YEP.
THANKS FER ALL YER HELP 'TIL NOW.
BURORORORO (RRRRRRR)
GN: YAMAMURA LIQUOR STORE
Act. 130
MANGA BA KAKUTOCHITA
(Translation: Drew a Manga, Apparently)

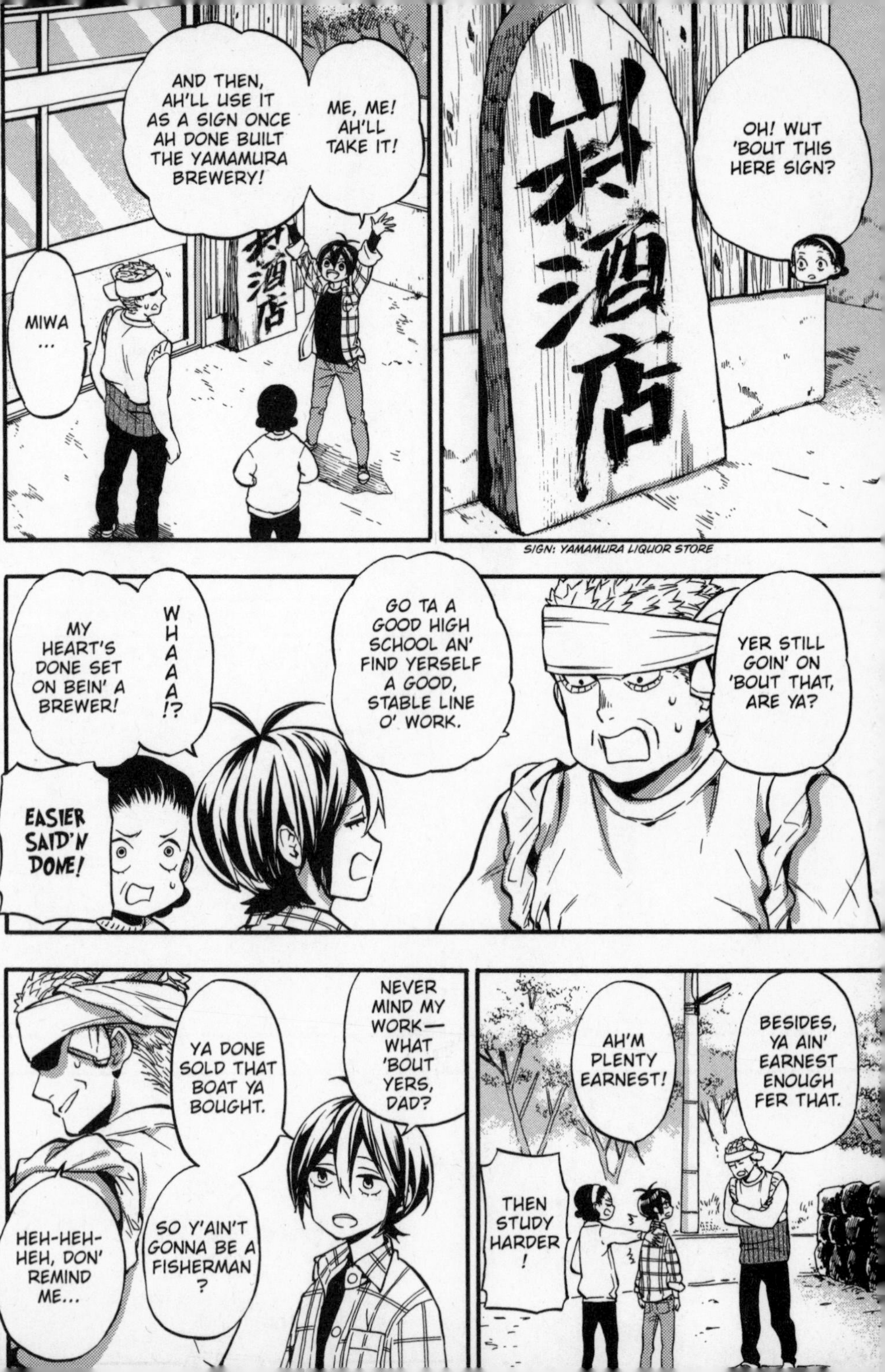
OH! WUT 'BOUT THIS HERE SIGN?
SIGN: YAMAMURA LIQUOR STORE
ME, ME! AH'LL TAKE IT!
AND THEN, AH'LL USE IT AS A SIGN ONCE AH DONE BUILT THE YAMAMURA BREWERY!
MIWA...
YER STILL GOIN' ON 'BOUT THAT, ARE YA?
GO TA A GOOD HIGH SCHOOL AN' FIND YERSELF A GOOD, STABLE LINE O' WORK.
WHAAAA!?
MY HEART'S DONE SET ON BEIN' A BREWER!
EASIER SAID'N DONE!
BESIDES, YA AIN' EARNEST ENOUGH FER THAT.
AH'M PLENTY EARNEST!
THEN STUDY HARDER!
NEVER MIND MY WORK— WHAT 'BOUT YERS, DAD?
YA DONE SOLD THAT BOAT YA BOUGHT.
SO Y'AIN'T GONNA BE A FISHERMAN?
HEH-HEH-HEH, DON' REMIND ME...

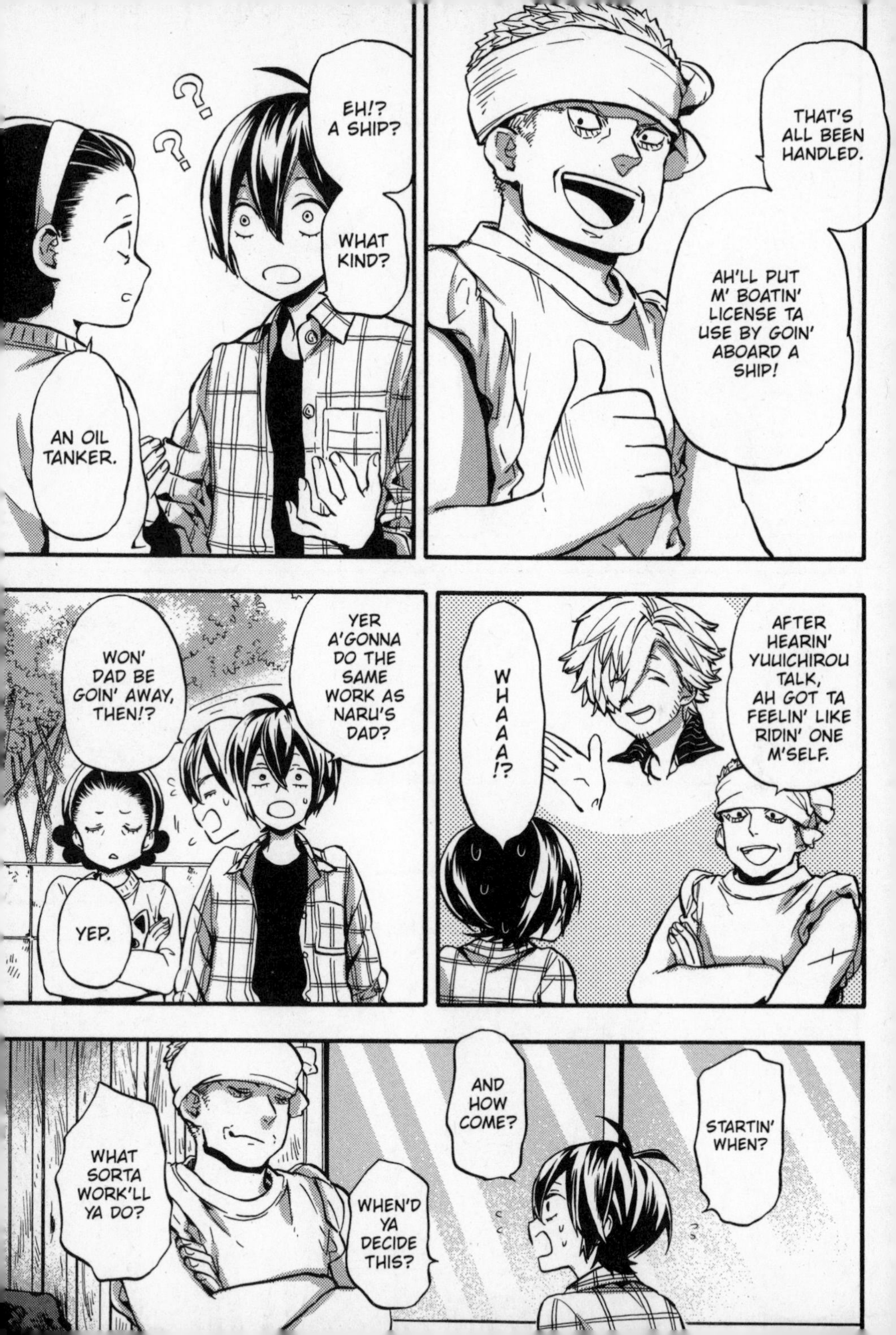
THAT'S ALL BEEN HANDLED.
AH'LL PUT M' BOATIN' LICENSE TA USE BY GOIN' ABOARD A SHIP!
EH!? A SHIP?
WHAT KIND?
AN OIL TANKER.
AFTER HEARIN' YUUICHIROU TALK, AH GOT TA FEELIN' LIKE RIDIN' ONE M'SELF.
WHAAAA!?
YER A'GONNA DO THE SAME WORK AS NARU'S DAD?
WON' DAD BE GOIN' AWAY, THEN!?
YEP.
STARTIN' WHEN?
AND HOW COME?
WHEN'D YA DECIDE THIS?
WHAT SORTA WORK'LL YA DO?

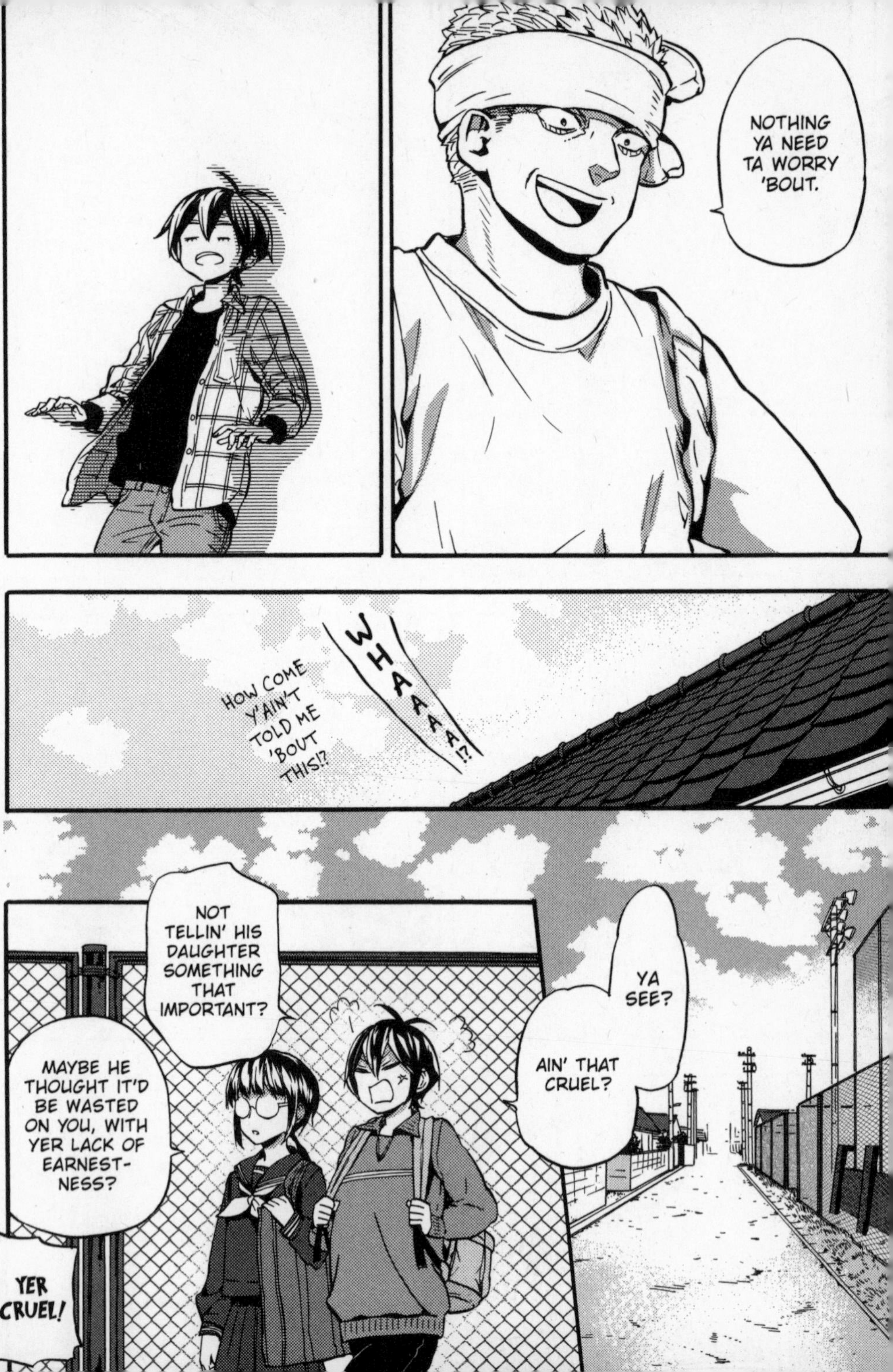
NOTHING YA NEED TA WORRY 'BOUT.
WHAAAAA!?
HOW COME Y'AIN'T TOLD ME 'BOUT THIS!?
YA SEE?
AIN' THAT CRUEL?
NOT TELLIN' HIS DAUGHTER SOMETHING THAT IMPORTANT?
MAYBE HE THOUGHT IT'D BE WASTED ON YOU, WITH YER LACK OF EARNEST-NESS?
YER CRUEL!

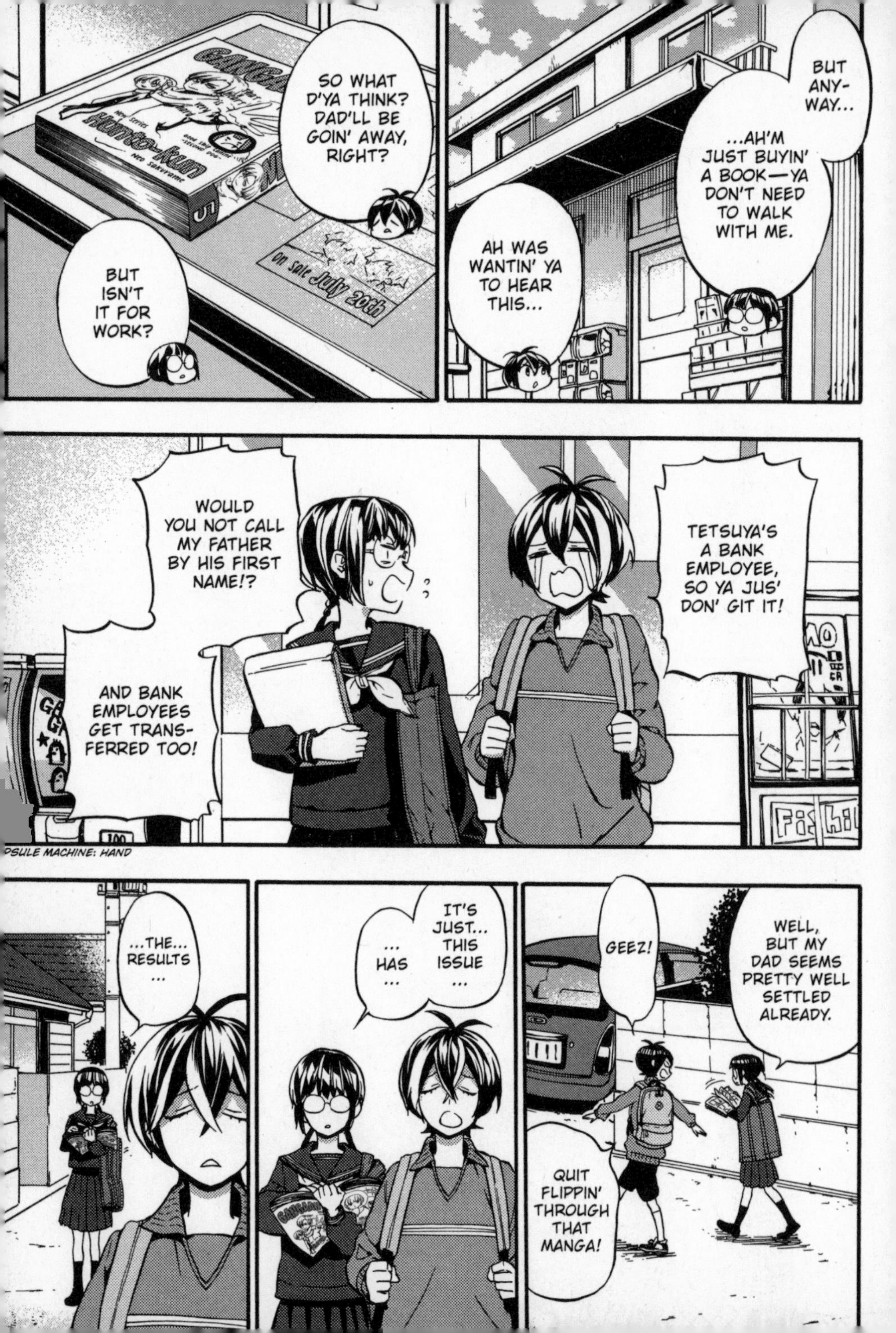
BUT ANY-WAY...
...AH'M JUST BUYIN' A BOOK—YA DON'T NEED TO WALK WITH ME.
AH WAS WANTIN' YA TO HEAR THIS...
SO WHAT D'YA THINK? DAD'LL BE GOIN' AWAY, RIGHT?
On sale July 20th
BUT ISN'T IT FOR WORK?
TETSUYA'S A BANK EMPLOYEE, SO YA JUS' DON' GIT IT!
WOULD YOU NOT CALL MY FATHER BY HIS FIRST NAME!?
AND BANK EMPLOYEES GET TRANS-FERRED TOO!
WELL, BUT MY DAD SEEMS PRETTY WELL SETTLED ALREADY.
GEEZ!
QUIT FLIPPIN' THROUGH THAT MANGA!
IT'S JUST... THIS ISSUE ...
... HAS ...
...THE... RESULTS ...
PSULE MACHINE: HAND

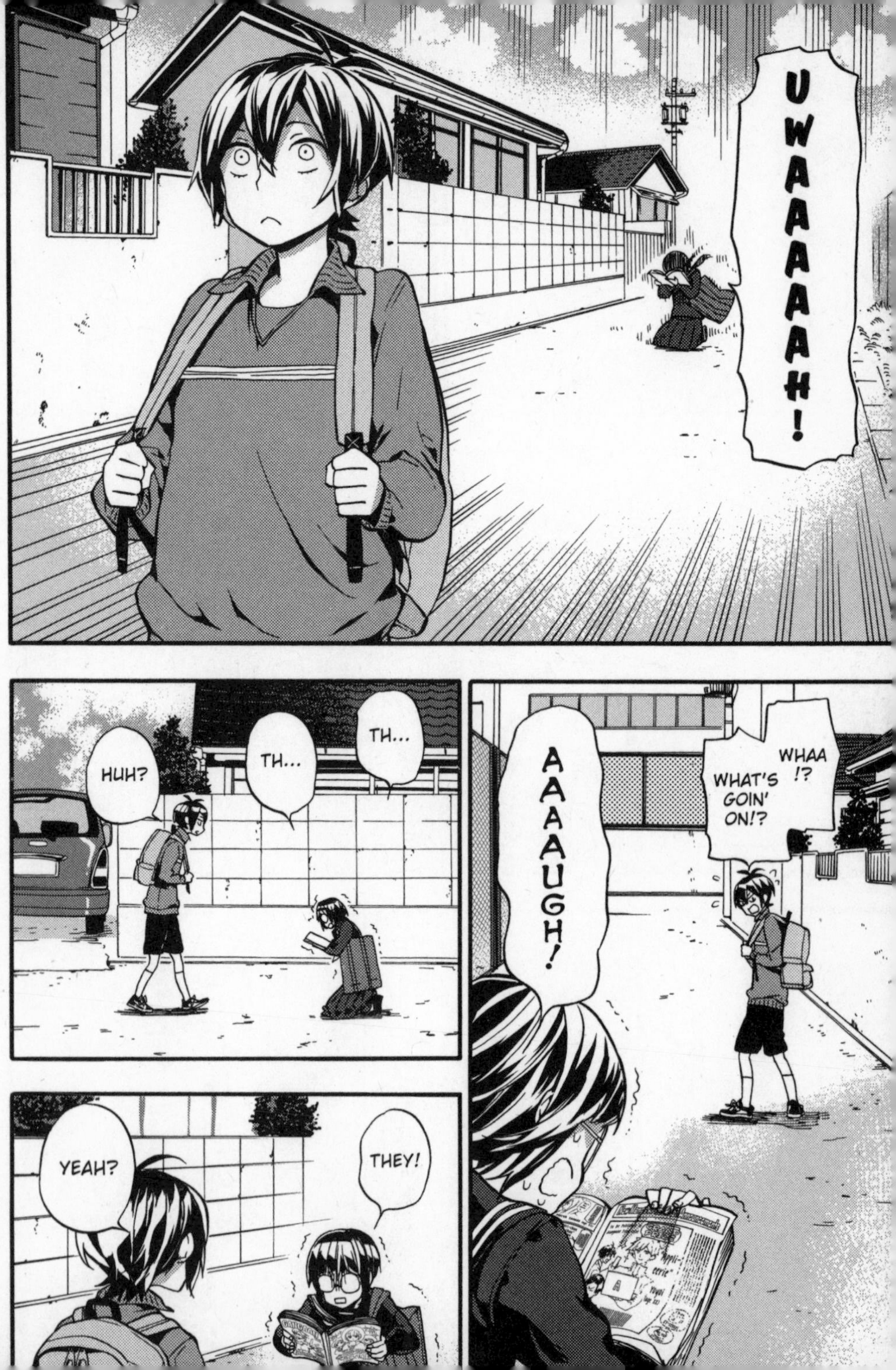
UWAAAAAAH!
WHAA!? WHAT'S GOIN' ON!?
AAAAAUGH!
TH...
TH...
HUH?
THEY!
YEAH?

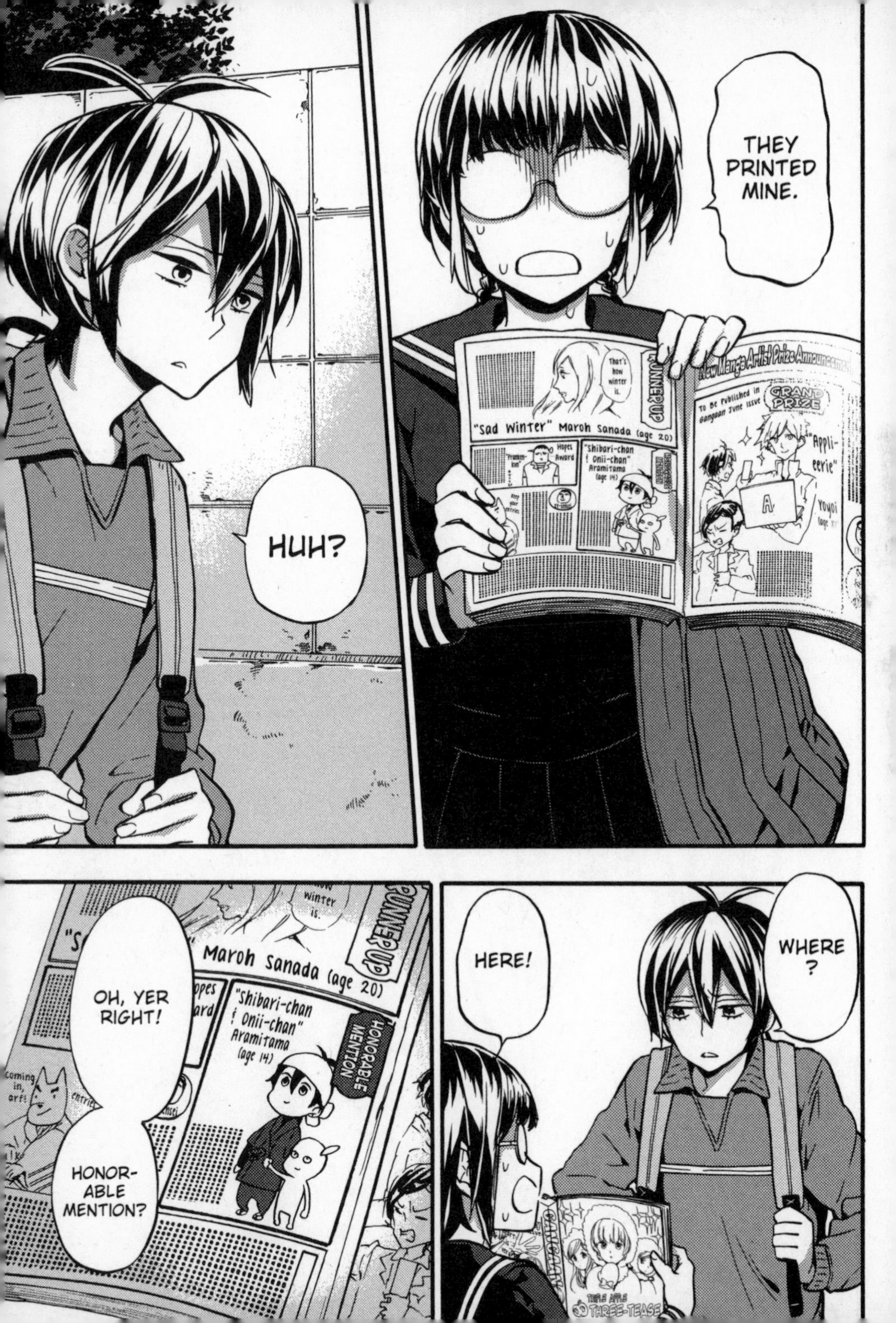
THEY PRINTED MINE.
RUNNER UP
That's how winter is.
"Sad Winter" Maroh Sanada (age 20)
"Shibari-chan & Onii-chan" Aramitama (age 14)
GRAND PRIZE
"Appli-eerie"
HUH?
WHERE ?
HERE!
RUNNER UP
Maroh Sanada (age 20)
"Shibari-chan & Onii-chan" Aramitama (age 14)
HONORABLE MENTION
OH, YER RIGHT!
HONOR-ABLE MENTION?

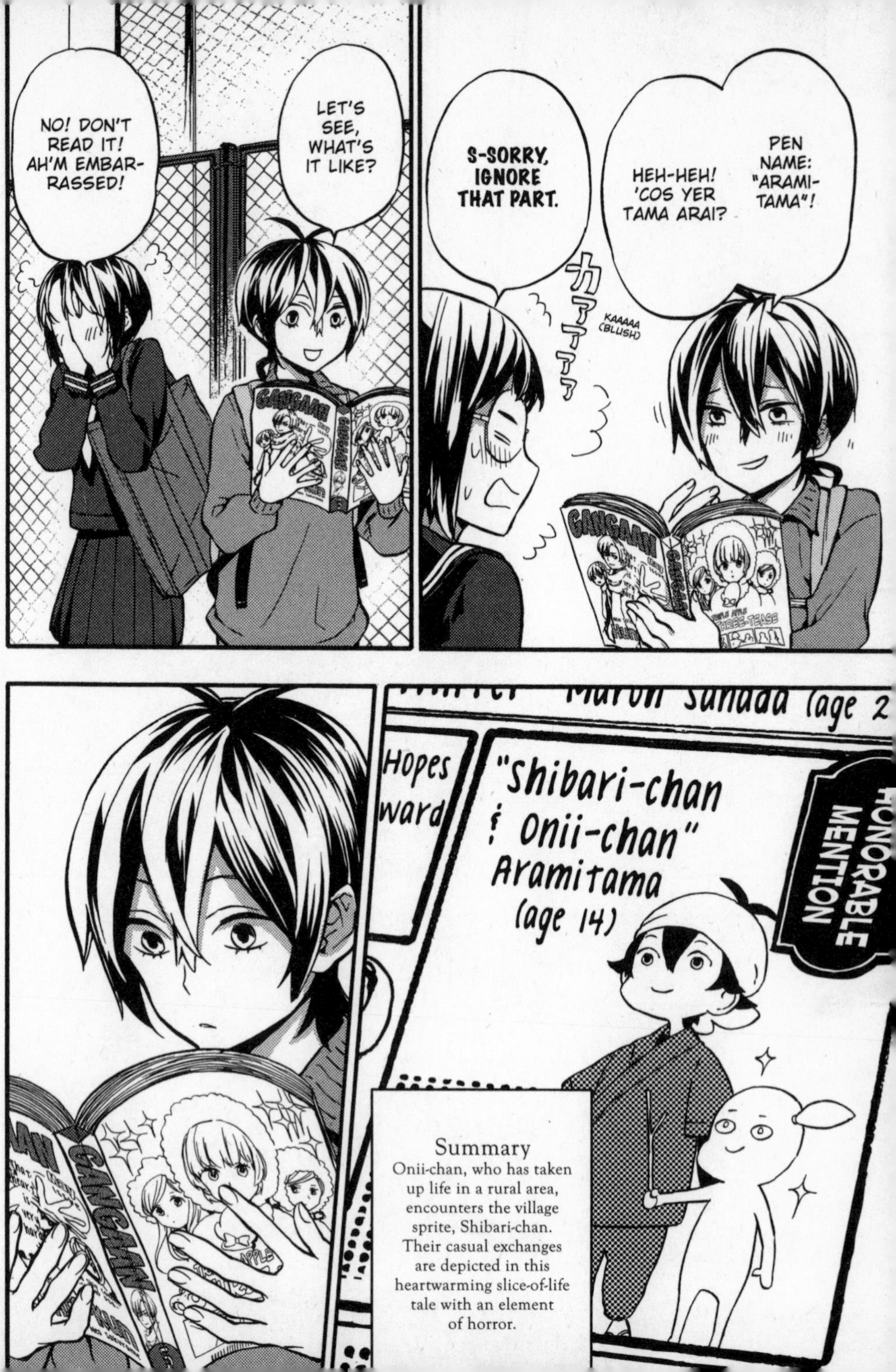
PEN NAME: "ARAMI-TAMA"!
HEH-HEH! 'COS YER TAMA ARAI?
S-SORRY, IGNORE THAT PART.
カァァァァ
KAAAAA (BLUSH)
LET'S SEE, WHAT'S IT LIKE?
NO! DON'T READ IT! AH'M EMBAR-RASSED!
Maron Sanada (age 2
Hopes
ward
HONORABLE MENTION
"Shibari-chan & Onii-chan"
Aramitama
(age 14)
Summary
Onii-chan, who has taken up life in a rural area, encounters the village sprite, Shibari-chan. Their casual exchanges are depicted in this heartwarming slice-of-life tale with an element of horror.

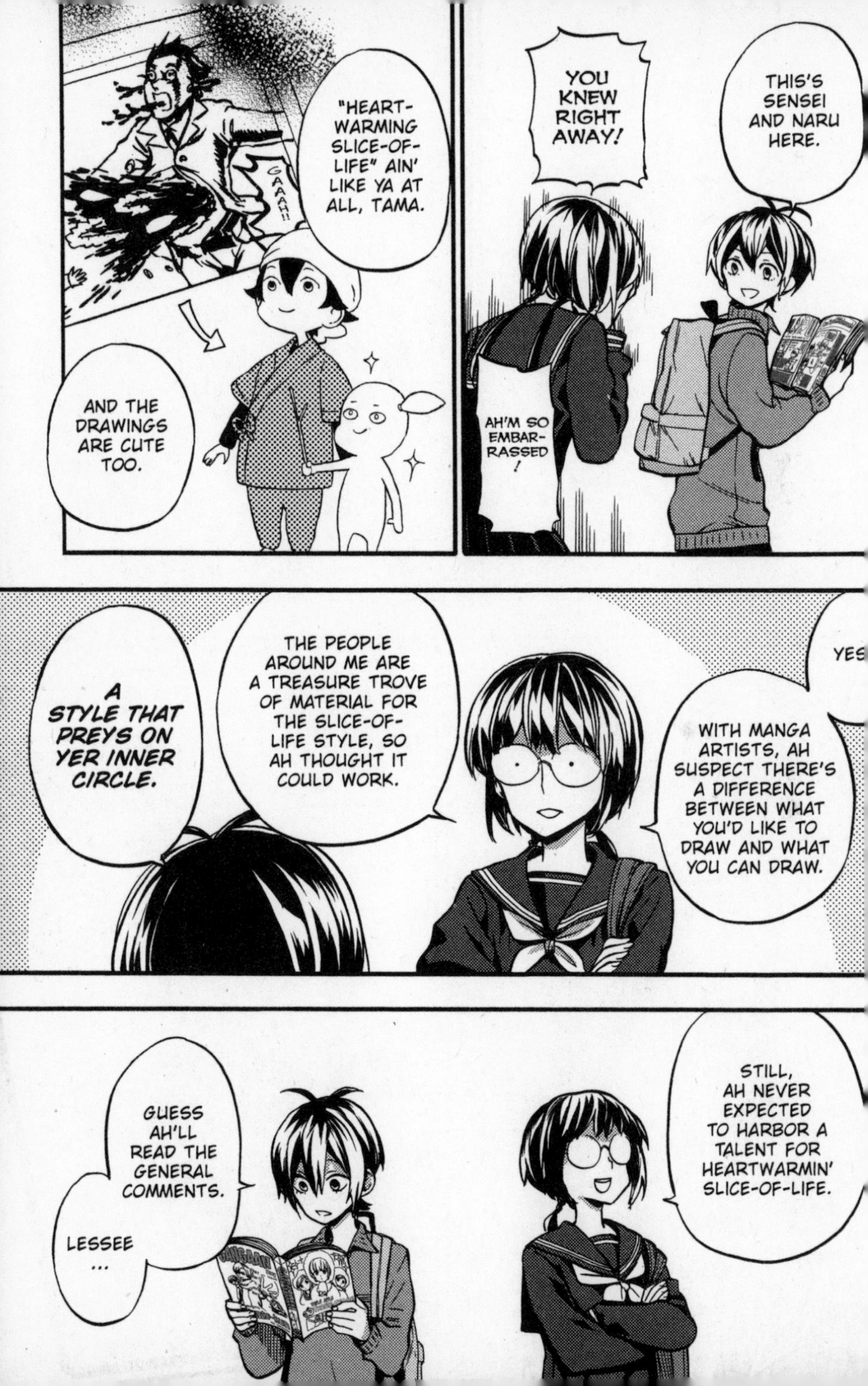
THIS'S SENSEI AND NARU HERE.
YOU KNEW RIGHT AWAY!
AH'M SO EMBARRASSED!
"HEART-WARMING SLICE-OF-LIFE" AIN' LIKE YA AT ALL, TAMA.
GAAAAH!!
AND THE DRAWINGS ARE CUTE TOO.
YES
WITH MANGA ARTISTS, AH SUSPECT THERE'S A DIFFERENCE BETWEEN WHAT YOU'D LIKE TO DRAW AND WHAT YOU CAN DRAW.
THE PEOPLE AROUND ME ARE A TREASURE TROVE OF MATERIAL FOR THE SLICE-OF-LIFE STYLE, SO AH THOUGHT IT COULD WORK.
A STYLE THAT PREYS ON YER INNER CIRCLE.
STILL, AH NEVER EXPECTED TO HARBOR A TALENT FOR HEARTWARMIN' SLICE-OF-LIFE.
GUESS AH'LL READ THE GENERAL COMMENTS.
LESSEE ...

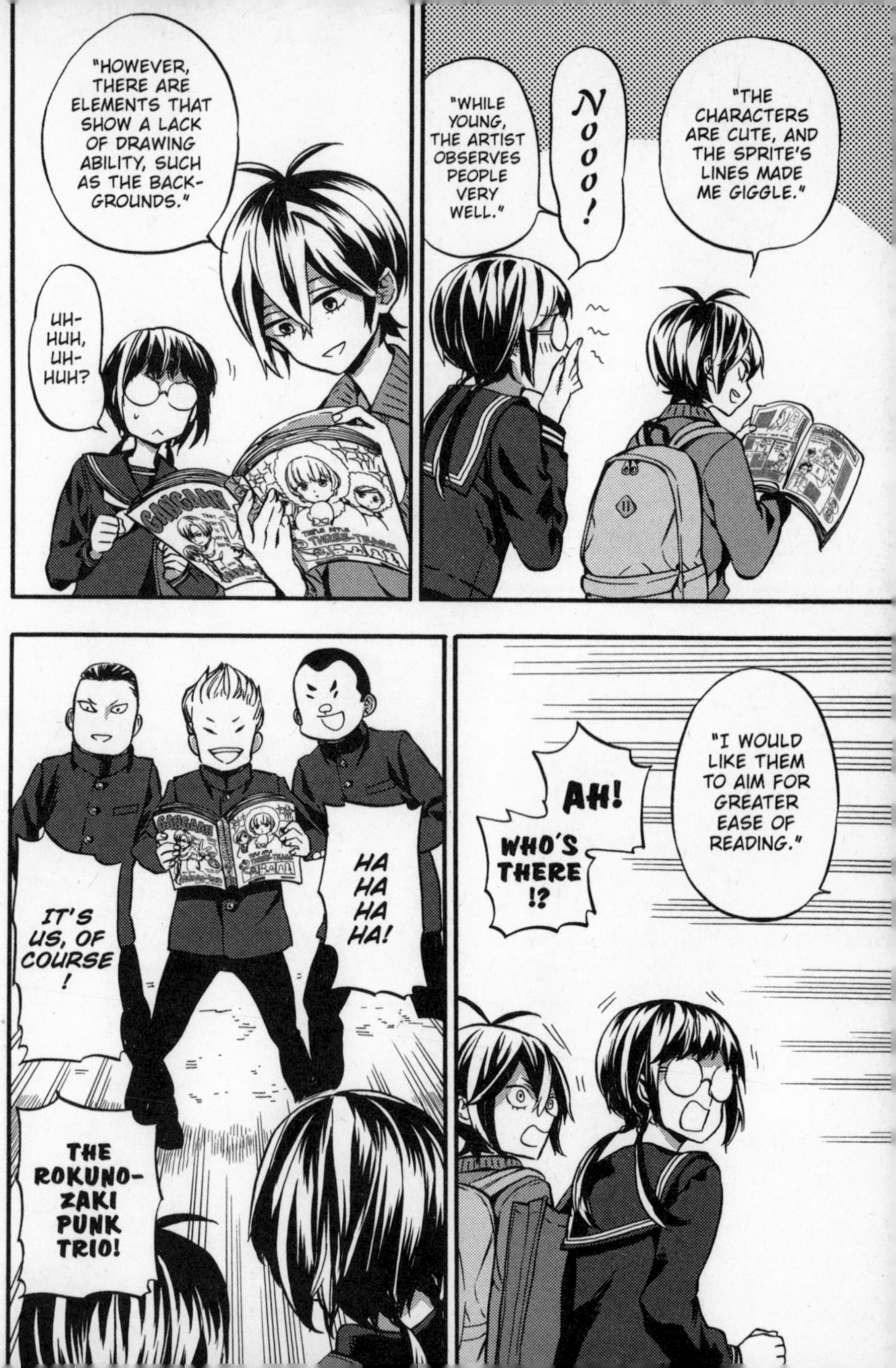
"THE CHARACTERS ARE CUTE, AND THE SPRITE'S LINES MADE ME GIGGLE."
Nooo!
"WHILE YOUNG, THE ARTIST OBSERVES PEOPLE VERY WELL."
"HOWEVER, THERE ARE ELEMENTS THAT SHOW A LACK OF DRAWING ABILITY, SUCH AS THE BACK-GROUNDS."
UH-HUH, UH-HUH?
"I WOULD LIKE THEM TO AIM FOR GREATER EASE OF READING."
AH!
WHO'S THERE!?
HA HA HA HA!
IT'S US, OF COURSE!
THE ROKUNO-ZAKI PUNK TRIO!

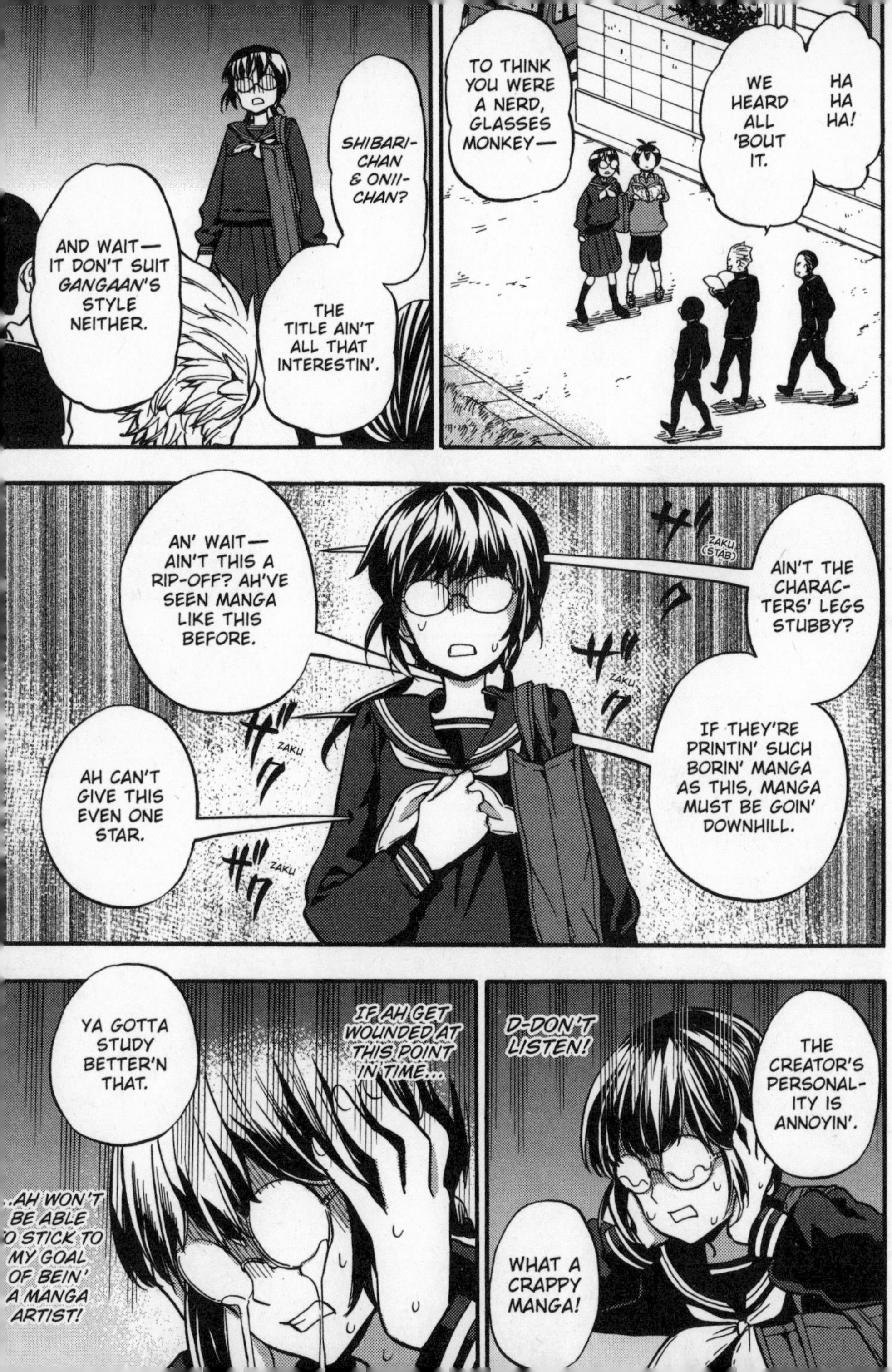
HA HA HA!
WE HEARD ALL 'BOUT IT.
TO THINK YOU WERE A NERD, GLASSES MONKEY—
SHIBARI-CHAN & ONII-CHAN?
THE TITLE AIN'T ALL THAT INTERESTIN'.
AND WAIT— IT DON'T SUIT GANGAAN'S STYLE NEITHER.
AIN'T THE CHARAC-TERS' LEGS STUBBY?
ZAKU (STAB)
AN' WAIT— AIN'T THIS A RIP-OFF? AH'VE SEEN MANGA LIKE THIS BEFORE.
IF THEY'RE PRINTIN' SUCH BORIN' MANGA AS THIS, MANGA MUST BE GOIN' DOWNHILL.
ZAKU
AH CAN'T GIVE THIS EVEN ONE STAR.
ZAKU
ZAKU
THE CREATOR'S PERSONAL-ITY IS ANNOYIN'.
D-DON'T LISTEN!
WHAT A CRAPPY MANGA!
IF AH GET WOUNDED AT THIS POINT IN TIME...
YA GOTTA STUDY BETTER'N THAT.
...AH WON'T BE ABLE TO STICK TO MY GOAL OF BEIN' A MANGA ARTIST!

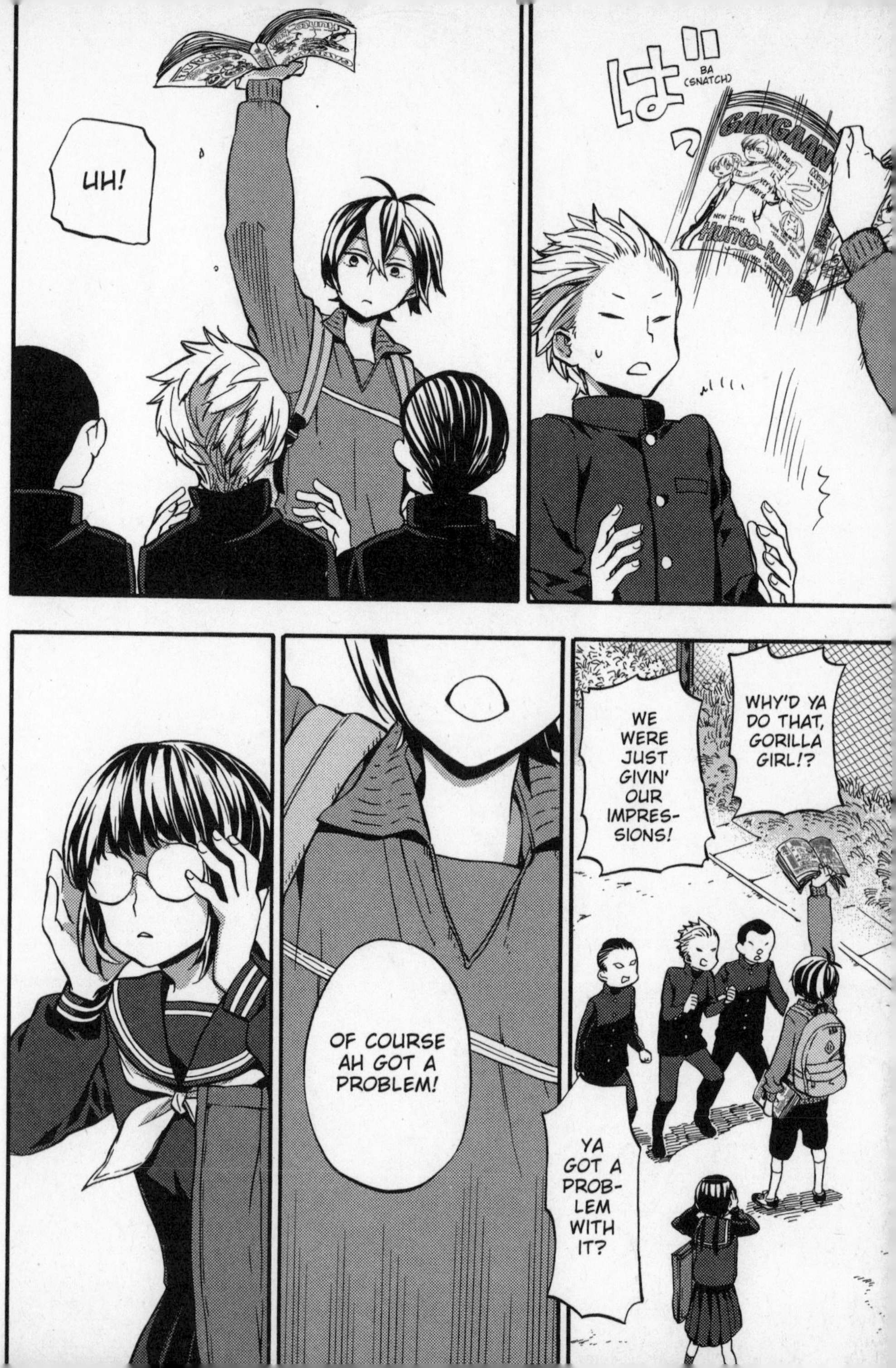
はっ
BA (SNATCH)
GANGAAN
May issue
New Series
Hunto-kun
UH!
WHY'D YA DO THAT, GORILLA GIRL!?
WE WERE JUST GIVIN' OUR IMPRES-SIONS!
YA GOT A PROB-LEM WITH IT?
OF COURSE AH GOT A PROBLEM!

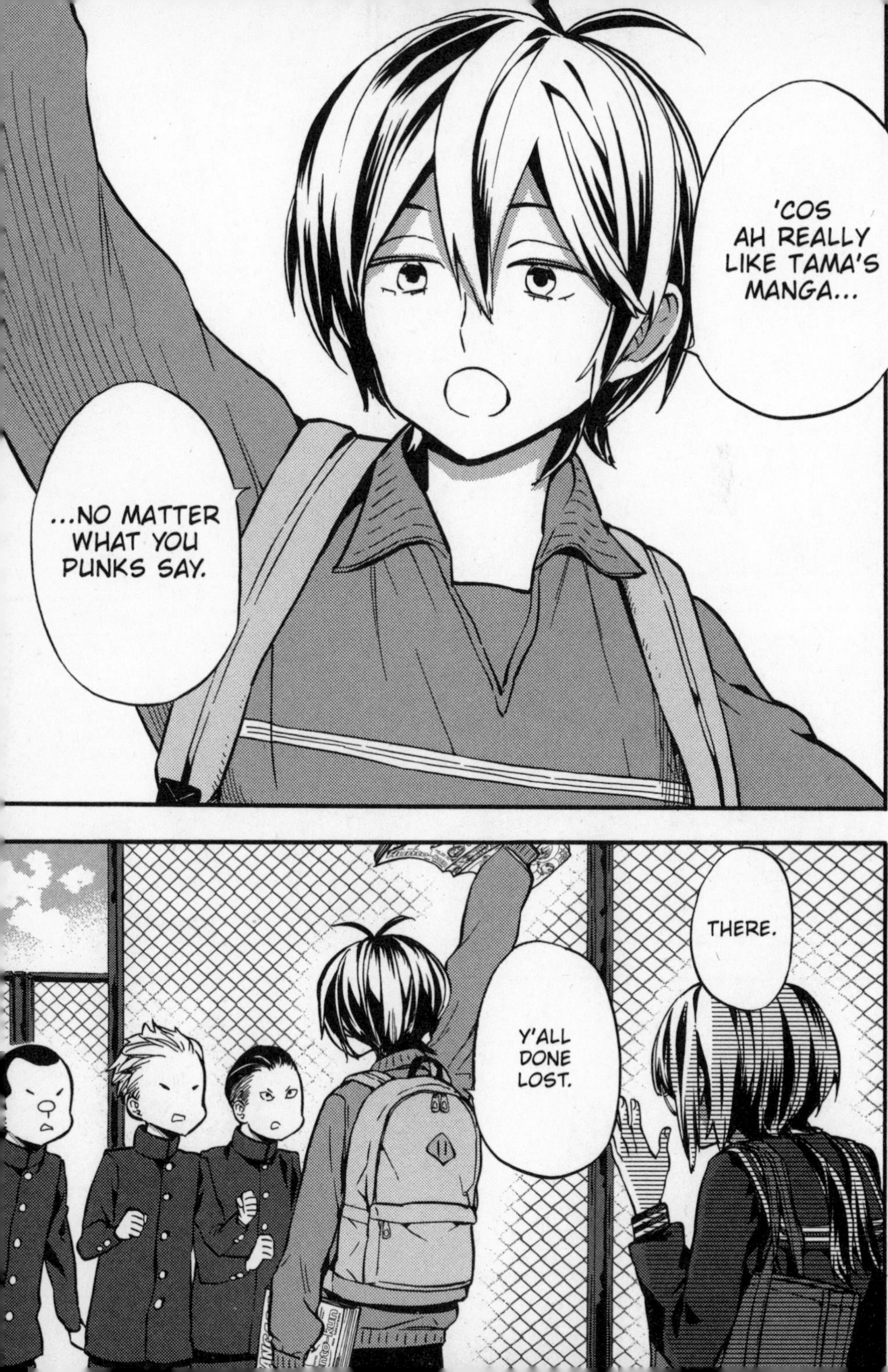
'COS AH REALLY LIKE TAMA'S MANGA...
...NO MATTER WHAT YOU PUNKS SAY.
THERE.
Y'ALL DONE LOST.

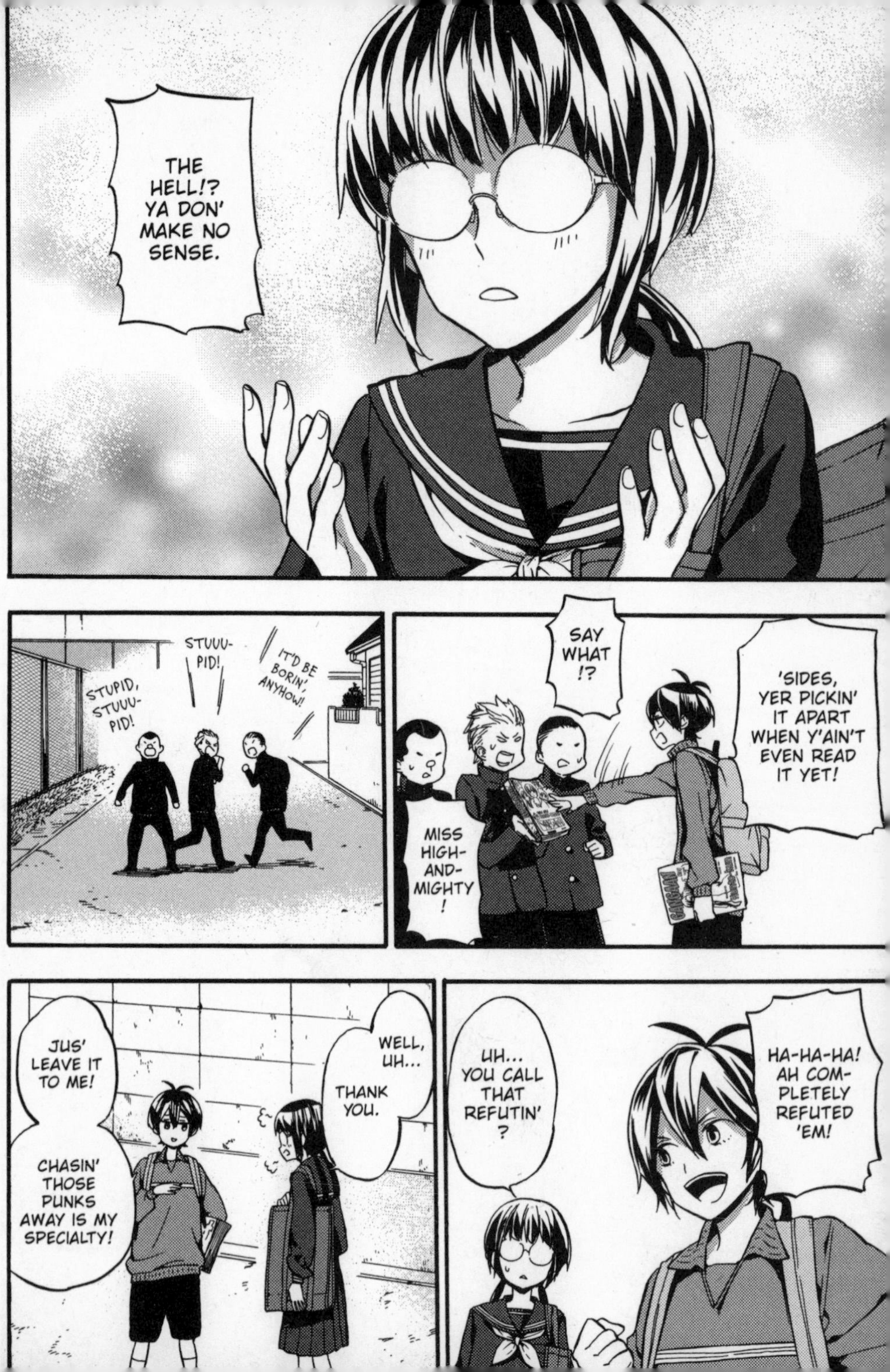
THE HELL!? YA DON' MAKE NO SENSE.
'SIDES, YER PICKIN' IT APART WHEN Y'AIN'T EVEN READ IT YET!
SAY WHAT !?
MISS HIGH-AND-MIGHTY !
IT'D BE BORIN', ANYHOW!
STUUU-PID!
STUPID, STUUU-PID!
HA-HA-HA! AH COMPLETELY REFUTED 'EM!
UH... YOU CALL THAT REFUTIN' ?
WELL, UH...
THANK YOU.
JUS' LEAVE IT TO ME!
CHASIN' THOSE PUNKS AWAY IS MY SPECIALTY!

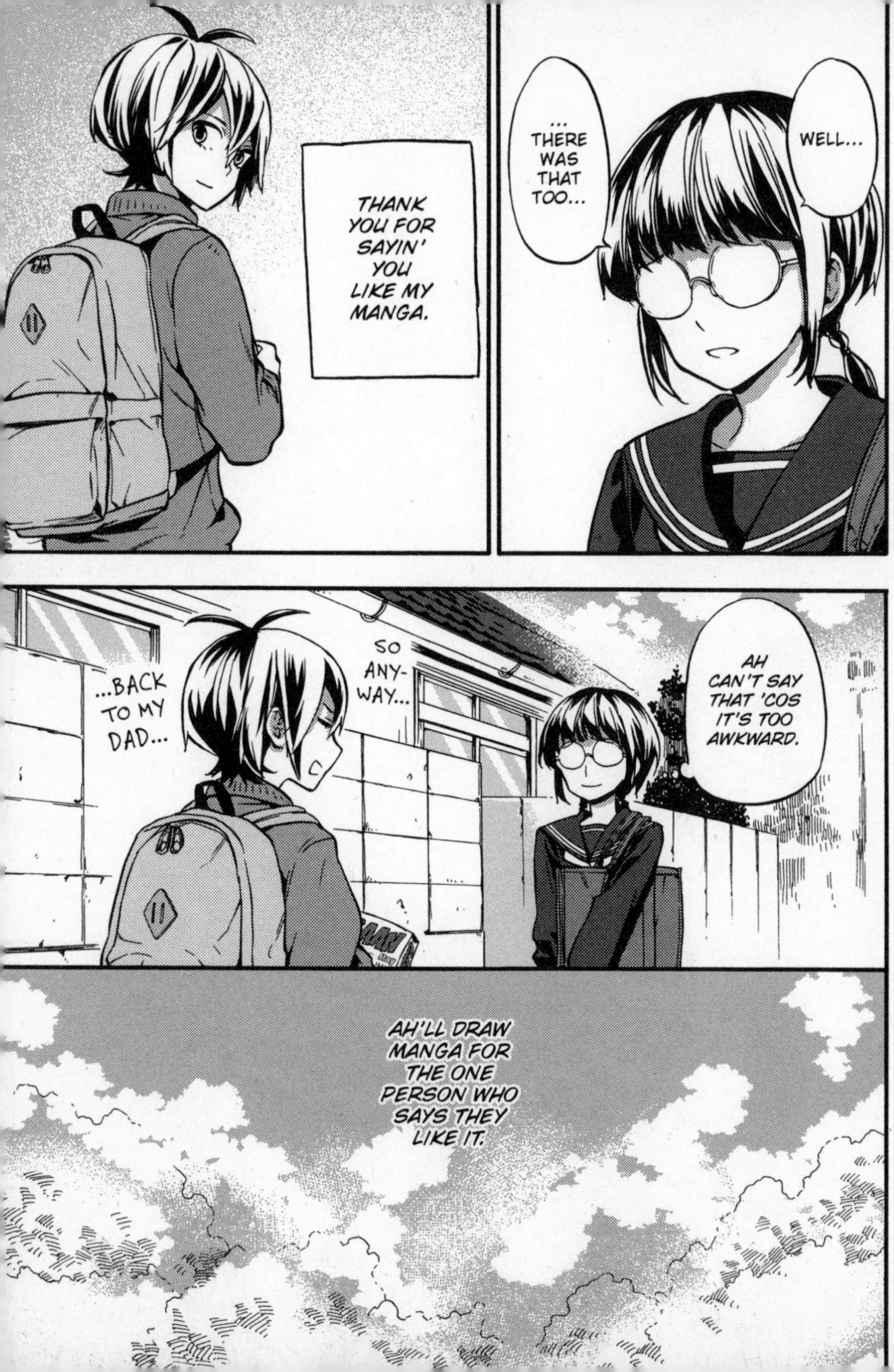
WELL...
...THERE WAS THAT TOO...
THANK YOU FOR SAYIN' YOU LIKE MY MANGA.
AH CAN'T SAY THAT 'COS IT'S TOO AWKWARD.
SO ANY-WAY...
...BACK TO MY DAD...
AH'LL DRAW MANGA FOR THE ONE PERSON WHO SAYS THEY LIKE IT.

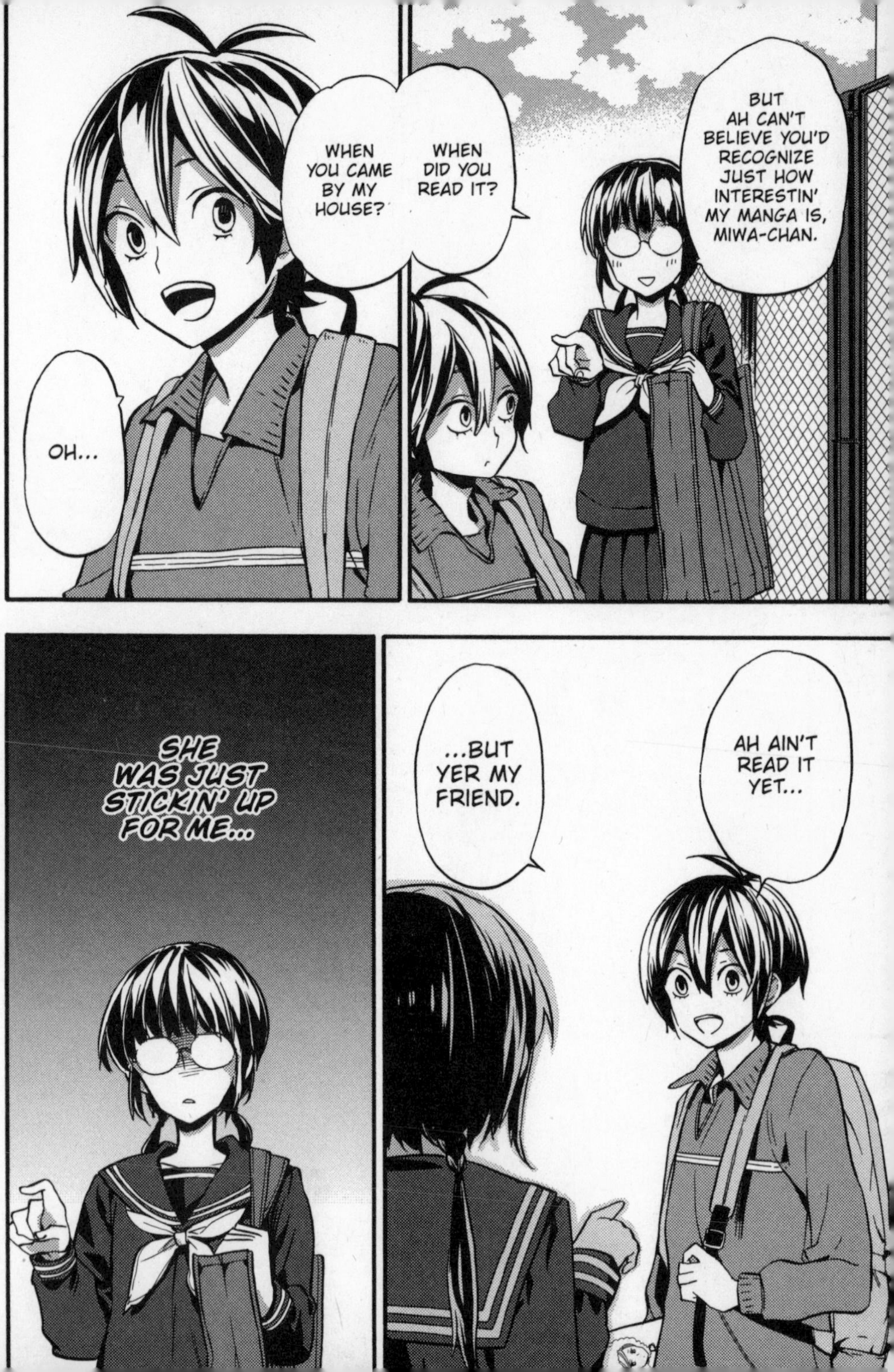
BUT AH CAN'T BELIEVE YOU'D RECOGNIZE JUST HOW INTERESTIN' MY MANGA IS, MIWA-CHAN.
WHEN DID YOU READ IT?
WHEN YOU CAME BY MY HOUSE?
OH...
AH AIN'T READ IT YET...
...BUT YER MY FRIEND.
SHE WAS JUST STICKIN' UP FOR ME...

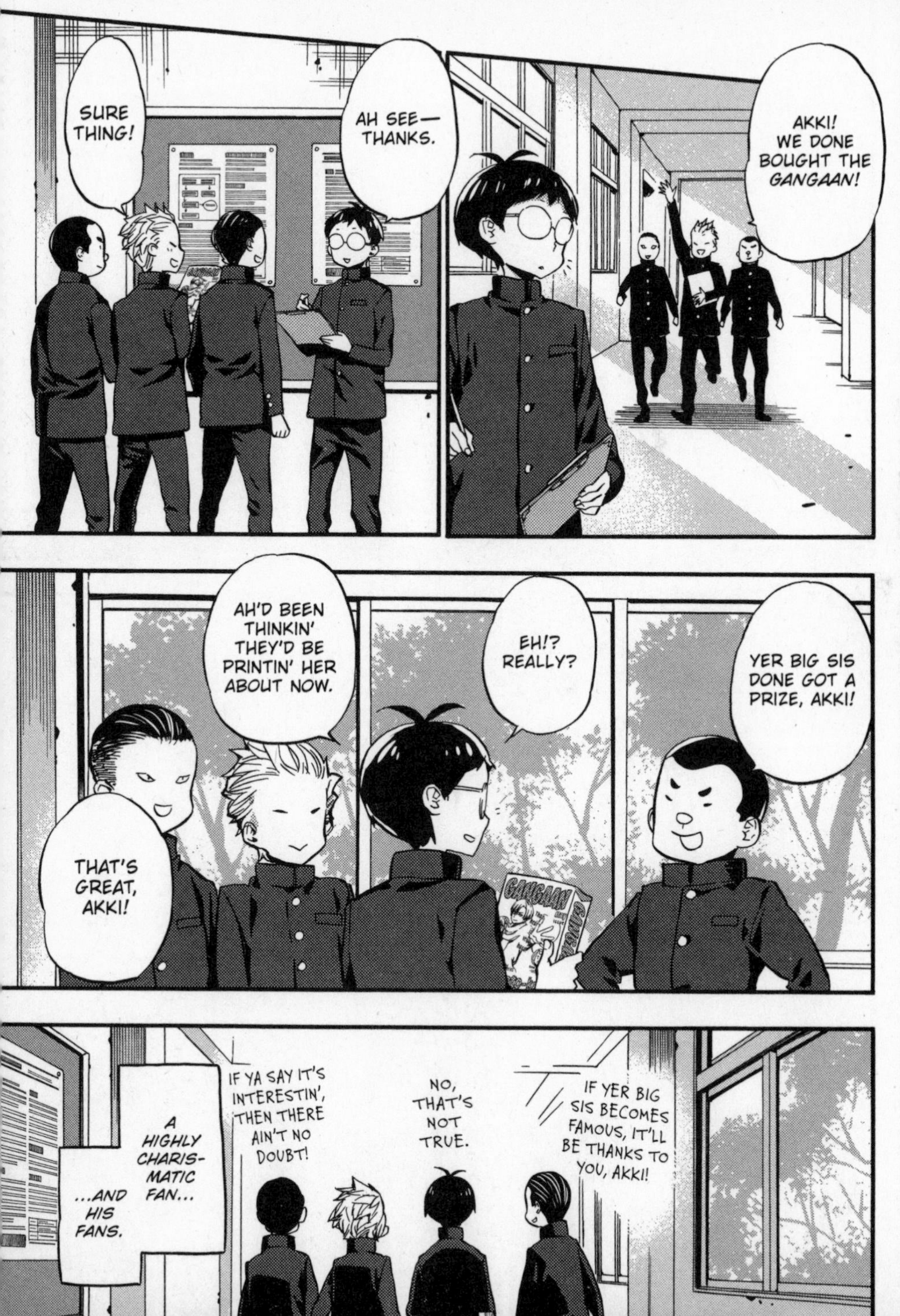
AKKI! WE DONE BOUGHT THE *GANGAAN*!
AH SEE—THANKS.
SURE THING!
YER BIG SIS DONE GOT A PRIZE, AKKI!
EH!? REALLY?
AH'D BEEN THINKIN' THEY'D BE PRINTIN' HER ABOUT NOW.
GANGAAN
THAT'S GREAT, AKKI!
IF YER BIG SIS BECOMES FAMOUS, IT'LL BE THANKS TO YOU, AKKI!
NO, THAT'S NOT TRUE.
IF YA SAY IT'S INTERESTIN', THEN THERE AIN'T NO DOUBT!
A HIGHLY CHARIS-MATIC FAN...
...AND HIS FANS.

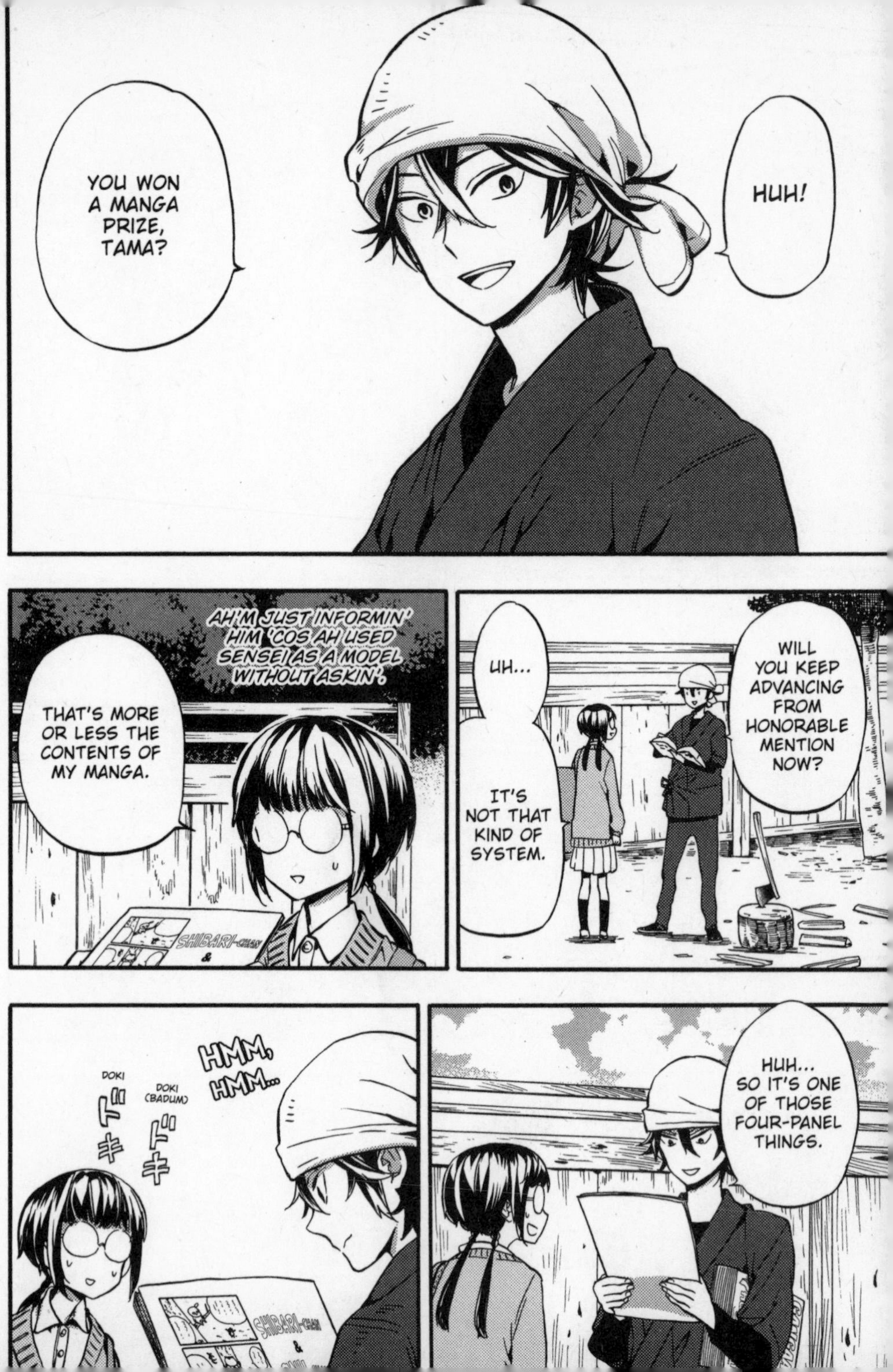
HUH!
YOU WON A MANGA PRIZE, TAMA?
WILL YOU KEEP ADVANCING FROM HONORABLE MENTION NOW?
UH... IT'S NOT THAT KIND OF SYSTEM.
AH'M JUST INFORMIN' HIM 'COS AH USED SENSEI AS A MODEL WITHOUT ASKIN'.
THAT'S MORE OR LESS THE CONTENTS OF MY MANGA.
SHIBARI-CHAN &
HUH... SO IT'S ONE OF THOSE FOUR-PANEL THINGS.
HMM, HMM...
ドキ DOKI
ドキ DOKI (BADUM)
SHIBARI-CHAN &

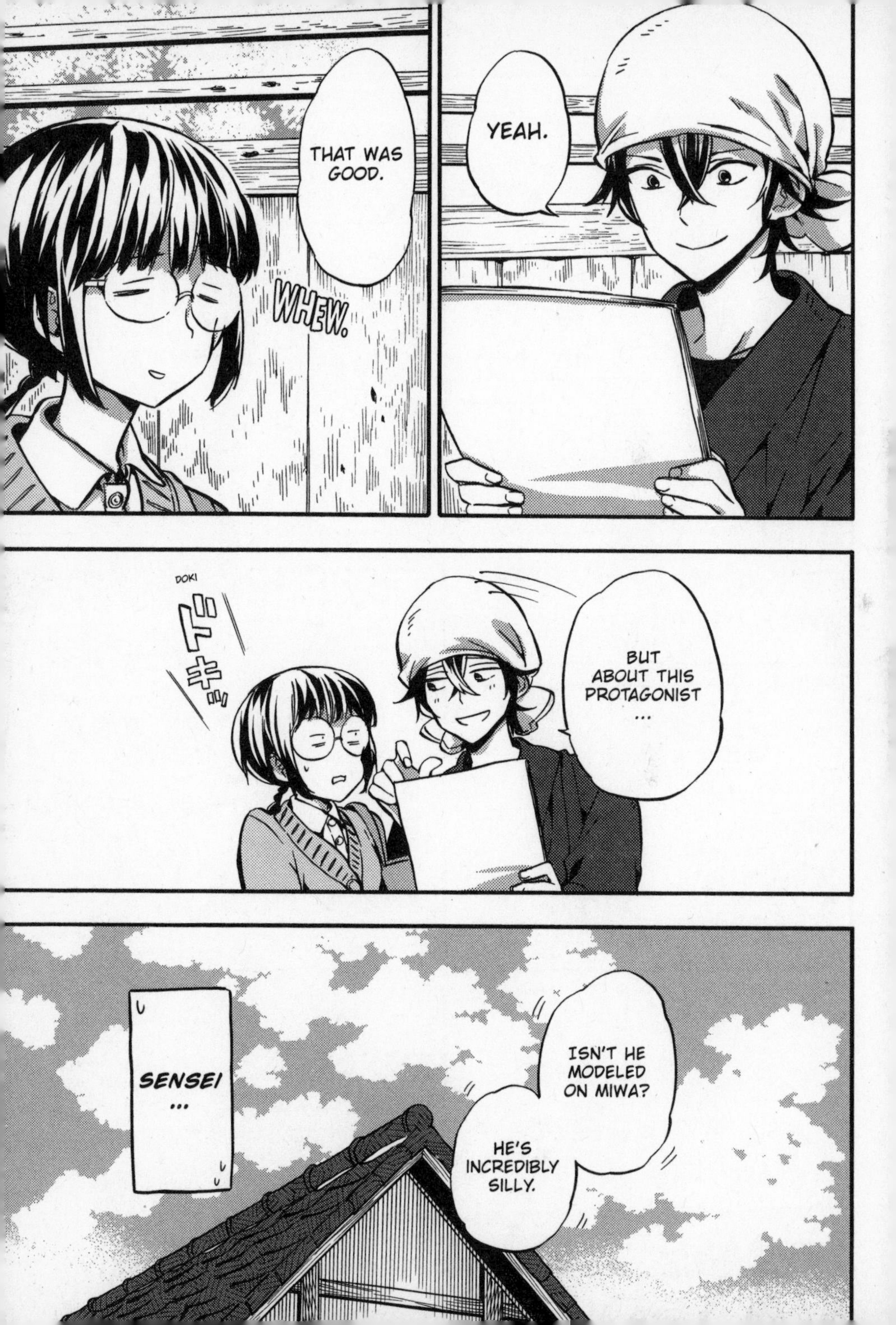
YEAH.
THAT WAS GOOD.
WHEW.
BUT ABOUT THIS PROTAGONIST ...
DOKI
ドキッ
ISN'T HE MODELED ON MIWA?
HE'S INCREDIBLY SILLY.
SENSEI ...

BONUS

SHIBARI-CHAN & ONII-CHAN

ARAMITAMA

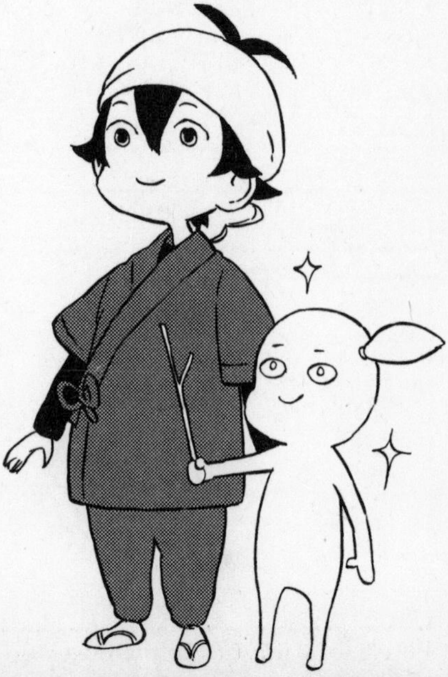

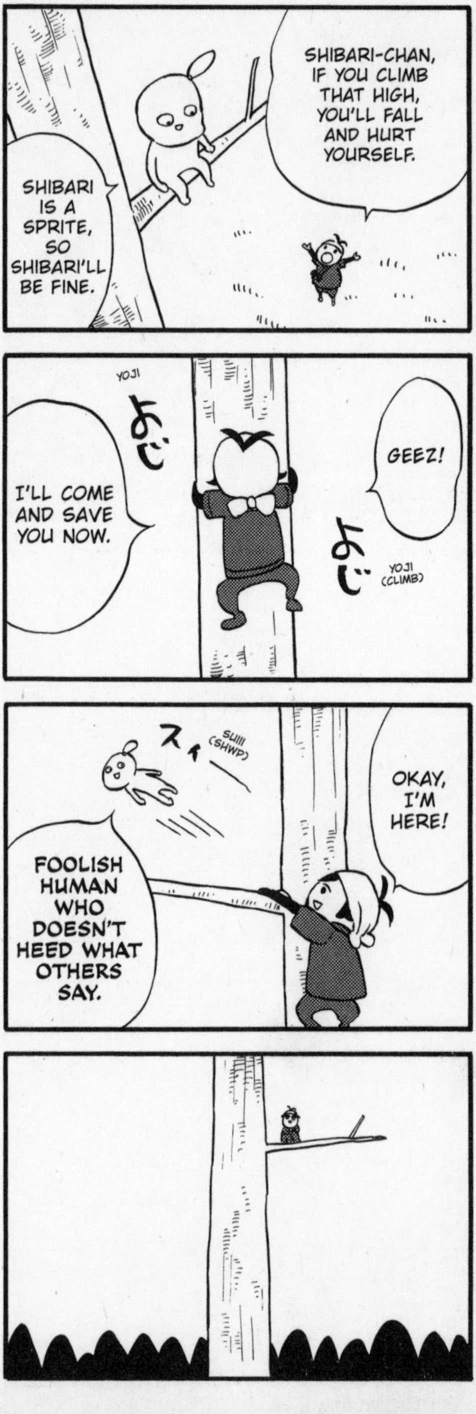

SHIBARI-CHAN, IF YOU CLIMB THAT HIGH, YOU'LL FALL AND HURT YOURSELF.
SHIBARI IS A SPRITE, SO SHIBARI'LL BE FINE.
GEEZ!
よじ
YOJI (CLIMB)
よじ
YOJI
I'LL COME AND SAVE YOU NOW.
OKAY, I'M HERE!
スィ
SUIII (SHWP)
FOOLISH HUMAN WHO DOESN'T HEED WHAT OTHERS SAY.

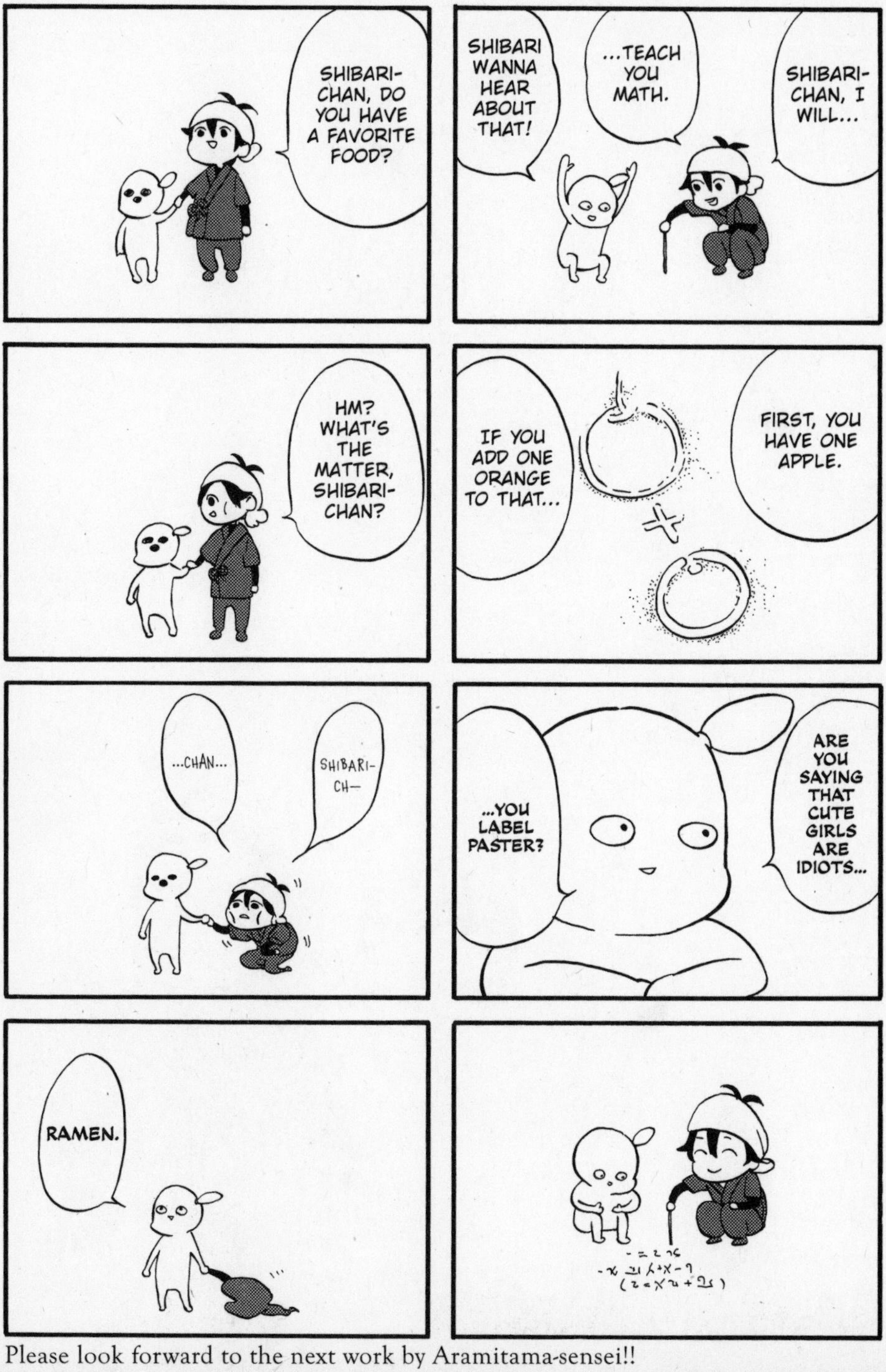
SHIBARI-CHAN, I WILL...
...TEACH YOU MATH.
SHIBARI WANNA HEAR ABOUT THAT!
SHIBARI-CHAN, DO YOU HAVE A FAVORITE FOOD?
FIRST, YOU HAVE ONE APPLE.
IF YOU ADD ONE ORANGE TO THAT...
HM? WHAT'S THE MATTER, SHIBARI-CHAN?
ARE YOU SAYING THAT CUTE GIRLS ARE IDIOTS...
...YOU LABEL PASTER?
SHIBARICH—
...CHAN...
RAMEN.

Please look forward to the next work by Aramitama-sensei!!

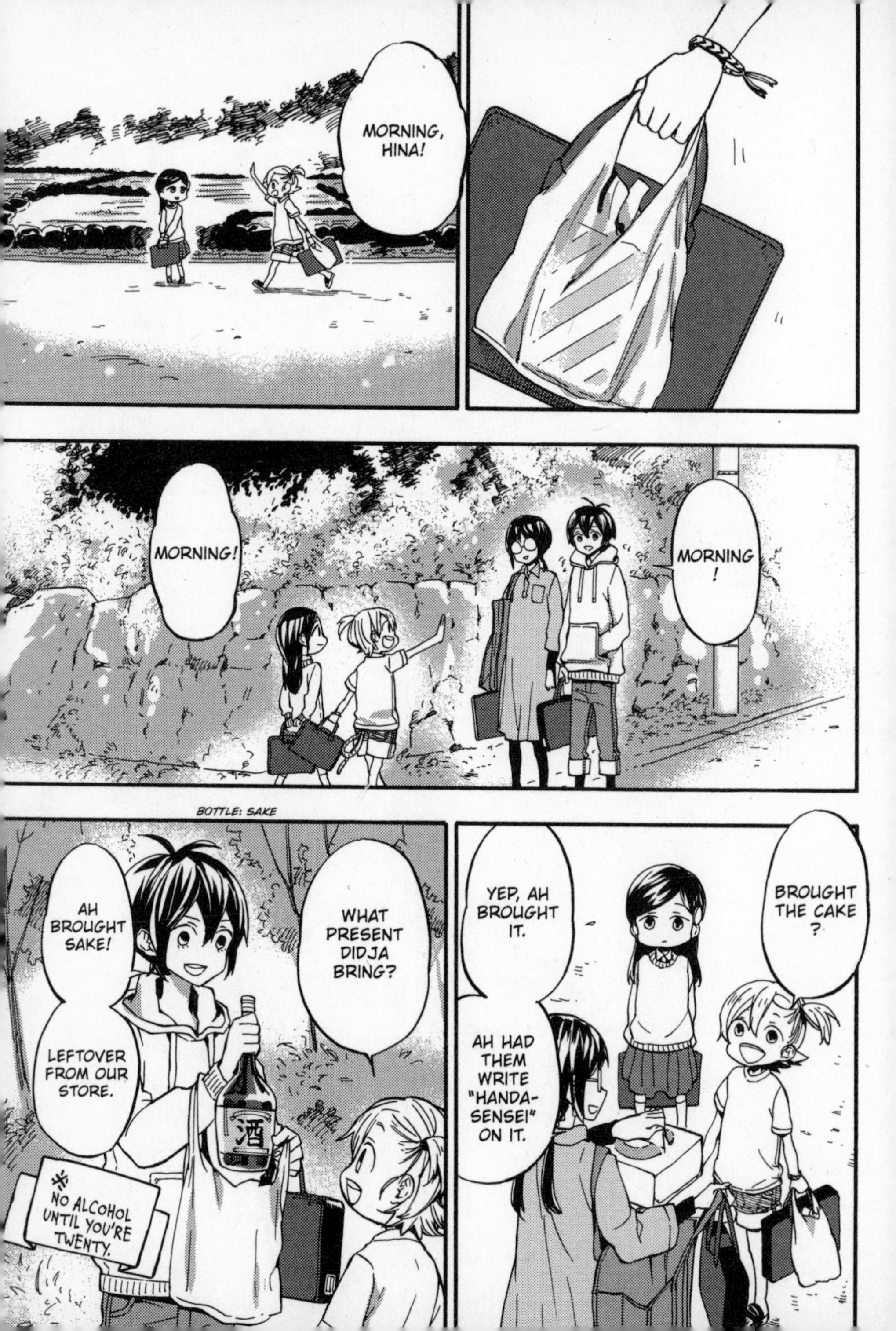
MORNING, HINA!
MORNING !
MORNING!
BROUGHT THE CAKE ?
YEP, AH BROUGHT IT.
AH HAD THEM WRITE "HANDA-SENSEI" ON IT.
WHAT PRESENT DIDJA BRING?
AH BROUGHT SAKE!
LEFTOVER FROM OUR STORE.
BOTTLE: SAKE
酒
※ NO ALCOHOL UNTIL YOU'RE TWENTY.

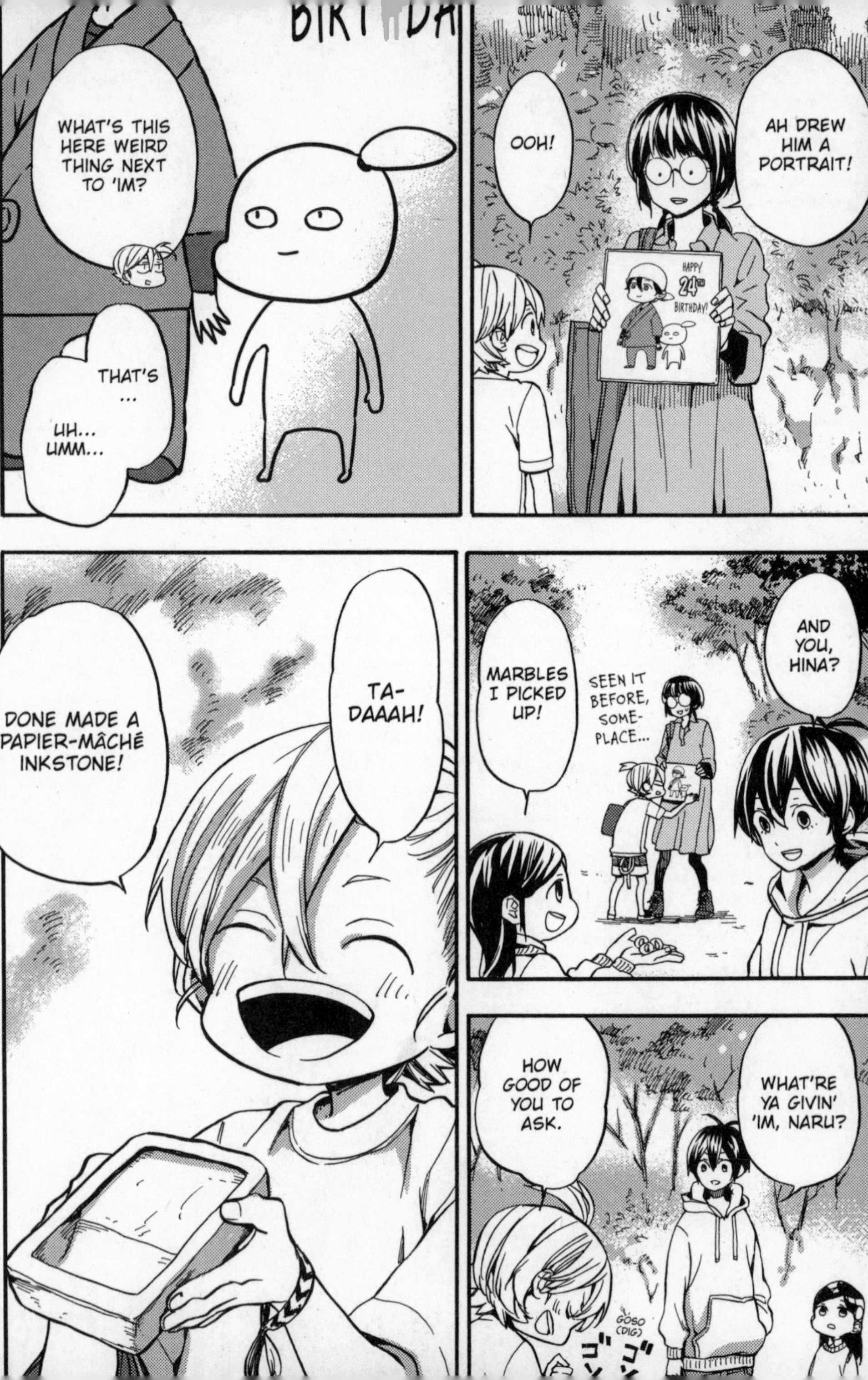
AH DREW HIM A PORTRAIT!
OOH!
HAPPY 24TH BIRTHDAY!
WHAT'S THIS HERE WEIRD THING NEXT TO 'IM?
THAT'S ...
UH... UMM...
AND YOU, HINA?
SEEN IT BEFORE, SOME-PLACE...
MARBLES I PICKED UP!
WHAT'RE YA GIVIN' 'IM, NARU?
HOW GOOD OF YOU TO ASK.
GOSO (DIG)
TA-DAAAH!
DONE MADE A PAPIER-MÂCHÉ INKSTONE!

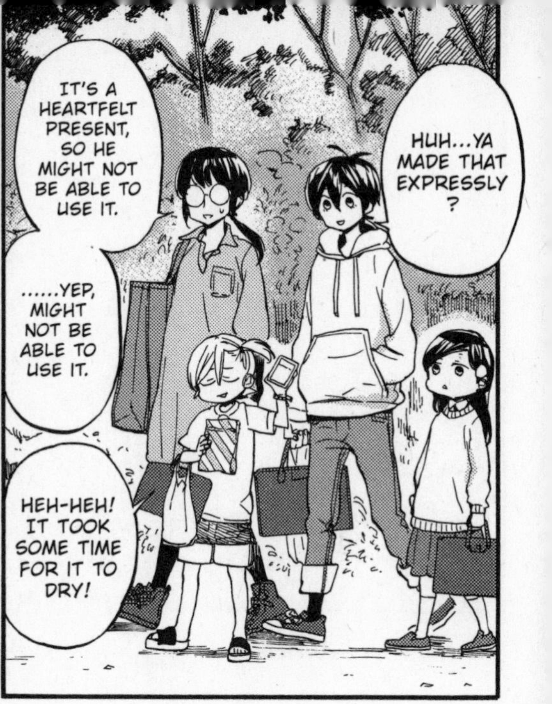
HUH...YA MADE THAT EXPRESSLY?
IT'S A HEARTFELT PRESENT, SO HE MIGHT NOT BE ABLE TO USE IT.
......YEP, MIGHT NOT BE ABLE TO USE IT.
HEH-HEH! IT TOOK SOME TIME FOR IT TO DRY!
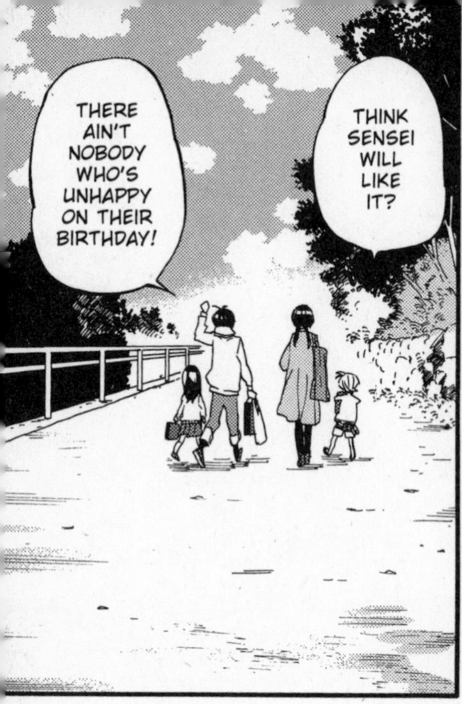
THINK SENSEI WILL LIKE IT?
THERE AIN'T NOBODY WHO'S UNHAPPY ON THEIR BIRTHDAY!

Act. 131
APRIL 15
(Translation: Handa-sensei's Birthday)

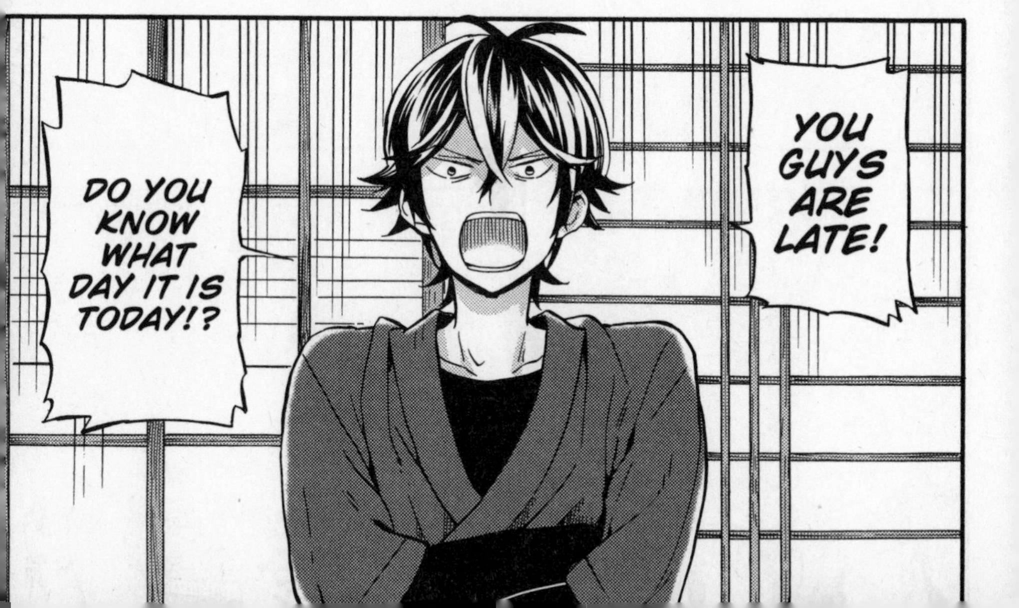
YOU GUYS ARE LATE!
DO YOU KNOW WHAT DAY IT IS TODAY!?

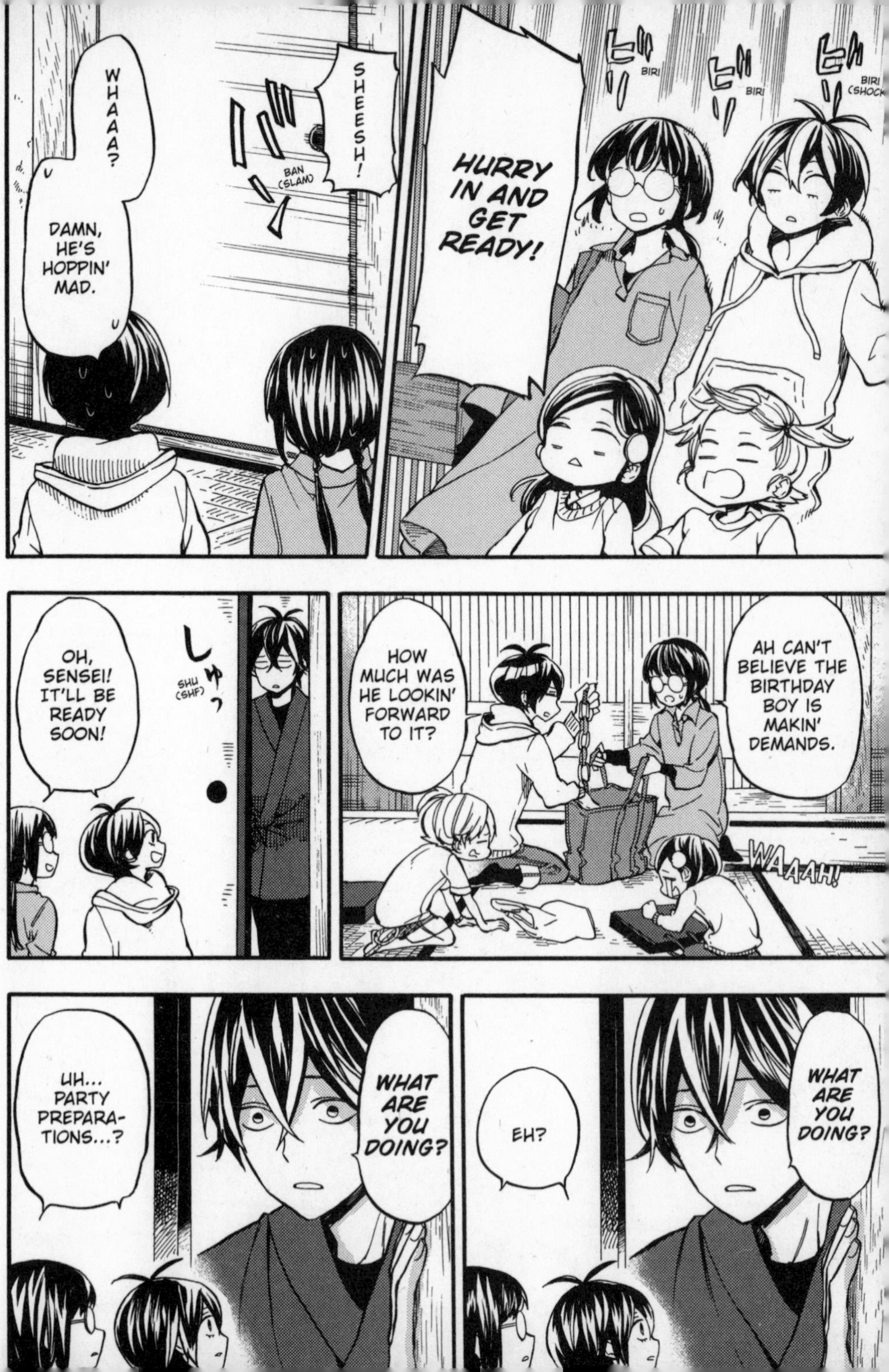
BIRI (SHOCK
BIRI
BIRI
HURRY IN AND GET READY!
SHEESH!
BAN (SLAM)
WHAAAA?
DAMN, HE'S HOPPIN' MAD.
AH CAN'T BELIEVE THE BIRTHDAY BOY IS MAKIN' DEMANDS.
HOW MUCH WAS HE LOOKIN' FORWARD TO IT?
WAAAH!
SHU (SHF)
OH, SENSEI! IT'LL BE READY SOON!
WHAT ARE YOU DOING?
EH?
WHAT ARE YOU DOING?
UH... PARTY PREPARA-TIONS...?

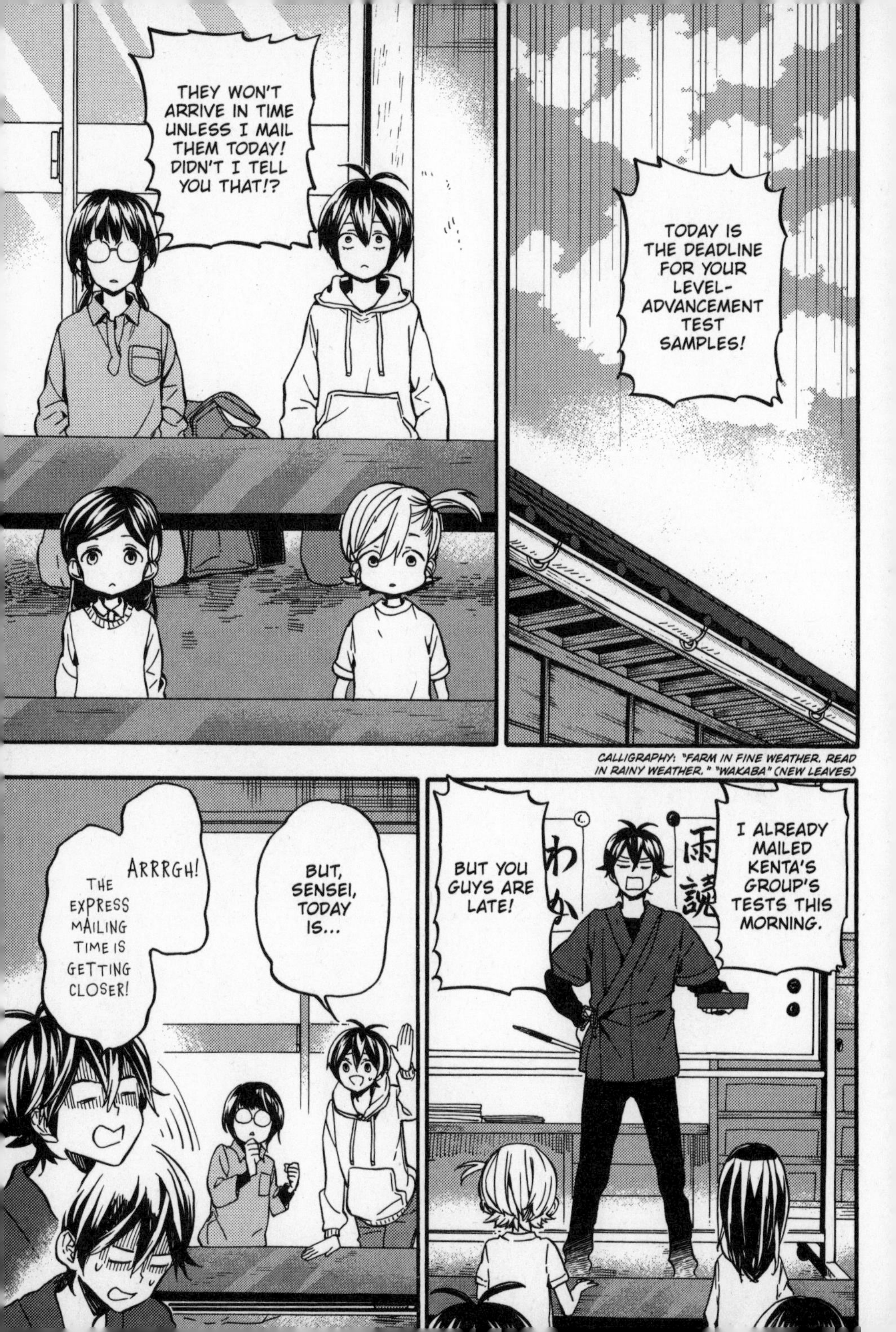
TODAY IS THE DEADLINE FOR YOUR LEVEL-ADVANCEMENT TEST SAMPLES!
THEY WON'T ARRIVE IN TIME UNLESS I MAIL THEM TODAY! DIDN'T I TELL YOU THAT!?
CALLIGRAPHY: "FARM IN FINE WEATHER. READ IN RAINY WEATHER." "WAKABA" (NEW LEAVES)
I ALREADY MAILED KENTA'S GROUP'S TESTS THIS MORNING.
BUT YOU GUYS ARE LATE!
BUT, SENSEI, TODAY IS...
ARRRGH! THE EXPRESS MAILING TIME IS GETTING CLOSER!

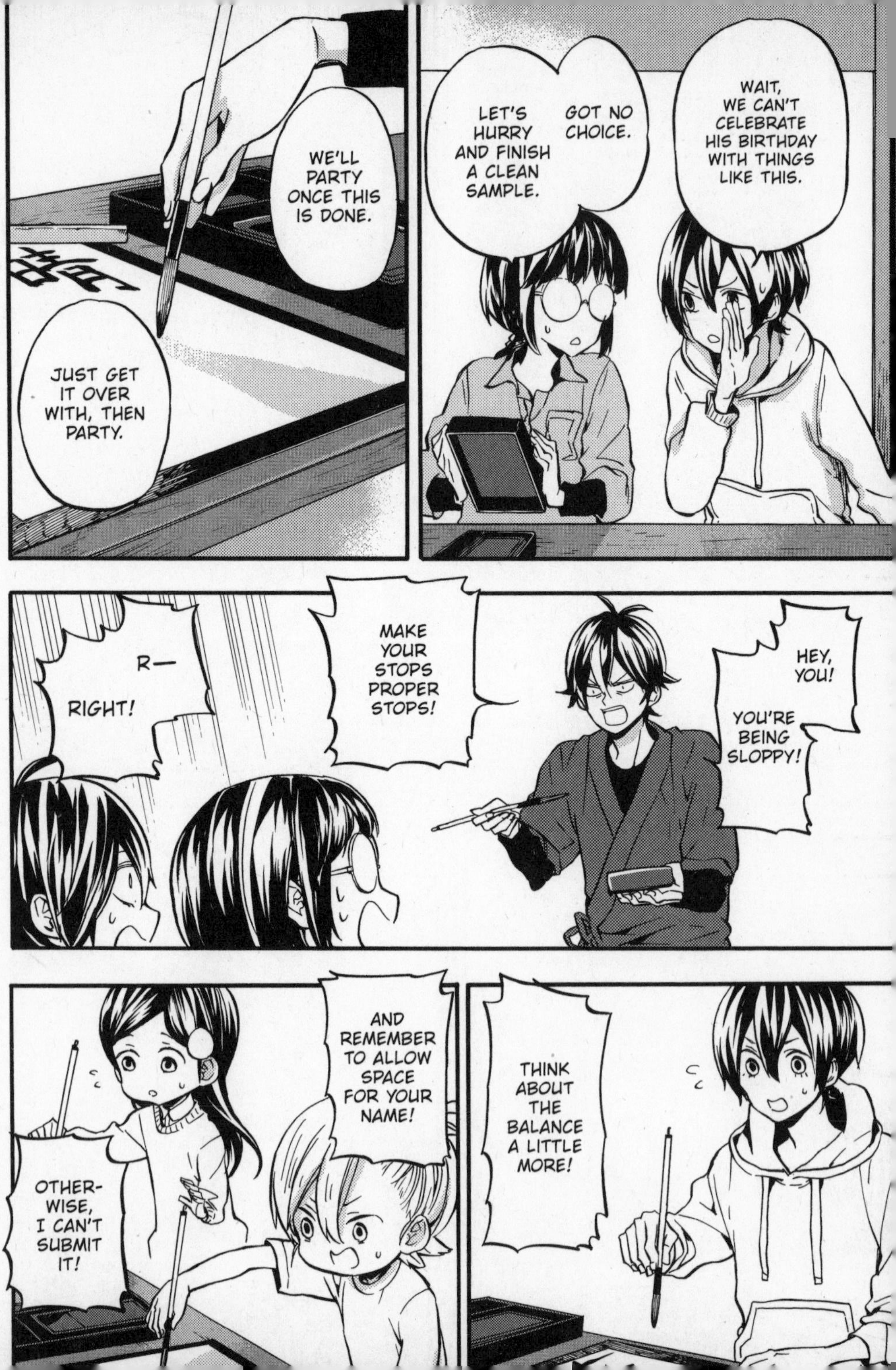
WAIT, WE CAN'T CELEBRATE HIS BIRTHDAY WITH THINGS LIKE THIS.
GOT NO CHOICE.
LET'S HURRY AND FINISH A CLEAN SAMPLE.
WE'LL PARTY ONCE THIS IS DONE.
JUST GET IT OVER WITH, THEN PARTY.
HEY, YOU!
YOU'RE BEING SLOPPY!
MAKE YOUR STOPS PROPER STOPS!
R— RIGHT!
THINK ABOUT THE BALANCE A LITTLE MORE!
AND REMEMBER TO ALLOW SPACE FOR YOUR NAME!
OTHER-WISE, I CAN'T SUBMIT IT!

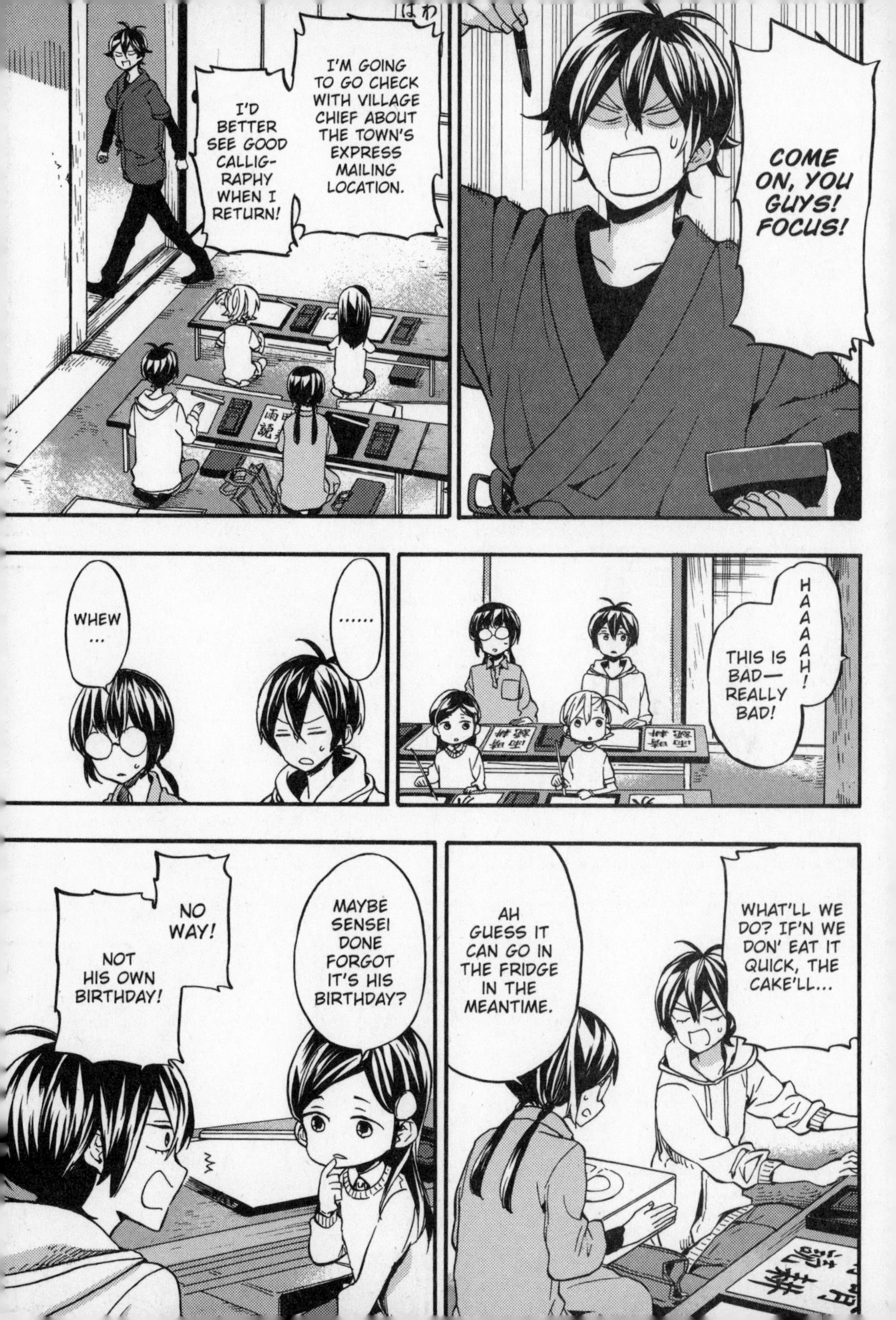
COME ON, YOU GUYS! FOCUS!
I'M GOING TO GO CHECK WITH VILLAGE CHIEF ABOUT THE TOWN'S EXPRESS MAILING LOCATION.
I'D BETTER SEE GOOD CALLIGRAPHY WHEN I RETURN!
HAAAAAH!
THIS IS BAD—REALLY BAD!
......
WHEW...
WHAT'LL WE DO? IF'N WE DON' EAT IT QUICK, THE CAKE'LL...
AH GUESS IT CAN GO IN THE FRIDGE IN THE MEANTIME.
MAYBE SENSEI DONE FORGOT IT'S HIS BIRTHDAY?
NO WAY!
NOT HIS OWN BIRTHDAY!

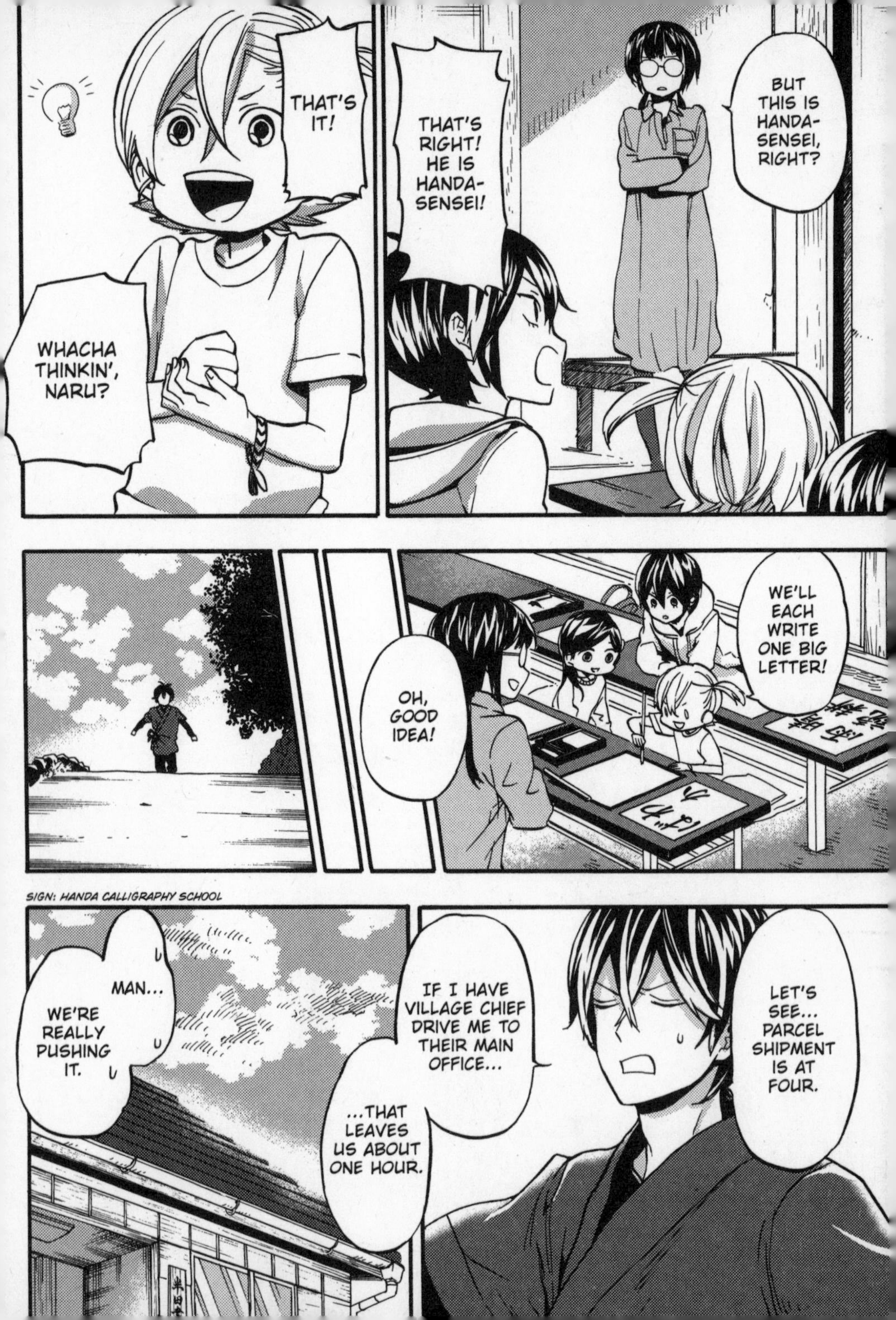
BUT THIS IS HANDA-SENSEI, RIGHT?
THAT'S RIGHT! HE IS HANDA-SENSEI!
THAT'S IT!
WHACHA THINKIN', NARU?
WE'LL EACH WRITE ONE BIG LETTER!
OH, GOOD IDEA!
LET'S SEE... PARCEL SHIPMENT IS AT FOUR.
IF I HAVE VILLAGE CHIEF DRIVE ME TO THEIR MAIN OFFICE...
...THAT LEAVES US ABOUT ONE HOUR.
MAN...
WE'RE REALLY PUSHING IT.
SIGN: HANDA CALLIGRAPHY SCHOOL

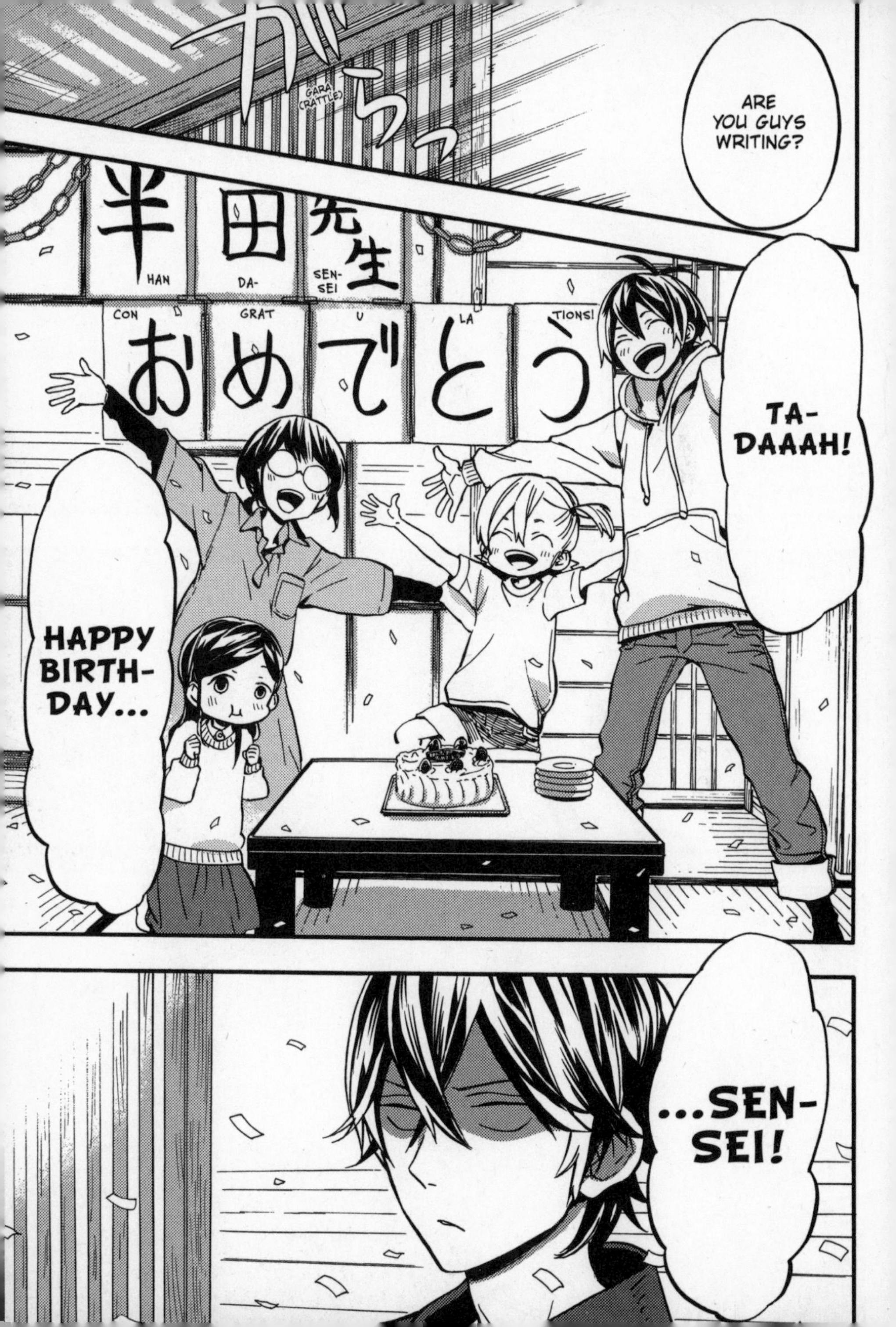
ARE YOU GUYS WRITING?
がらっ
GARA (RATTLE)
半田先生
HAN DA- SEN- SEI
おめでとう
CON GRAT U LA TIONS!
TA-DAAAH!
HAPPY BIRTH-DAY...
...SEN-SEI!

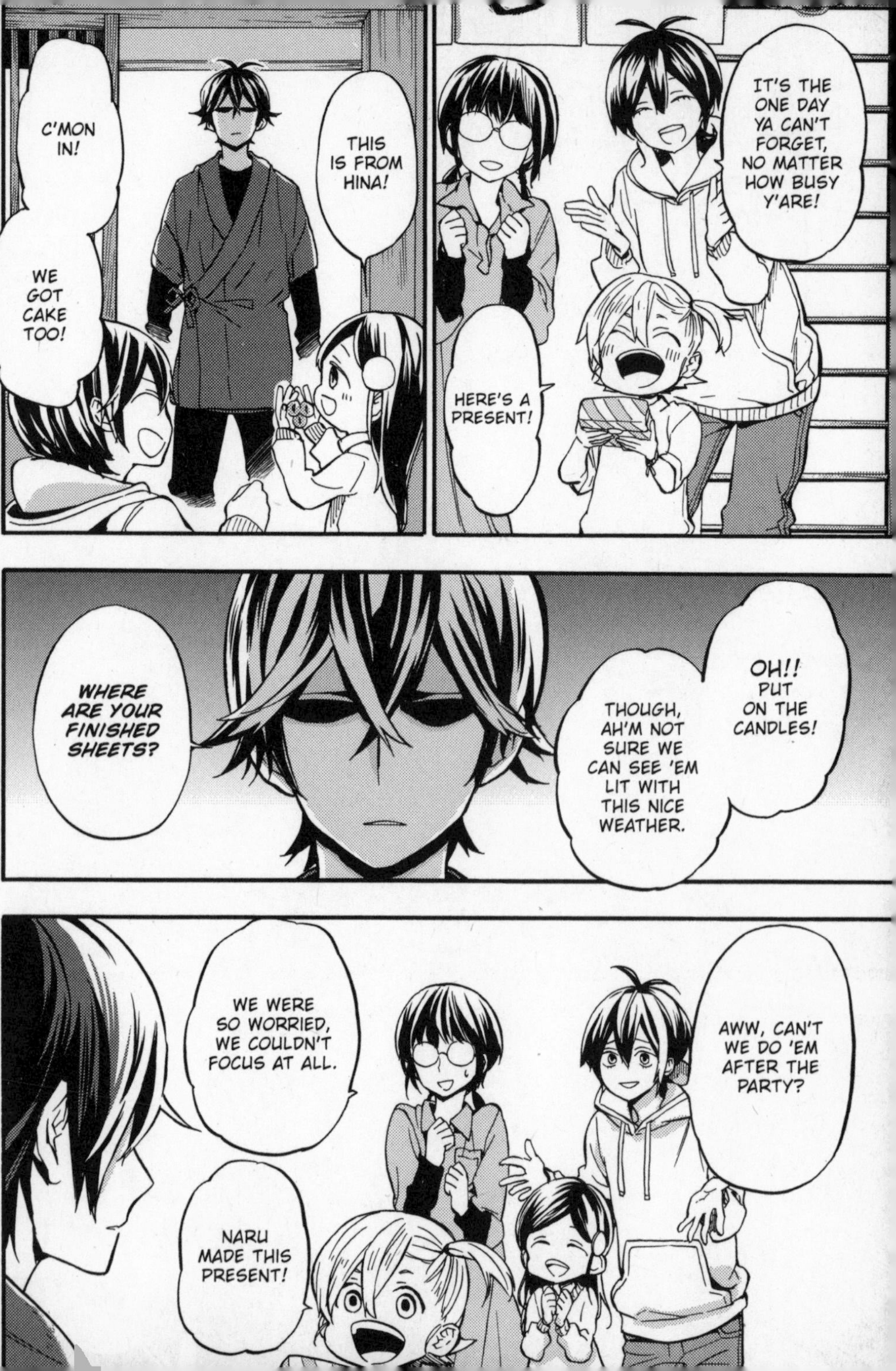
IT'S THE ONE DAY YA CAN'T FORGET, NO MATTER HOW BUSY Y'ARE!
HERE'S A PRESENT!
THIS IS FROM HINA!
C'MON IN!
WE GOT CAKE TOO!
OH!! PUT ON THE CANDLES!
THOUGH, AH'M NOT SURE WE CAN SEE 'EM LIT WITH THIS NICE WEATHER.
WHERE ARE YOUR FINISHED SHEETS?
AWW, CAN'T WE DO 'EM AFTER THE PARTY?
WE WERE SO WORRIED, WE COULDN'T FOCUS AT ALL.
NARU MADE THIS PRESENT!

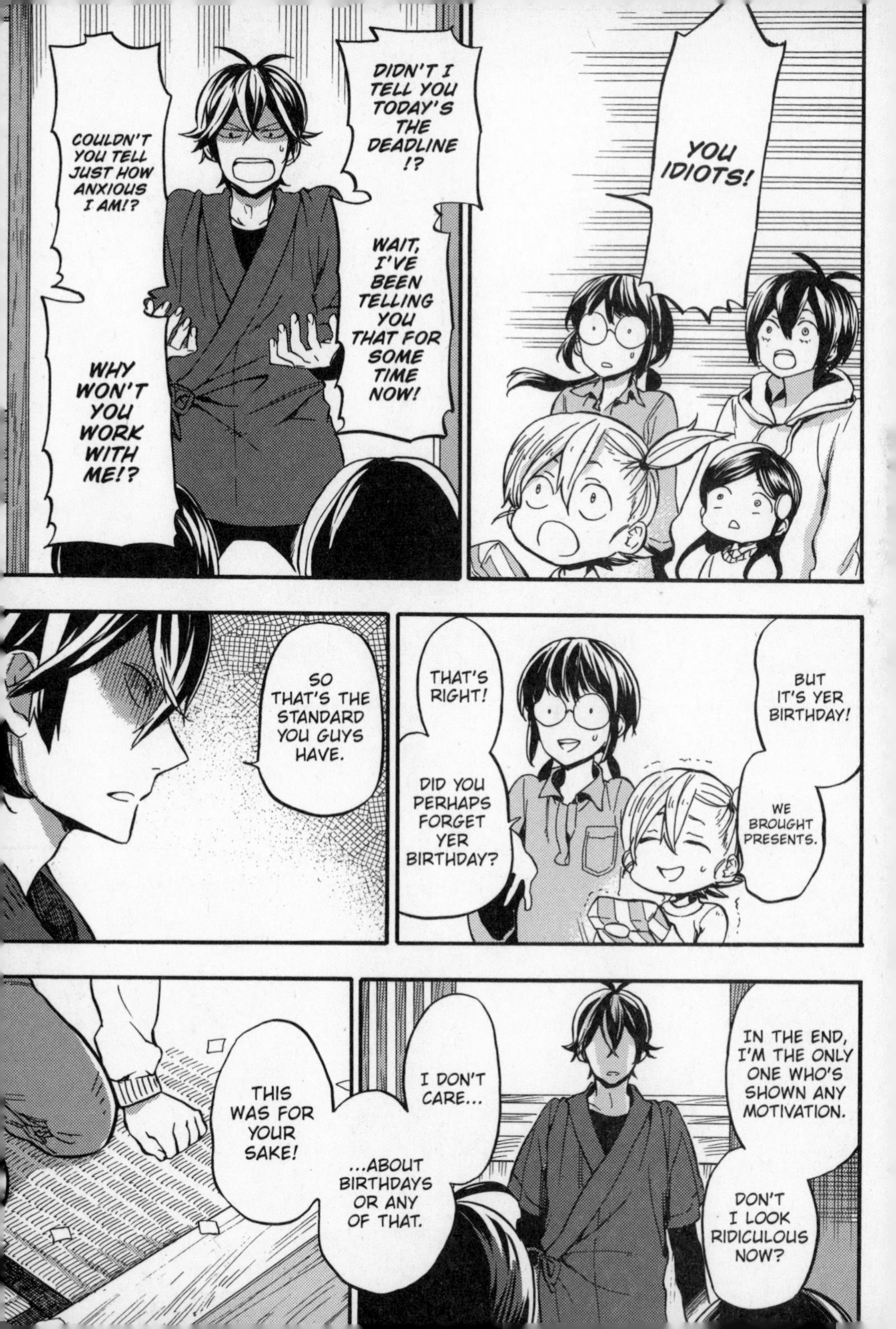
YOU IDIOTS!
DIDN'T I TELL YOU TODAY'S THE DEADLINE !?
WAIT, I'VE BEEN TELLING YOU THAT FOR SOME TIME NOW!
COULDN'T YOU TELL JUST HOW ANXIOUS I AM!?
WHY WON'T YOU WORK WITH ME!?
BUT IT'S YER BIRTHDAY!
WE BROUGHT PRESENTS.
THAT'S RIGHT!
DID YOU PERHAPS FORGET YER BIRTHDAY?
SO THAT'S THE STANDARD YOU GUYS HAVE.
IN THE END, I'M THE ONLY ONE WHO'S SHOWN ANY MOTIVATION.
DON'T I LOOK RIDICULOUS NOW?
I DON'T CARE...
...ABOUT BIRTHDAYS OR ANY OF THAT.
THIS WAS FOR YOUR SAKE!

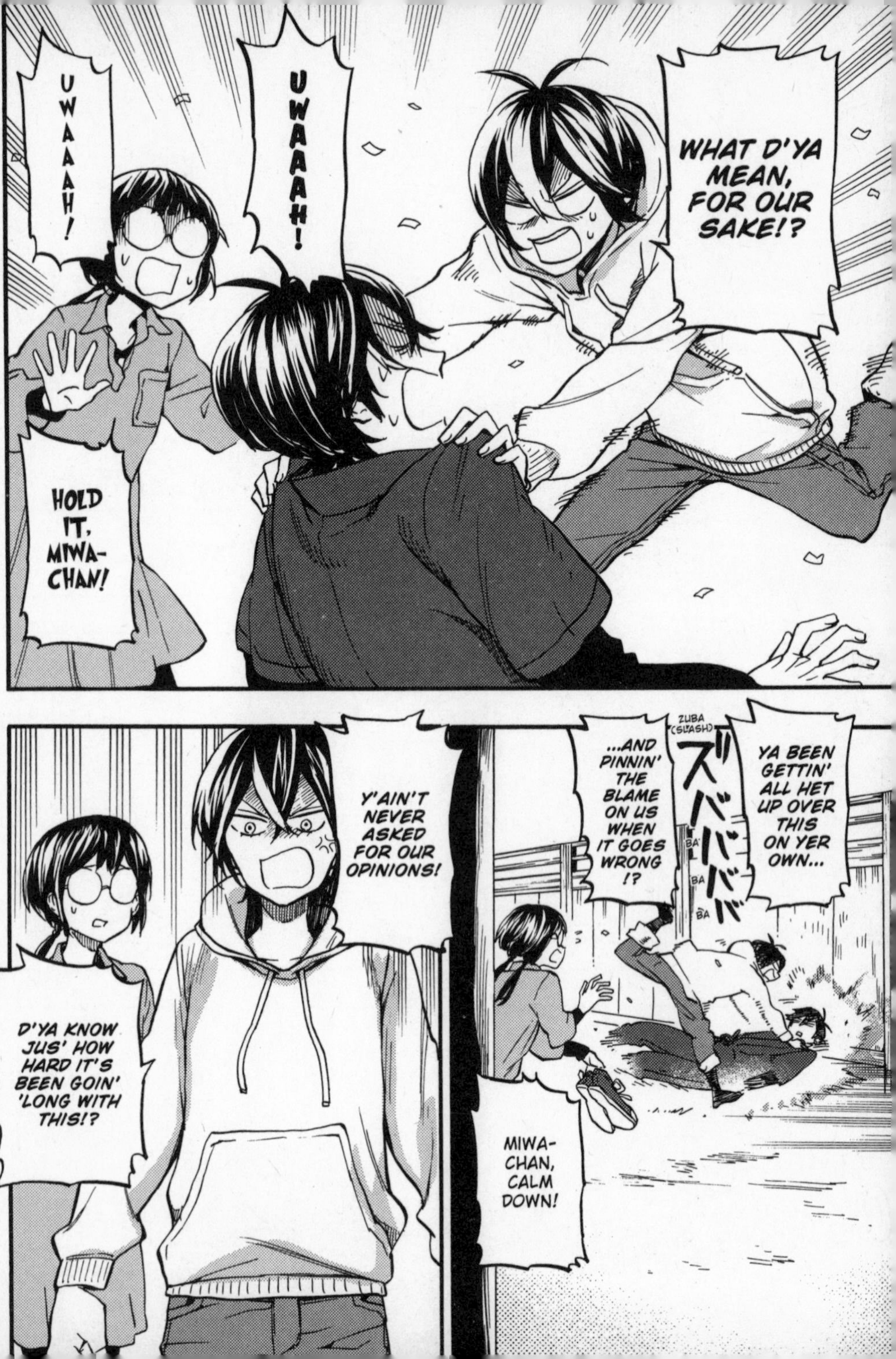
WHAT D'YA MEAN, FOR OUR SAKE!?
UWAAAAH!
UWAAAAH!
HOLD IT, MIWA-CHAN!
YA BEEN GETTIN' ALL HET UP OVER THIS ON YER OWN...
ZUBA (SLASH)
ズババババ
BA BA BA
...AND PINNIN' THE BLAME ON US WHEN IT GOES WRONG!?
MIWA-CHAN, CALM DOWN!
Y'AIN'T NEVER ASKED FOR OUR OPINIONS!
D'YA KNOW JUS' HOW HARD IT'S BEEN GOIN' 'LONG WITH THIS!?

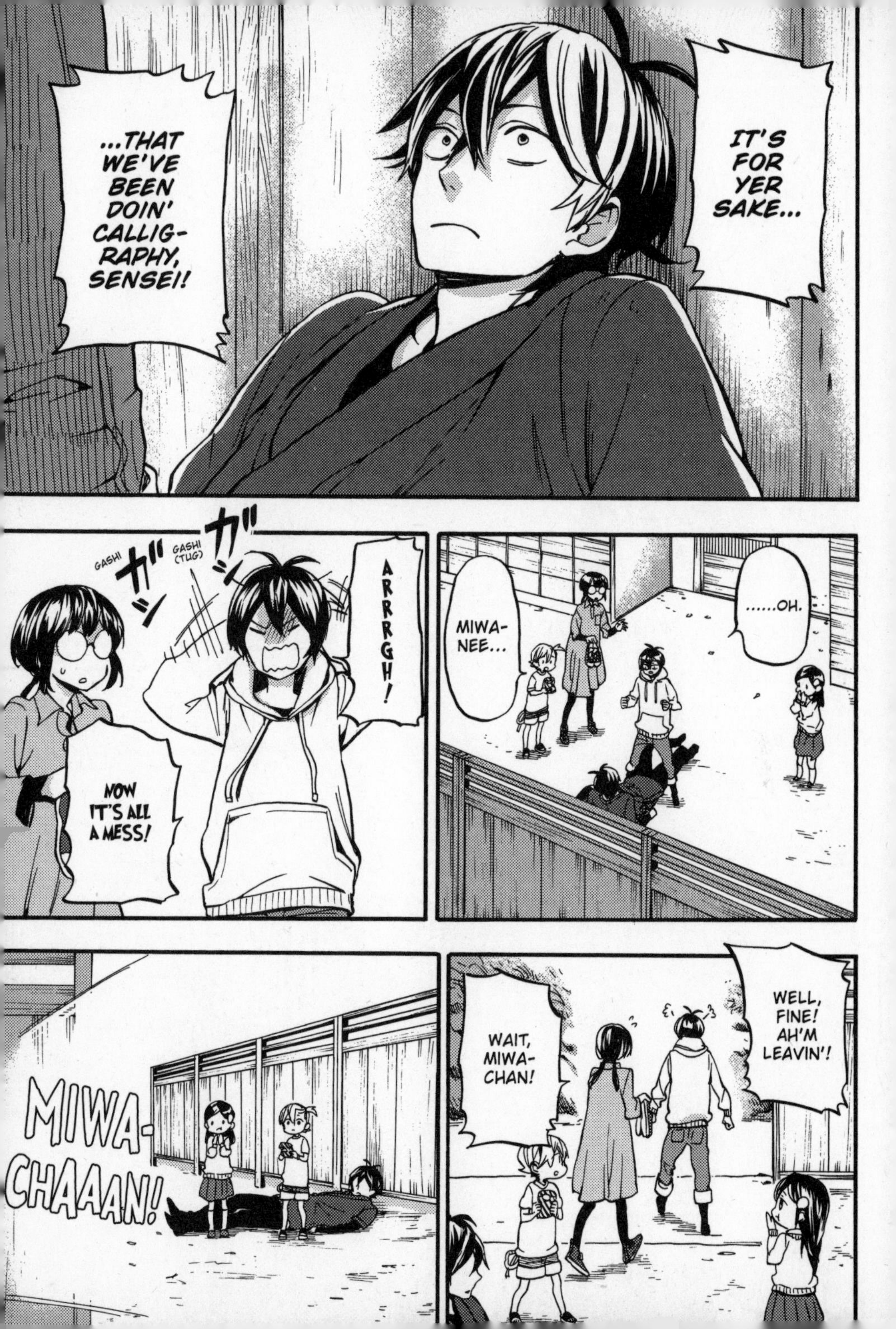
IT'S FOR YER SAKE...
...THAT WE'VE BEEN DOIN' CALLIGRAPHY, SENSEI!
......OH.
MIWA-NEE...
ARRRGH!
GASHI (TUG)
GASHI
NOW IT'S ALL A MESS!
WELL, FINE! AH'M LEAVIN'!
WAIT, MIWA-CHAN!
MIWA-CHAAAN!

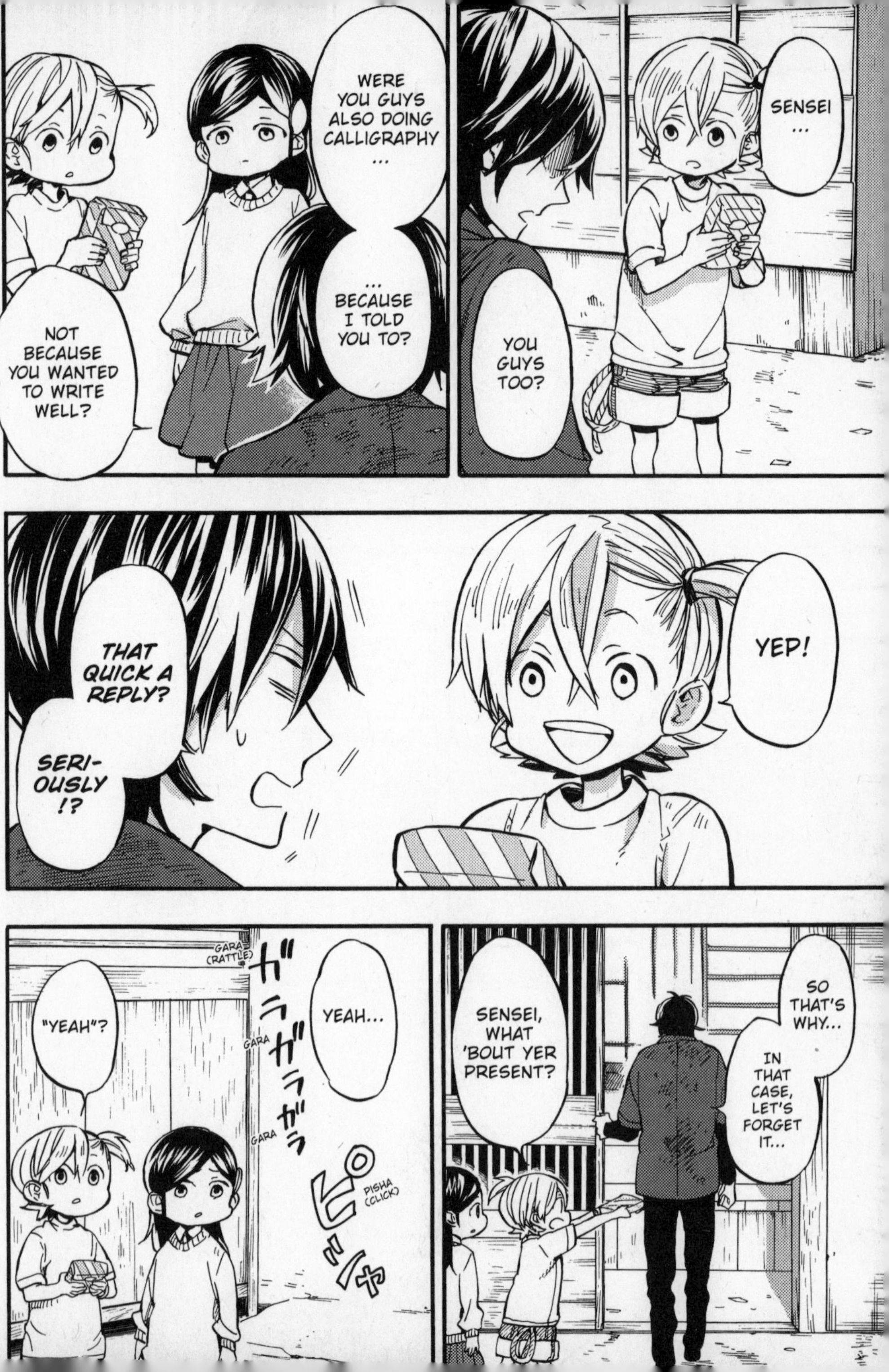
SENSEI ...
YOU GUYS TOO?
WERE YOU GUYS ALSO DOING CALLIGRAPHY ...
... BECAUSE I TOLD YOU TO?
NOT BECAUSE YOU WANTED TO WRITE WELL?
YEP!
THAT QUICK A REPLY?
SERI-OUSLY !?
SO THAT'S WHY...
IN THAT CASE, LET'S FORGET IT...
SENSEI, WHAT 'BOUT YER PRESENT?
YEAH...
GARA (RATTLE)
GARA
GARA
PISHA (CLICK)
"YEAH"?

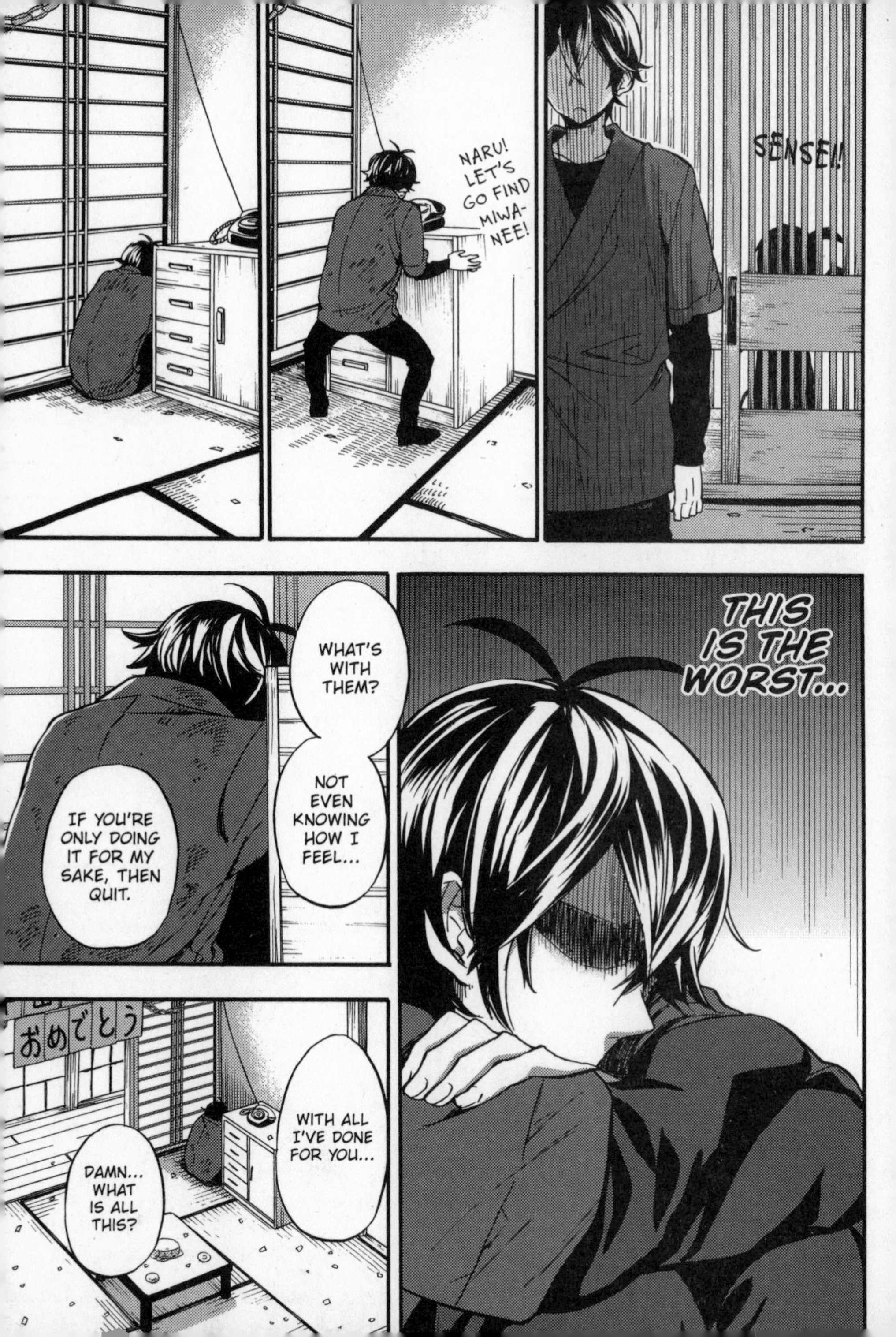
SENSEI!!
NARU! LET'S GO FIND MIWA-NEE!
THIS IS THE WORST...
WHAT'S WITH THEM?
NOT EVEN KNOWING HOW I FEEL...
IF YOU'RE ONLY DOING IT FOR MY SAKE, THEN QUIT.
おめでとう
WITH ALL I'VE DONE FOR YOU...
DAMN... WHAT IS ALL THIS?

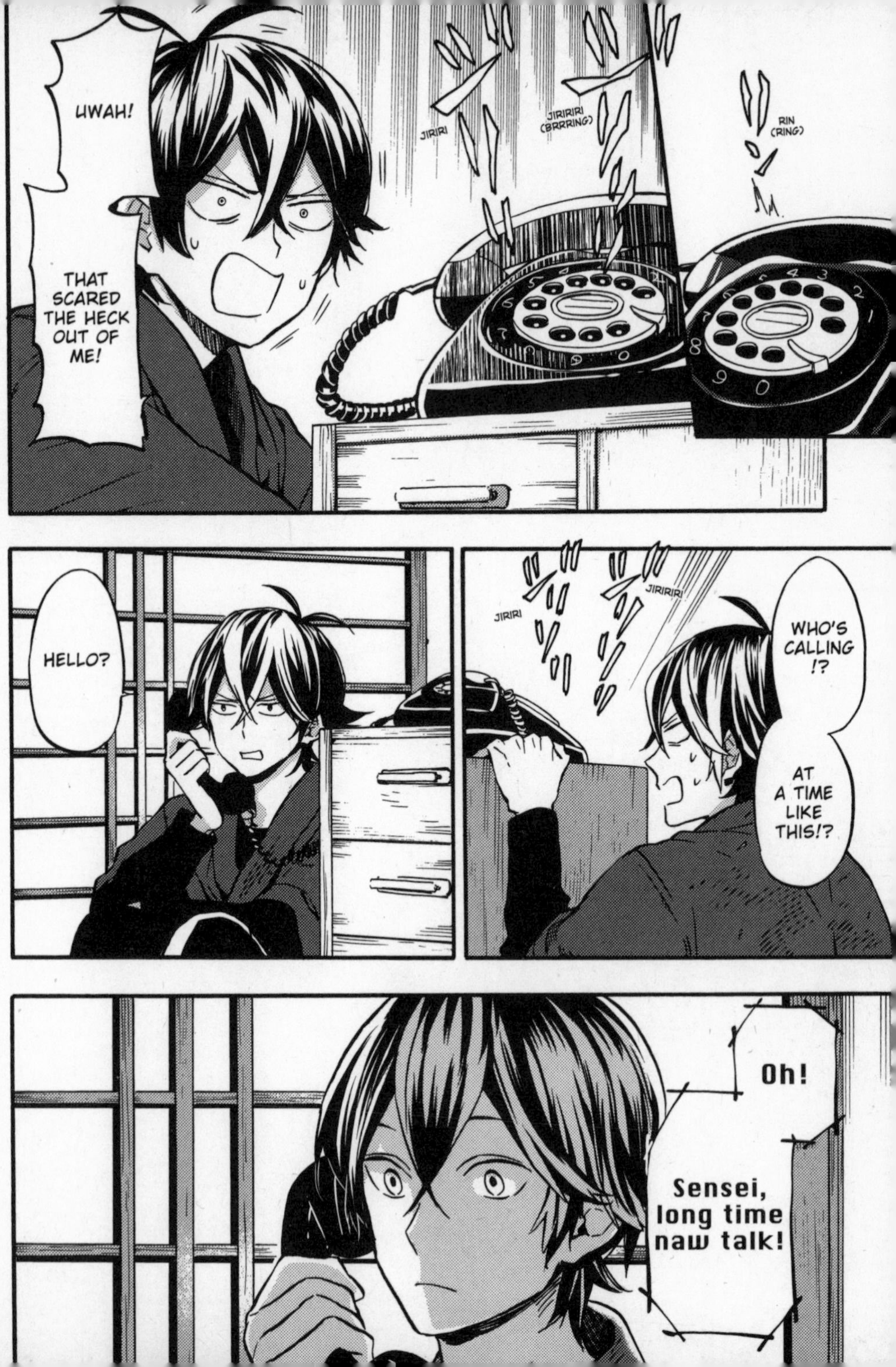
RIN (RING)
JIRIRIRI (BRRRING)
JIRIRI
UWAH!
THAT SCARED THE HECK OUT OF ME!
JIRIRIRI
JIRIRI
WHO'S CALLING!?
AT A TIME LIKE THIS!?
HELLO?
Oh!
Sensei, long time naw talk!

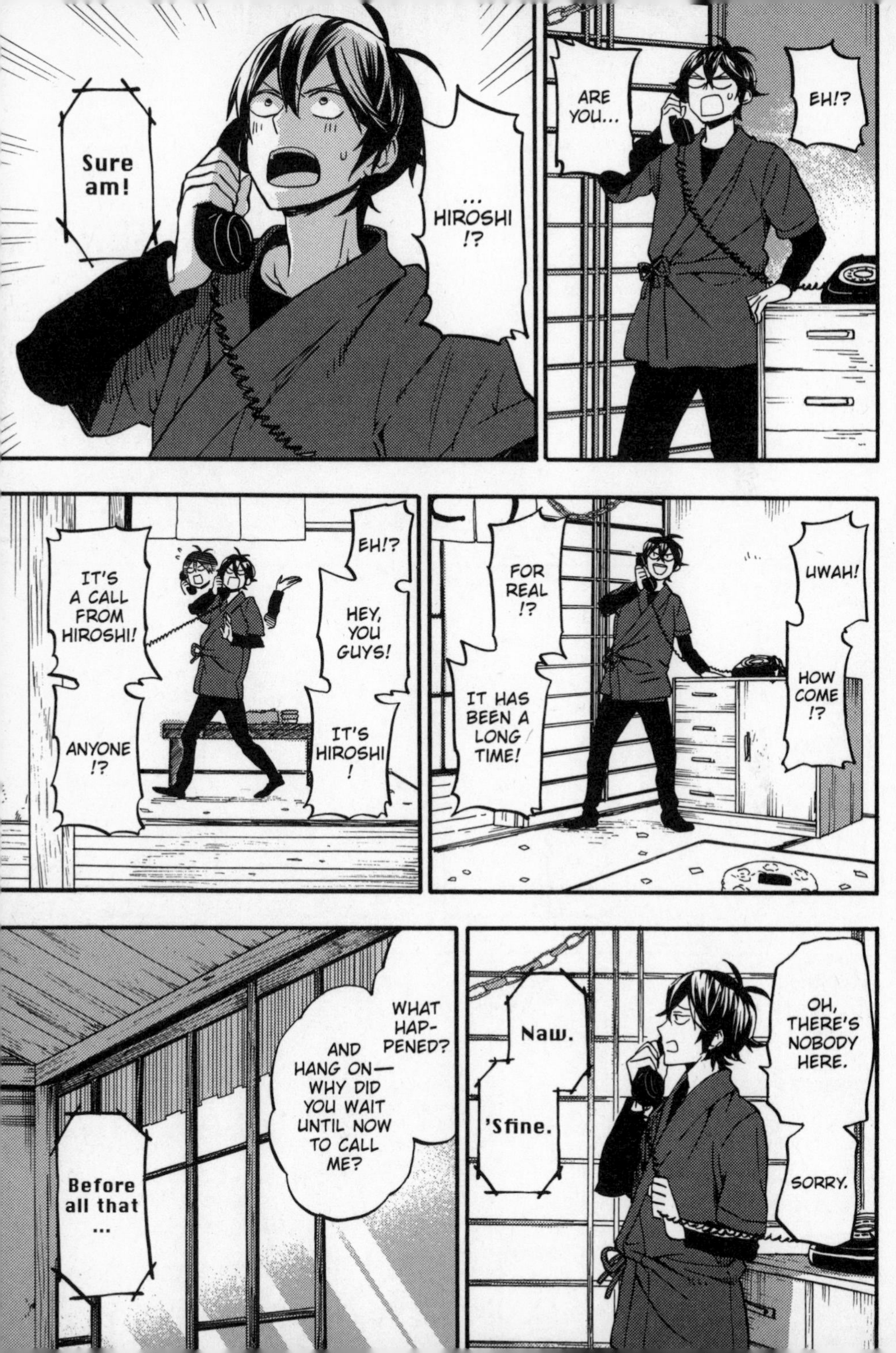
EH!?
ARE YOU...
...HIROSHI!?
Sure am!
UWAH!
HOW COME!?
FOR REAL!?
IT HAS BEEN A LONG TIME!
EH!?
HEY, YOU GUYS!
IT'S HIROSHI!
IT'S A CALL FROM HIROSHI!
ANYONE!?
OH, THERE'S NOBODY HERE.
SORRY.
Naw.
'Sfine.
WHAT HAPPENED?
AND HANG ON—WHY DID YOU WAIT UNTIL NOW TO CALL ME?
Before all that...

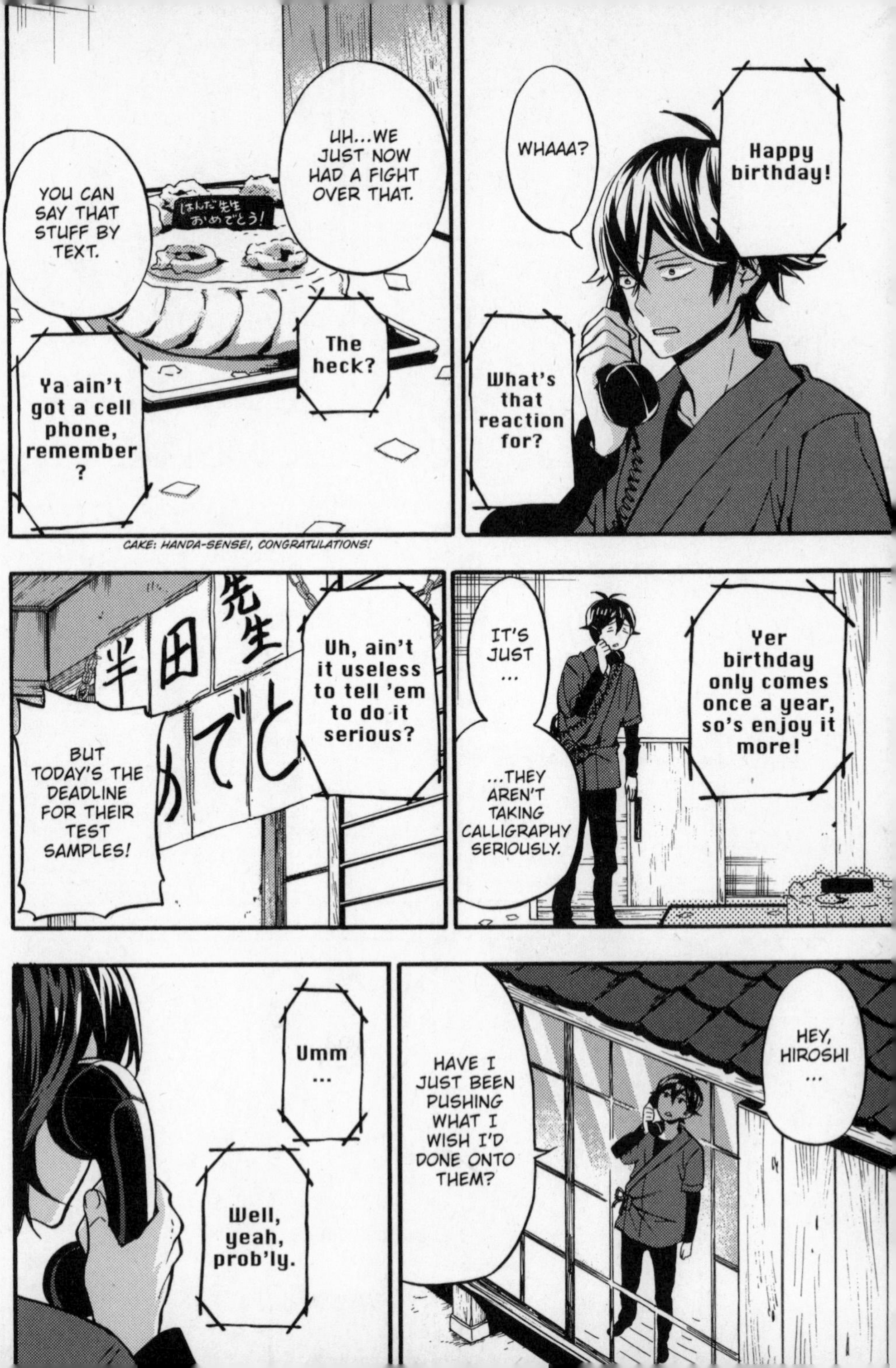
Happy birthday!
WHAAA?
What's that reaction for?
UH...WE JUST NOW HAD A FIGHT OVER THAT.
The heck?
はんだ先生 おめでとう!
YOU CAN SAY THAT STUFF BY TEXT.
Ya ain't got a cell phone, remember?
CAKE: HANDA-SENSEI, CONGRATULATIONS!
Yer birthday only comes once a year, so's enjoy it more!
IT'S JUST...
...THEY AREN'T TAKING CALLIGRAPHY SERIOUSLY.
Uh, ain't it useless to tell 'em to do it serious?
半田先生
BUT TODAY'S THE DEADLINE FOR THEIR TEST SAMPLES!
HEY, HIROSHI...
HAVE I JUST BEEN PUSHING WHAT I WISH I'D DONE ONTO THEM?
Umm...
Well, yeah, prob'ly.

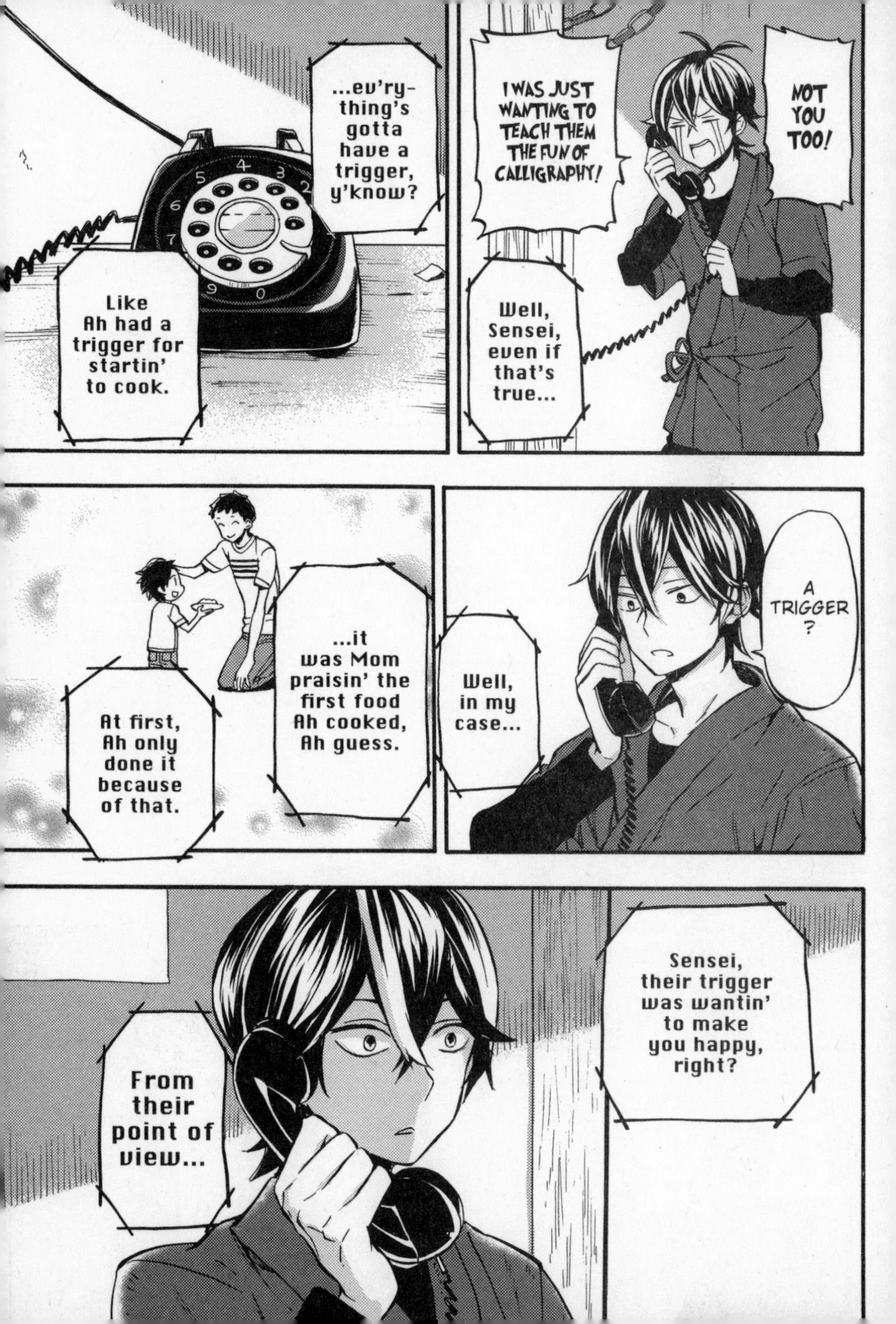
NOT YOU TOO!
I WAS JUST WANTING TO TEACH THEM THE FUN OF CALLIGRAPHY!
Well, Sensei, even if that's true...
...ev'ry-thing's gotta have a trigger, y'know?
Like Ah had a trigger for startin' to cook.
A TRIGGER?
Well, in my case...
...it was Mom praisin' the first food Ah cooked, Ah guess.
At first, Ah only done it because of that.
Sensei, their trigger was wantin' to make you happy, right?
From their point of view...

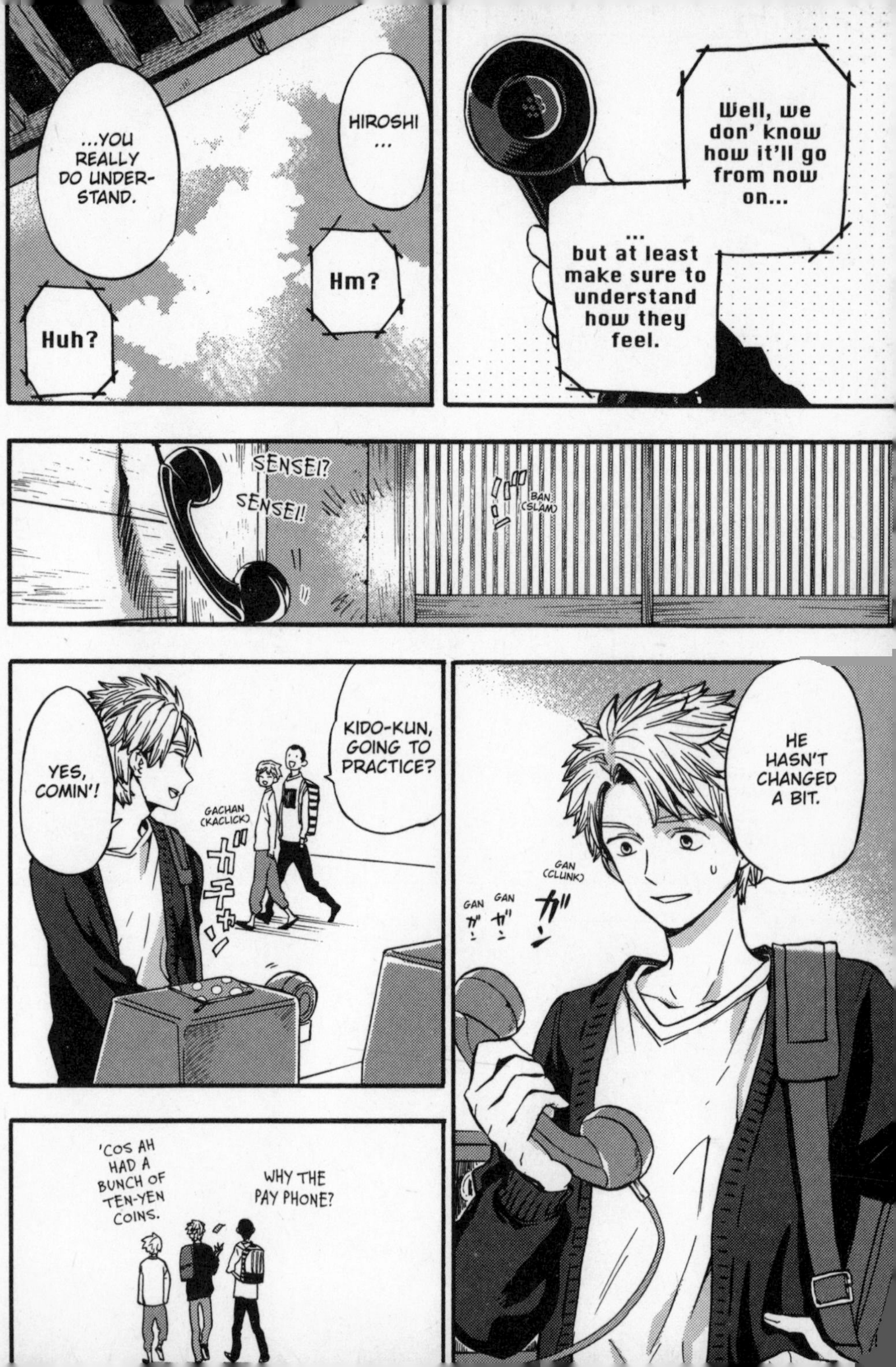
Well, we don' know how it'll go from now on...
... but at least make sure to understand how they feel.
HIROSHI ...
...YOU REALLY DO UNDER-STAND.
Hm?
Huh?
SENSEI!?
SENSEI!
BAN (SLAM)
HE HASN'T CHANGED A BIT.
GAN (CLUNK)
GAN
GAN
KIDO-KUN, GOING TO PRACTICE?
YES, COMIN'!
GACHAN (KACLICK)
WHY THE PAY PHONE?
'COS AH HAD A BUNCH OF TEN-YEN COINS.

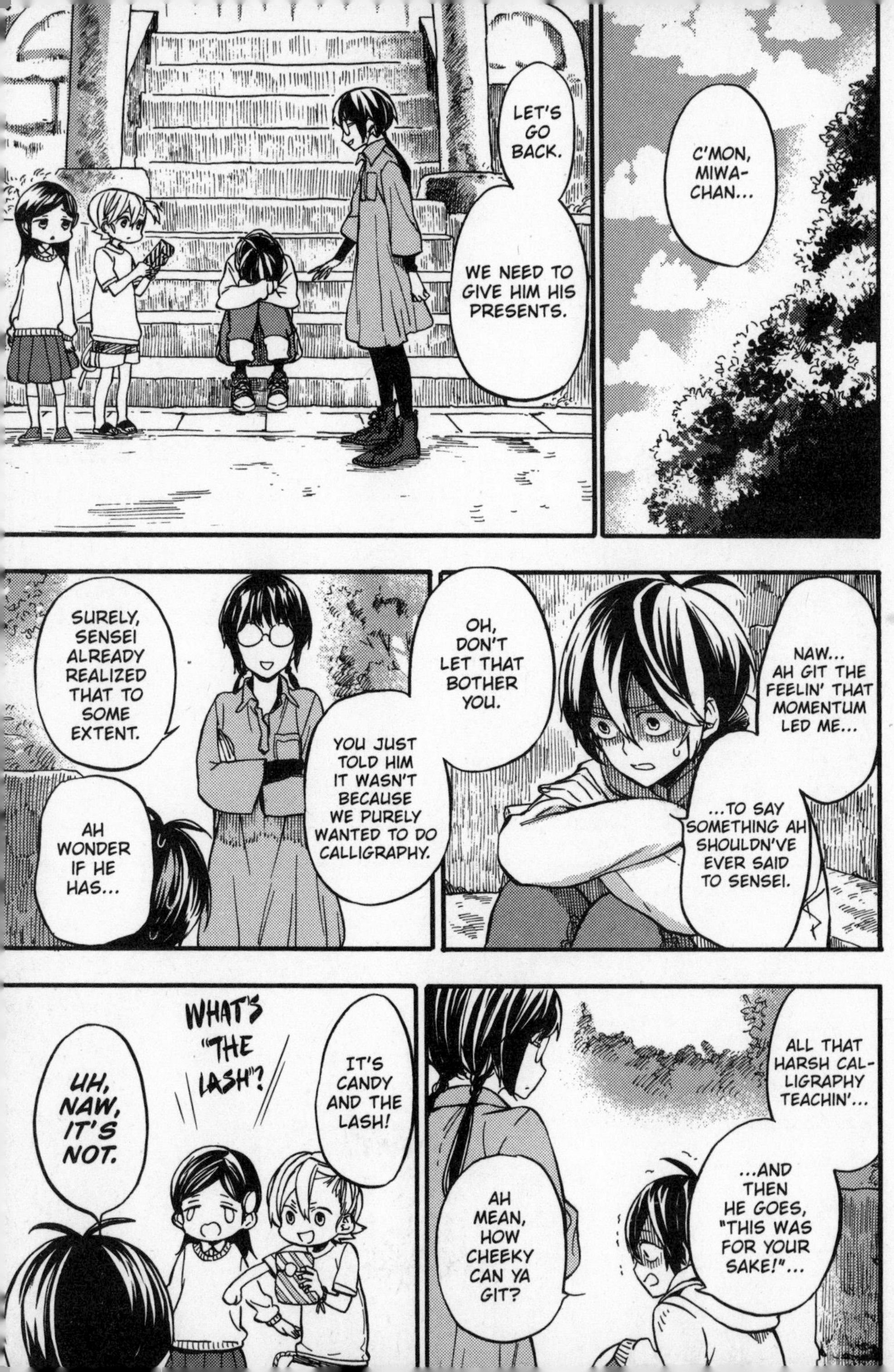
C'MON, MIWA-CHAN...
LET'S GO BACK.
WE NEED TO GIVE HIM HIS PRESENTS.
NAW... AH GIT THE FEELIN' THAT MOMENTUM LED ME...
...TO SAY SOMETHING AH SHOULDN'VE EVER SAID TO SENSEI.
OH, DON'T LET THAT BOTHER YOU.
YOU JUST TOLD HIM IT WASN'T BECAUSE WE PURELY WANTED TO DO CALLIGRAPHY.
SURELY, SENSEI ALREADY REALIZED THAT TO SOME EXTENT.
AH WONDER IF HE HAS...
ALL THAT HARSH CALLIGRAPHY TEACHIN'...
...AND THEN HE GOES, "THIS WAS FOR YOUR SAKE!"...
AH MEAN, HOW CHEEKY CAN YA GIT?
IT'S CANDY AND THE LASH!
WHAT'S "THE LASH"?
UH, NAW, IT'S NOT.

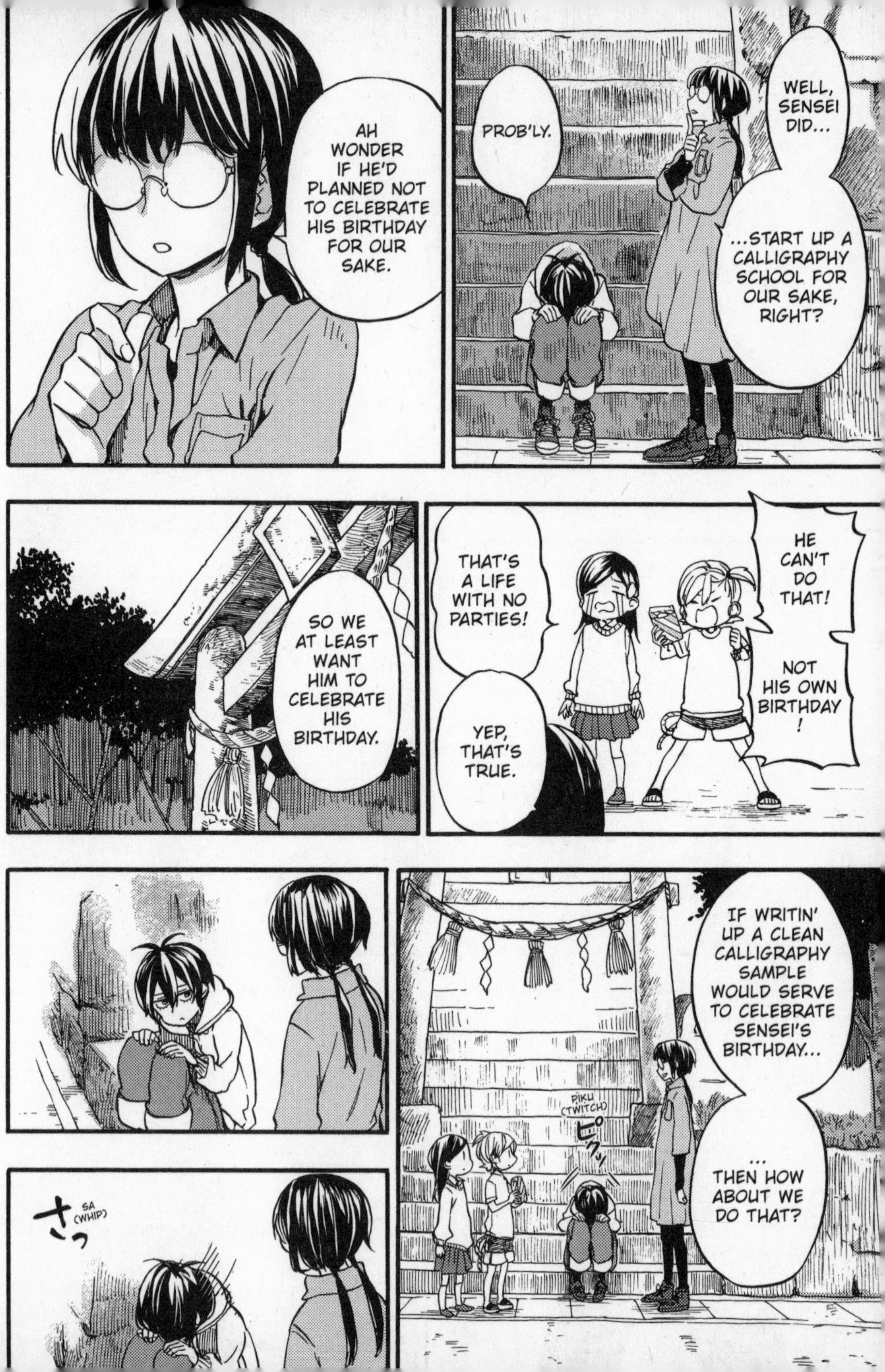
WELL, SENSEI DID...
...START UP A CALLIGRAPHY SCHOOL FOR OUR SAKE, RIGHT?
PROB'LY.
AH WONDER IF HE'D PLANNED NOT TO CELEBRATE HIS BIRTHDAY FOR OUR SAKE.
HE CAN'T DO THAT!
THAT'S A LIFE WITH NO PARTIES!
NOT HIS OWN BIRTHDAY!
YEP, THAT'S TRUE.
SO WE AT LEAST WANT HIM TO CELEBRATE HIS BIRTHDAY.
IF WRITIN' UP A CLEAN CALLIGRAPHY SAMPLE WOULD SERVE TO CELEBRATE SENSEI'S BIRTHDAY...
PIKU (TWITCH)
...THEN HOW ABOUT WE DO THAT?
SA (WHIP)

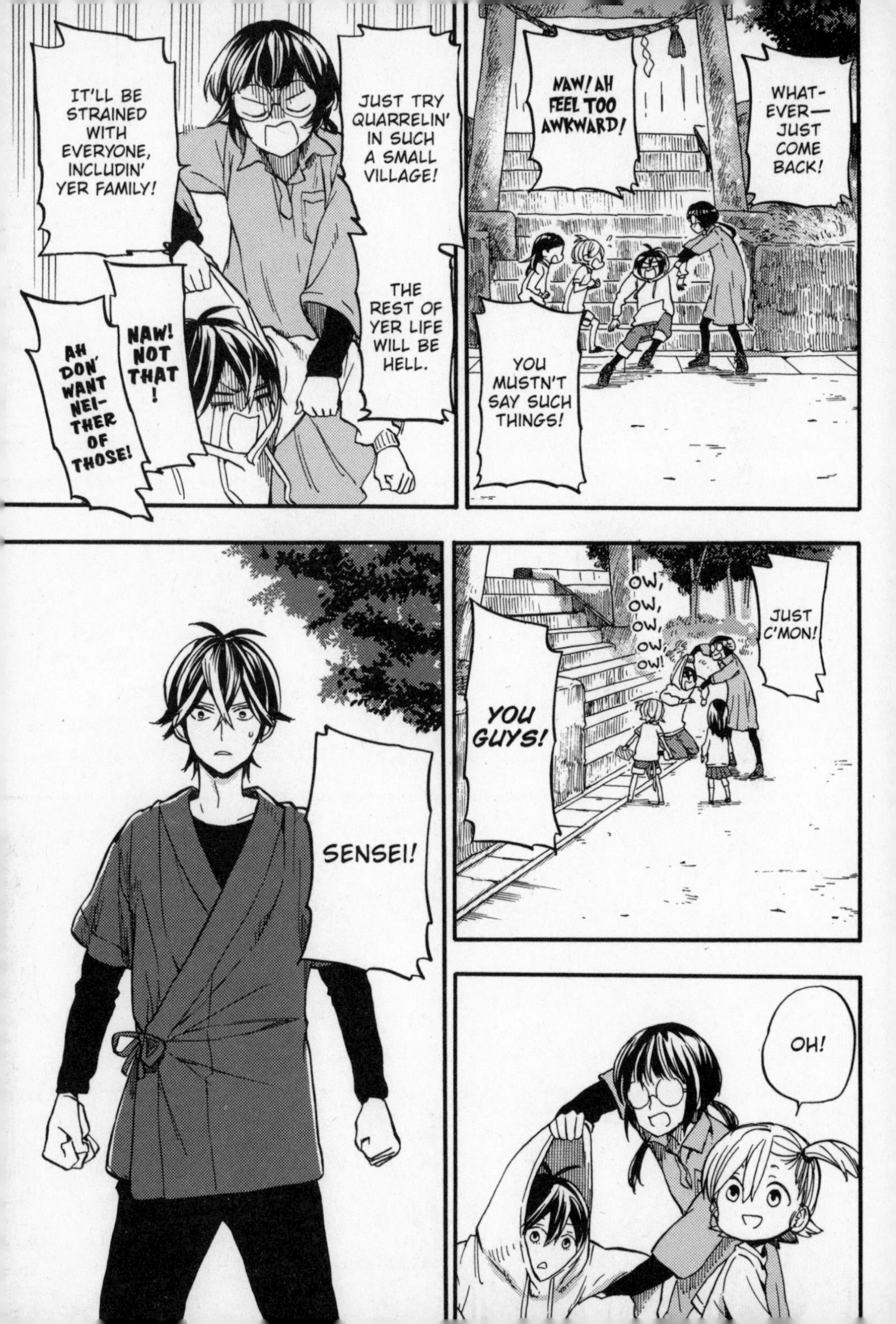
WHAT-EVER—JUST COME BACK!
NAW! AH FEEL TOO AWKWARD!
YOU MUSTN'T SAY SUCH THINGS!
JUST TRY QUARRELIN' IN SUCH A SMALL VILLAGE!
IT'LL BE STRAINED WITH EVERYONE, INCLUDIN' YER FAMILY!
THE REST OF YER LIFE WILL BE HELL.
NAW! NOT THAT!
AH DON' WANT NEI-THER OF THOSE!
JUST C'MON!
OW, OW, OW, OW, OW!
YOU GUYS!
OH!
SENSEI!

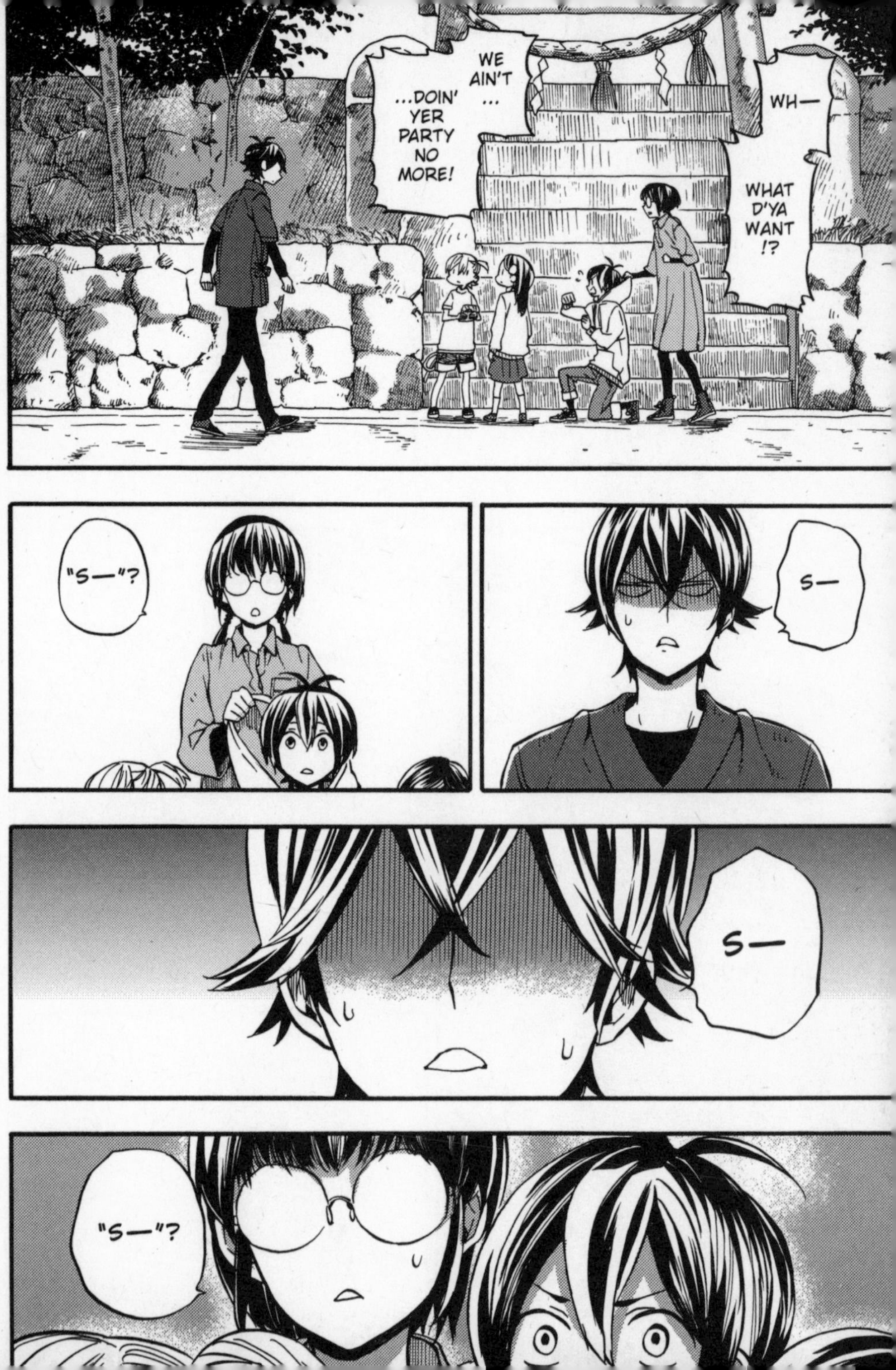
WH—
WHAT D'YA WANT!?
WE AIN'T ...
...DOIN' YER PARTY NO MORE!
S—
"S—"?
S—
"S—"?

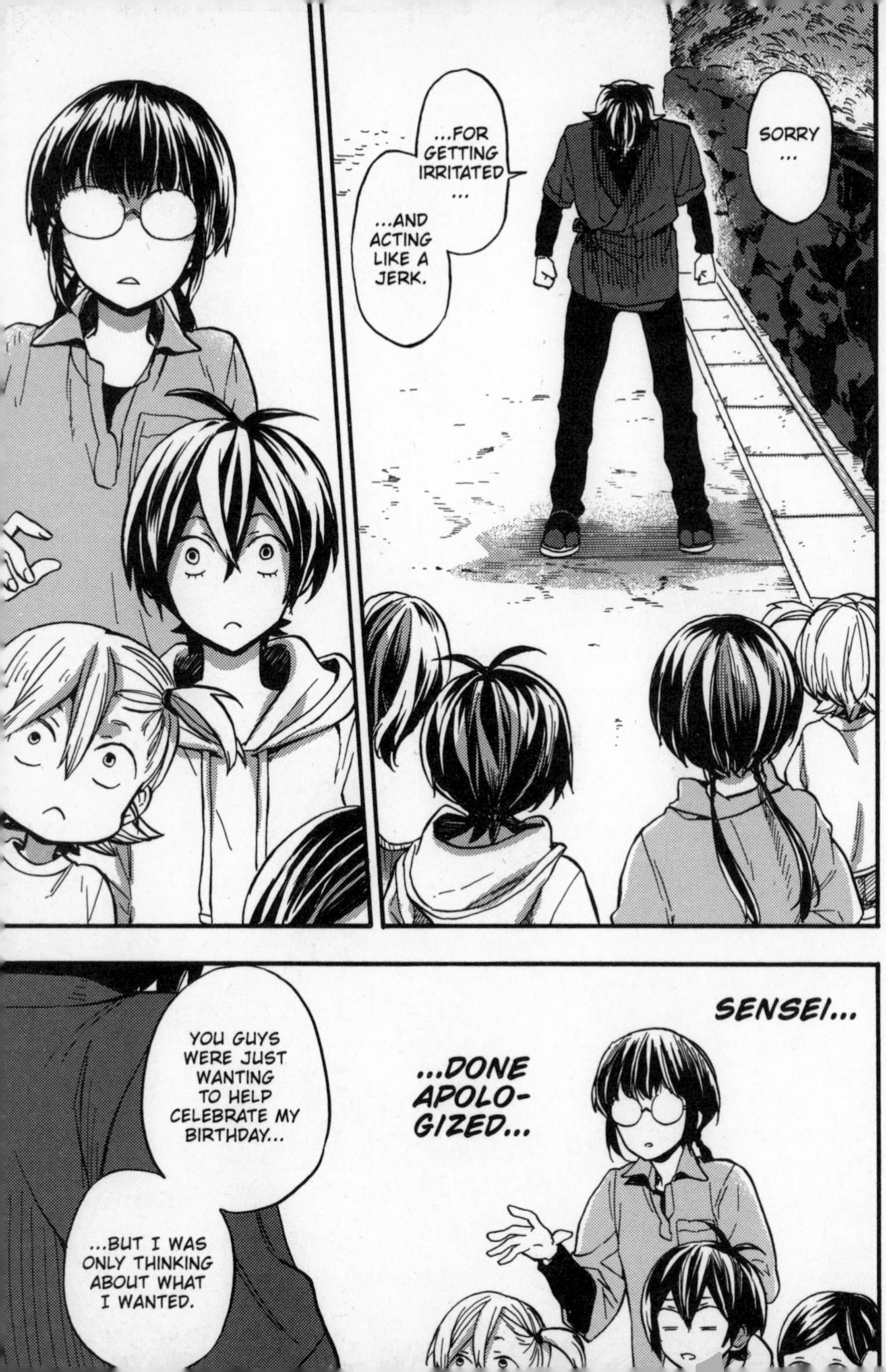
SORRY ...
...FOR GETTING IRRITATED ...
...AND ACTING LIKE A JERK.
SENSEI...
...DONE APOLO-GIZED...
YOU GUYS WERE JUST WANTING TO HELP CELEBRATE MY BIRTHDAY...
...BUT I WAS ONLY THINKING ABOUT WHAT I WANTED.

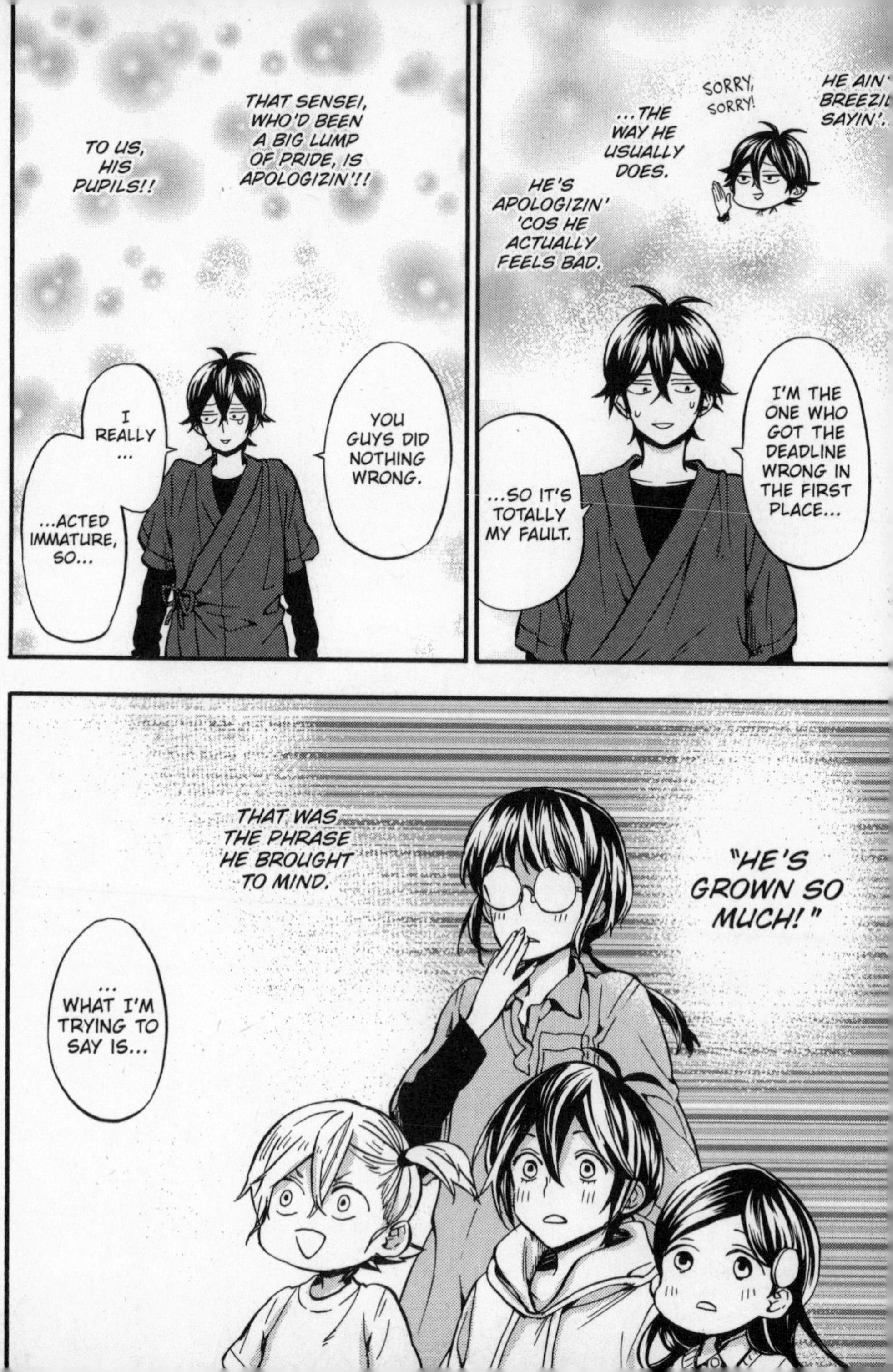
HE AIN' BREEZI SAYIN'.
SORRY, SORRY!
...THE WAY HE USUALLY DOES.
HE'S APOLOGIZIN' 'COS HE ACTUALLY FEELS BAD.
I'M THE ONE WHO GOT THE DEADLINE WRONG IN THE FIRST PLACE...
...SO IT'S TOTALLY MY FAULT.
THAT SENSEI, WHO'D BEEN A BIG LUMP OF PRIDE, IS APOLOGIZIN'!!
TO US, HIS PUPILS!!
YOU GUYS DID NOTHING WRONG.
I REALLY ...
...ACTED IMMATURE, SO...
"HE'S GROWN SO MUCH!"
THAT WAS THE PHRASE HE BROUGHT TO MIND.
... WHAT I'M TRYING TO SAY IS...

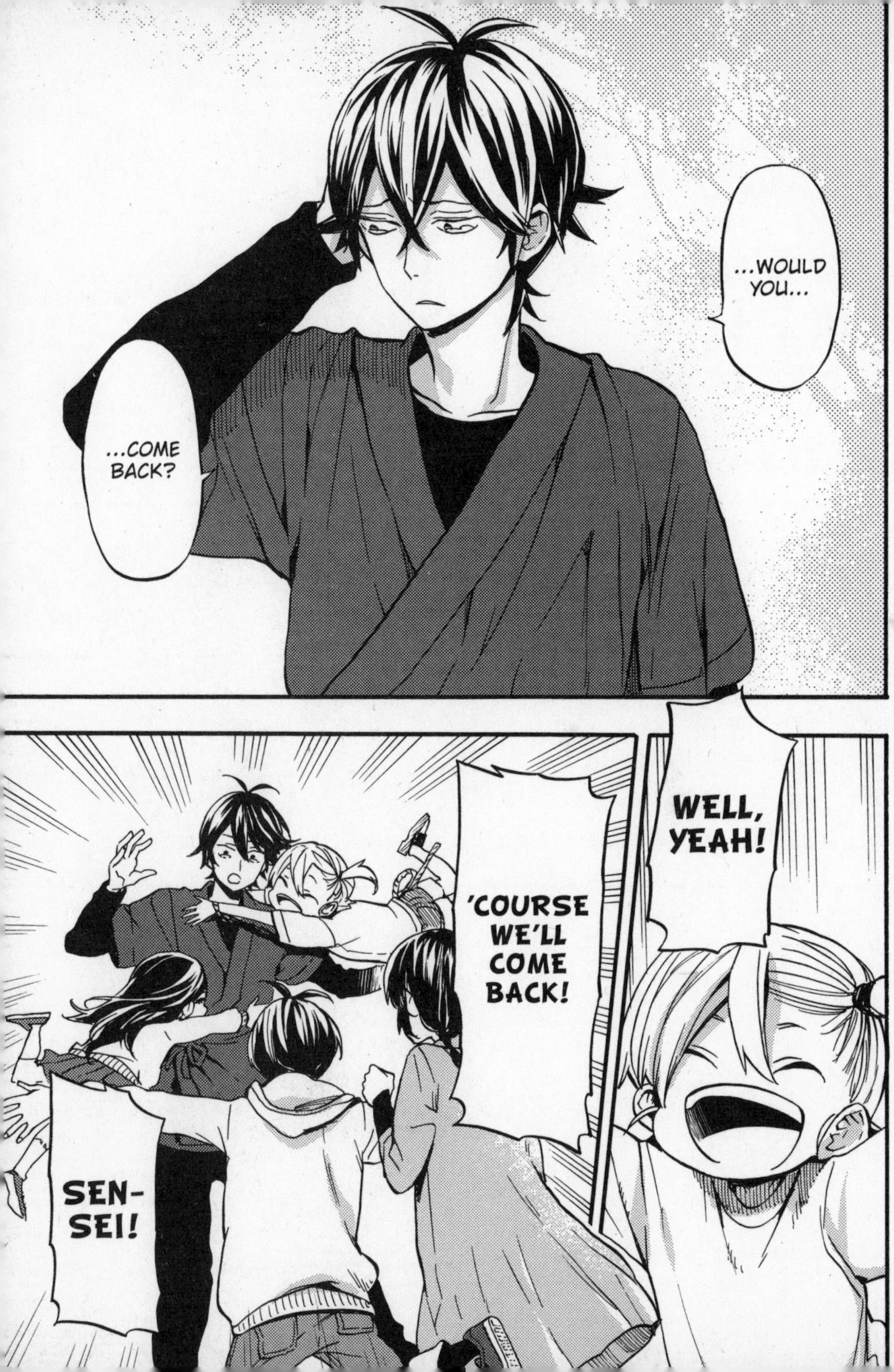
...WOULD YOU...
...COME BACK?
WELL, YEAH!
'COURSE WE'LL COME BACK!
SEN-SEI!

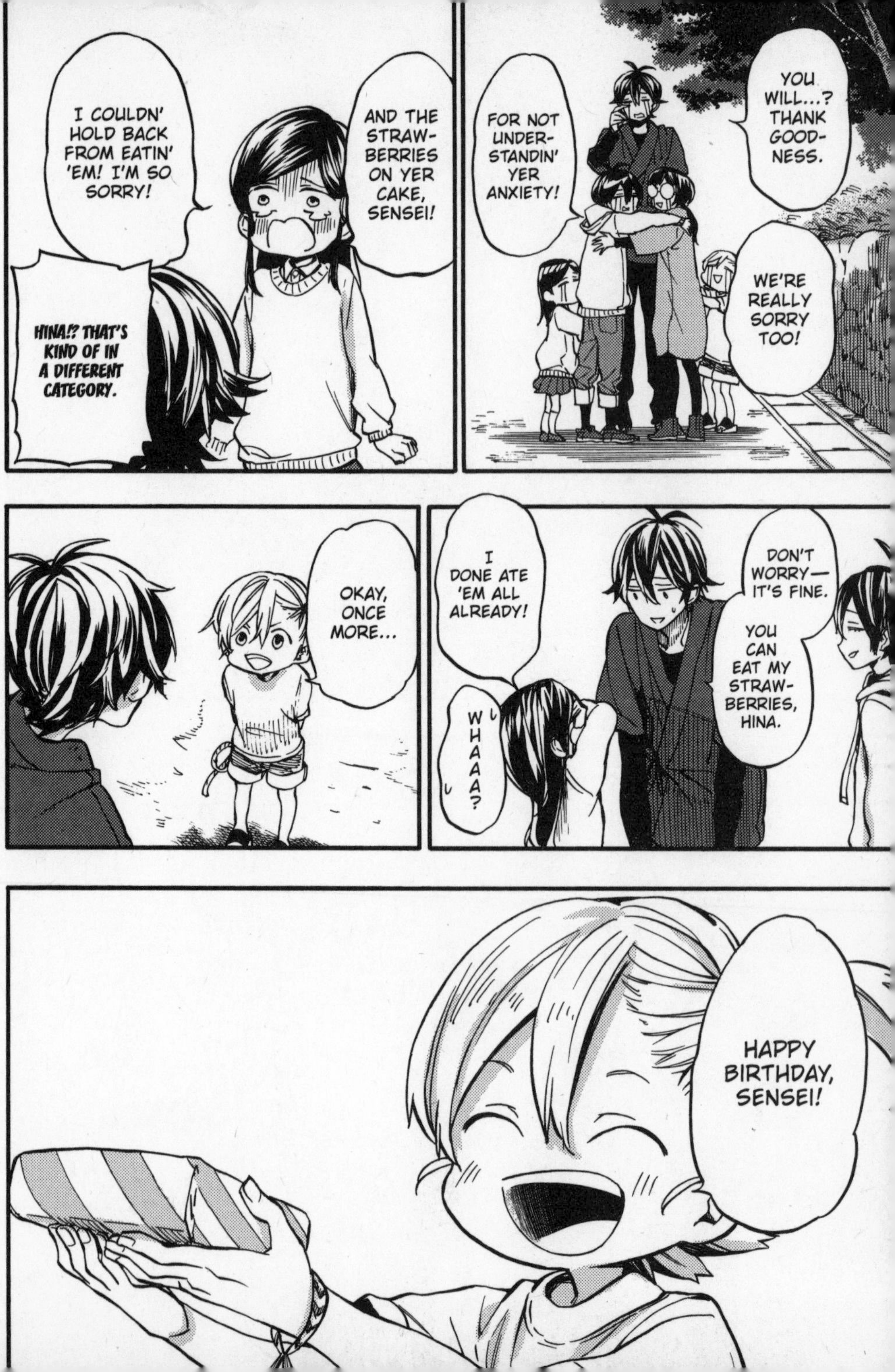
YOU WILL...? THANK GOOD-NESS.
WE'RE REALLY SORRY TOO!
FOR NOT UNDER-STANDIN' YER ANXIETY!
AND THE STRAW-BERRIES ON YER CAKE, SENSEI!
I COULDN' HOLD BACK FROM EATIN' 'EM! I'M SO SORRY!
HINA!? THAT'S KIND OF IN A DIFFERENT CATEGORY.
DON'T WORRY—IT'S FINE.
YOU CAN EAT MY STRAW-BERRIES, HINA.
I DONE ATE 'EM ALL ALREADY!
WHAAAA?
OKAY, ONCE MORE...
HAPPY BIRTHDAY, SENSEI!

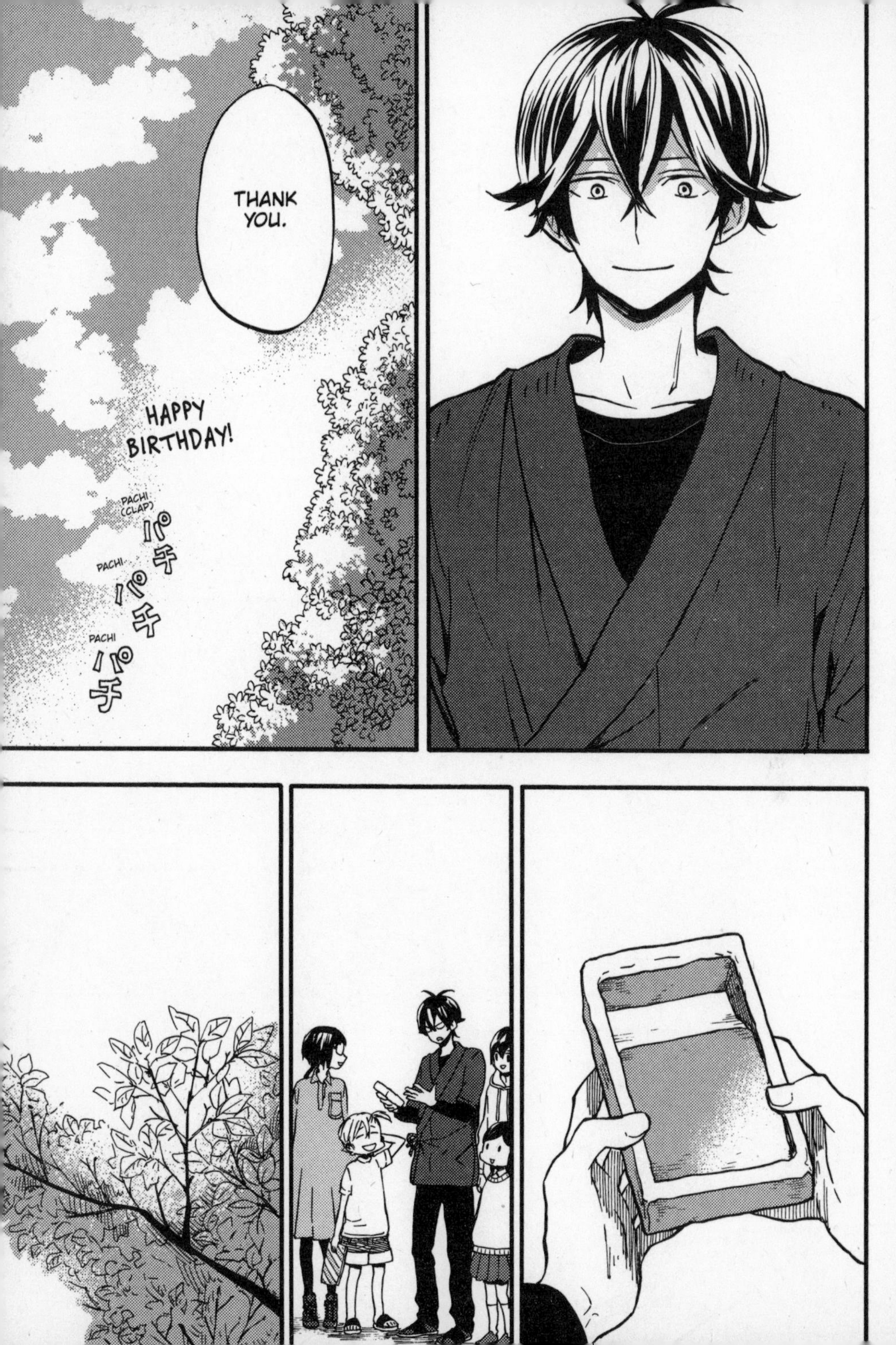
THANK YOU.
HAPPY BIRTHDAY!
PACHI (CLAP)
パチ
PACHI
パチ
PACHI
パチ

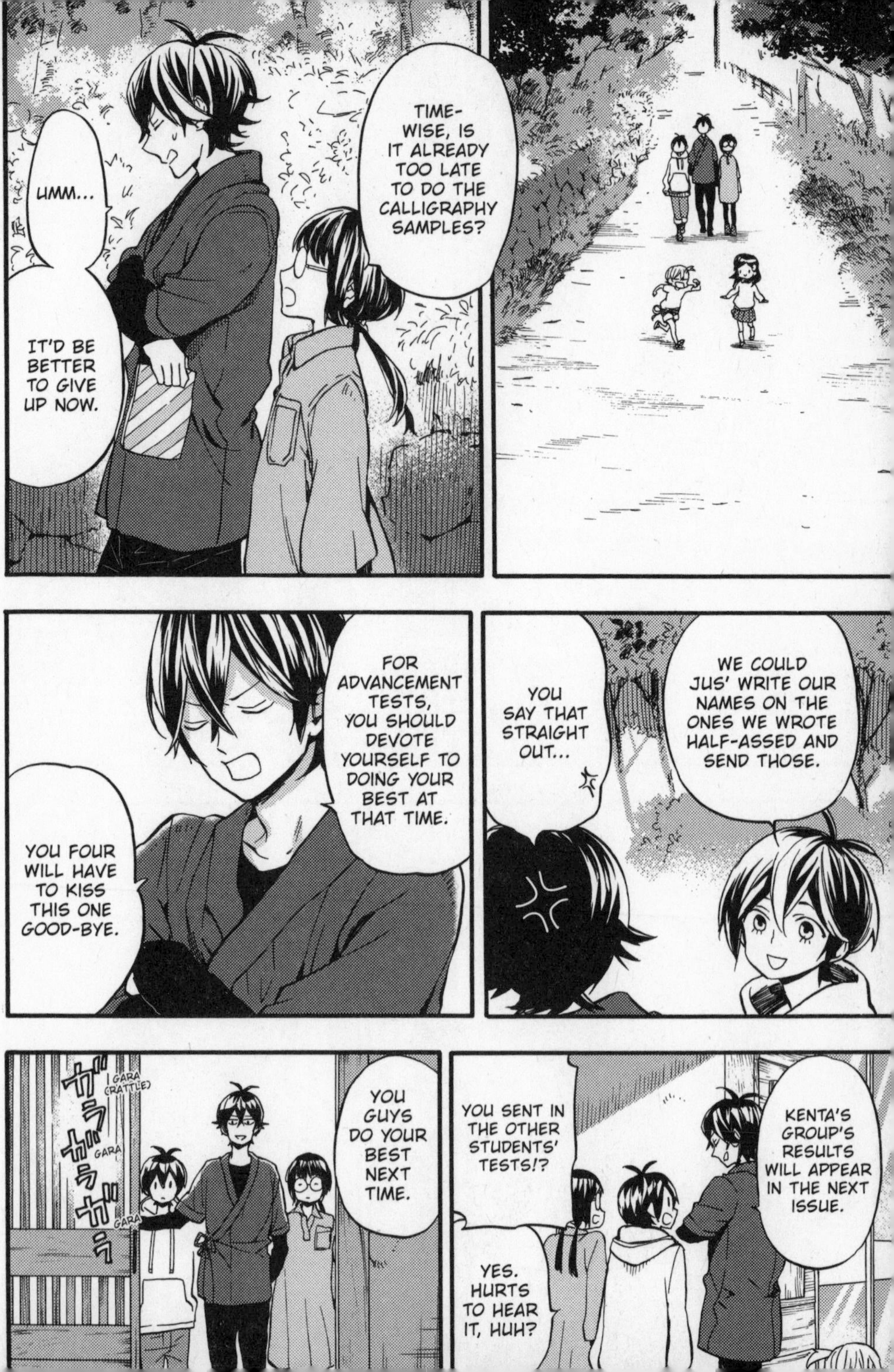
TIME-WISE, IS IT ALREADY TOO LATE TO DO THE CALLIGRAPHY SAMPLES?
UMM...
IT'D BE BETTER TO GIVE UP NOW.
WE COULD JUS' WRITE OUR NAMES ON THE ONES WE WROTE HALF-ASSED AND SEND THOSE.
YOU SAY THAT STRAIGHT OUT...
FOR ADVANCEMENT TESTS, YOU SHOULD DEVOTE YOURSELF TO DOING YOUR BEST AT THAT TIME.
YOU FOUR WILL HAVE TO KISS THIS ONE GOOD-BYE.
KENTA'S GROUP'S RESULTS WILL APPEAR IN THE NEXT ISSUE.
YOU SENT IN THE OTHER STUDENTS' TESTS!?
YES. HURTS TO HEAR IT, HUH?
YOU GUYS DO YOUR BEST NEXT TIME.
GARA (RATTLE)
GARA
GARA

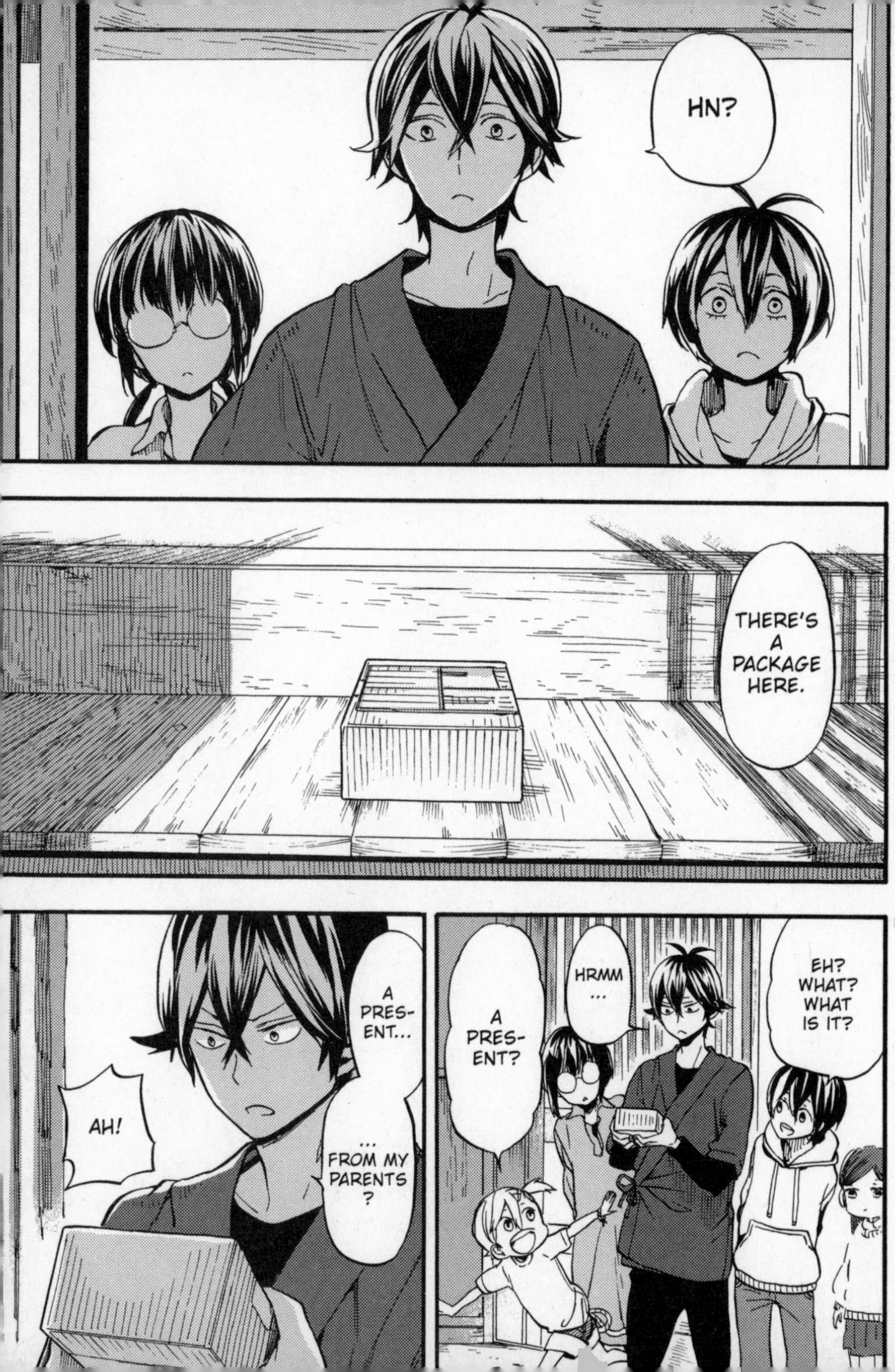
HN?
THERE'S A PACKAGE HERE.
EH? WHAT? WHAT IS IT?
HRMM ...
A PRESENT?
A PRESENT...
... FROM MY PARENTS ?
AH!

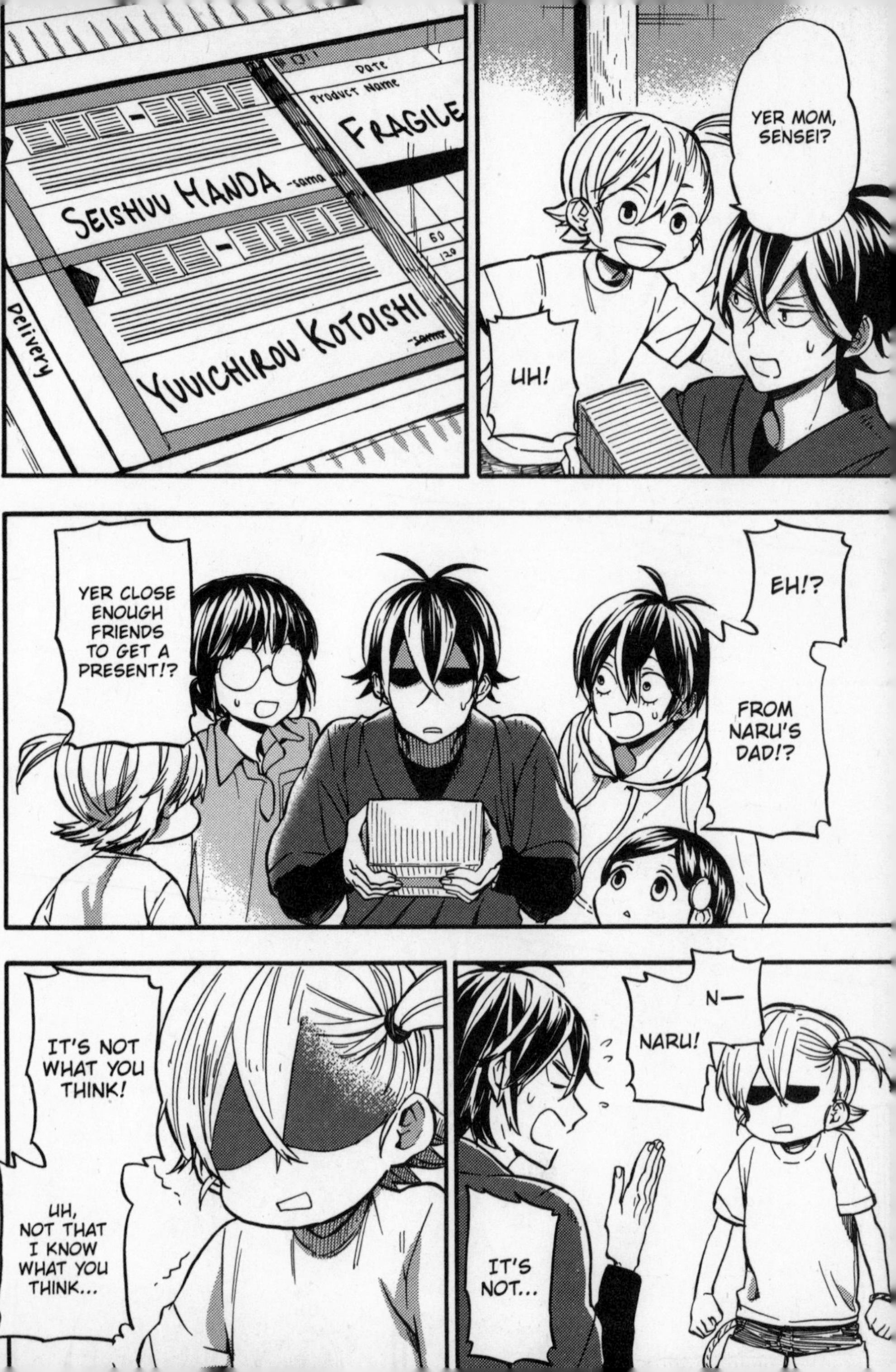
YER MOM, SENSEI?
UH!
Date
Product Name
FRAGILE
SEISHUU HANDA -sama
60
120
YUUICHIROU KOTOISHI
Delivery
EH!?
FROM NARU'S DAD!?
YER CLOSE ENOUGH FRIENDS TO GET A PRESENT!?
N—
NARU!
IT'S NOT...
IT'S NOT WHAT YOU THINK!
UH, NOT THAT I KNOW WHAT YOU THINK...

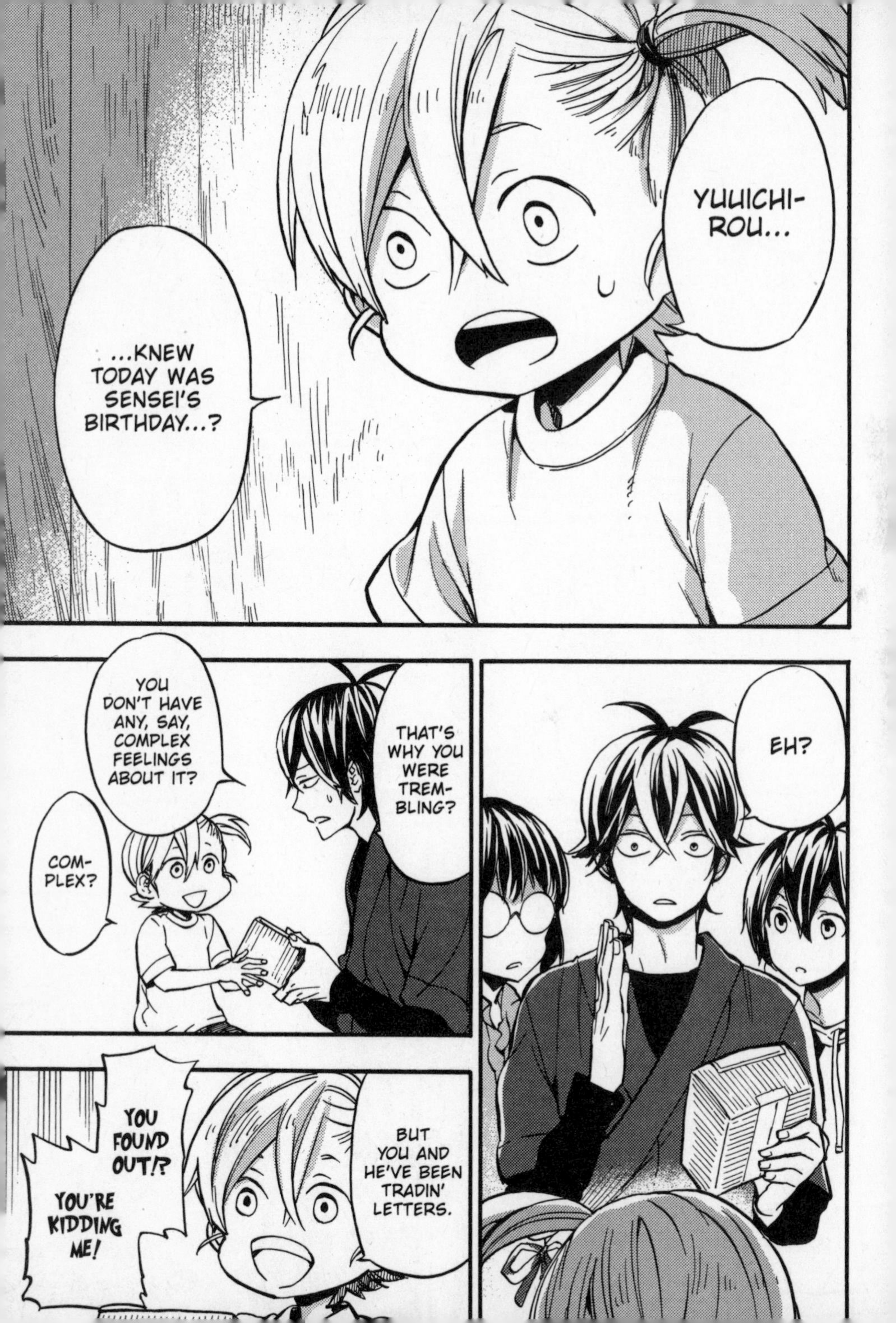
YUUICHI-ROU...
...KNEW TODAY WAS SENSEI'S BIRTHDAY...?
EH?
THAT'S WHY YOU WERE TREM-BLING?
YOU DON'T HAVE ANY, SAY, COMPLEX FEELINGS ABOUT IT?
COM-PLEX?
BUT YOU AND HE'VE BEEN TRADIN' LETTERS.
YOU FOUND OUT!?
YOU'RE KIDDING ME!

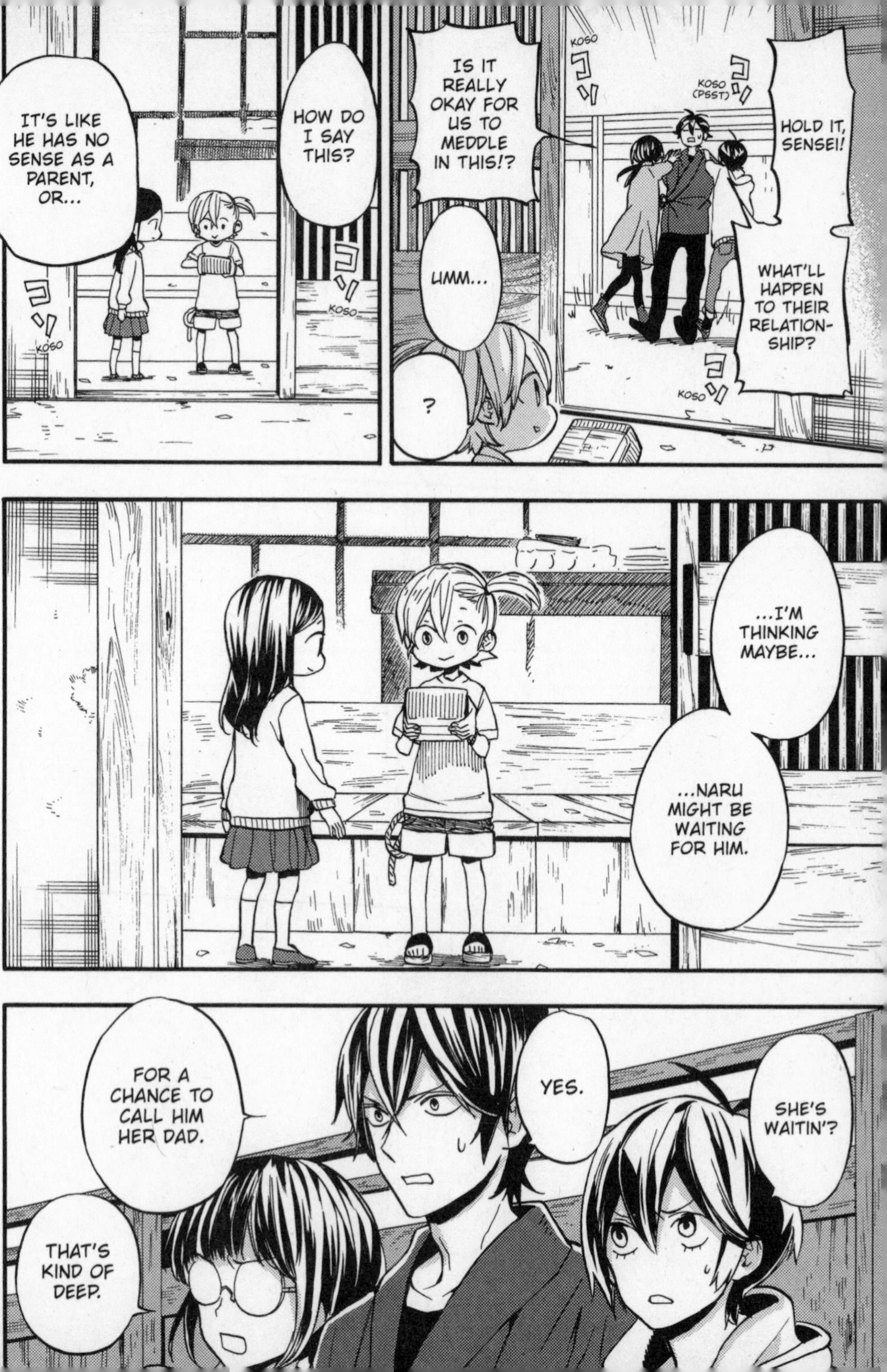

KOSO (PSST)
HOLD IT, SENSEI!
WHAT'LL HAPPEN TO THEIR RELATIONSHIP?
KOSO
KOSO
IS IT REALLY OKAY FOR US TO MEDDLE IN THIS!?
UMM...
?
KOSO
HOW DO I SAY THIS?
IT'S LIKE HE HAS NO SENSE AS A PARENT, OR...
KOSO
...I'M THINKING MAYBE...
...NARU MIGHT BE WAITING FOR HIM.
SHE'S WAITIN'?
YES.
FOR A CHANCE TO CALL HIM HER DAD.
THAT'S KIND OF DEEP.

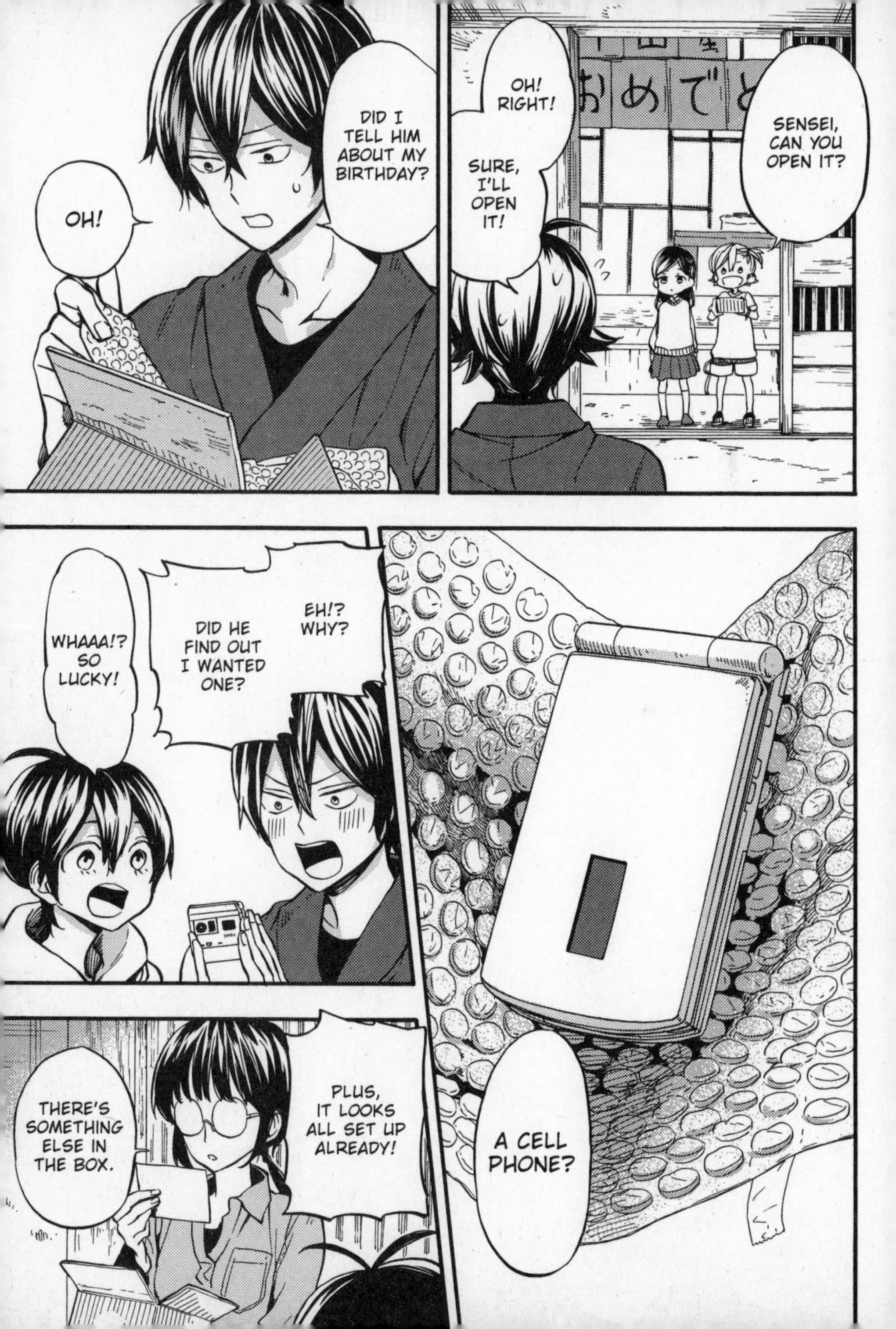

おめでと
SENSEI, CAN YOU OPEN IT?
OH! RIGHT!
SURE, I'LL OPEN IT!
DID I TELL HIM ABOUT MY BIRTHDAY?
OH!
A CELL PHONE?
EH!? WHY?
DID HE FIND OUT I WANTED ONE?
WHAAA!? SO LUCKY!
PLUS, IT LOOKS ALL SET UP ALREADY!
THERE'S SOMETHING ELSE IN THE BOX.

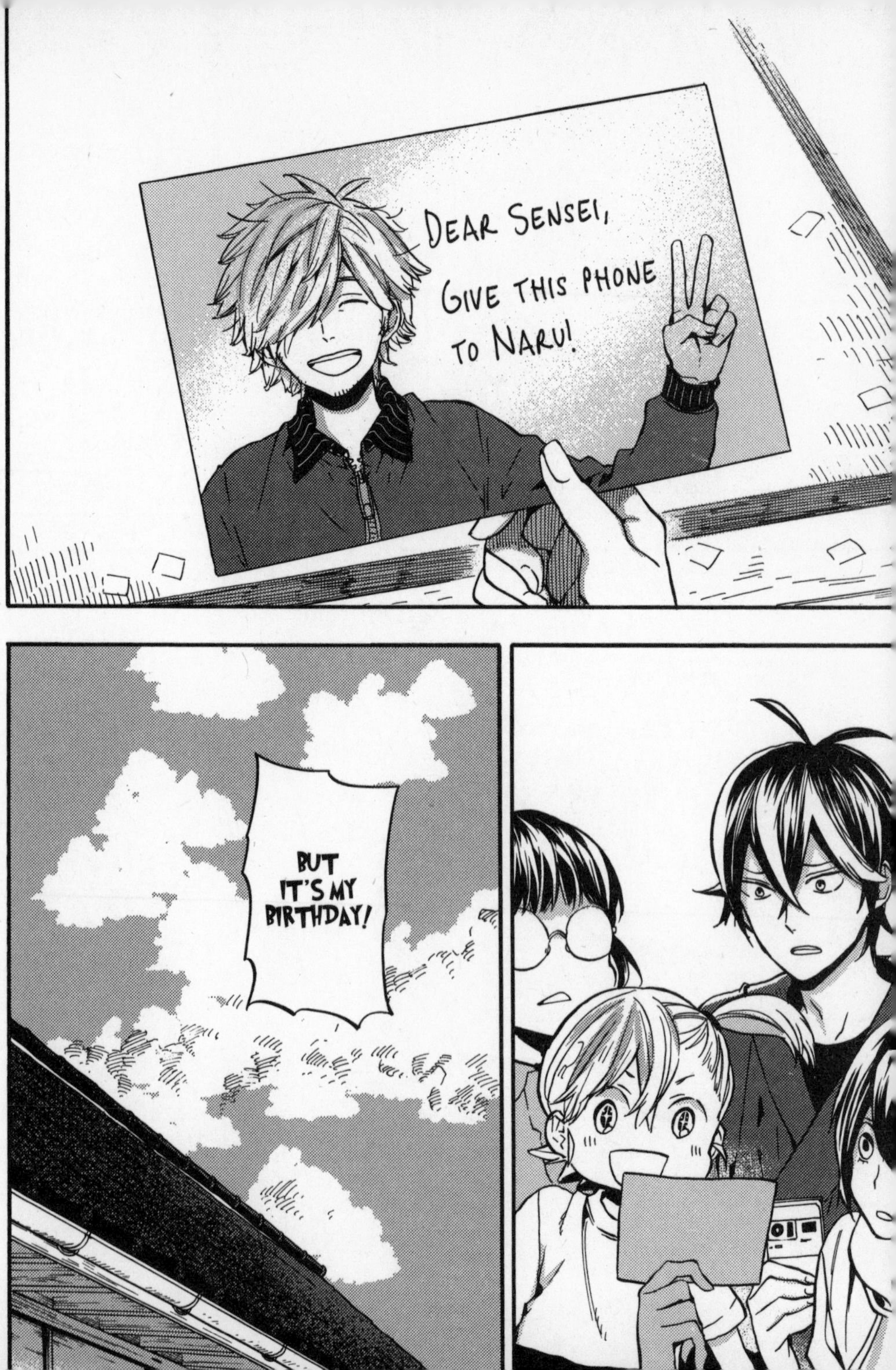
Dear Sensei,
Give this phone to Naru!
BUT IT'S MY BIRTHDAY!

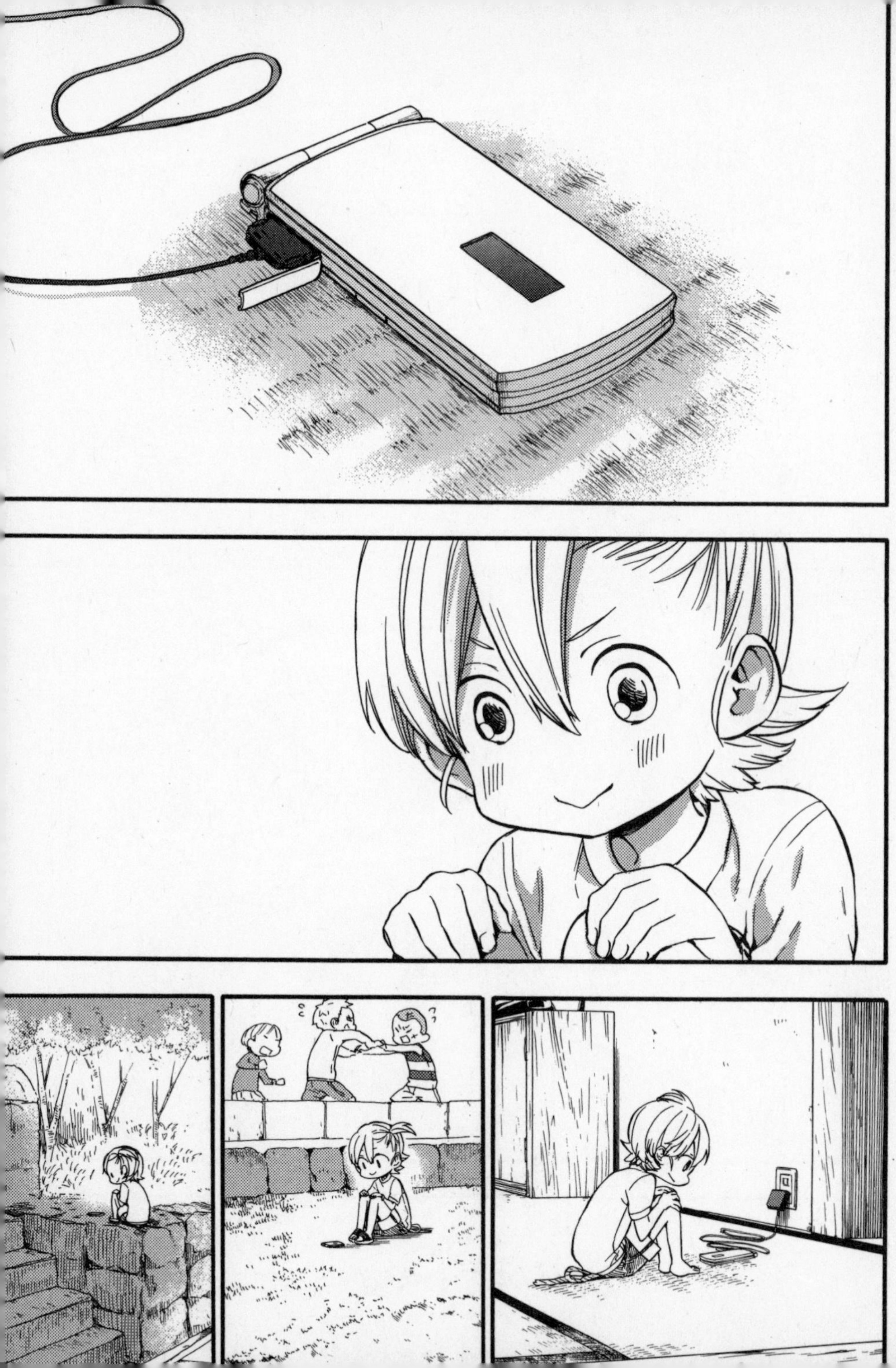

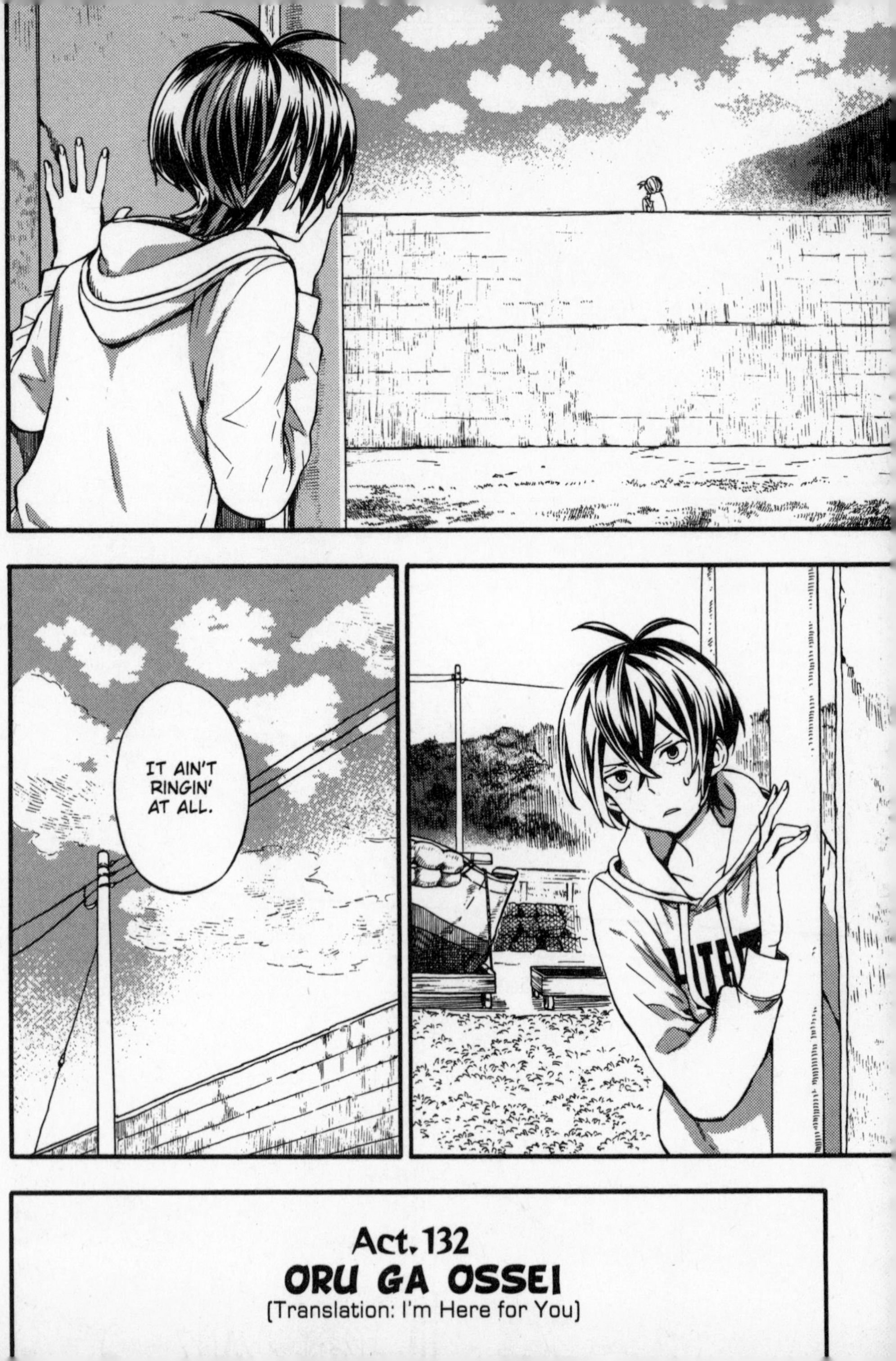
IT AIN'T RINGIN' AT ALL.

Act. 132
ORU GA OSSEI
[Translation: I'm Here for You]

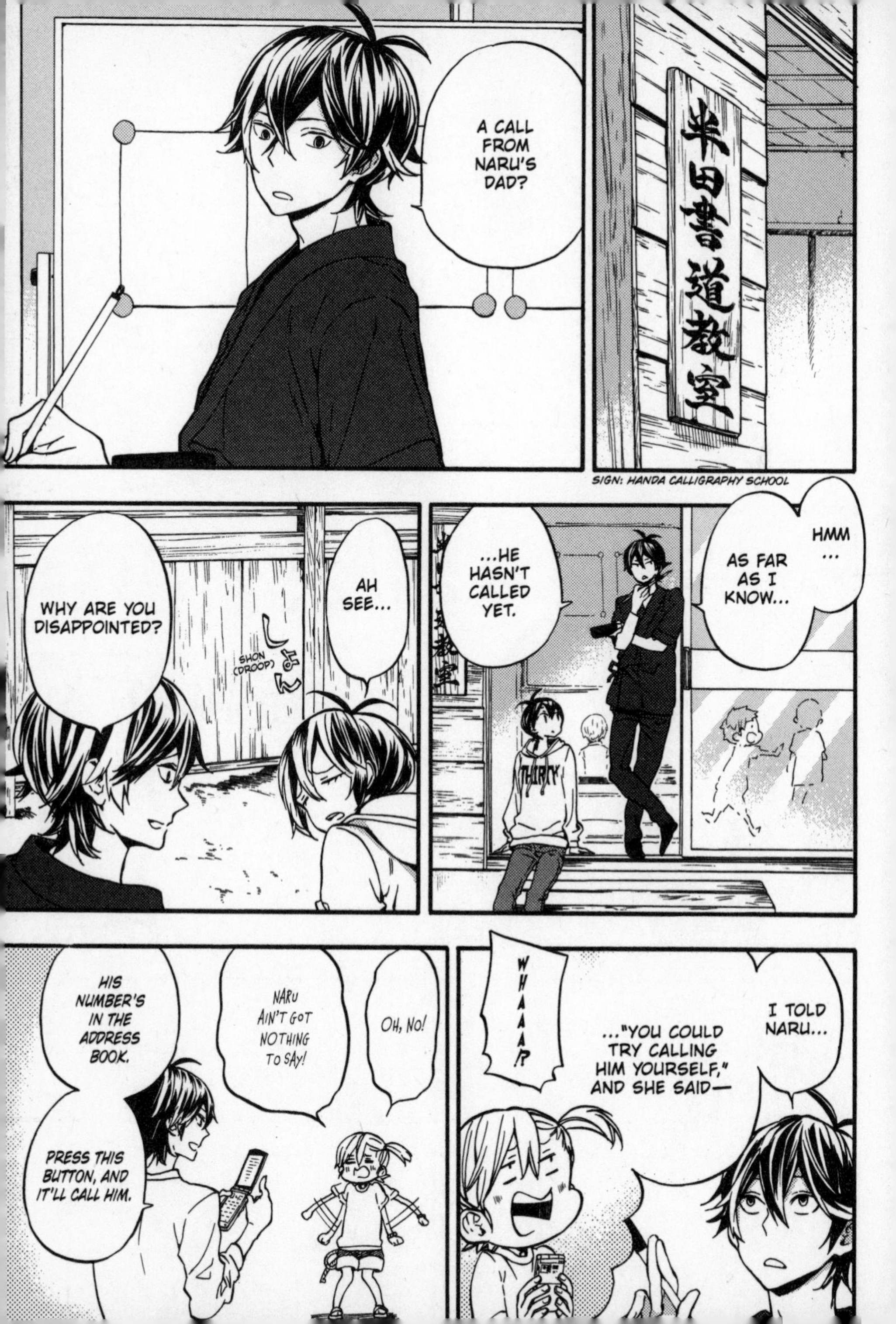
半田書道教室
SIGN: HANDA CALLIGRAPHY SCHOOL
A CALL FROM NARU'S DAD?
HMM...
AS FAR AS I KNOW...
...HE HASN'T CALLED YET.
AH SEE...
しょん
SHON (DROOP)
WHY ARE YOU DISAPPOINTED?
I TOLD NARU...
..."YOU COULD TRY CALLING HIM YOURSELF," AND SHE SAID—
WHAAAA!?
OH, NO!
NARU AIN'T GOT NOTHING TO SAY!
HIS NUMBER'S IN THE ADDRESS BOOK.
PRESS THIS BUTTON, AND IT'LL CALL HIM.

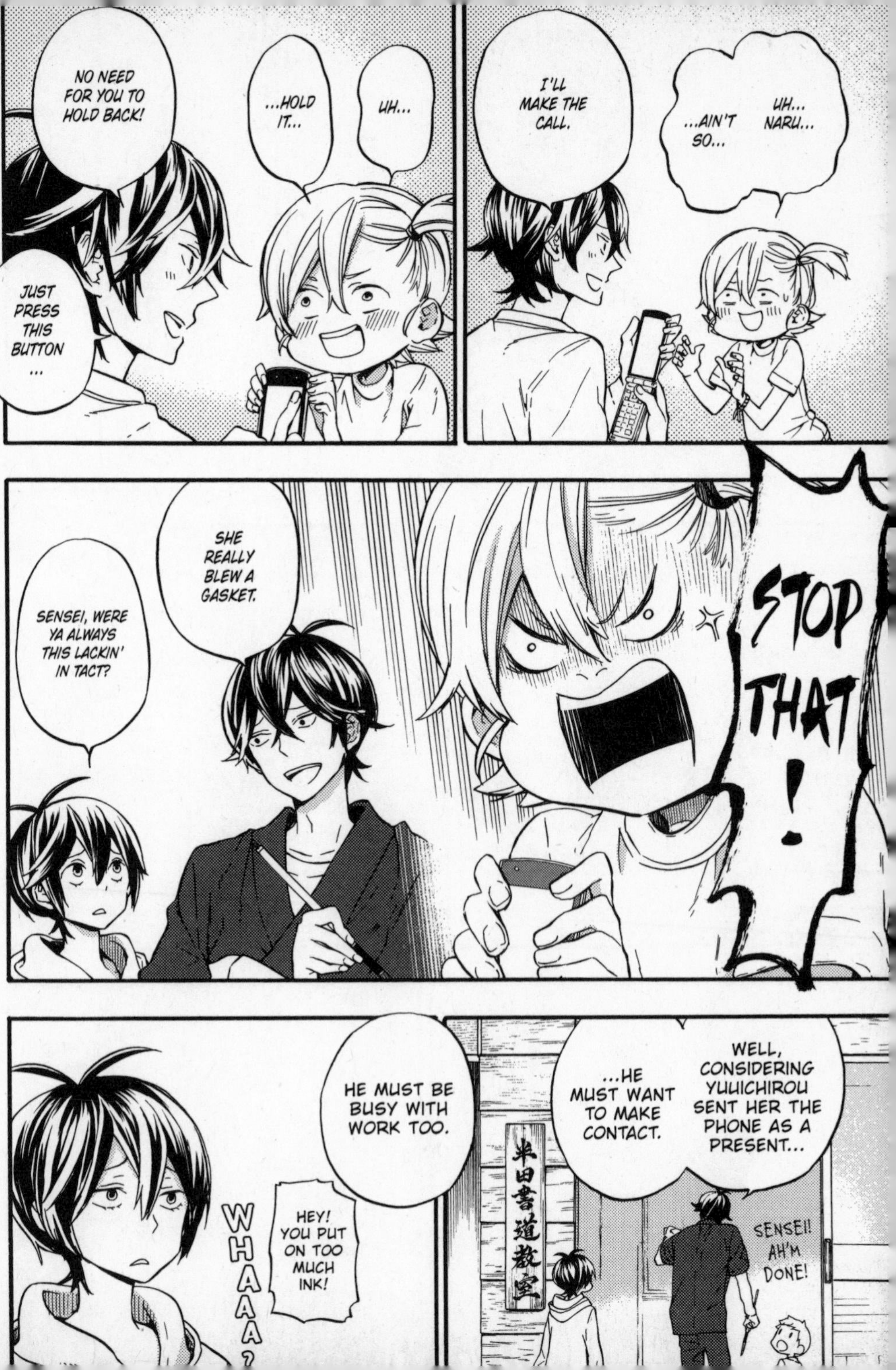
UH... NARU...
...AIN'T SO...
I'LL MAKE THE CALL.
UH...
...HOLD IT...
NO NEED FOR YOU TO HOLD BACK!
JUST PRESS THIS BUTTON...
STOP THAT!
SHE REALLY BLEW A GASKET.
SENSEI, WERE YA ALWAYS THIS LACKIN' IN TACT?
WELL, CONSIDERING YUUICHIROU SENT HER THE PHONE AS A PRESENT...
...HE MUST WANT TO MAKE CONTACT.
SENSEI! AH'M DONE!
半田書道教室
HE MUST BE BUSY WITH WORK TOO.
HEY! YOU PUT ON TOO MUCH INK!
WHAAAA?

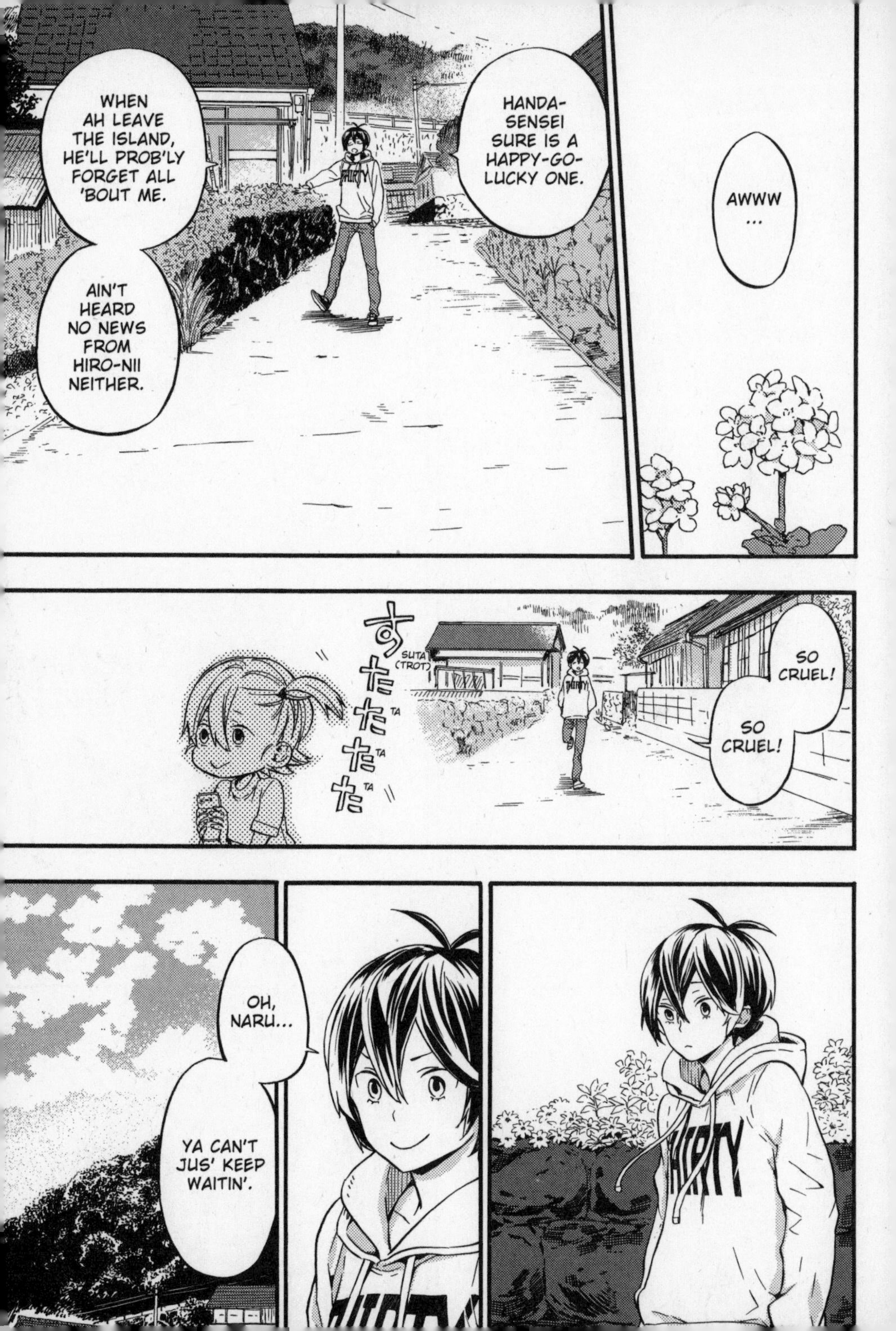
AWWW...
HANDA-SENSEI SURE IS A HAPPY-GO-LUCKY ONE.
WHEN AH LEAVE THE ISLAND, HE'LL PROB'LY FORGET ALL 'BOUT ME.
AIN'T HEARD NO NEWS FROM HIRO-NII NEITHER.
SO CRUEL!
SO CRUEL!
すたたたた
SUTA (TROT)
TA TA TA
OH, NARU...
YA CAN'T JUS' KEEP WAITIN'.

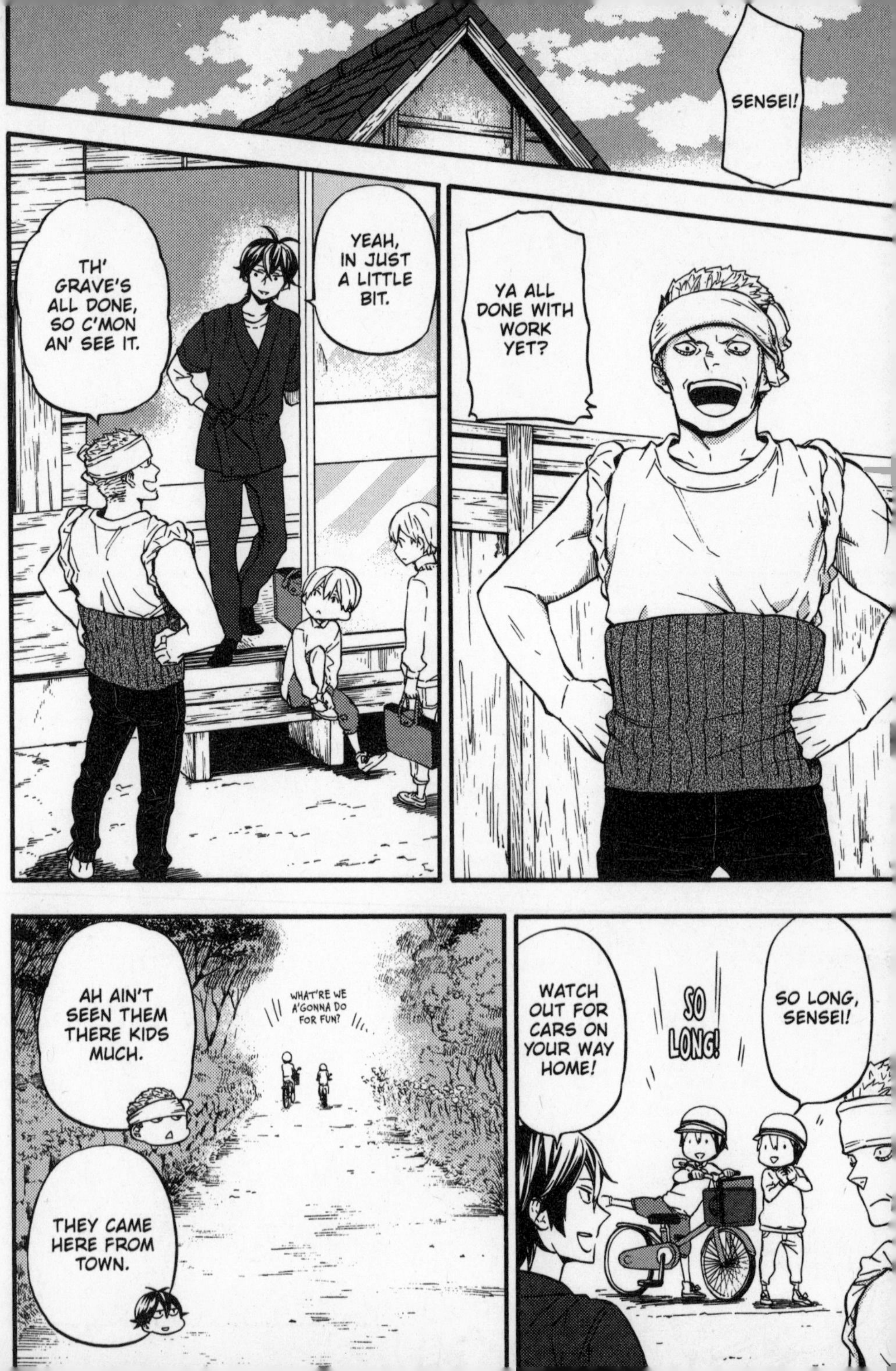
SENSEI!
YA ALL DONE WITH WORK YET?
YEAH, IN JUST A LITTLE BIT.
TH' GRAVE'S ALL DONE, SO C'MON AN' SEE IT.
SO LONG, SENSEI!
SO LONG!
WATCH OUT FOR CARS ON YOUR WAY HOME!
WHAT'RE WE A'GONNA DO FOR FUN?
AH AIN'T SEEN THEM THERE KIDS MUCH.
THEY CAME HERE FROM TOWN.

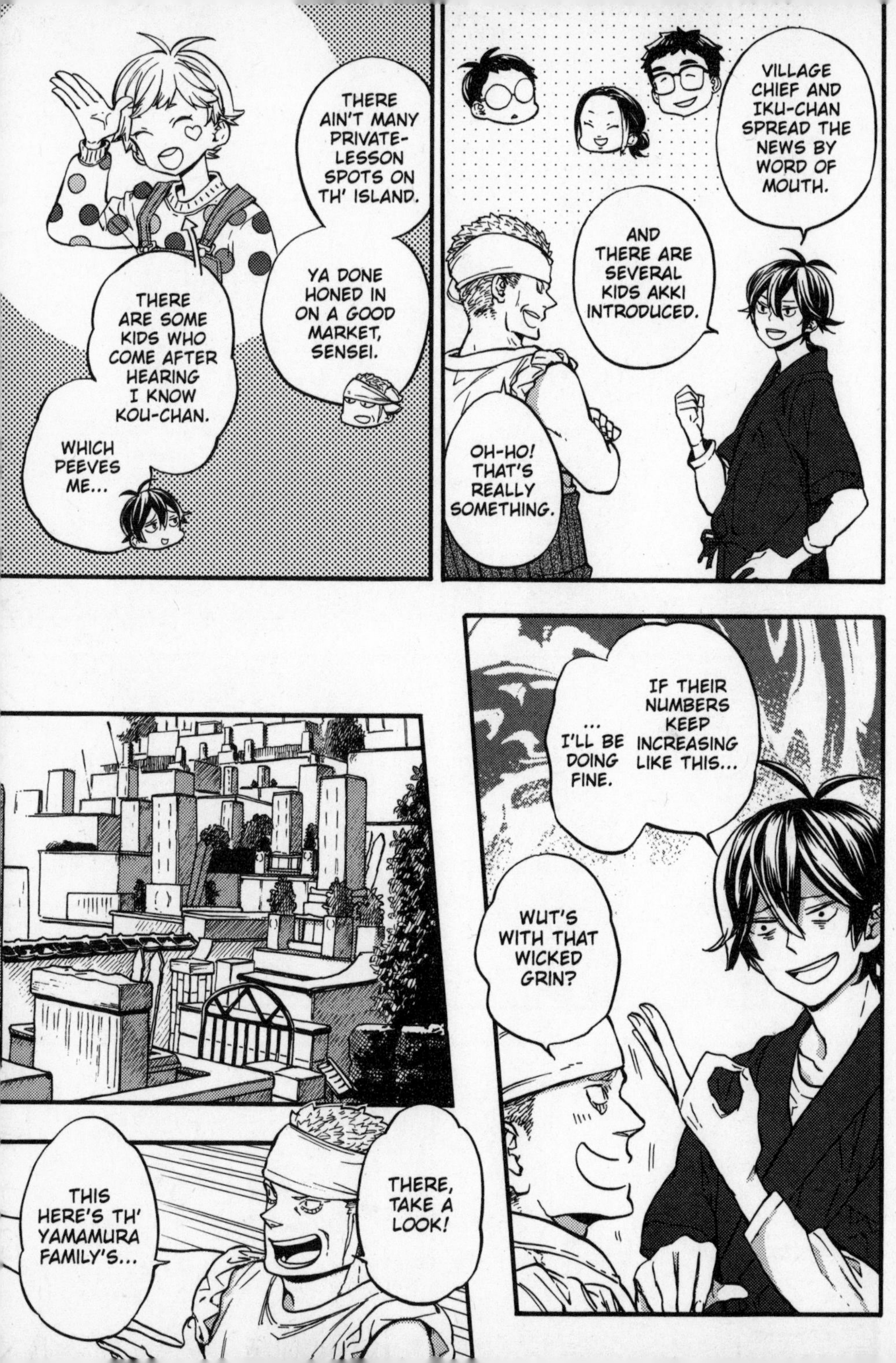
VILLAGE CHIEF AND IKU-CHAN SPREAD THE NEWS BY WORD OF MOUTH.
AND THERE ARE SEVERAL KIDS AKKI INTRODUCED.
OH-HO! THAT'S REALLY SOMETHING.
THERE AIN'T MANY PRIVATE-LESSON SPOTS ON TH' ISLAND.
YA DONE HONED IN ON A GOOD MARKET, SENSEI.
THERE ARE SOME KIDS WHO COME AFTER HEARING I KNOW KOU-CHAN.
WHICH PEEVES ME...
IF THEIR NUMBERS KEEP INCREASING LIKE THIS...
... I'LL BE DOING FINE.
WUT'S WITH THAT WICKED GRIN?
THERE, TAKE A LOOK!
THIS HERE'S TH' YAMAMURA FAMILY'S...

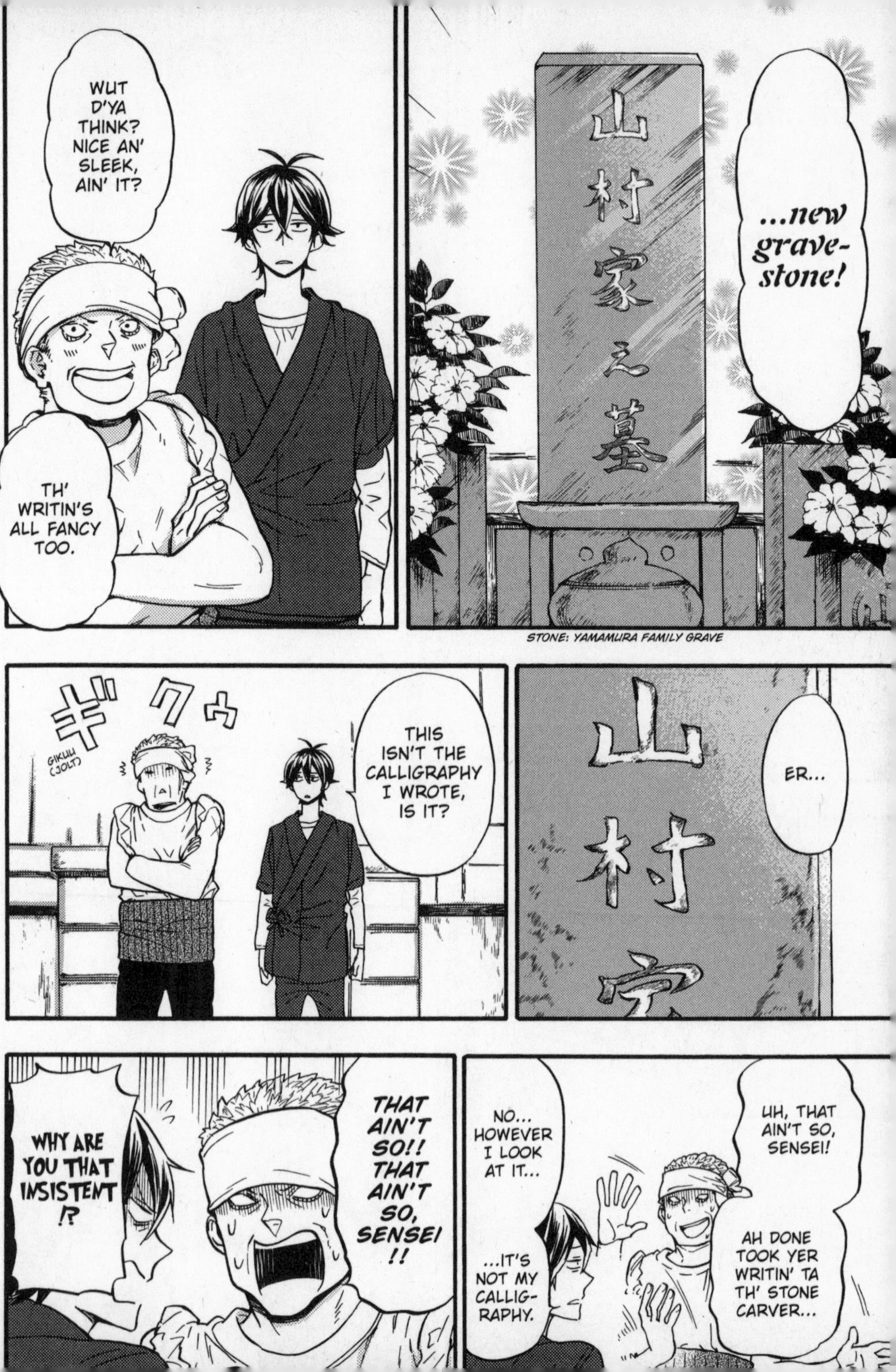
...new grave-stone!
山村家之墓
STONE: YAMAMURA FAMILY GRAVE
WUT D'YA THINK? NICE AN' SLEEK, AIN' IT?
TH' WRITIN'S ALL FANCY TOO.
ER...
THIS ISN'T THE CALLIGRAPHY I WROTE, IS IT?
ギクゥ
GIKUU (JOLT)
UH, THAT AIN'T SO, SENSEI!
AH DONE TOOK YER WRITIN' TA TH' STONE CARVER...
NO... HOWEVER I LOOK AT IT...
...IT'S NOT MY CALLIGRAPHY.
THAT AIN'T SO!! THAT AIN'T SO, SENSEI!!
WHY ARE YOU THAT INSISTENT!?

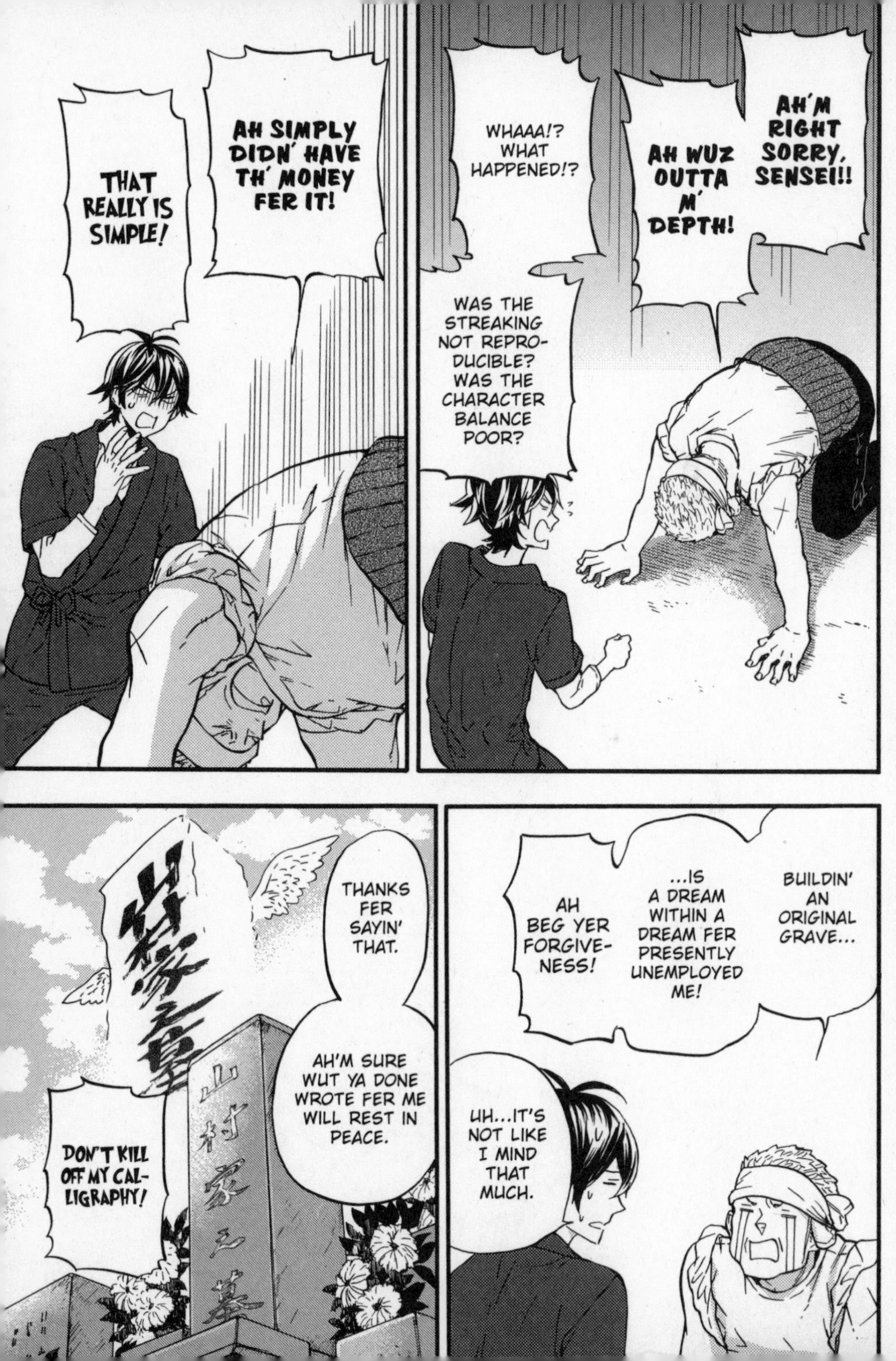
AH'M RIGHT SORRY, SENSEI!!
AH WUZ OUTTA M' DEPTH!
WHAAA!? WHAT HAPPENED!?
WAS THE STREAKING NOT REPRO-DUCIBLE? WAS THE CHARACTER BALANCE POOR?
AH SIMPLY DIDN' HAVE TH' MONEY FER IT!
THAT REALLY IS SIMPLE!
BUILDIN' AN ORIGINAL GRAVE...
...IS A DREAM WITHIN A DREAM FER PRESENTLY UNEMPLOYED ME!
AH BEG YER FORGIVE-NESS!
UH...IT'S NOT LIKE I MIND THAT MUCH.
THANKS FER SAYIN' THAT.
AH'M SURE WUT YA DONE WROTE FER ME WILL REST IN PEACE.
DON'T KILL OFF MY CAL-LIGRAPHY!
山村家之墓

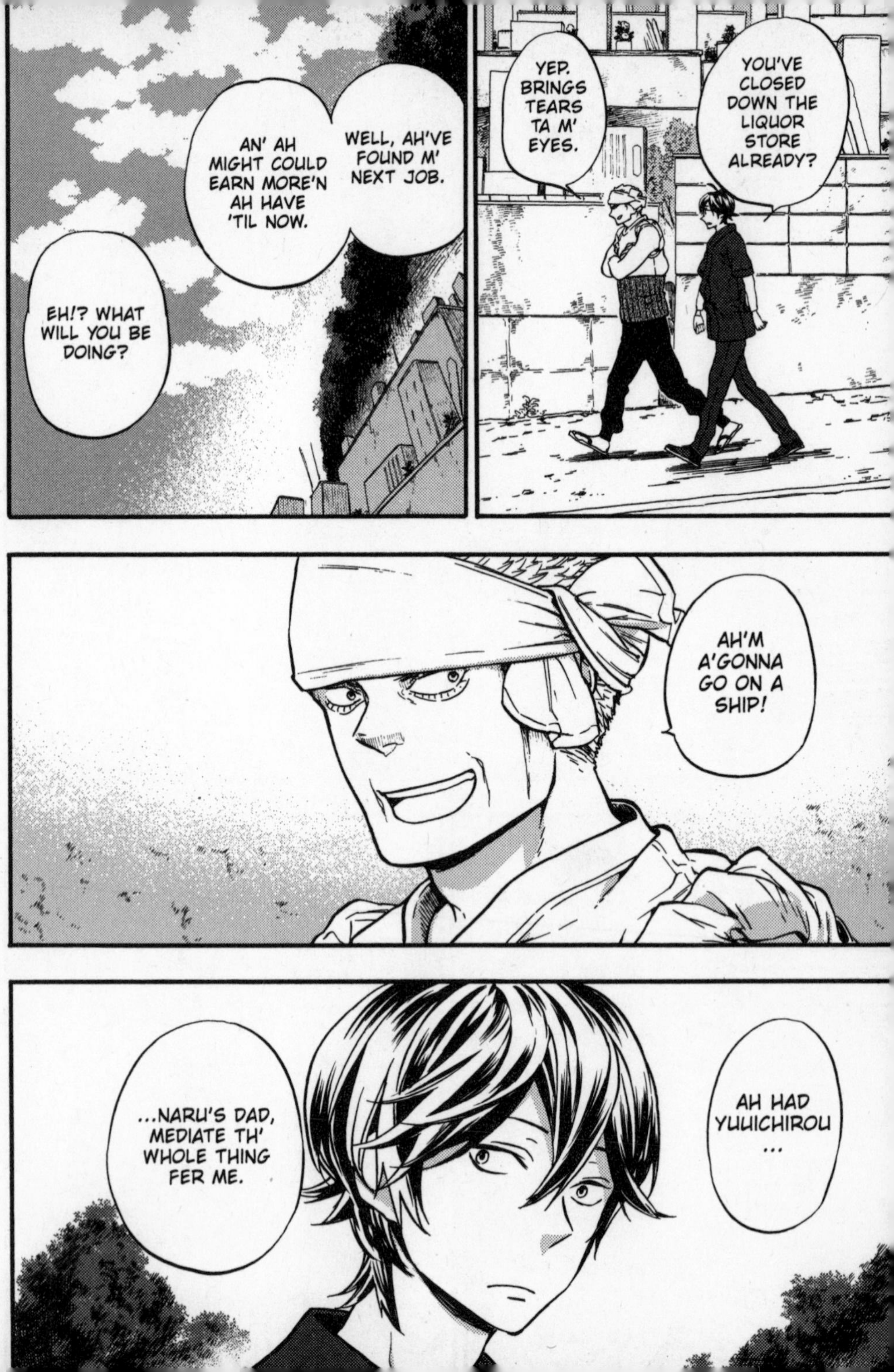
YOU'VE CLOSED DOWN THE LIQUOR STORE ALREADY?
YEP. BRINGS TEARS TA M' EYES.
WELL, AH'VE FOUND M' NEXT JOB.
AN' AH MIGHT COULD EARN MORE'N AH HAVE 'TIL NOW.
EH!? WHAT WILL YOU BE DOING?
AH'M A'GONNA GO ON A SHIP!
AH HAD YUUICHIROU ...
...NARU'S DAD, MEDIATE TH' WHOLE THING FER ME.

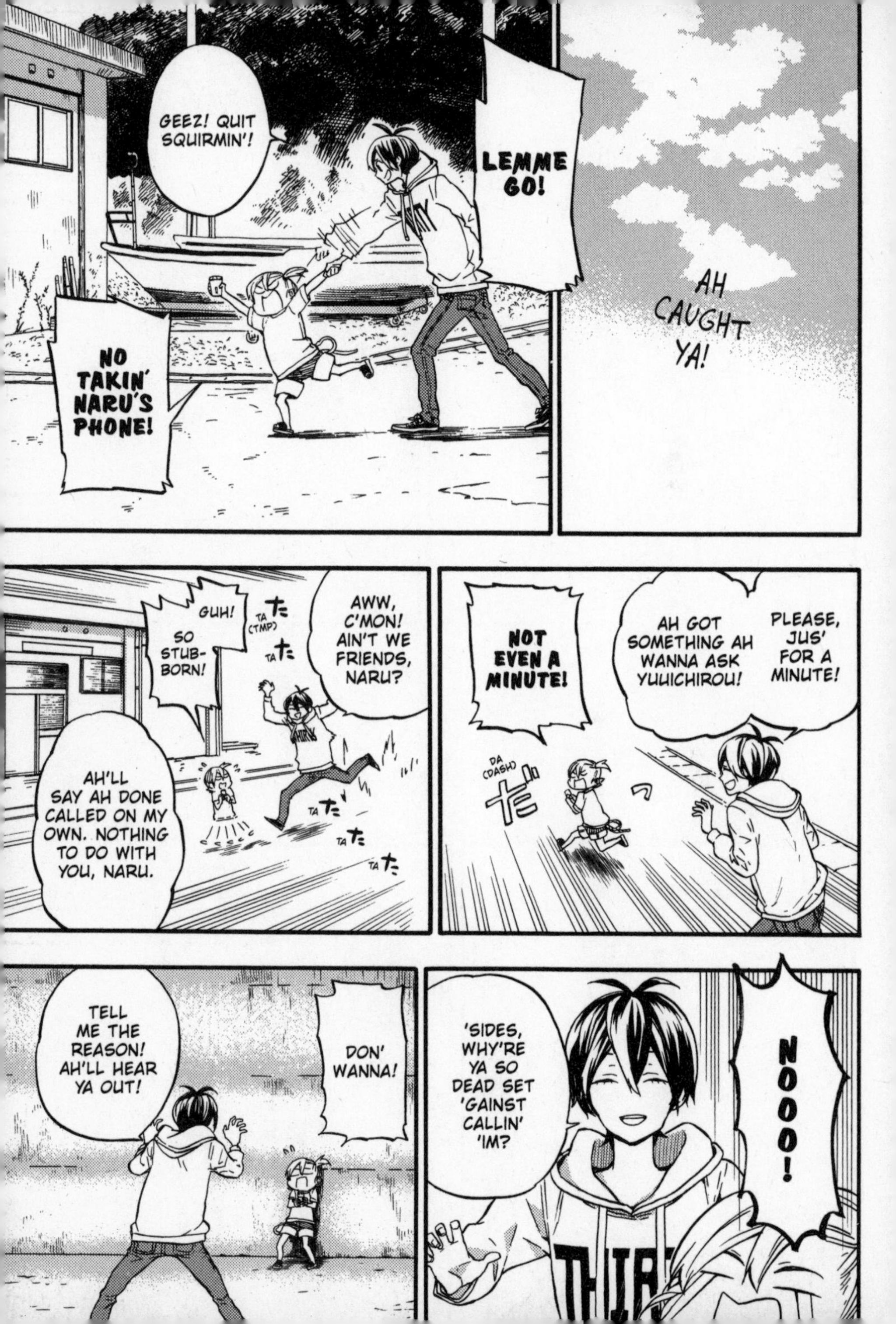
AH CAUGHT YA!
LEMME GO!
GEEZ! QUIT SQUIRMIN'!
NO TAKIN' NARU'S PHONE!
PLEASE, JUS' FOR A MINUTE!
AH GOT SOMETHING AH WANNA ASK YUUICHIROU!
NOT EVEN A MINUTE!
DA (DASH) だ
AWW, C'MON! AIN'T WE FRIENDS, NARU?
TA (TMP) た
TA た
GUH! SO STUBBORN!
AH'LL SAY AH DONE CALLED ON MY OWN. NOTHING TO DO WITH YOU, NARU.
TA た
TA た
TA た
NOOO!
'SIDES, WHY'RE YA SO DEAD SET 'GAINST CALLIN' 'IM?
DON' WANNA!
TELL ME THE REASON! AH'LL HEAR YA OUT!

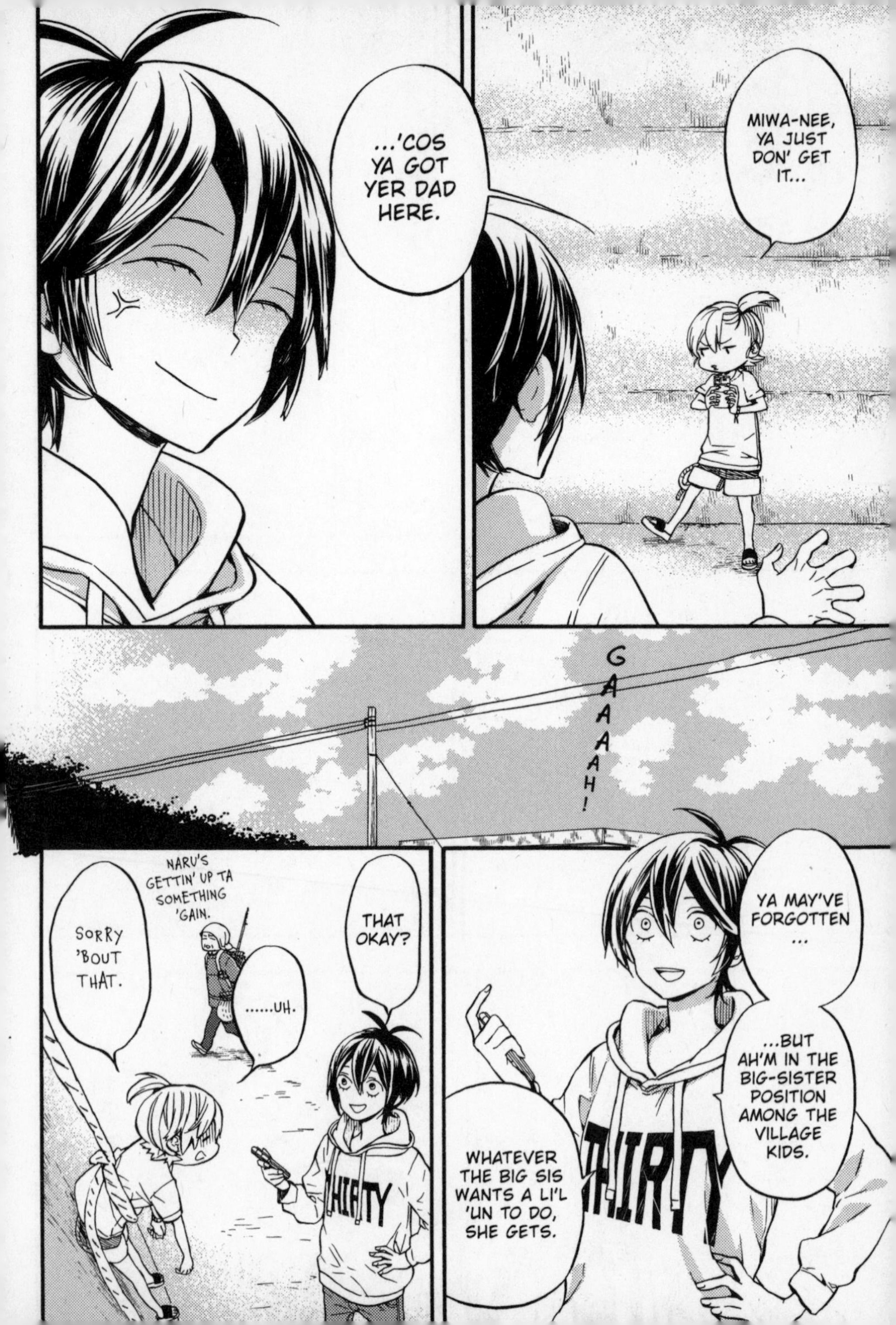
MIWA-NEE, YA JUST DON' GET IT...
...'COS YA GOT YER DAD HERE.
GAAAAAH!
YA MAY'VE FORGOTTEN ...
...BUT AH'M IN THE BIG-SISTER POSITION AMONG THE VILLAGE KIDS.
WHATEVER THE BIG SIS WANTS A LI'L 'UN TO DO, SHE GETS.
THAT OKAY?
......UH.
NARU'S GETTIN' UP TA SOMETHING 'GAIN.
SORRY 'BOUT THAT.

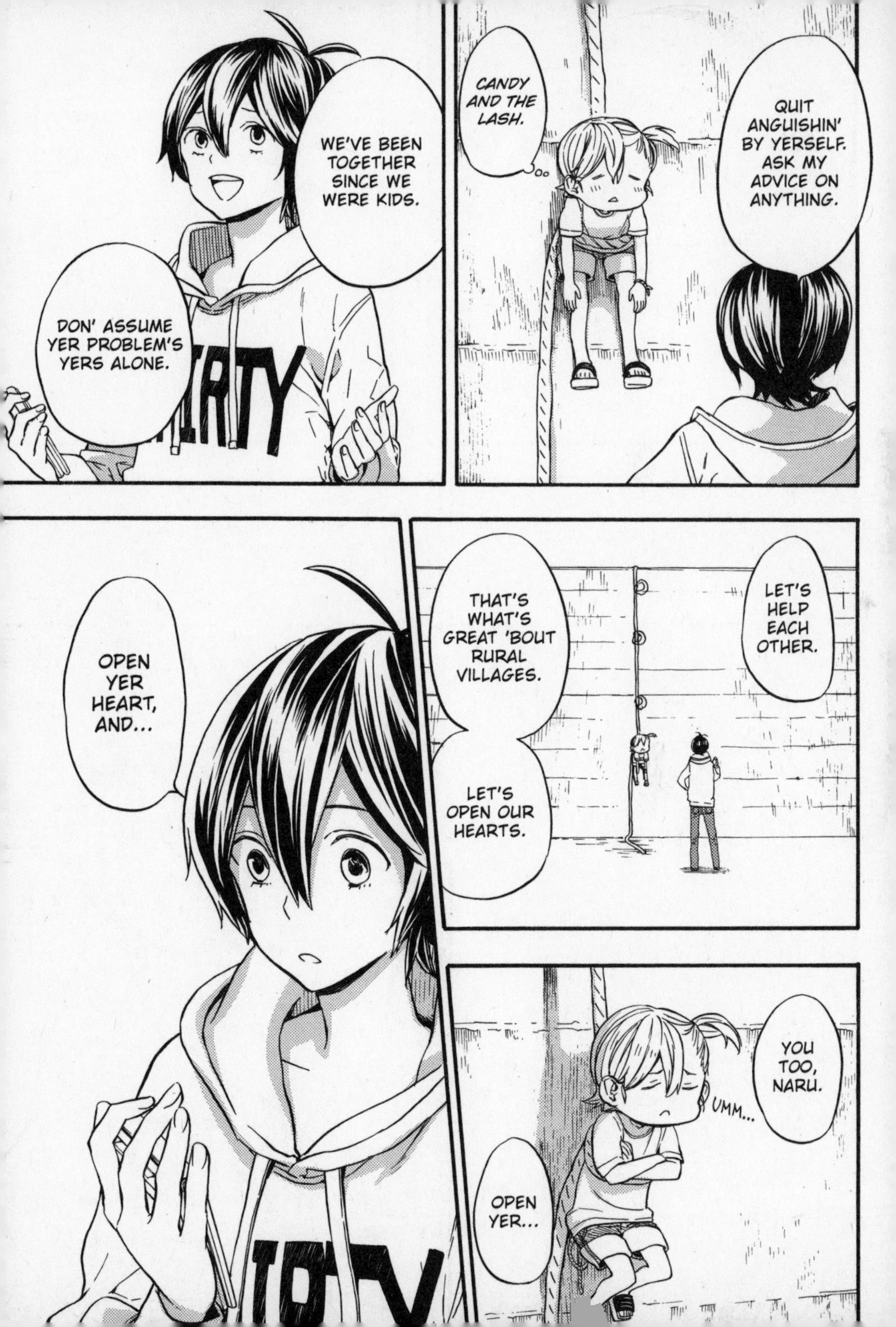
QUIT ANGUISHIN' BY YERSELF. ASK MY ADVICE ON ANYTHING.
CANDY AND THE LASH.
WE'VE BEEN TOGETHER SINCE WE WERE KIDS.
DON' ASSUME YER PROBLEM'S YERS ALONE.
LET'S HELP EACH OTHER.
THAT'S WHAT'S GREAT 'BOUT RURAL VILLAGES.
LET'S OPEN OUR HEARTS.
YOU TOO, NARU.
UMM...
OPEN YER...
OPEN YER HEART, AND...

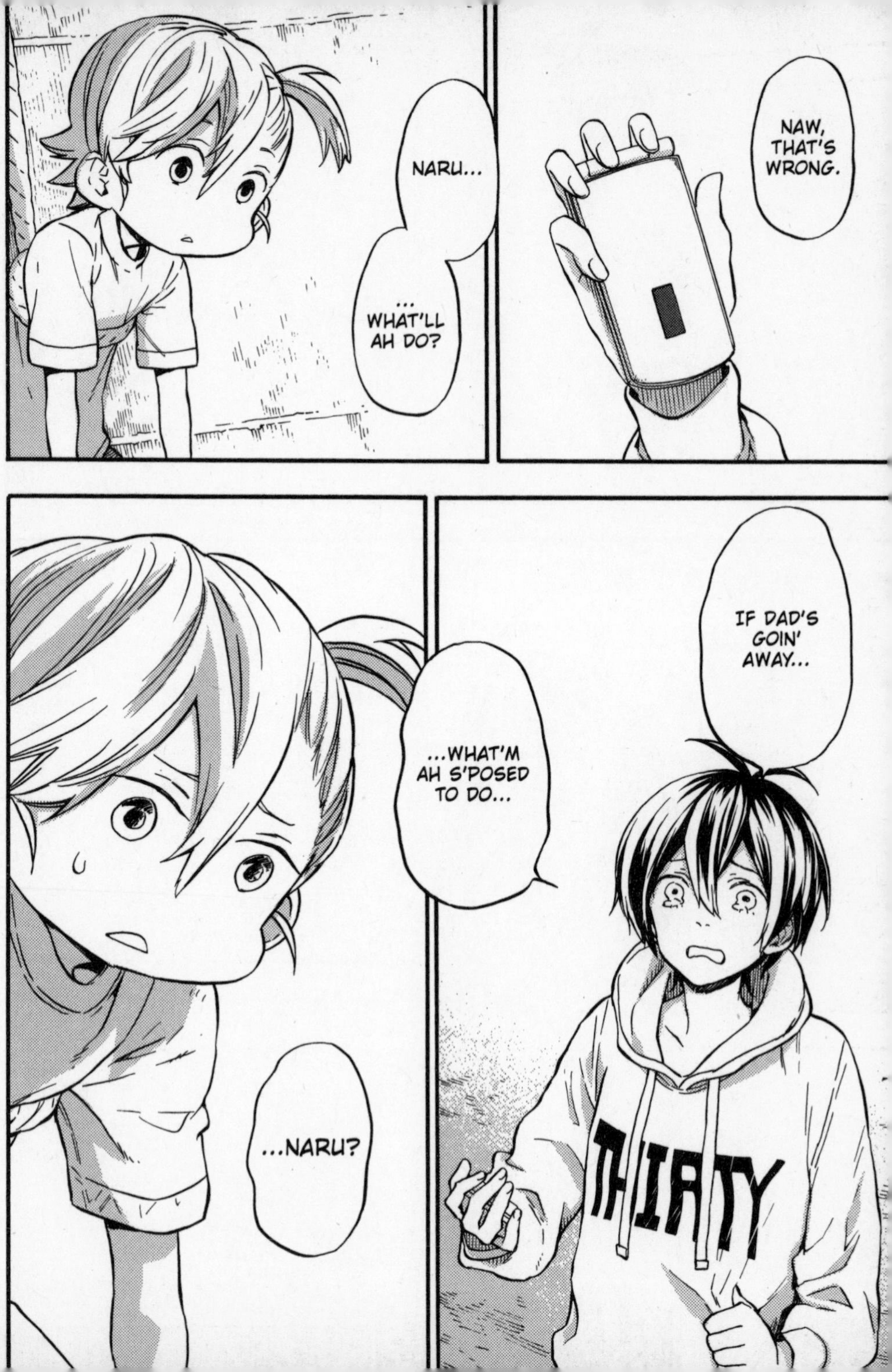
NAW, THAT'S WRONG.
NARU...
...WHAT'LL AH DO?
IF DAD'S GOIN' AWAY...
...WHAT'M AH S'POSED TO DO...
THIRTY
...NARU?

SO THAT'S IT...
MIWA-NEE'S IWAO-BAN IS GOIN' ON A SHIP.
YEP. THE SAME AS YER YUUICHIROU, NARU.
HE'LL BE LEAVIN' REAL SOON.
NARU IS...THE SENPAI HERE, HUH...?
KIRI (SERIOUS)
YEP... SOMETHING LIKE THAT.
MORE'N WANTIN' TO CALL 'COS AH WAS WORRIED 'BOUT YOU, NARU...
...AH WAS WANTIN' TO ASK 'BOUT THE SORTA PLACE DAD WOULD BE WORKIN'.
WHAT MUST IT BE LIKE, LIVIN' OFF THE ISLAND?
FOR HIRO-NII TOO.
GUESS IT MAKES ME A BIT LONELY...

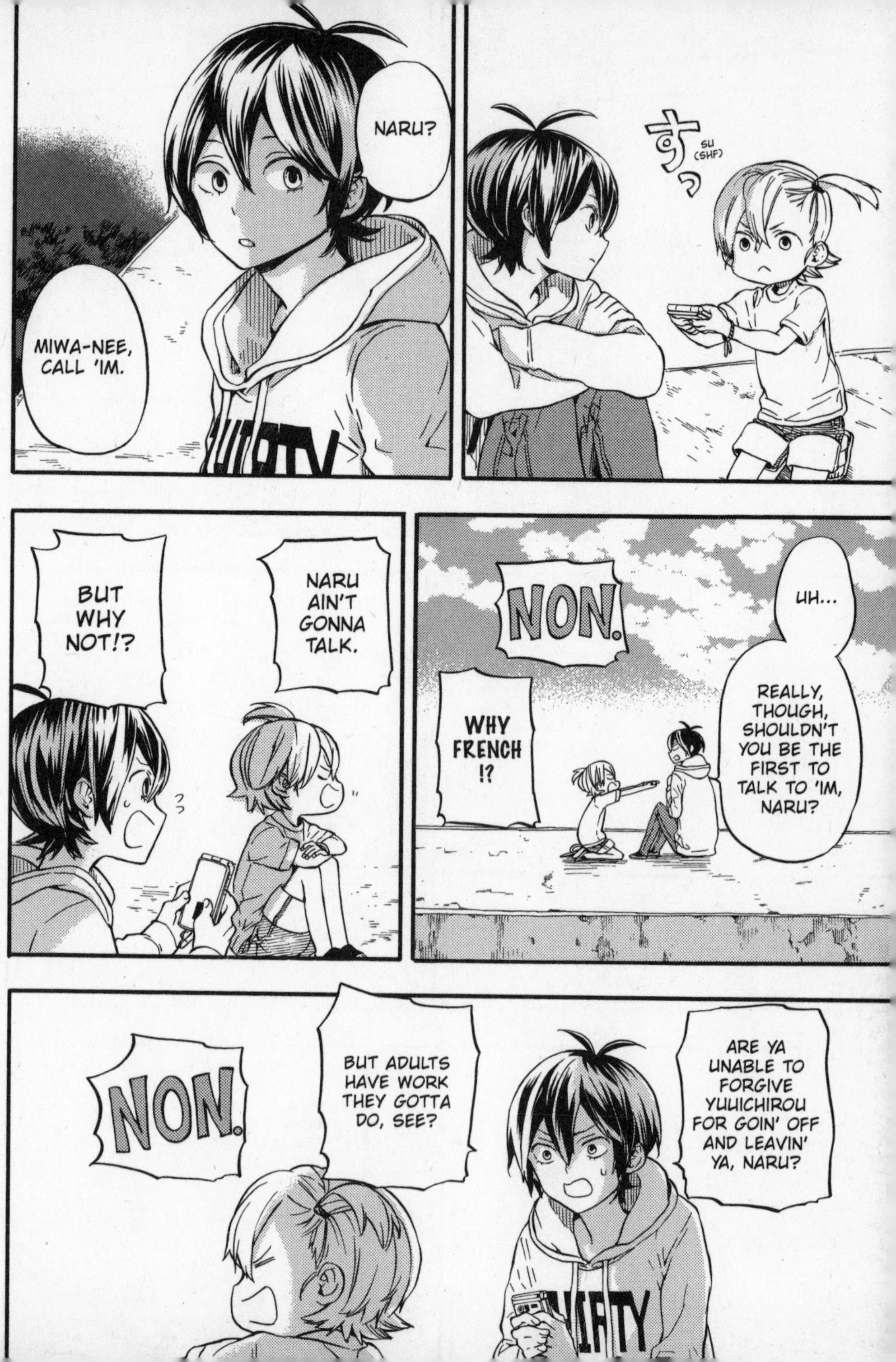

すっ
SU (SHF)
NARU?
MIWA-NEE, CALL 'IM.
UH...
REALLY, THOUGH, SHOULDN'T YOU BE THE FIRST TO TALK TO 'IM, NARU?
NON.
WHY FRENCH!?
NARU AIN'T GONNA TALK.
BUT WHY NOT!?
ARE YA UNABLE TO FORGIVE YUUICHIROU FOR GOIN' OFF AND LEAVIN' YA, NARU?
BUT ADULTS HAVE WORK THEY GOTTA DO, SEE?
NON.

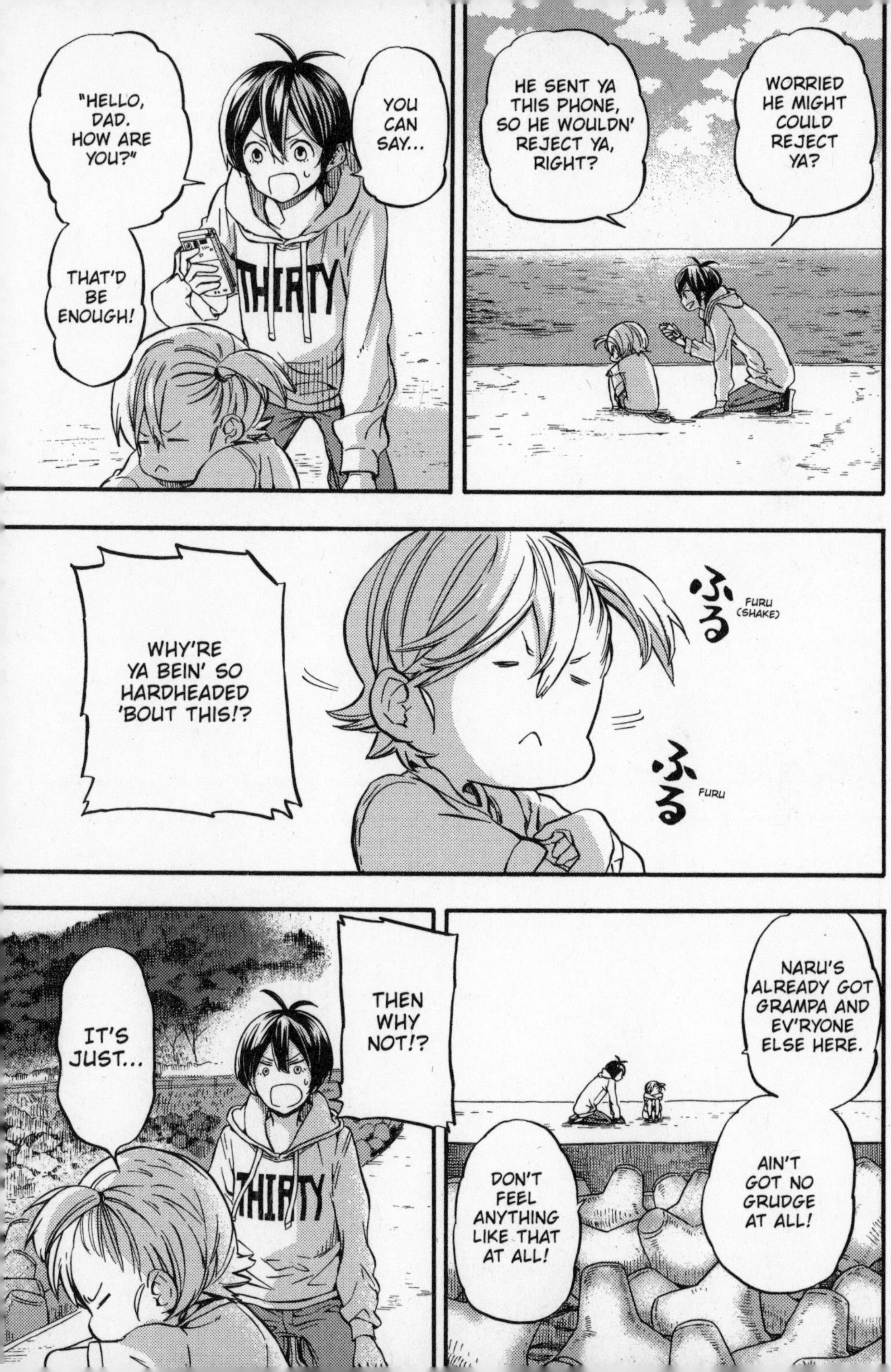
WORRIED HE MIGHT COULD REJECT YA?
HE SENT YA THIS PHONE, SO HE WOULDN' REJECT YA, RIGHT?
YOU CAN SAY...
"HELLO, DAD. HOW ARE YOU?"
THAT'D BE ENOUGH!
THIRTY
ふる
FURU (SHAKE)
ふる
FURU
WHY'RE YA BEIN' SO HARDHEADED 'BOUT THIS!?
NARU'S ALREADY GOT GRAMPA AND EV'RYONE ELSE HERE.
AIN'T GOT NO GRUDGE AT ALL!
DON'T FEEL ANYTHING LIKE THAT AT ALL!
THEN WHY NOT!?
IT'S JUST...
THIRTY

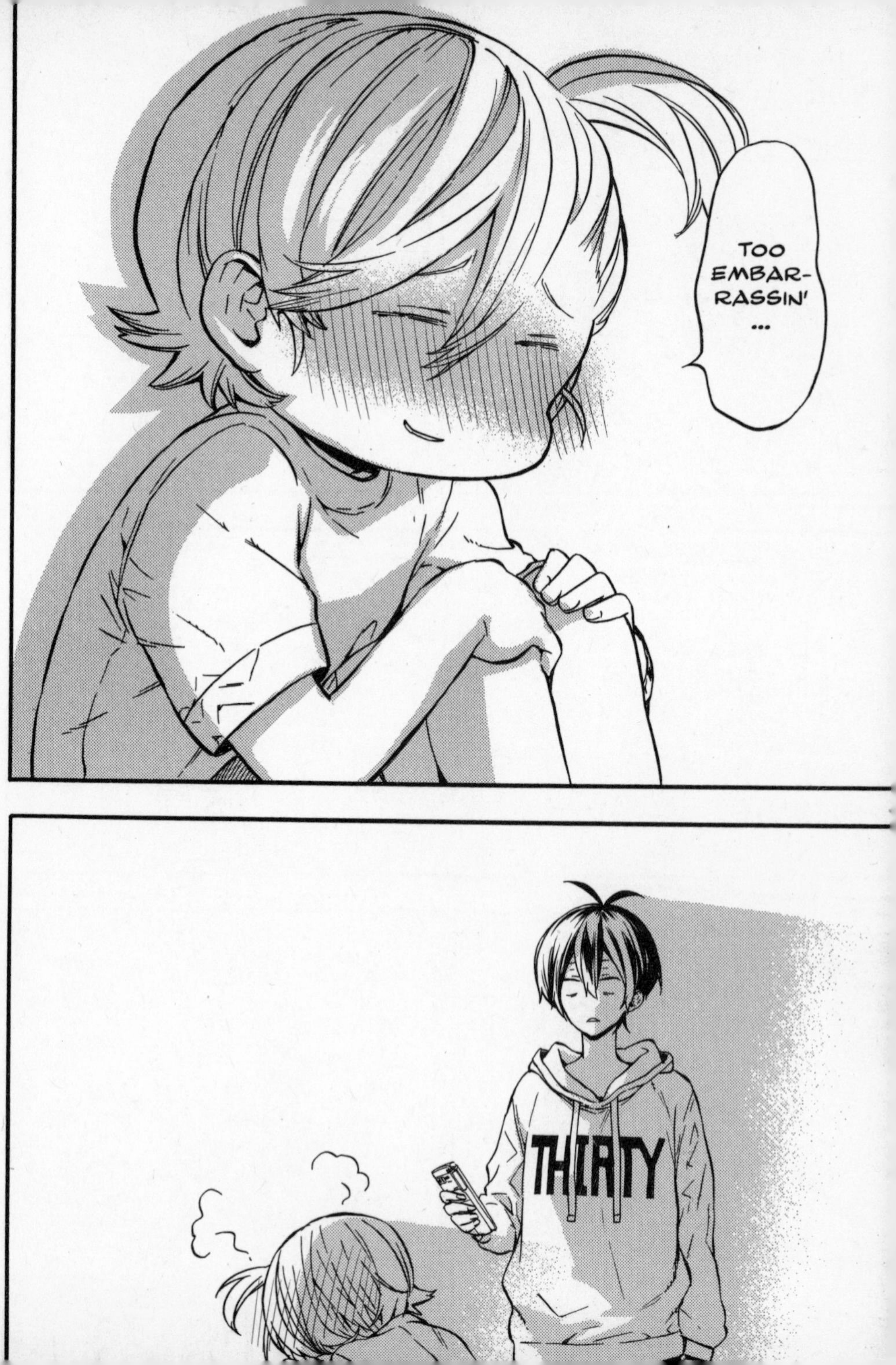
TOO EMBAR-RASSIN'...
THIRTY

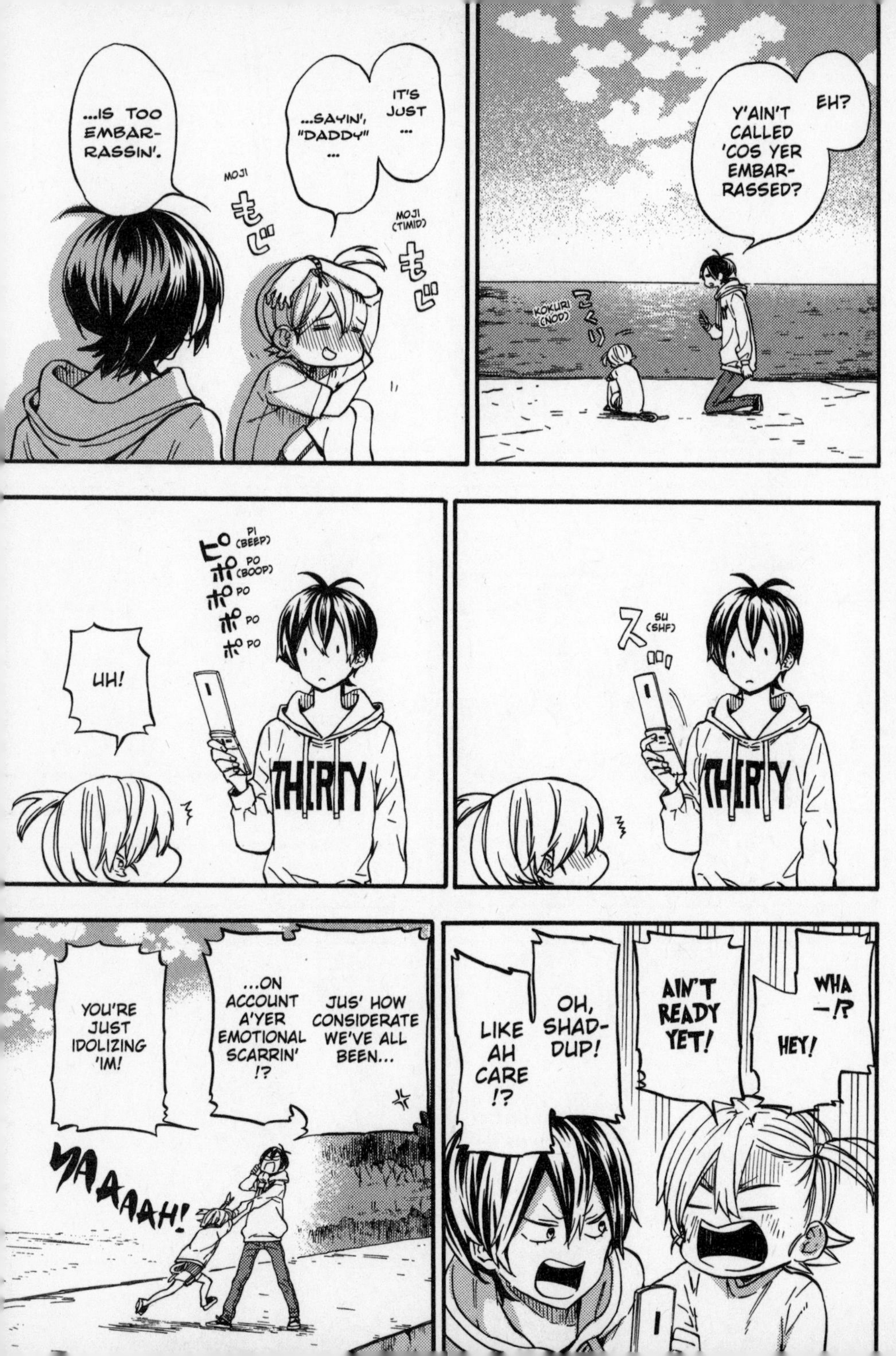
EH?
Y'AIN'T CALLED 'COS YER EMBAR-RASSED?
KOKURI (NOD)
こくり
IT'S JUST ...
...SAYIN', "DADDY" ...
...IS TOO EMBAR-RASSIN'.
MOJI (TIMID)
もじ
MOJI
もじ
SU (SHF)
ス
PI (BEEP)
ピ
PO (BOOP)
ポ
PO
ポ
PO
ポ
PO
ポ
UH!
WHA—!?
HEY!
AIN'T READY YET!
OH, SHAD-DUP!
LIKE AH CARE!?
JUS' HOW CONSIDERATE WE'VE ALL BEEN...
...ON ACCOUNT A'YER EMOTIONAL SCARRIN'!?
YOU'RE JUST IDOLIZING 'IM!
YAAAAAH!

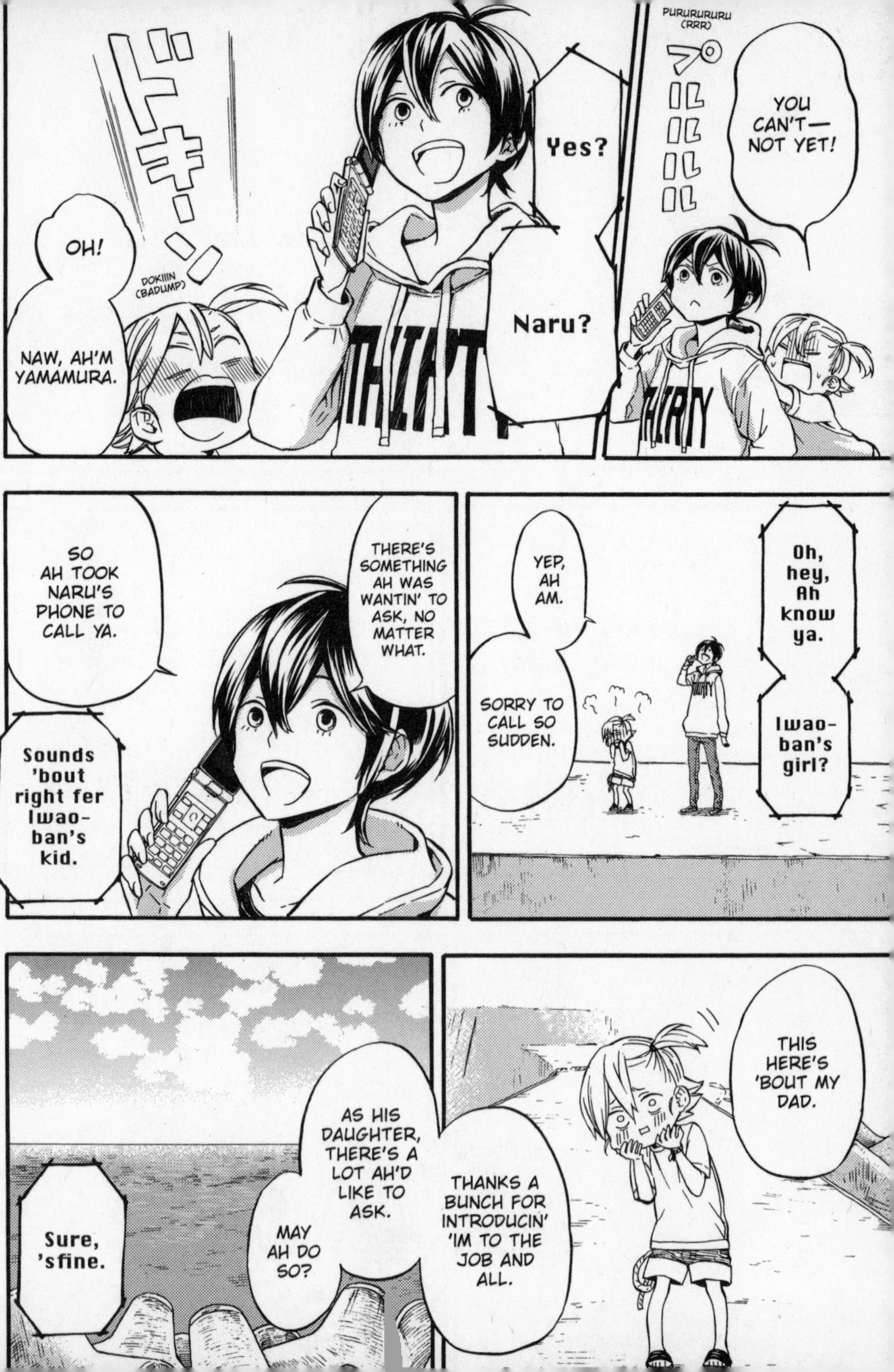
プルルルル
PURURURURU (RRR)
YOU CAN'T— NOT YET!
Yes?
Naru?
ドキーン
DOKIIIN (BADUMP)
OH!
NAW, AH'M YAMAMURA.
Oh, hey, Ah know ya.
Iwao-ban's girl?
YEP, AH AM.
SORRY TO CALL SO SUDDEN.
THERE'S SOMETHING AH WAS WANTIN' TO ASK, NO MATTER WHAT.
SO AH TOOK NARU'S PHONE TO CALL YA.
Sounds 'bout right fer Iwao-ban's kid.
THIS HERE'S 'BOUT MY DAD.
THANKS A BUNCH FOR INTRODUCIN' 'IM TO THE JOB AND ALL.
AS HIS DAUGHTER, THERE'S A LOT AH'D LIKE TO ASK.
MAY AH DO SO?
Sure, 'sfine.

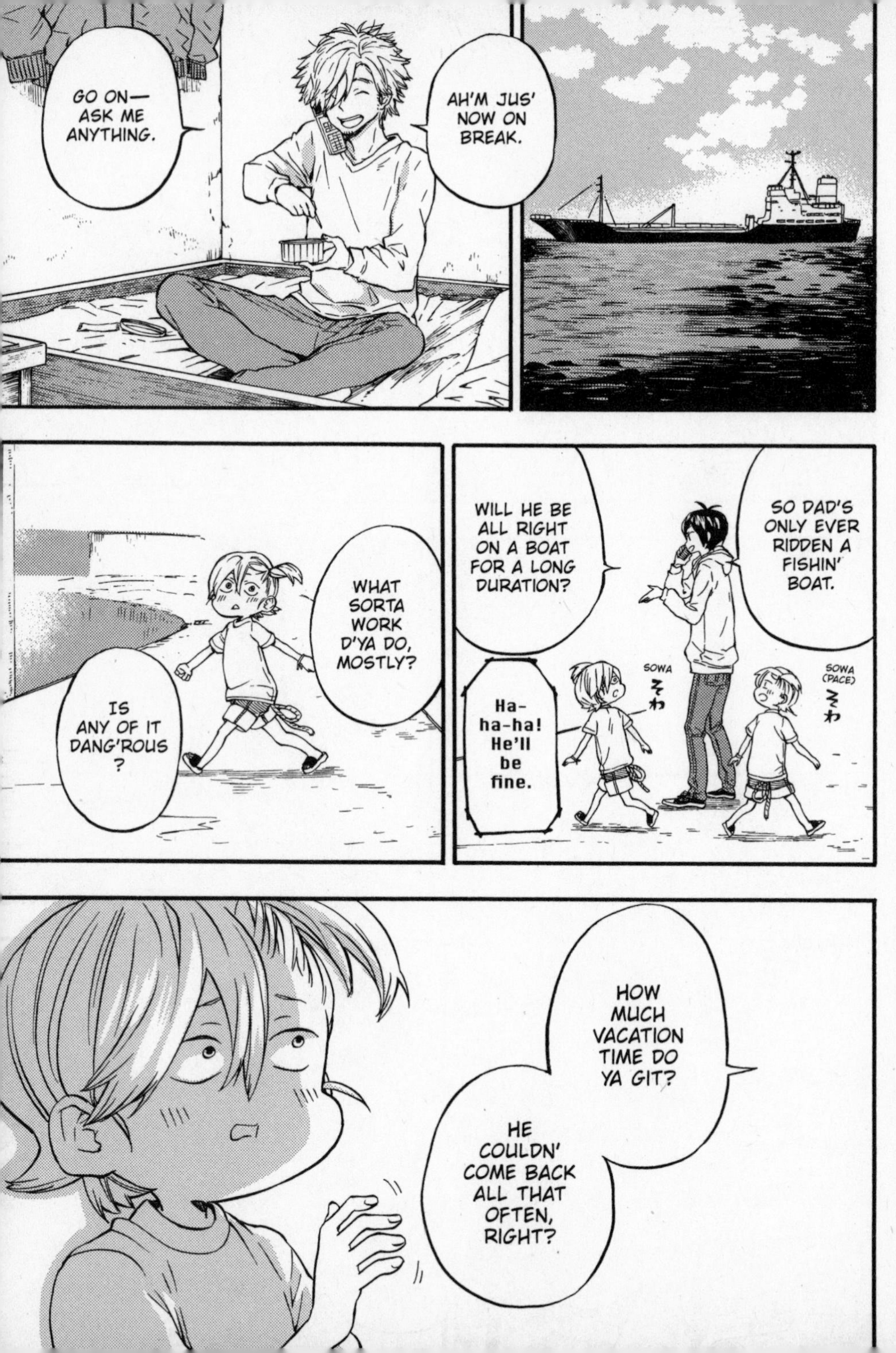
AH'M JUS' NOW ON BREAK.
GO ON— ASK ME ANYTHING.
SO DAD'S ONLY EVER RIDDEN A FISHIN' BOAT.
WILL HE BE ALL RIGHT ON A BOAT FOR A LONG DURATION?
SOWA (PACE)
そわ
SOWA
そわ
Ha-ha-ha! He'll be fine.
WHAT SORTA WORK D'YA DO, MOSTLY?
IS ANY OF IT DANG'ROUS?
HOW MUCH VACATION TIME DO YA GIT?
HE COULDN' COME BACK ALL THAT OFTEN, RIGHT?

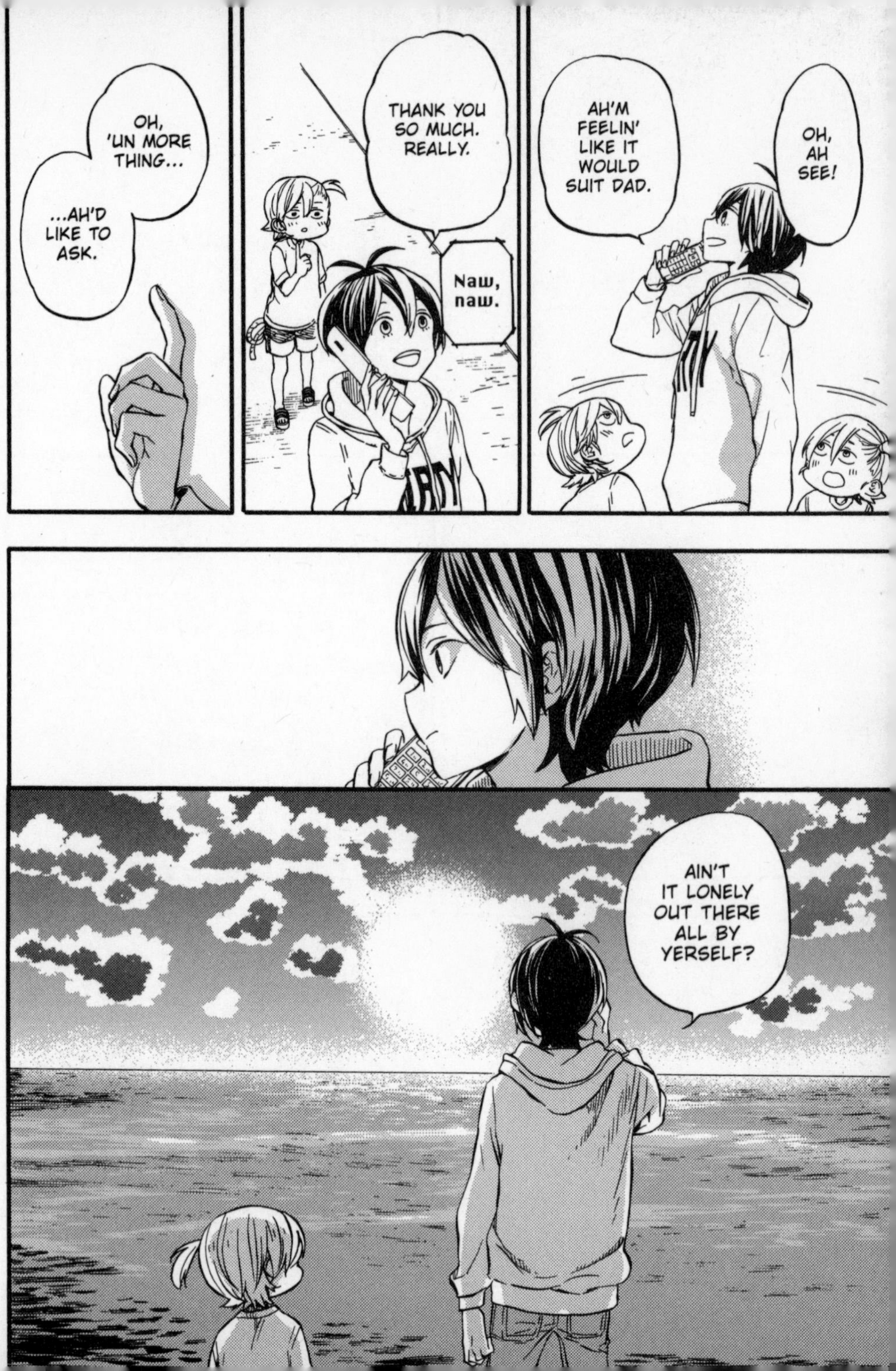
OH, AH SEE!
AH'M FEELIN' LIKE IT WOULD SUIT DAD.
THANK YOU SO MUCH. REALLY.
Naw, naw.
OH, 'UN MORE THING...
...AH'D LIKE TO ASK.
AIN'T IT LONELY OUT THERE ALL BY YERSELF?

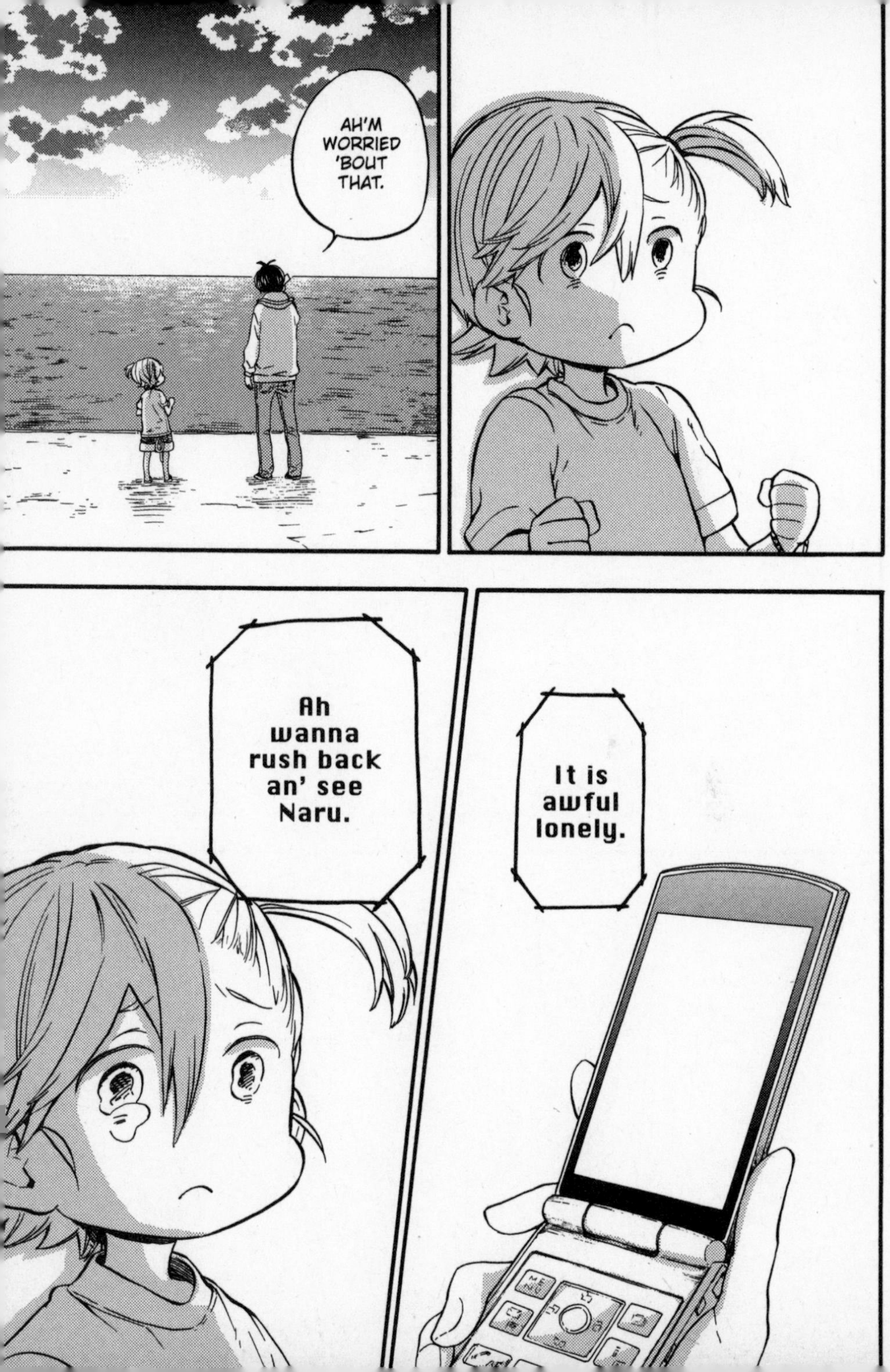
AH'M WORRIED 'BOUT THAT.
It is awful lonely.
Ah wanna rush back an' see Naru.

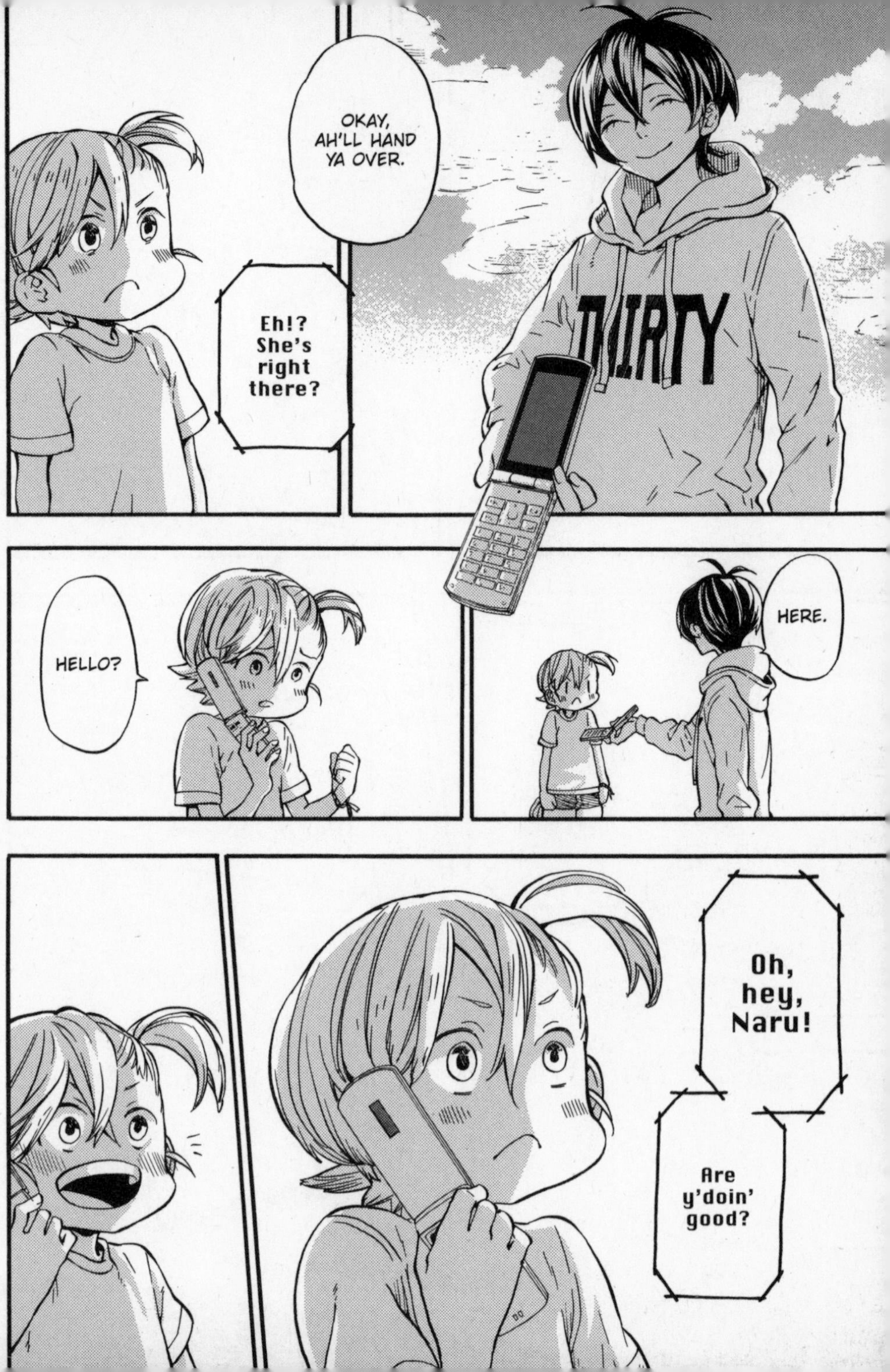
OKAY, AH'LL HAND YA OVER.
Eh!? She's right there?
HERE.
HELLO?
Oh, hey, Naru!
Are y'doin' good?

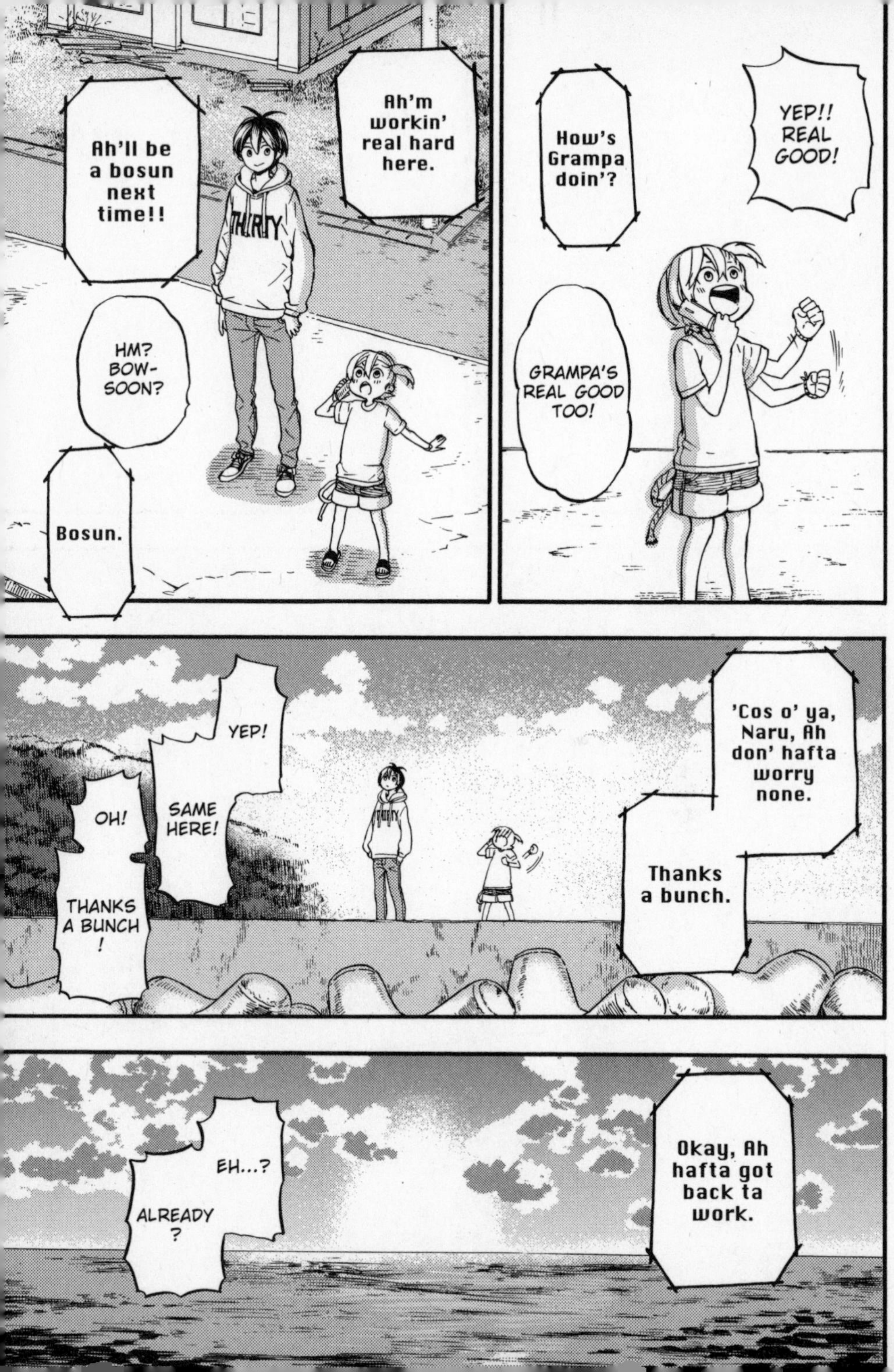
YEP!! REAL GOOD!
How's Grampa doin'?
GRAMPA'S REAL GOOD TOO!
Ah'm workin' real hard here.
Ah'll be a bosun next time!!
HM? BOW-SOON?
Bosun.
'Cos o' ya, Naru, Ah don' hafta worry none.
Thanks a bunch.
YEP!
SAME HERE!
OH!
THANKS A BUNCH!
Okay, Ah hafta got back ta work.
EH...?
ALREADY?

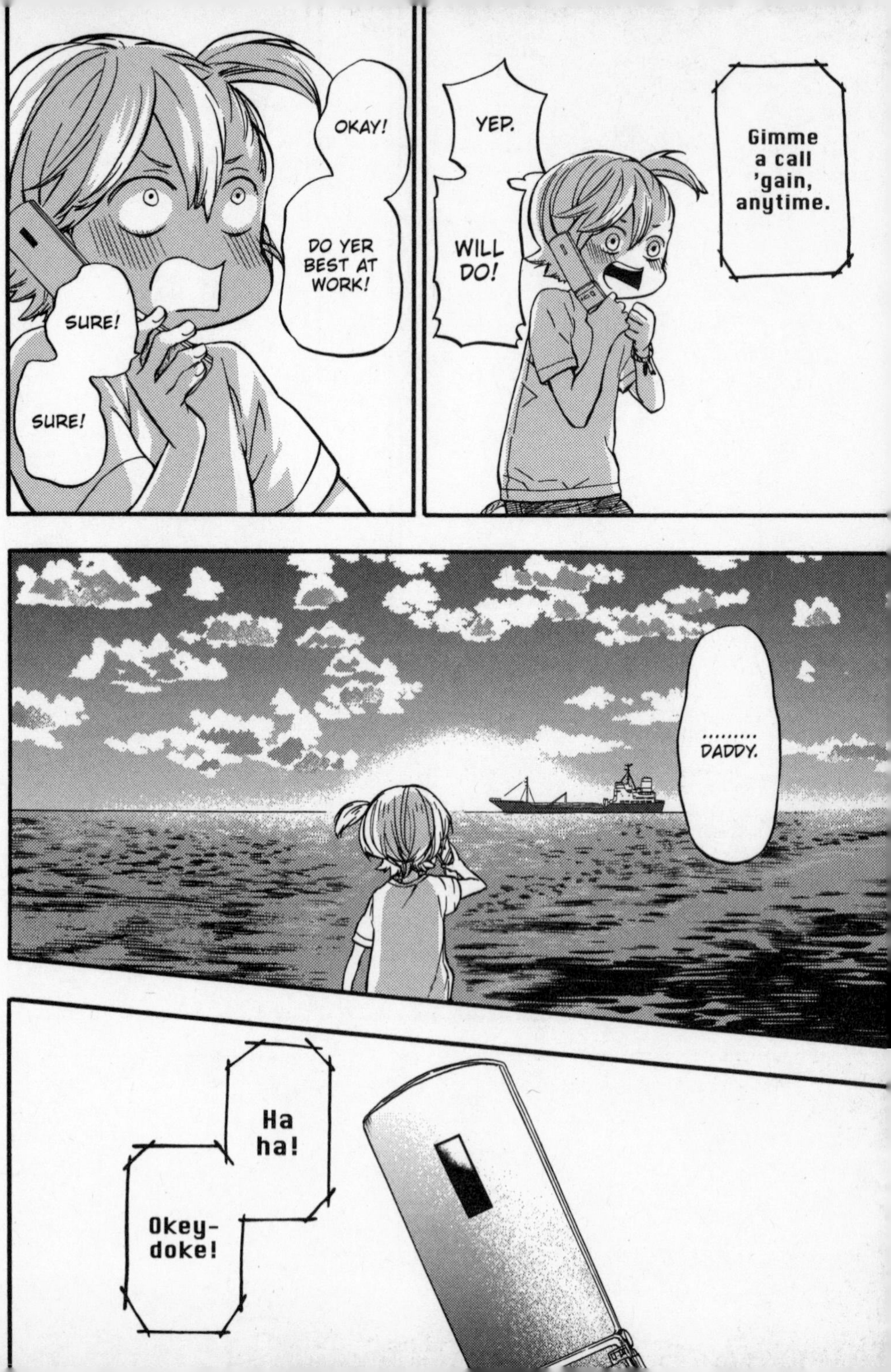
Gimme a call 'gain, anytime.
YEP.
WILL DO!
OKAY!
DO YER BEST AT WORK!
SURE!
SURE!
.... DADDY.
Ha ha!
Okey-doke!

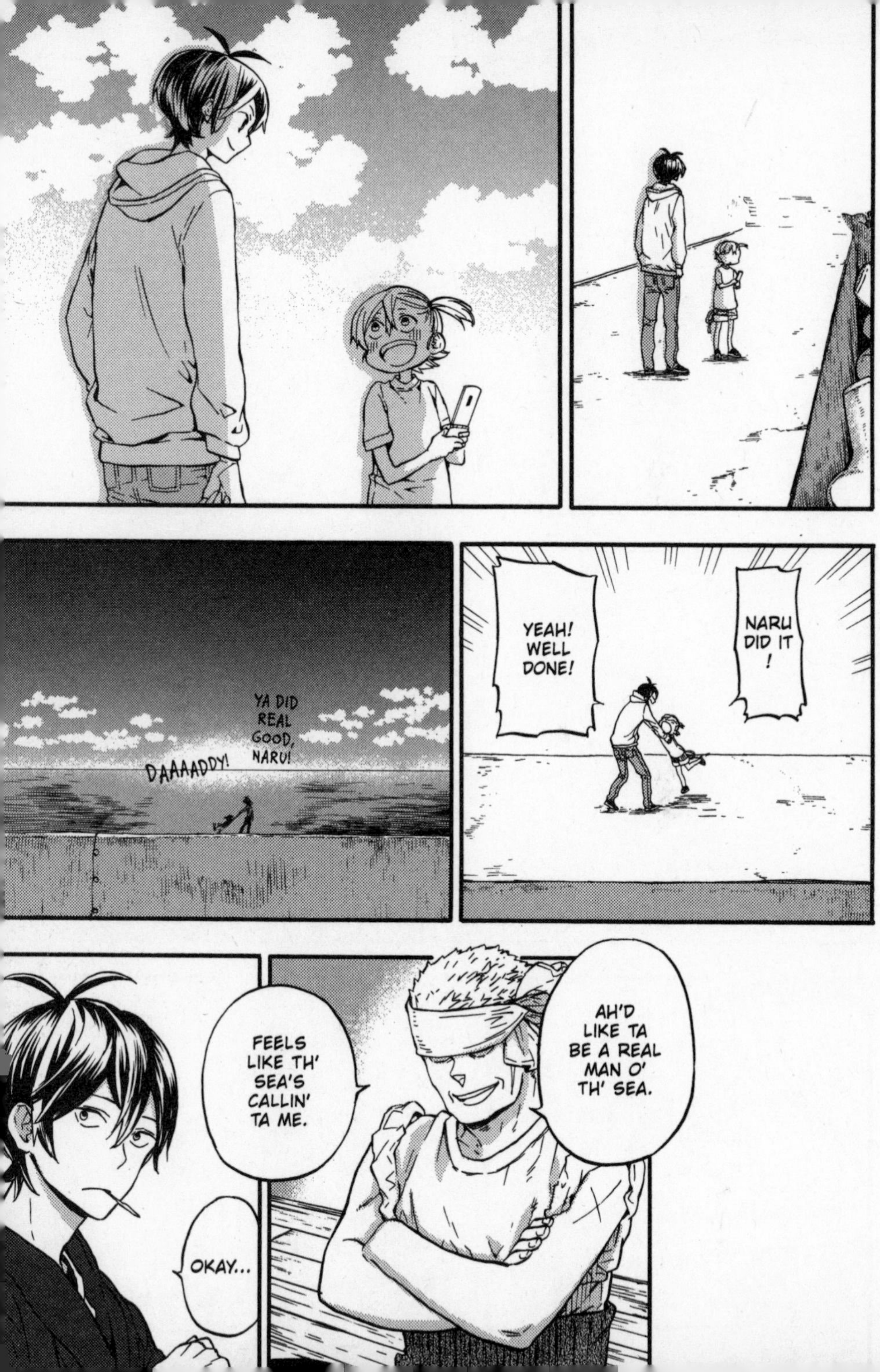
NARU DID IT!
YEAH! WELL DONE!
YA DID REAL GOOD, NARU!
DAAAADDY!
AH'D LIKE TA BE A REAL MAN O' TH' SEA.
FEELS LIKE TH' SEA'S CALLIN' TA ME.
OKAY...

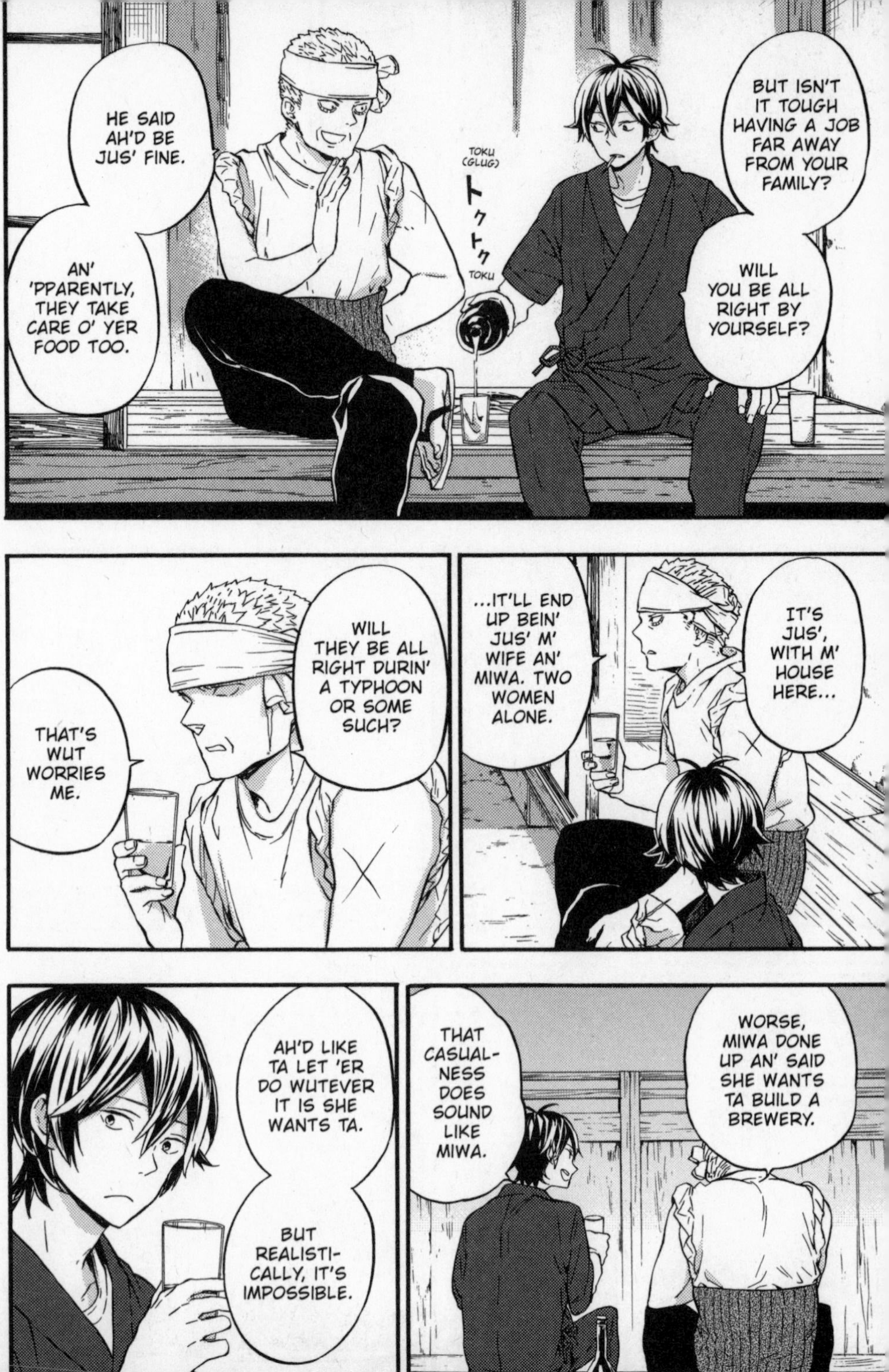
BUT ISN'T IT TOUGH HAVING A JOB FAR AWAY FROM YOUR FAMILY?
WILL YOU BE ALL RIGHT BY YOURSELF?
TOKU (GLUG)
トクトク
TOKU
HE SAID AH'D BE JUS' FINE.
AN' 'PPARENTLY, THEY TAKE CARE O' YER FOOD TOO.
IT'S JUS', WITH M' HOUSE HERE...
...IT'LL END UP BEIN' JUS' M' WIFE AN' MIWA. TWO WOMEN ALONE.
WILL THEY BE ALL RIGHT DURIN' A TYPHOON OR SOME SUCH?
THAT'S WUT WORRIES ME.
WORSE, MIWA DONE UP AN' SAID SHE WANTS TA BUILD A BREWERY.
THAT CASUAL-NESS DOES SOUND LIKE MIWA.
AH'D LIKE TA LET 'ER DO WUTEVER IT IS SHE WANTS TA.
BUT REALISTI-CALLY, IT'S IMPOSSIBLE.

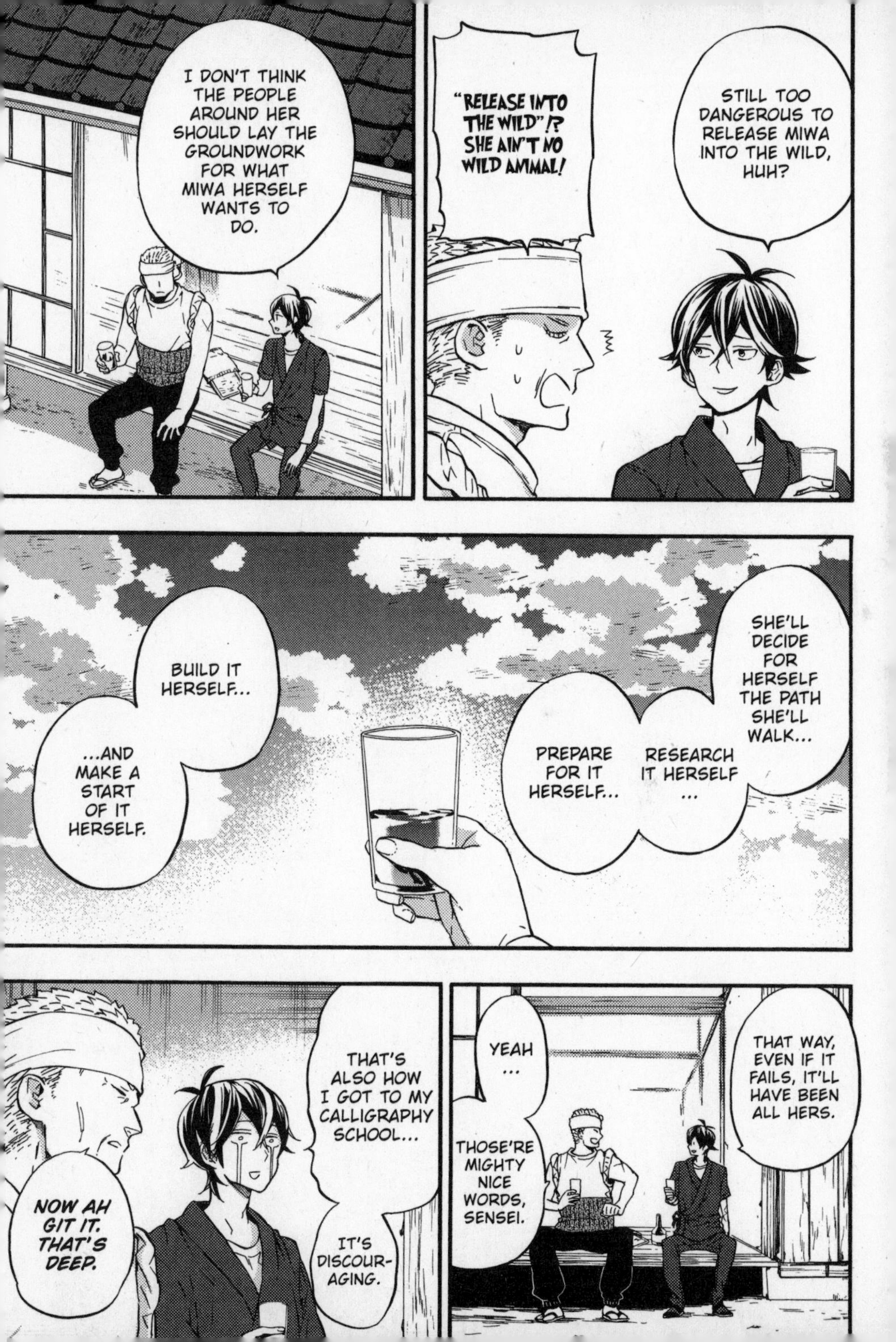
STILL TOO DANGEROUS TO RELEASE MIWA INTO THE WILD, HUH?
"RELEASE INTO THE WILD"!? SHE AIN'T NO WILD ANIMAL!
I DON'T THINK THE PEOPLE AROUND HER SHOULD LAY THE GROUNDWORK FOR WHAT MIWA HERSELF WANTS TO DO.
SHE'LL DECIDE FOR HERSELF THE PATH SHE'LL WALK...
RESEARCH IT HERSELF ...
PREPARE FOR IT HERSELF...
BUILD IT HERSELF...
...AND MAKE A START OF IT HERSELF.
THAT WAY, EVEN IF IT FAILS, IT'LL HAVE BEEN ALL HERS.
YEAH ...
THOSE'RE MIGHTY NICE WORDS, SENSEI.
THAT'S ALSO HOW I GOT TO MY CALLIGRAPHY SCHOOL...
NOW AH GIT IT. THAT'S DEEP.
IT'S DISCOURAGING.

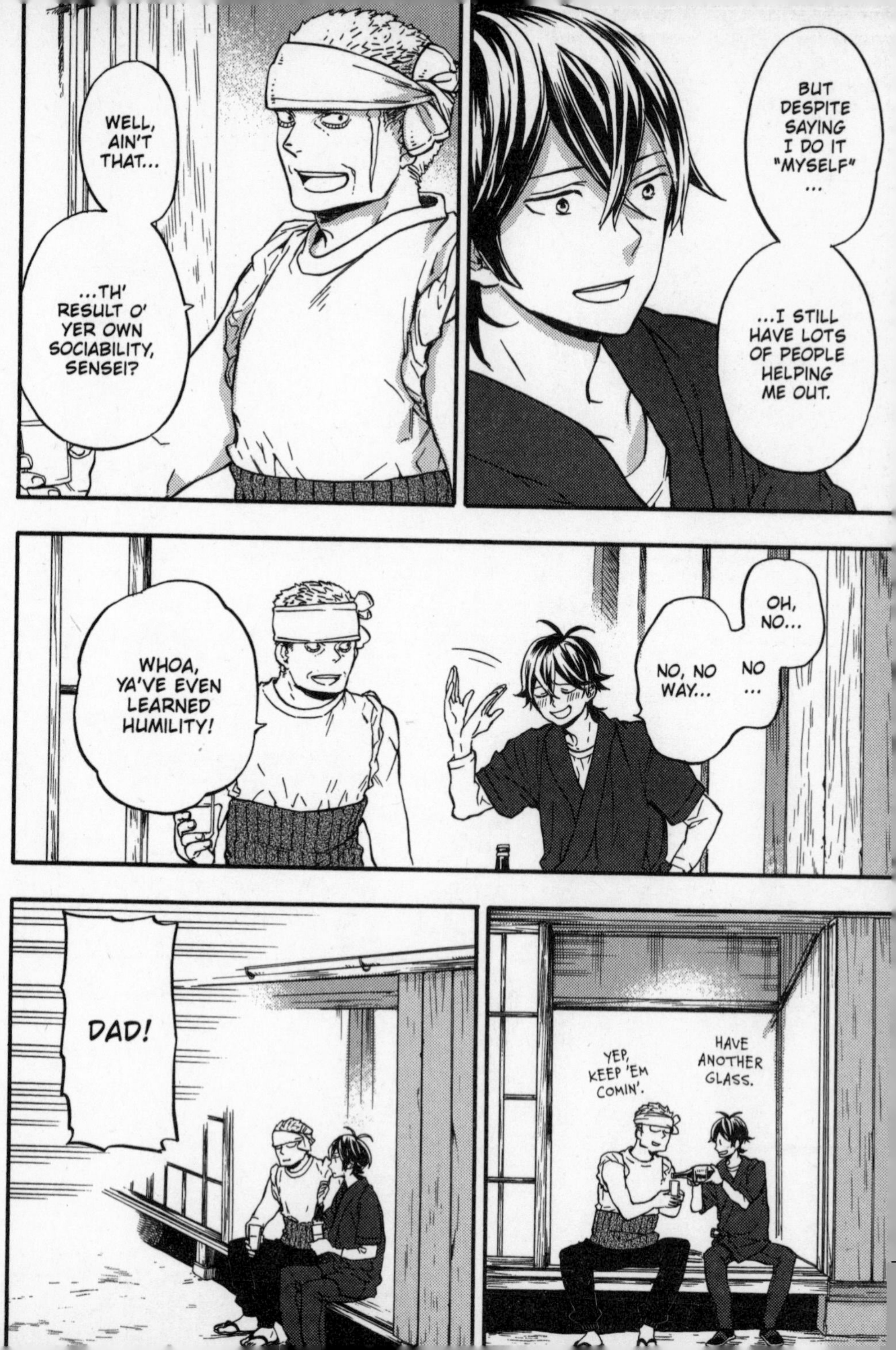
BUT DESPITE SAYING I DO IT "MYSELF" ...
...I STILL HAVE LOTS OF PEOPLE HELPING ME OUT.
WELL, AIN'T THAT...
...TH' RESULT O' YER OWN SOCIABILITY, SENSEI?
OH, NO... NO ... NO, NO WAY...
WHOA, YA'VE EVEN LEARNED HUMILITY!
HAVE ANOTHER GLASS.
YEP, KEEP 'EM COMIN'.
DAD!

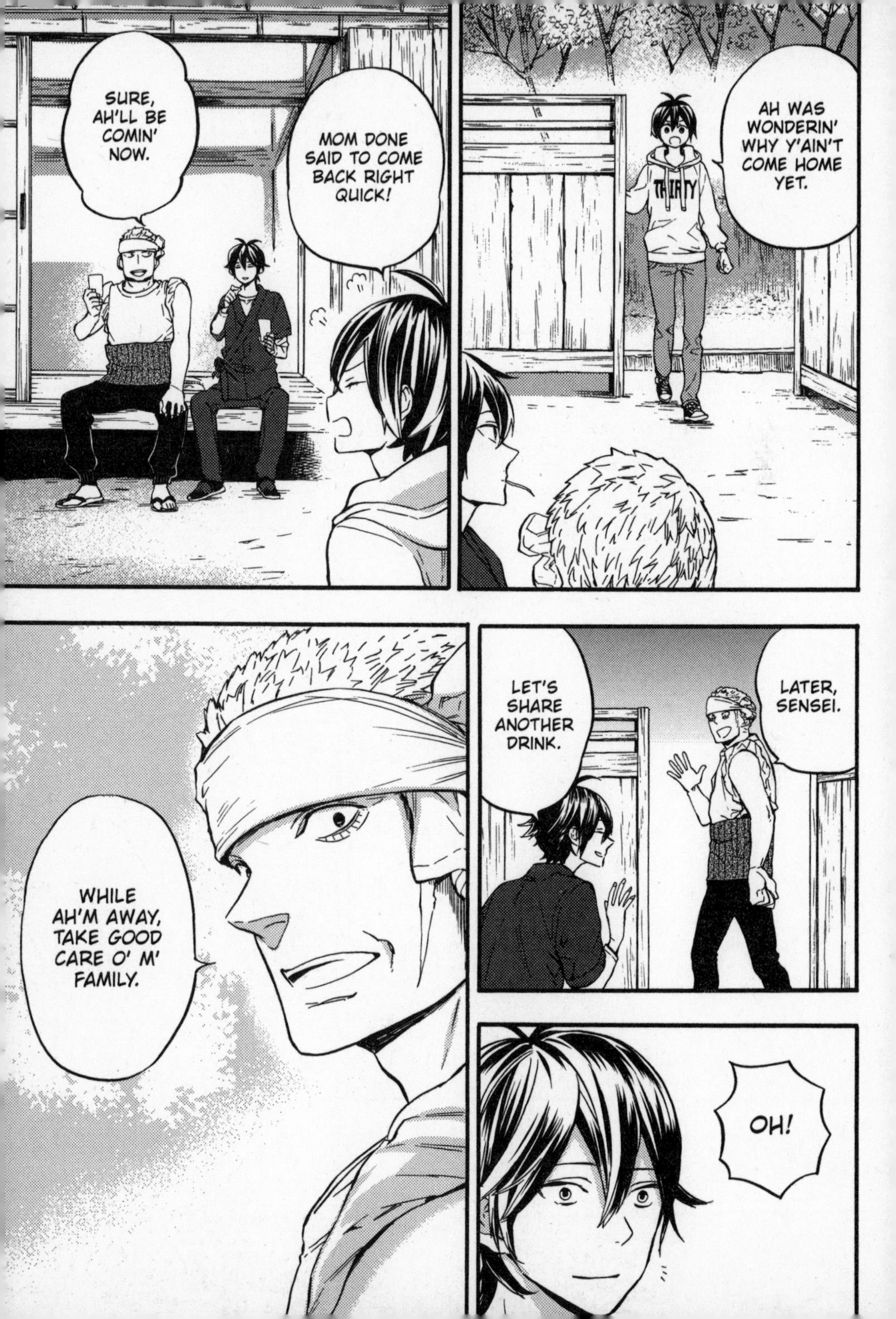
AH WAS WONDERIN' WHY Y'AIN'T COME HOME YET.
MOM DONE SAID TO COME BACK RIGHT QUICK!
SURE, AH'LL BE COMIN' NOW.
LATER, SENSEI.
LET'S SHARE ANOTHER DRINK.
OH!
WHILE AH'M AWAY, TAKE GOOD CARE O' M' FAMILY.

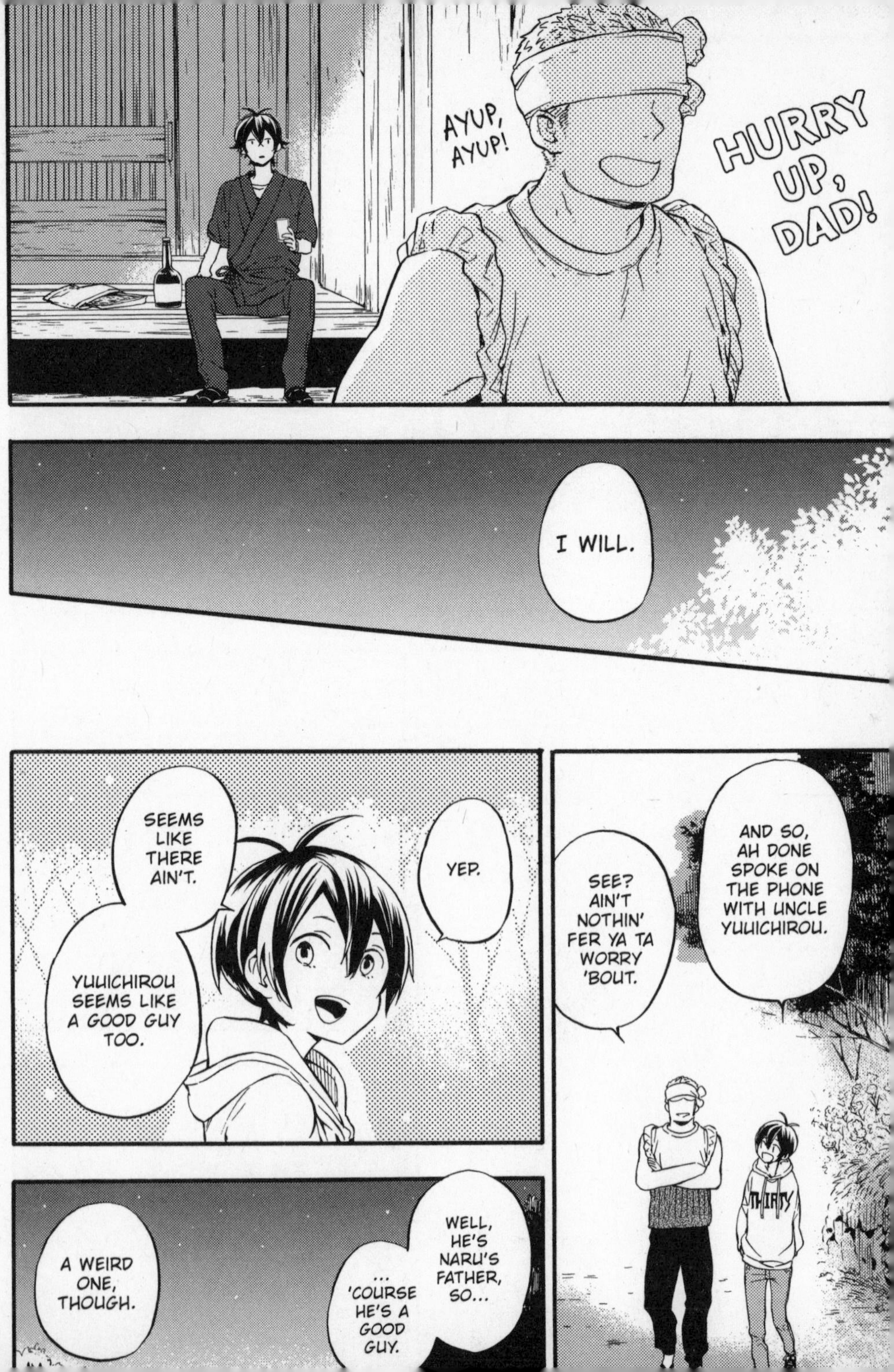
HURRY UP, DAD!
AYUP, AYUP!
I WILL.
AND SO, AH DONE SPOKE ON THE PHONE WITH UNCLE YUUICHIROU.
SEE? AIN'T NOTHIN' FER YA TA WORRY 'BOUT.
YEP.
SEEMS LIKE THERE AIN'T.
YUUICHIROU SEEMS LIKE A GOOD GUY TOO.
WELL, HE'S NARU'S FATHER, SO...
...'COURSE HE'S A GOOD GUY.
A WEIRD ONE, THOUGH.

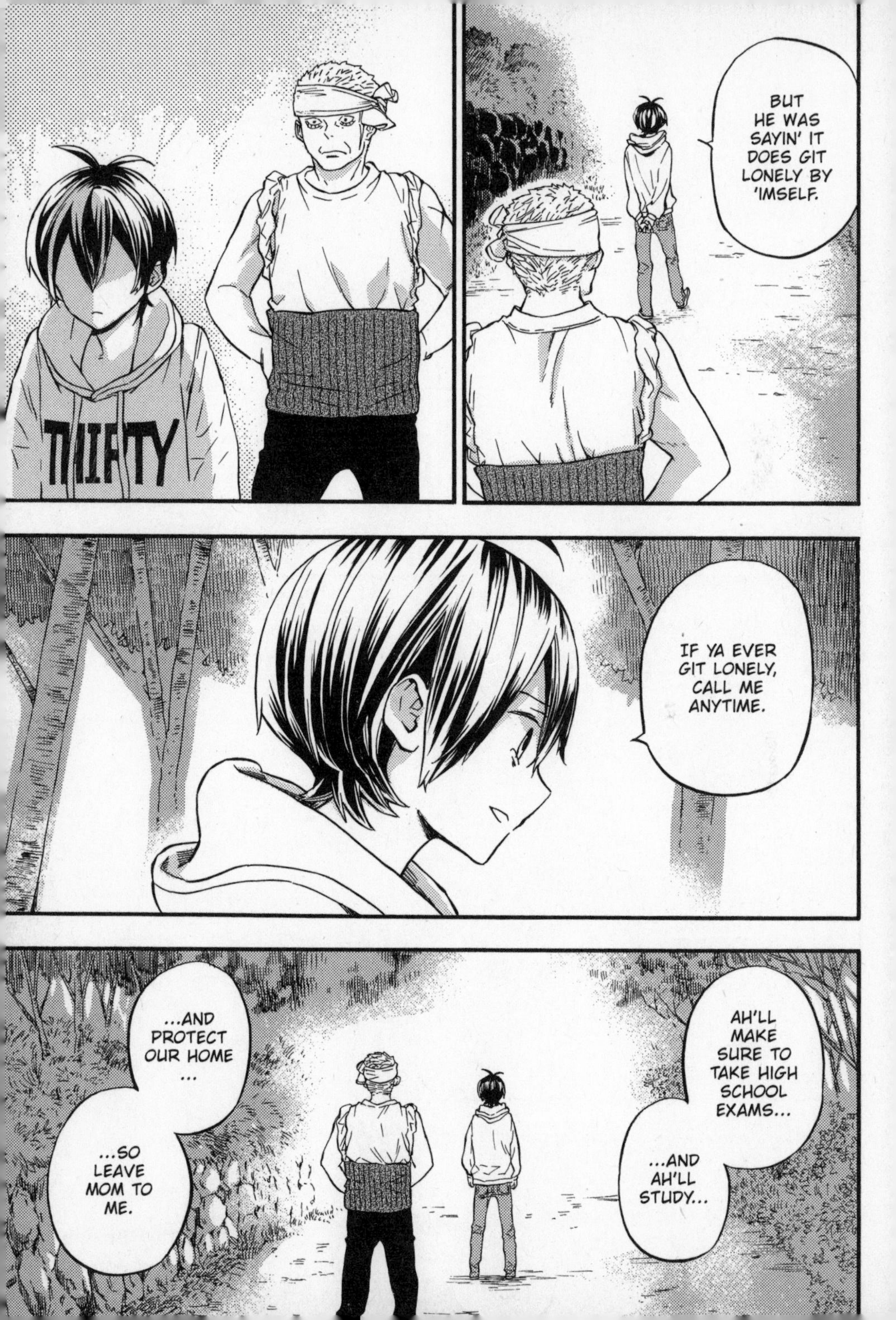
BUT HE WAS SAYIN' IT DOES GIT LONELY BY 'IMSELF.
THIRTY
IF YA EVER GIT LONELY, CALL ME ANYTIME.
AH'LL MAKE SURE TO TAKE HIGH SCHOOL EXAMS...
...AND AH'LL STUDY...
...AND PROTECT OUR HOME ...
...SO LEAVE MOM TO ME.

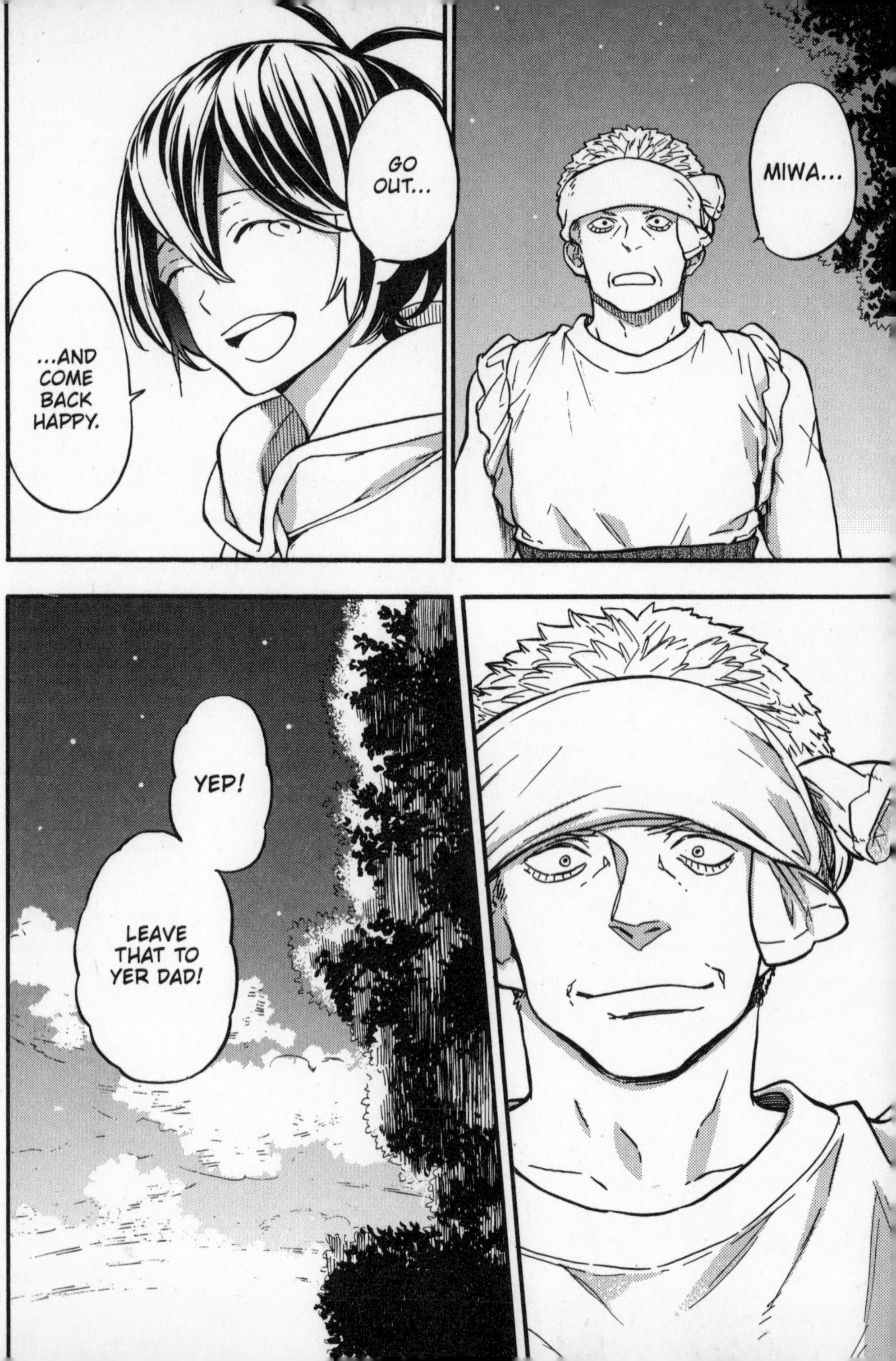
MIWA...
GO OUT...
...AND COME BACK HAPPY.
YEP!
LEAVE THAT TO YER DAD!

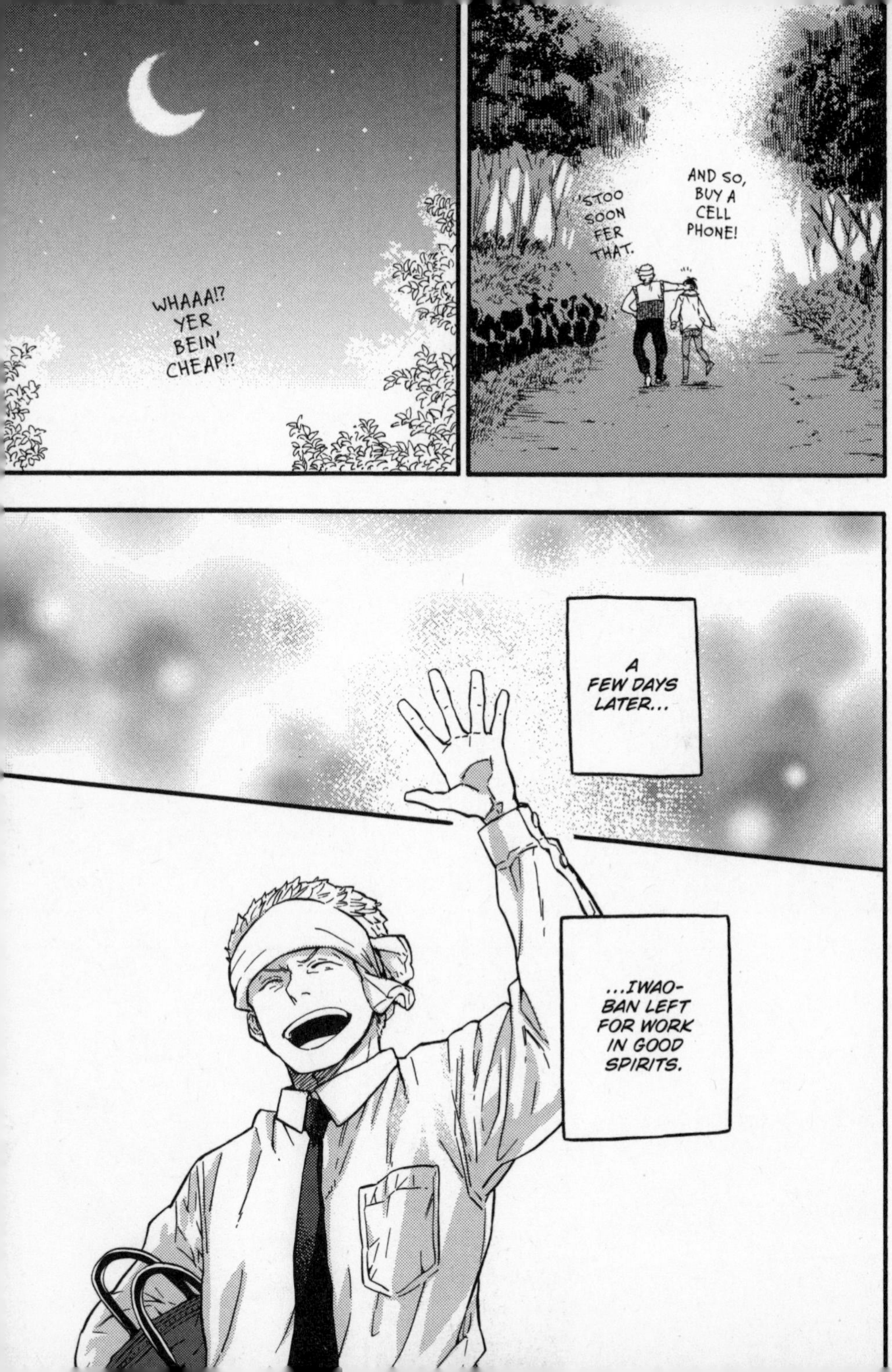
AND SO, BUY A CELL PHONE!
'STOO SOON FER THAT.
WHAAA!? YER BEIN' CHEAP!?
A FEW DAYS LATER...
...IWAO-BAN LEFT FOR WORK IN GOOD SPIRITS.

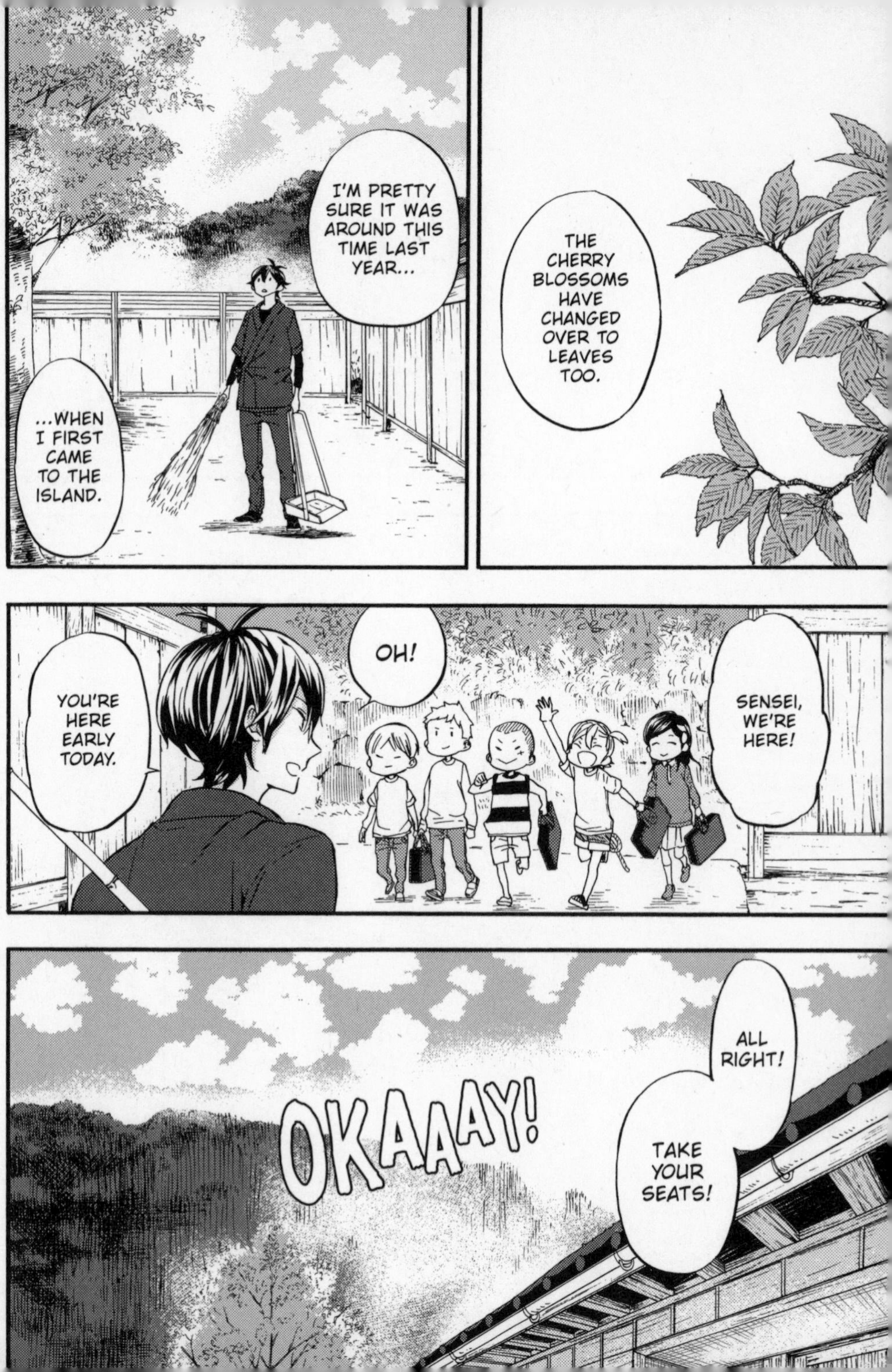
THE CHERRY BLOSSOMS HAVE CHANGED OVER TO LEAVES TOO.
I'M PRETTY SURE IT WAS AROUND THIS TIME LAST YEAR...
...WHEN I FIRST CAME TO THE ISLAND.
SENSEI, WE'RE HERE!
OH!
YOU'RE HERE EARLY TODAY.
ALL RIGHT!
TAKE YOUR SEATS!
OKAAAY!

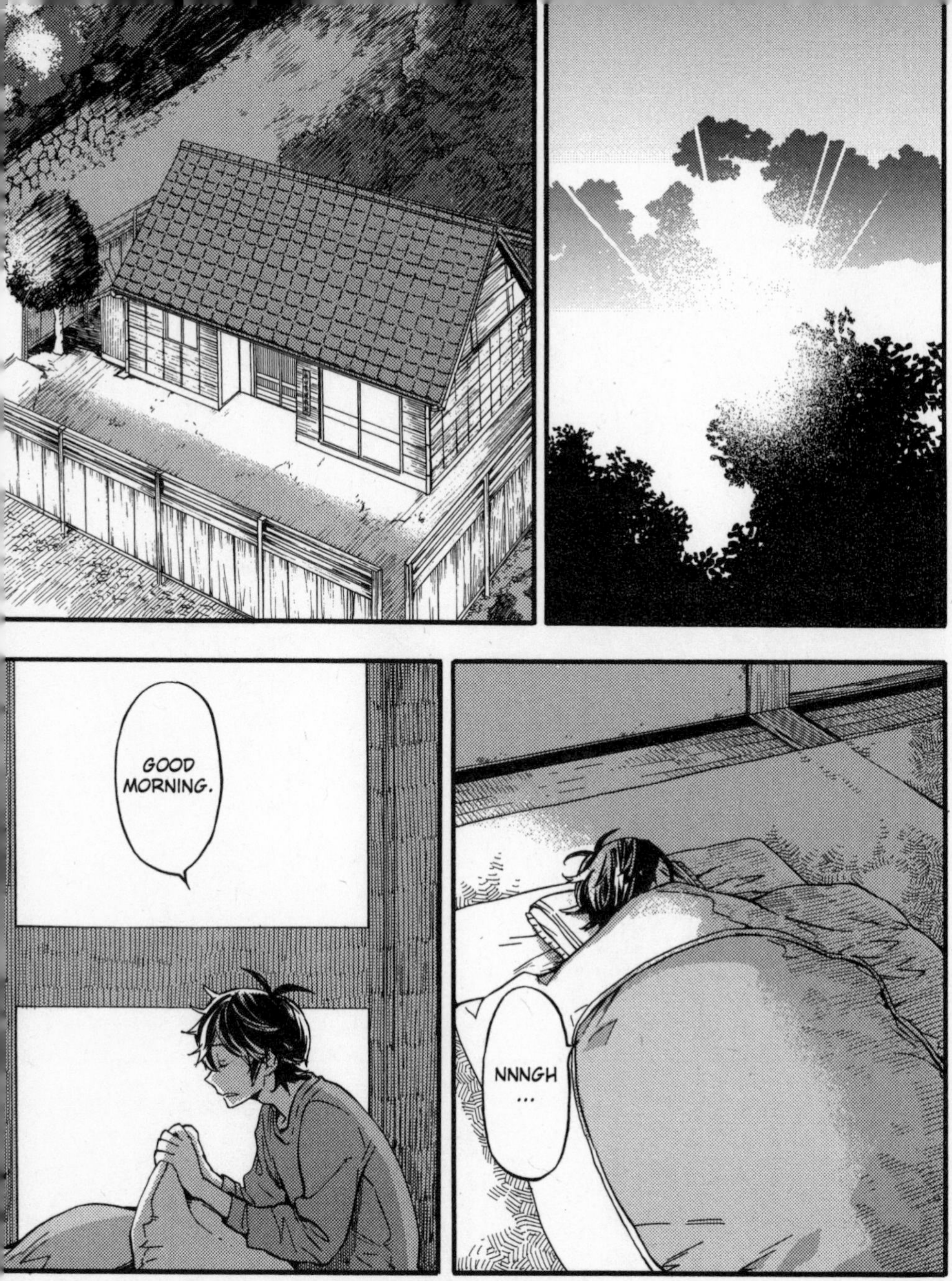
NNNGH ...
GOOD MORNING.

Act. 133
OGGA ICHINCHI
(Translation: One Day in My Life)

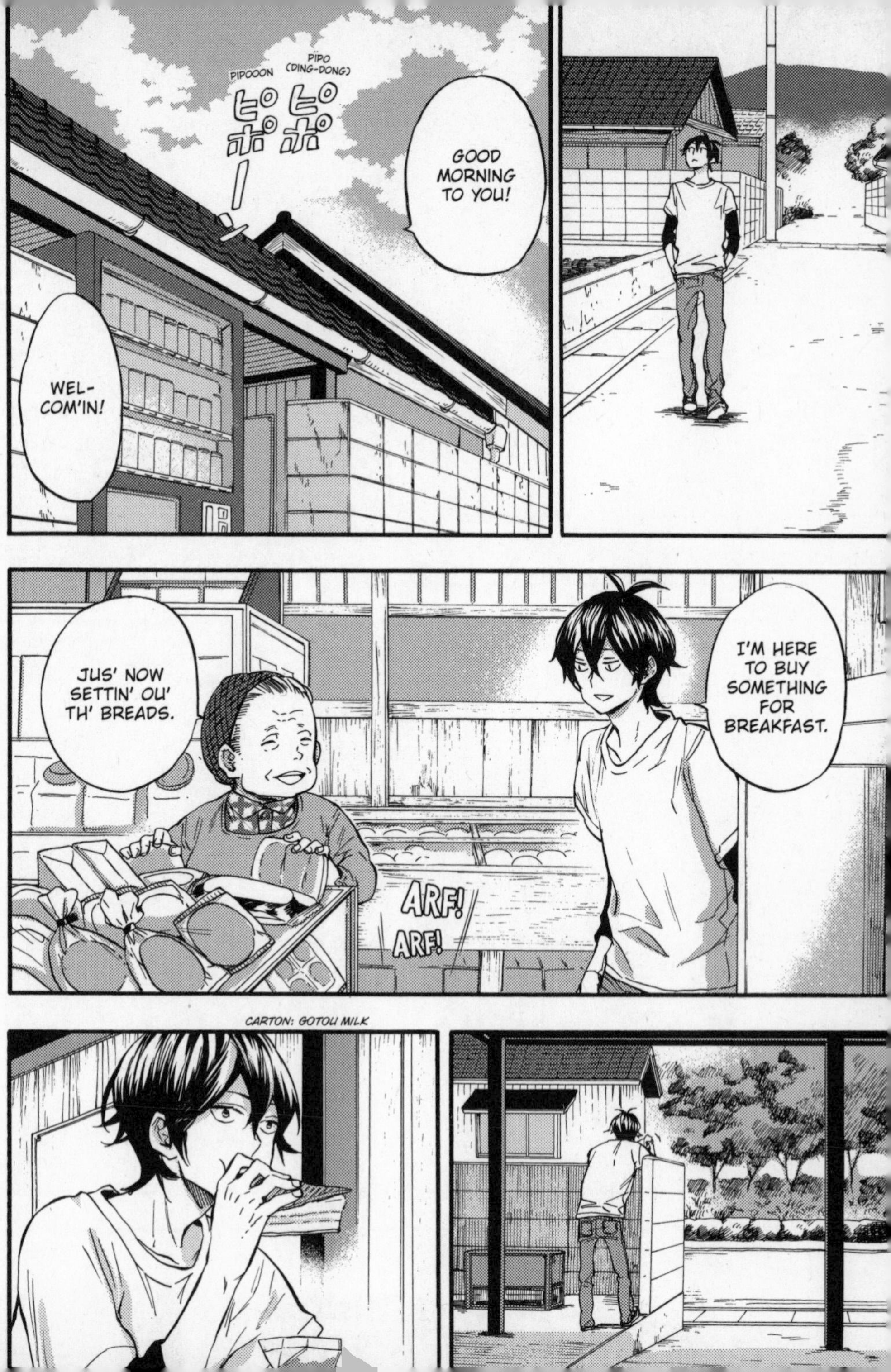
GOOD MORNING TO YOU!
PIPO (DING-DONG)
ピポ
PIPOOON
ピポー
WEL-COM'IN!
I'M HERE TO BUY SOMETHING FOR BREAKFAST.
JUS' NOW SETTIN' OU' TH' BREADS.
ARF!
ARF!
CARTON: GOTOU MILK

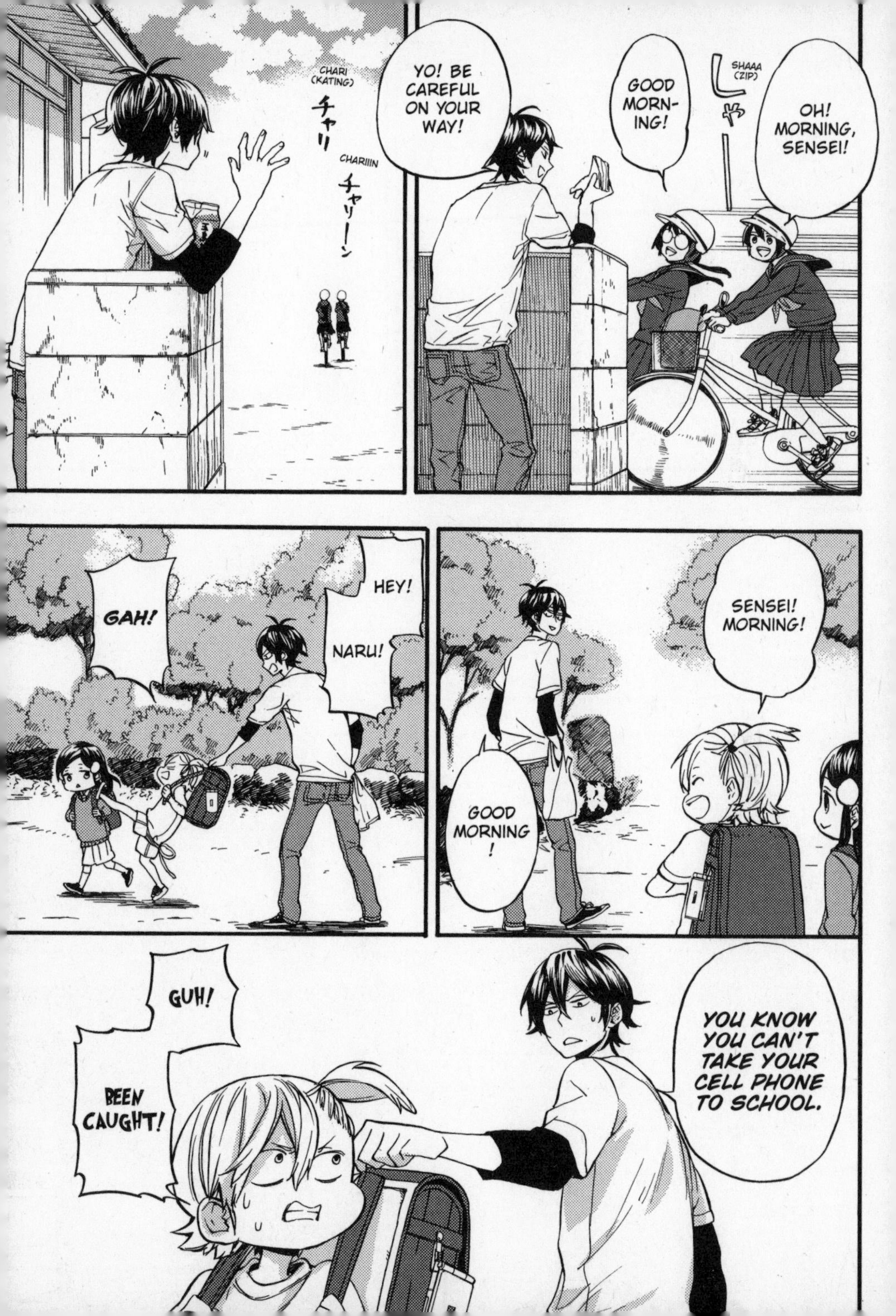
OH! MORNING, SENSEI!
SHAAA (ZIP)
しゃ
GOOD MORNING!
YO! BE CAREFUL ON YOUR WAY!
CHARI (KATING)
チャリ
CHARIIIN
チャリーン
SENSEI! MORNING!
GOOD MORNING!
HEY!
NARU!
GAH!
YOU KNOW YOU CAN'T TAKE YOUR CELL PHONE TO SCHOOL.
GUH!
BEEN CAUGHT!

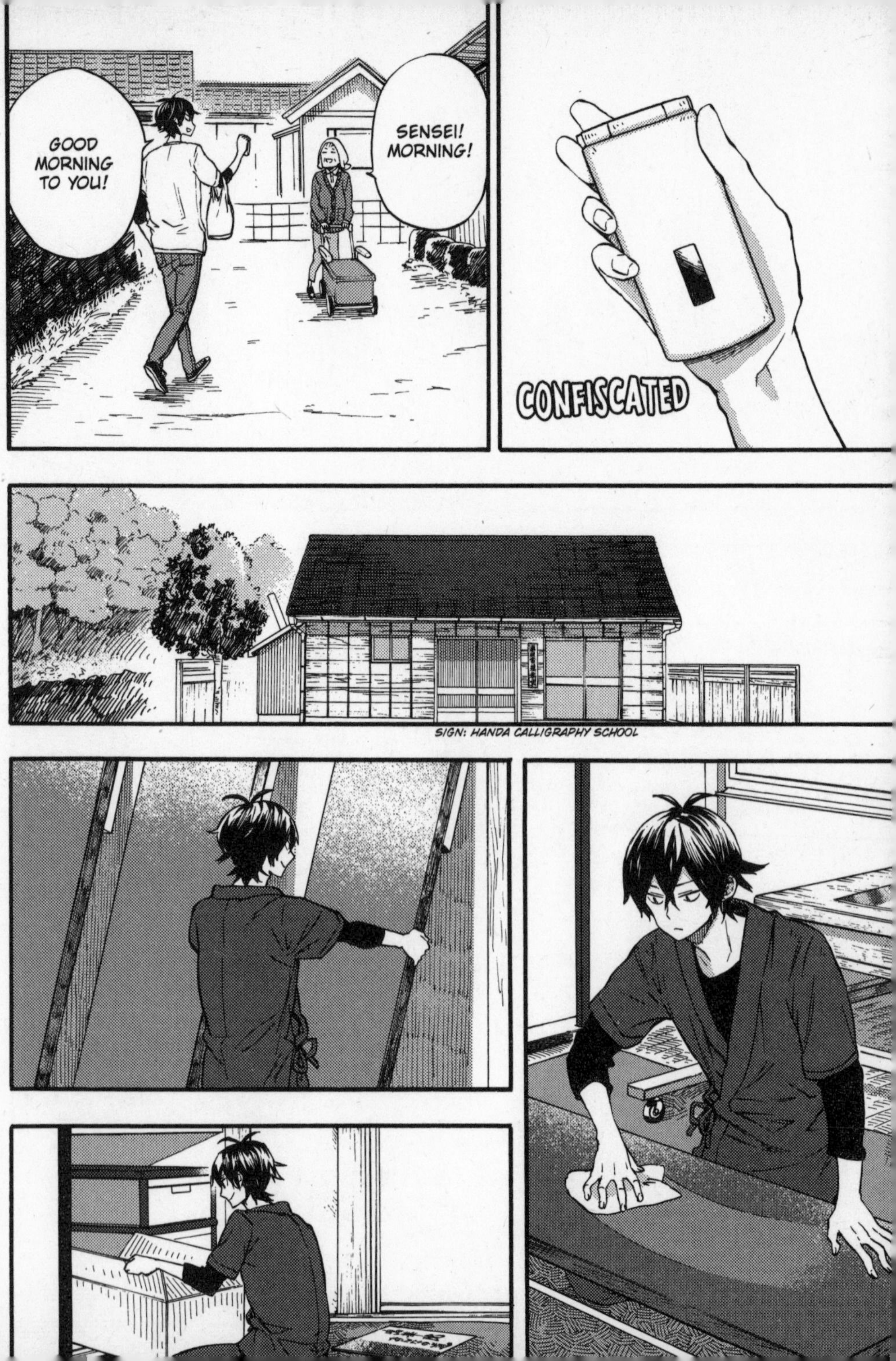
CONFISCATED
SENSEI! MORNING!
GOOD MORNING TO YOU!
SIGN: HANDA CALLIGRAPHY SCHOOL

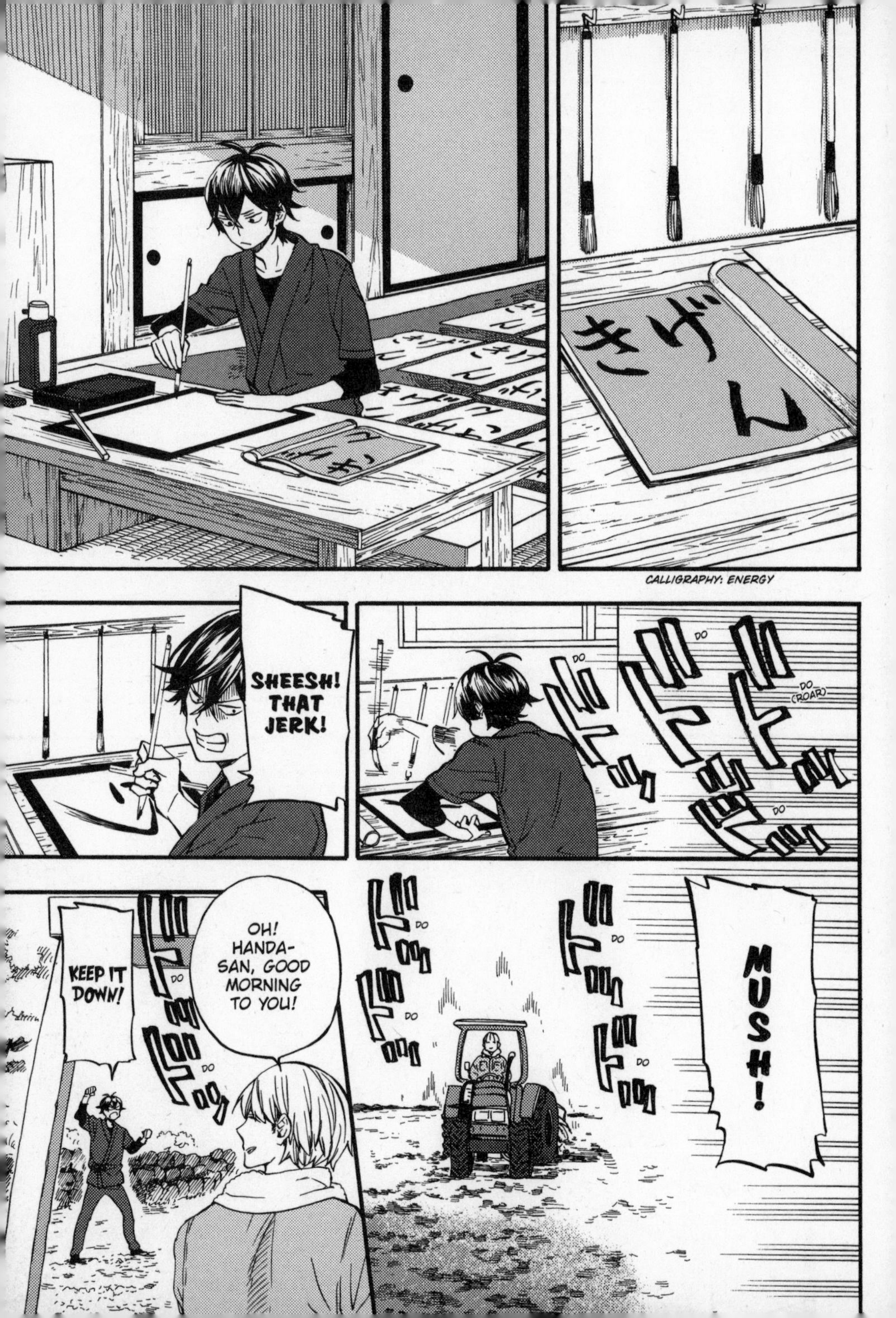
きげん
CALLIGRAPHY: ENERGY
DO
DO
DO (ROAR)
DO
SHEESH! THAT JERK!
MUSH!
DO
DO
DO
DO
OH! HANDA-SAN, GOOD MORNING TO YOU!
DO
DO
KEEP IT DOWN!

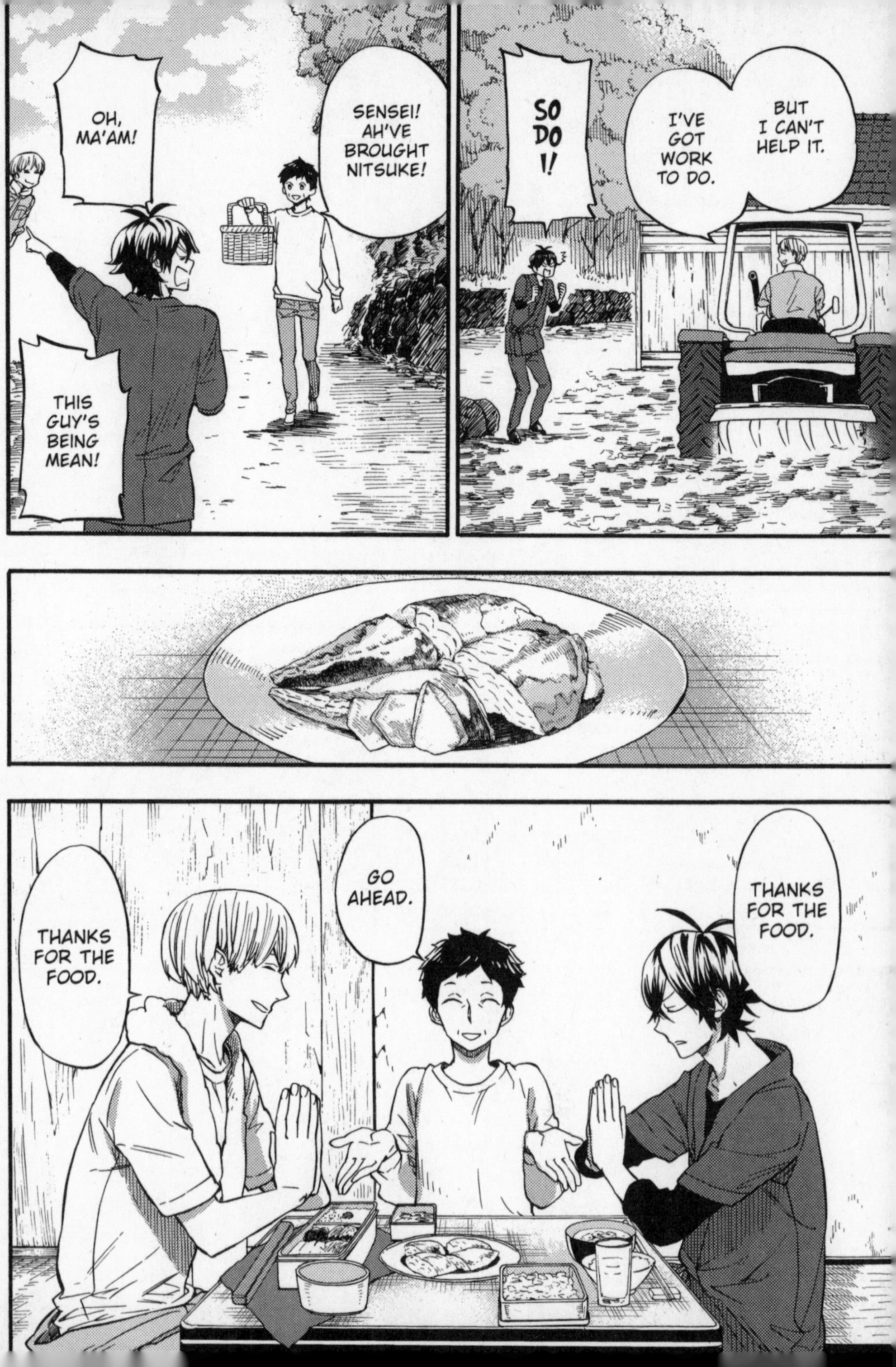
BUT I CAN'T HELP IT.
I'VE GOT WORK TO DO.
SO DO I!
SENSEI! AH'VE BROUGHT NITSUKE!
OH, MA'AM!
THIS GUY'S BEING MEAN!
THANKS FOR THE FOOD.
GO AHEAD.
THANKS FOR THE FOOD.

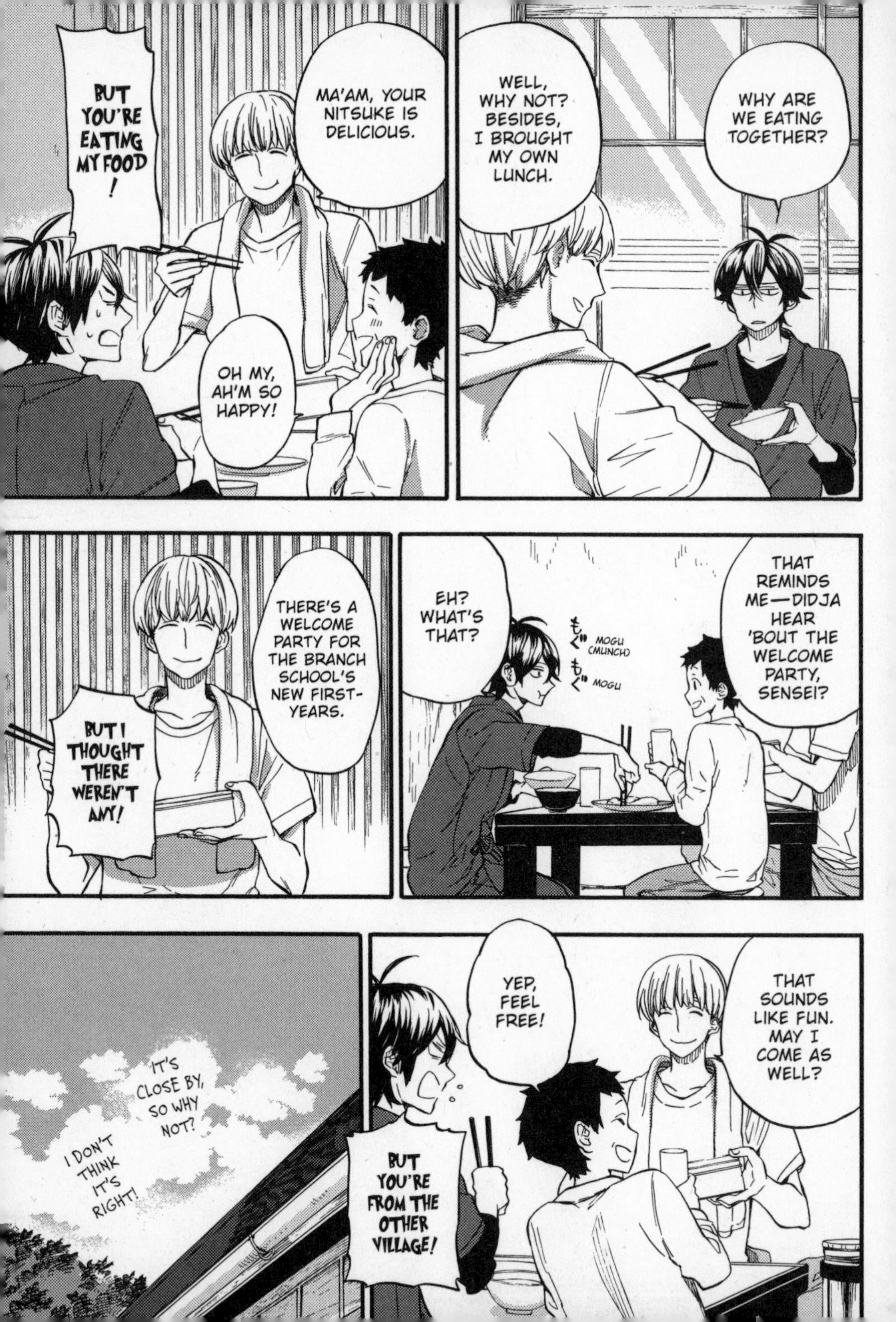
WHY ARE WE EATING TOGETHER?
WELL, WHY NOT? BESIDES, I BROUGHT MY OWN LUNCH.
MA'AM, YOUR NITSUKE IS DELICIOUS.
BUT YOU'RE EATING MY FOOD!
OH MY, AH'M SO HAPPY!
THAT REMINDS ME—DIDJA HEAR 'BOUT THE WELCOME PARTY, SENSEI?
EH? WHAT'S THAT?
もぐ MOGU (MUNCH)
もぐ MOGU
THERE'S A WELCOME PARTY FOR THE BRANCH SCHOOL'S NEW FIRST-YEARS.
BUT I THOUGHT THERE WEREN'T ANY!
THAT SOUNDS LIKE FUN. MAY I COME AS WELL?
YEP, FEEL FREE!
BUT YOU'RE FROM THE OTHER VILLAGE!
IT'S CLOSE BY, SO WHY NOT?
I DON'T THINK IT'S RIGHT!

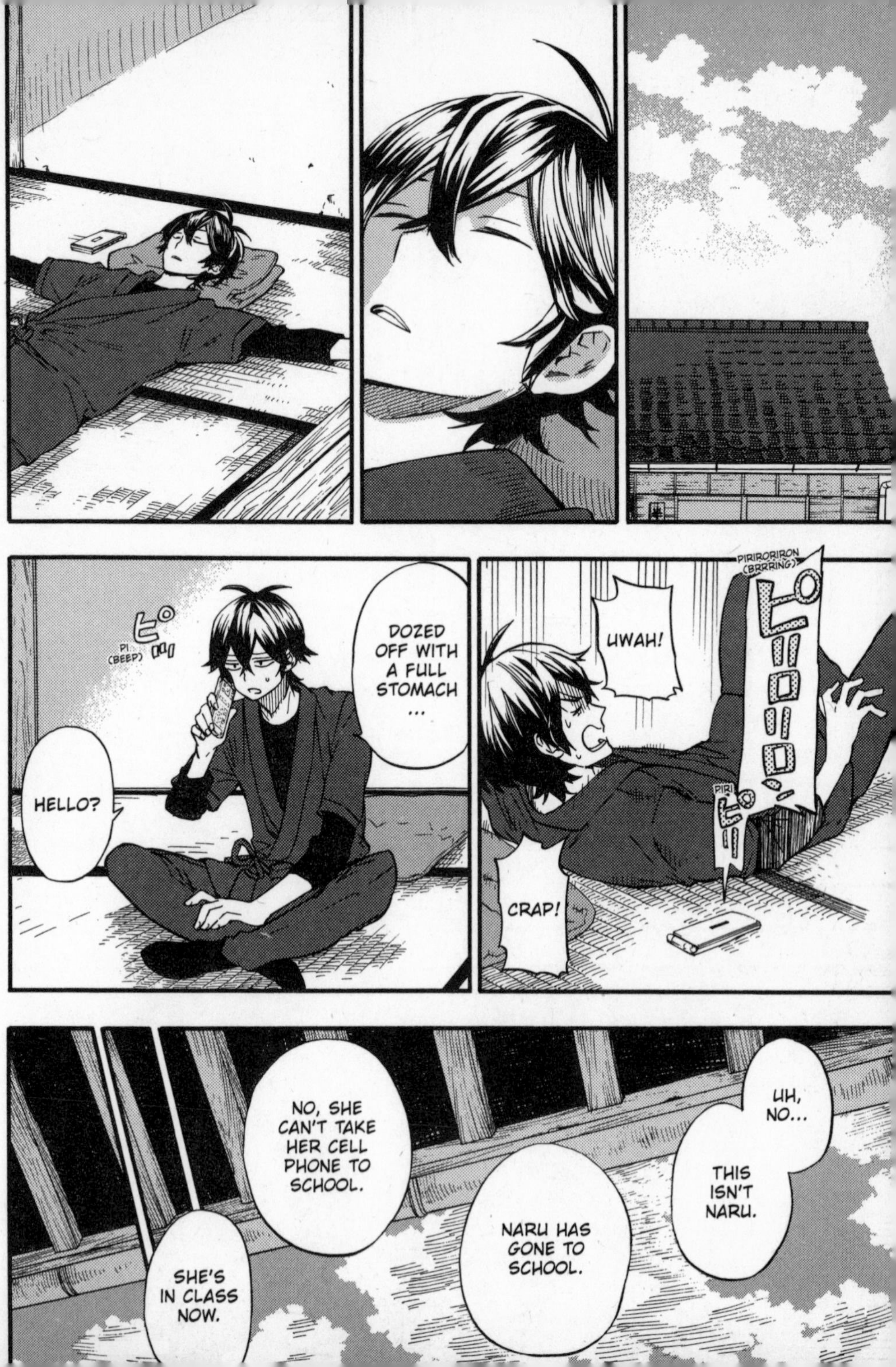
PIRIRORIRON (BRRRING)
UWAH!
PIRI
CRAP!
DOZED OFF WITH A FULL STOMACH ...
PI (BEEP)
HELLO?
UH, NO...
THIS ISN'T NARU.
NARU HAS GONE TO SCHOOL.
NO, SHE CAN'T TAKE HER CELL PHONE TO SCHOOL.
SHE'S IN CLASS NOW.

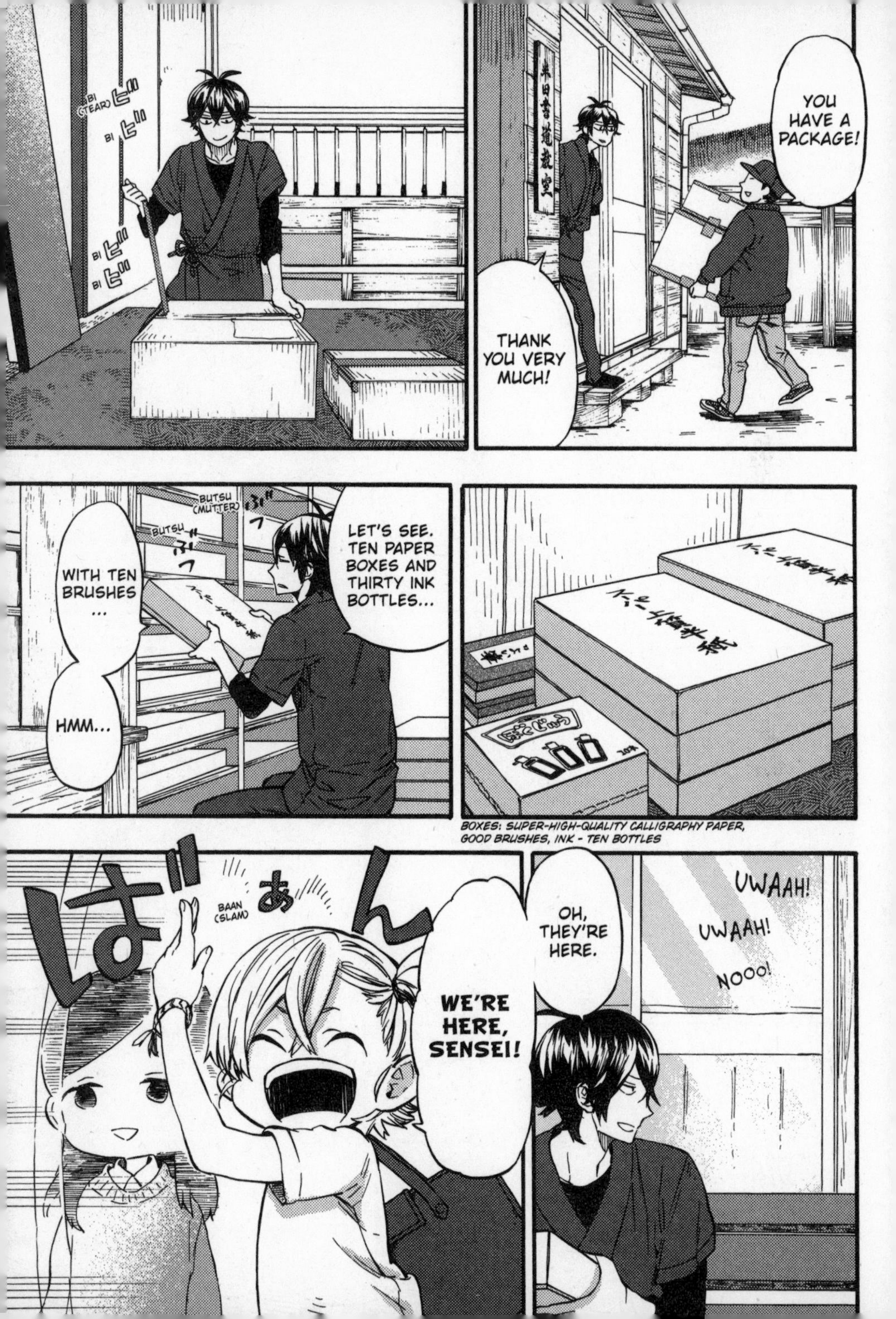
YOU HAVE A PACKAGE!
THANK YOU VERY MUCH!
BI (TEAR)
BI
BI
BI
BOXES: SUPER-HIGH-QUALITY CALLIGRAPHY PAPER, GOOD BRUSHES, INK - TEN BOTTLES
LET'S SEE. TEN PAPER BOXES AND THIRTY INK BOTTLES...
BUTSU (MUTTER)
BUTSU
WITH TEN BRUSHES...
HMM...
UWAAH!
UWAAH!
NOOO!
OH, THEY'RE HERE.
WE'RE HERE, SENSEI!
BAAN (SLAM)

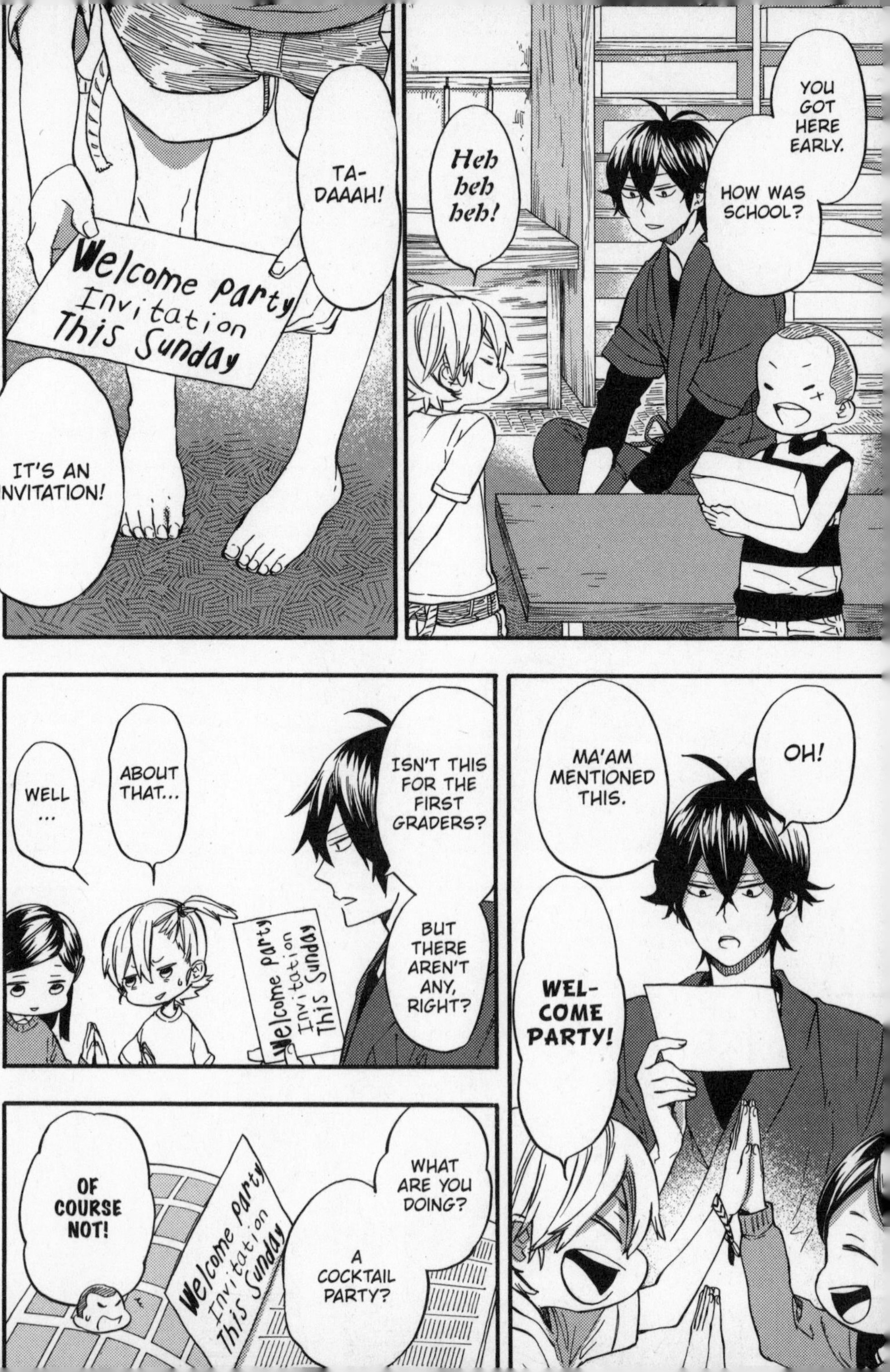
YOU GOT HERE EARLY.
HOW WAS SCHOOL?
Heh heh heh!
TA-DAAAH!
Welcome party Invitation This Sunday
IT'S AN INVITATION!
OH!
MA'AM MENTIONED THIS.
WEL-COME PARTY!
ISN'T THIS FOR THE FIRST GRADERS?
BUT THERE AREN'T ANY, RIGHT?
ABOUT THAT...
WELL ...
Welcome party Invitation This Sunday
WHAT ARE YOU DOING?
A COCKTAIL PARTY?
OF COURSE NOT!
Welcome party Invitation This Sunday

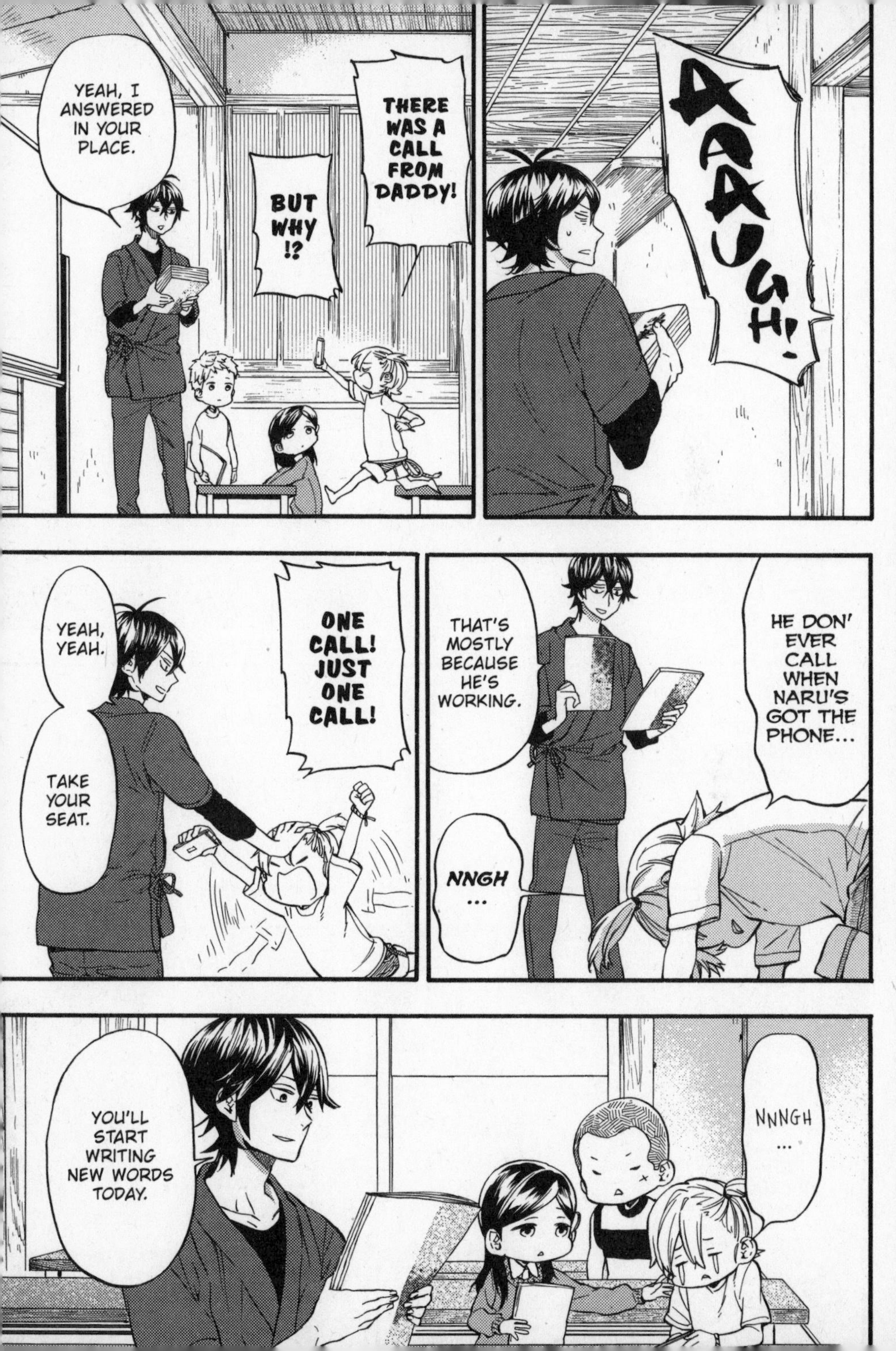
AAAUGH!
THERE WAS A CALL FROM DADDY!
BUT WHY!?
YEAH, I ANSWERED IN YOUR PLACE.
HE DON' EVER CALL WHEN NARU'S GOT THE PHONE...
THAT'S MOSTLY BECAUSE HE'S WORKING.
NNGH...
ONE CALL! JUST ONE CALL!
YEAH, YEAH.
TAKE YOUR SEAT.
NNNGH...
YOU'LL START WRITING NEW WORDS TODAY.

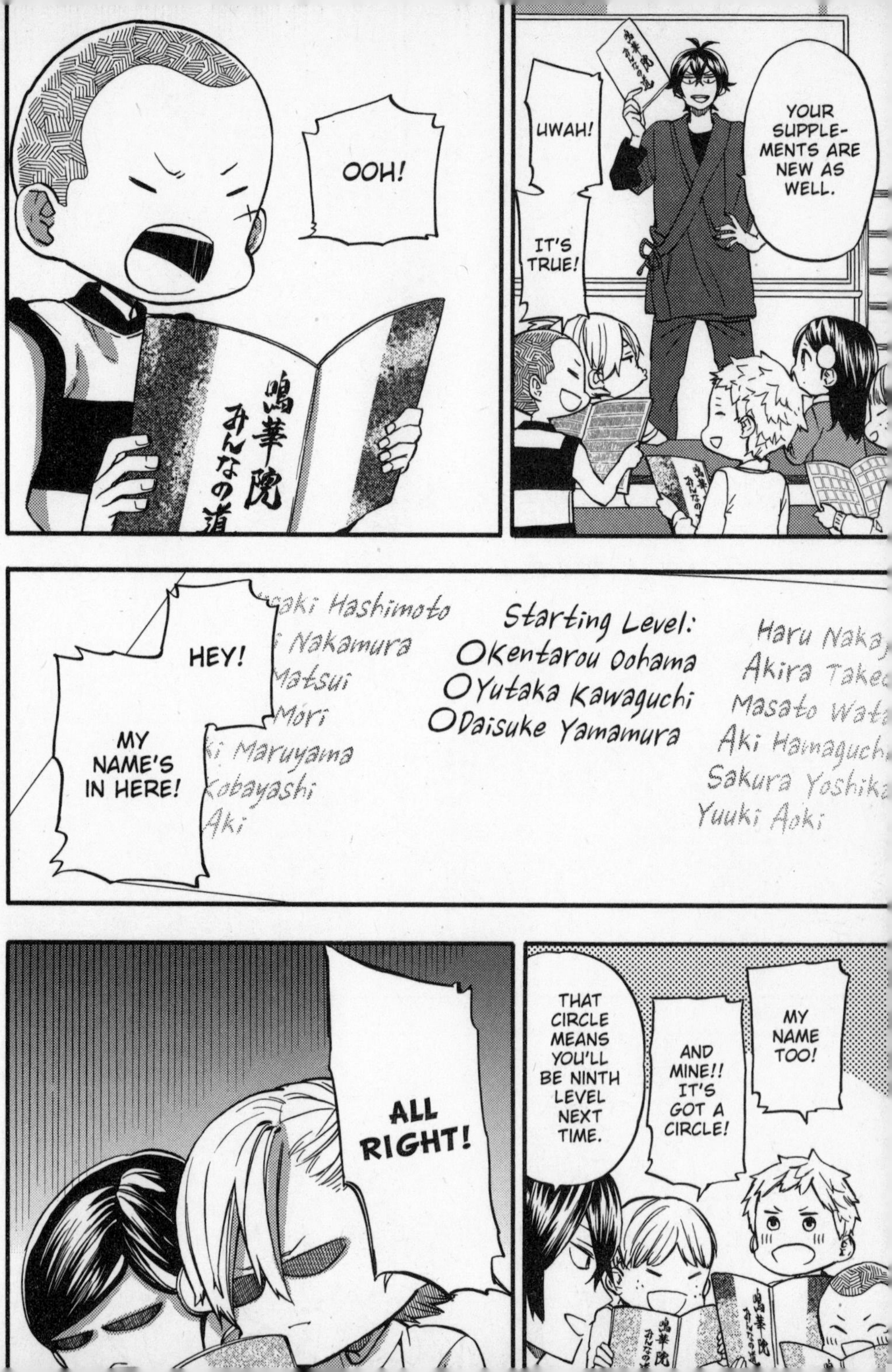
YOUR SUPPLE-MENTS ARE NEW AS WELL.
UWAH!
IT'S TRUE!
OOH!
鳴華院 みんなの道
Haru Naka
Akira Take
Masato Wat
Aki Hamaguch
Sakura Yoshik
Yuuki Aoki
Starting Level:
OKentarou Oohama
OYutaka Kawaguchi
ODaisuke Yamamura
aki Hashimoto
Nakamura
Matsui
Mori
i Maruyama
Kobayashi
Aki
HEY!
MY NAME'S IN HERE!
MY NAME TOO!
AND MINE!! IT'S GOT A CIRCLE!
THAT CIRCLE MEANS YOU'LL BE NINTH LEVEL NEXT TIME.
ALL RIGHT!

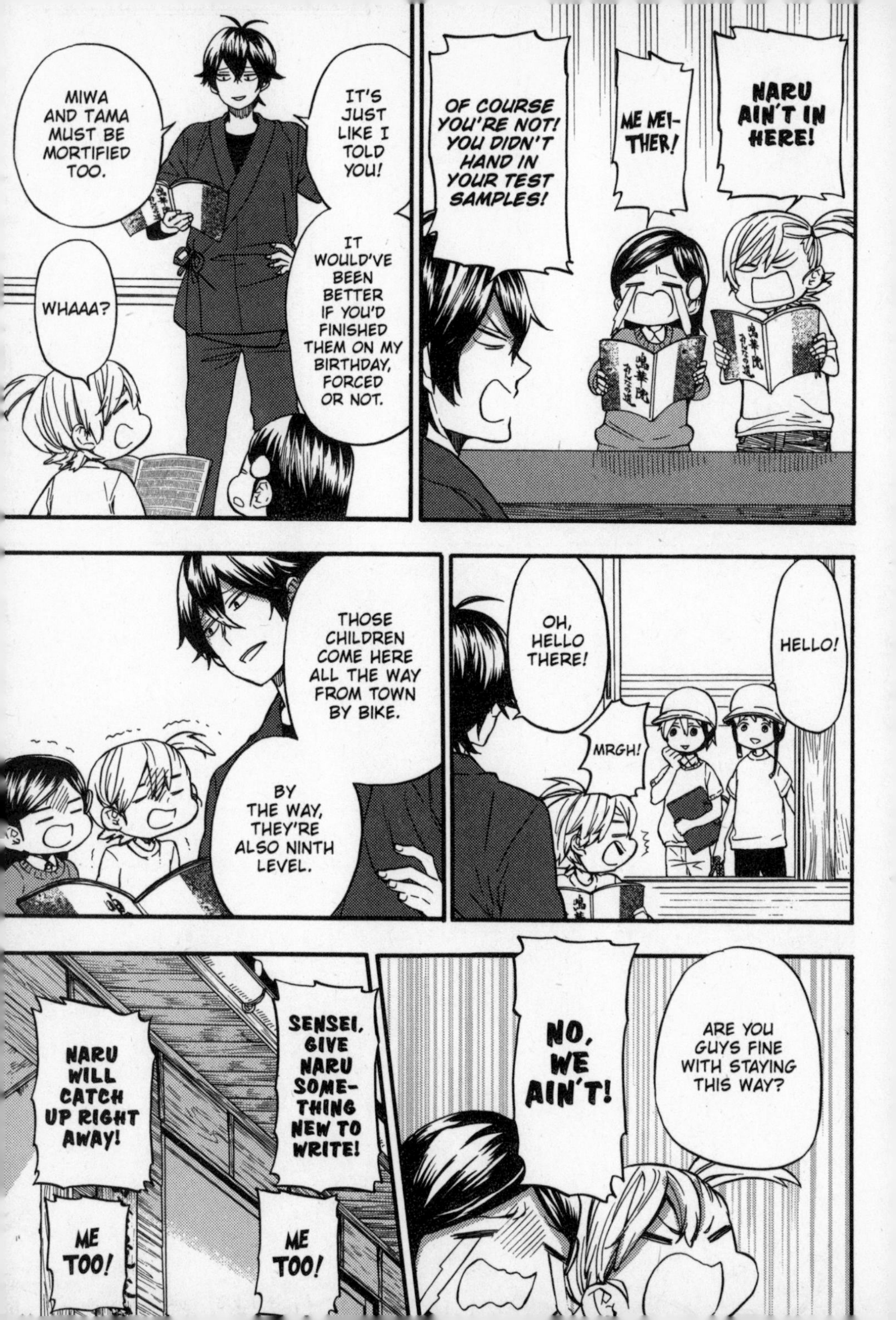
NARU AIN'T IN HERE!
ME NEI-THER!
OF COURSE YOU'RE NOT! YOU DIDN'T HAND IN YOUR TEST SAMPLES!
IT'S JUST LIKE I TOLD YOU!
MIWA AND TAMA MUST BE MORTIFIED TOO.
IT WOULD'VE BEEN BETTER IF YOU'D FINISHED THEM ON MY BIRTHDAY, FORCED OR NOT.
WHAAA?
HELLO!
OH, HELLO THERE!
MRGH!
THOSE CHILDREN COME HERE ALL THE WAY FROM TOWN BY BIKE.
BY THE WAY, THEY'RE ALSO NINTH LEVEL.
ARE YOU GUYS FINE WITH STAYING THIS WAY?
NO, WE AIN'T!
SENSEI, GIVE NARU SOME-THING NEW TO WRITE!
NARU WILL CATCH UP RIGHT AWAY!
ME TOO!
ME TOO!

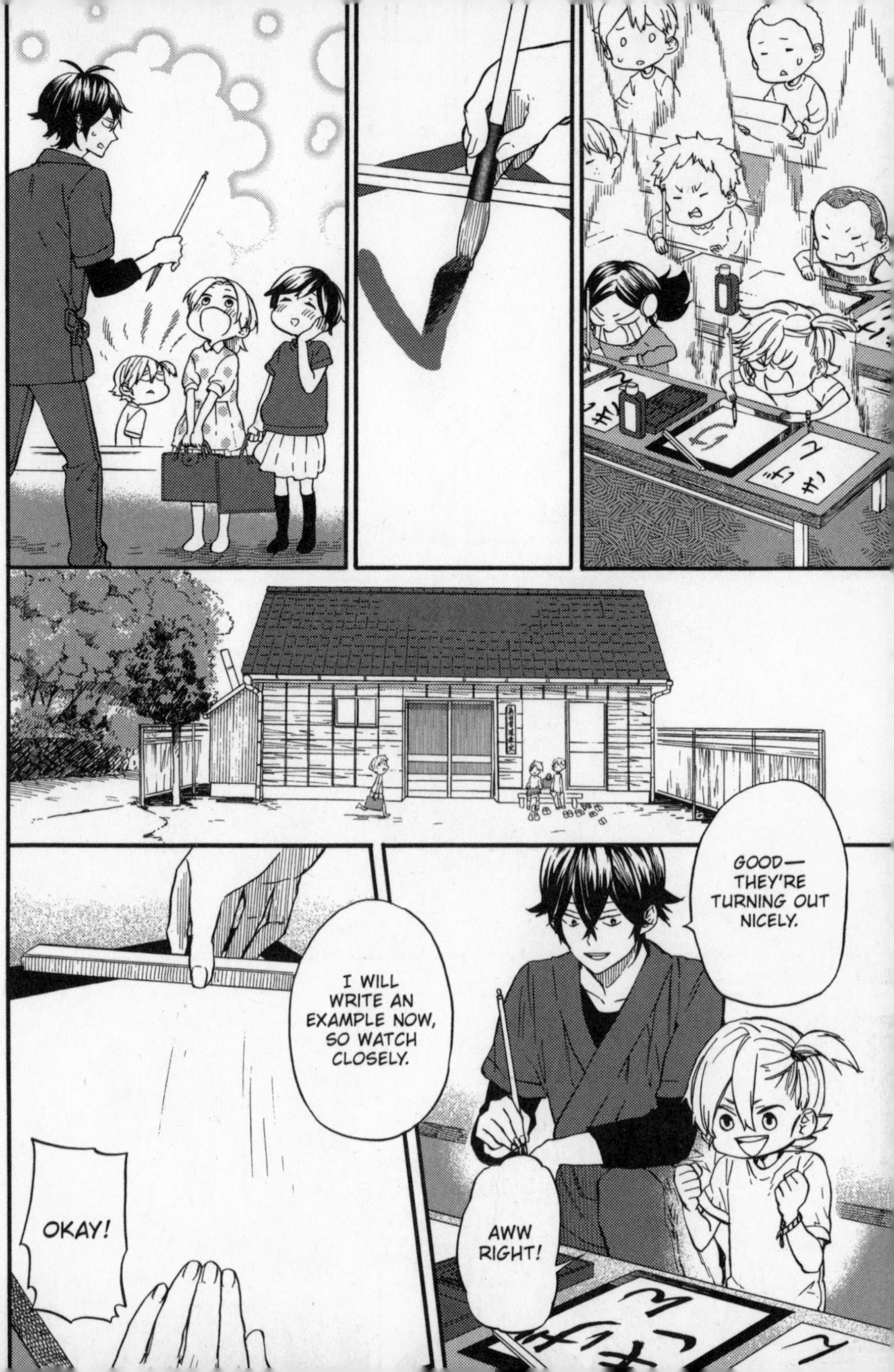
GOOD— THEY'RE TURNING OUT NICELY.
AWW RIGHT!
I WILL WRITE AN EXAMPLE NOW, SO WATCH CLOSELY.
OKAY!

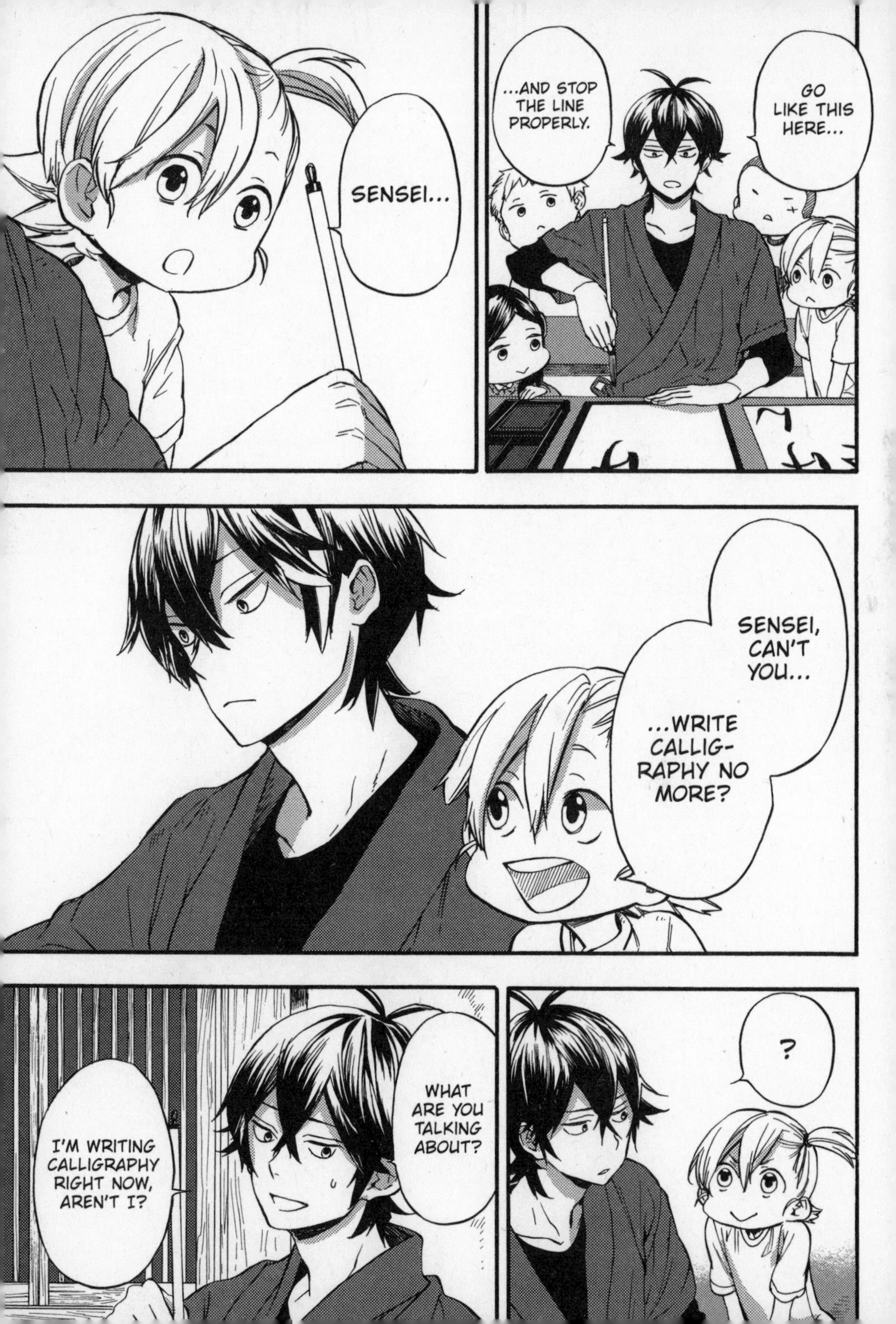
GO LIKE THIS HERE...
...AND STOP THE LINE PROPERLY.
SENSEI...
SENSEI, CAN'T YOU...
...WRITE CALLIG-RAPHY NO MORE?
?
WHAT ARE YOU TALKING ABOUT?
I'M WRITING CALLIGRAPHY RIGHT NOW, AREN'T I?

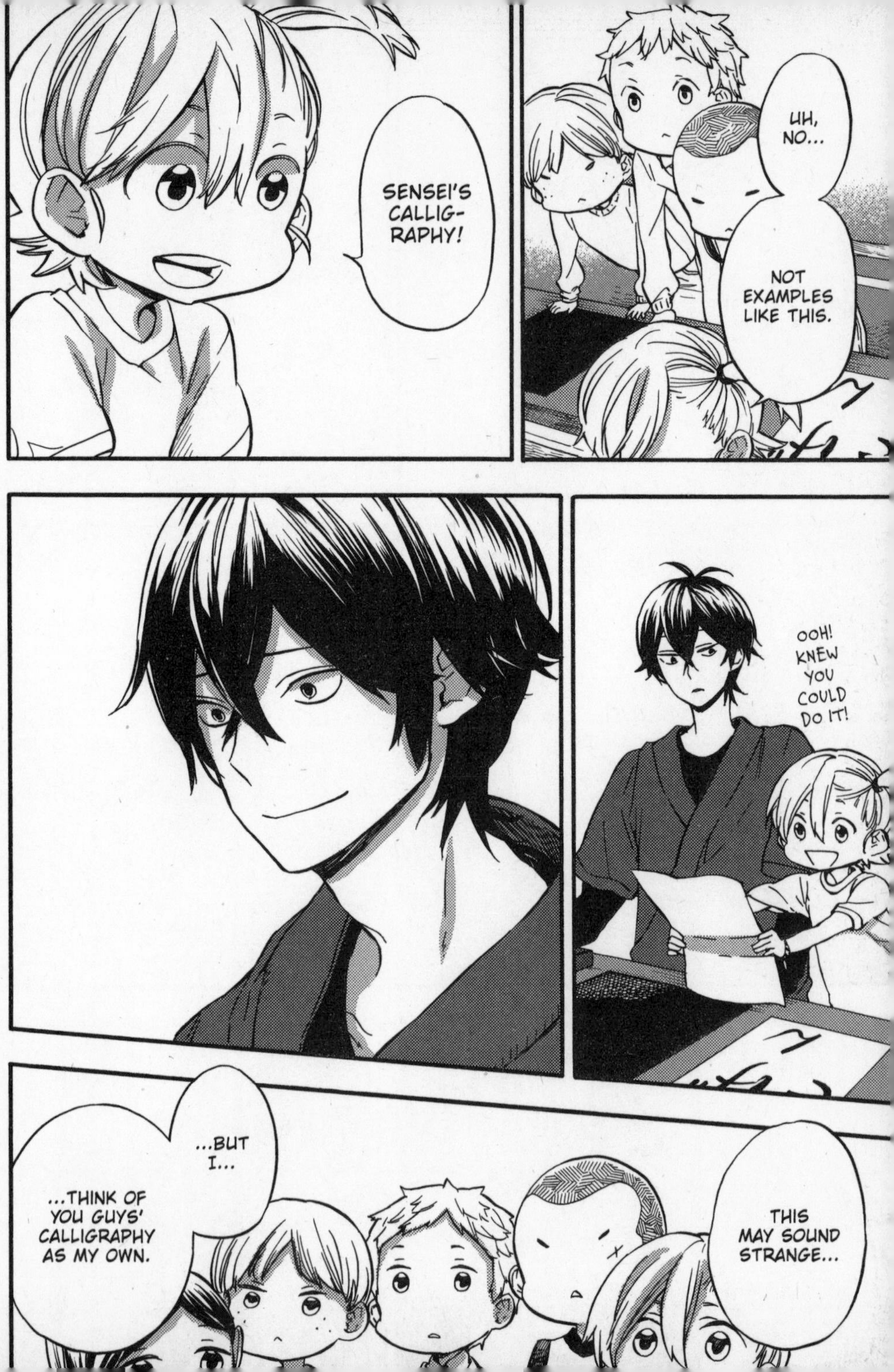
UH, NO...
NOT EXAMPLES LIKE THIS.
SENSEI'S CALLIGRAPHY!
OOH! KNEW YOU COULD DO IT!
THIS MAY SOUND STRANGE...
...BUT I...
...THINK OF YOU GUYS' CALLIGRAPHY AS MY OWN.

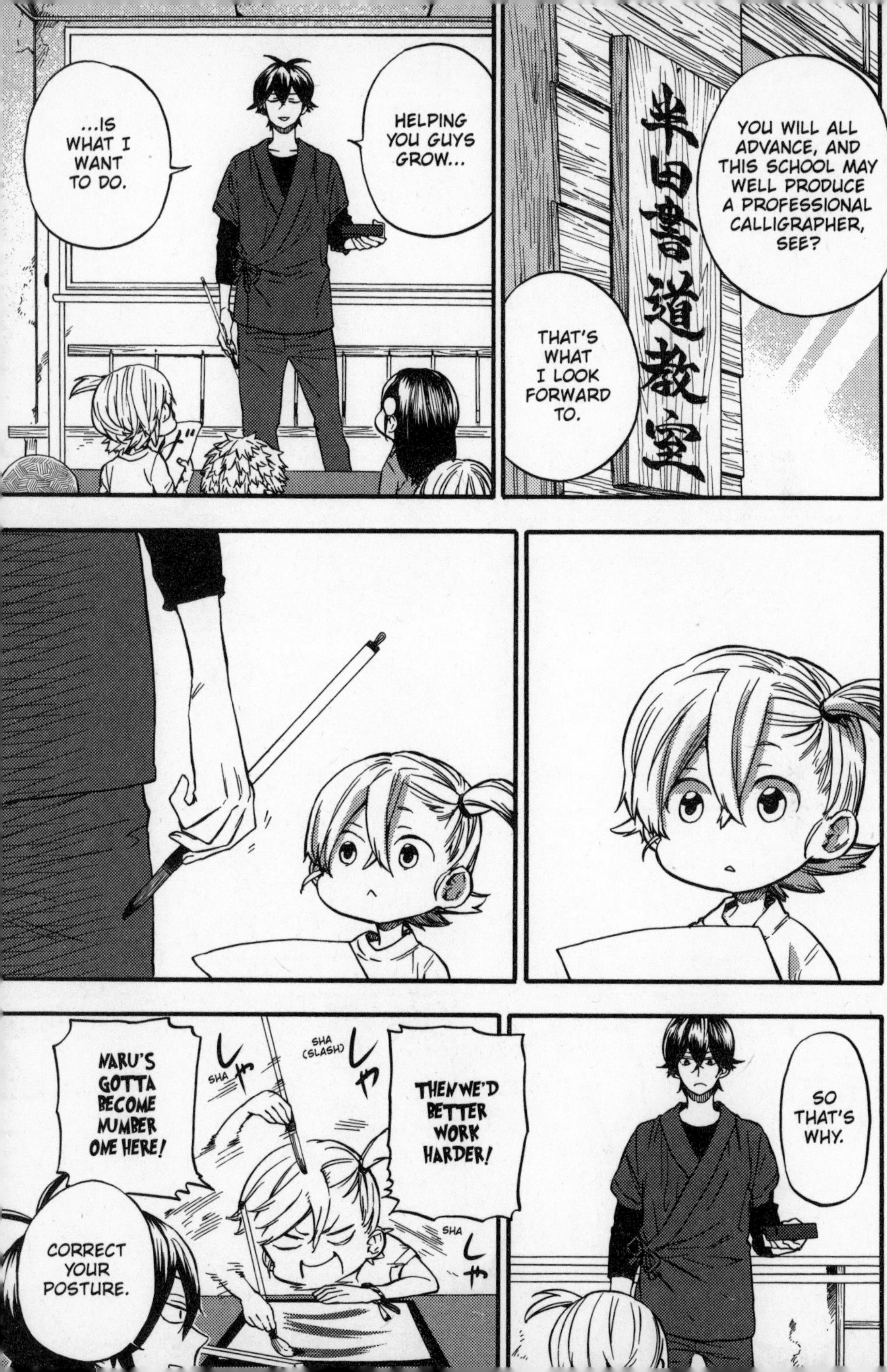
半田書道教室
YOU WILL ALL ADVANCE, AND THIS SCHOOL MAY WELL PRODUCE A PROFESSIONAL CALLIGRAPHER, SEE?
THAT'S WHAT I LOOK FORWARD TO.
HELPING YOU GUYS GROW...
...IS WHAT I WANT TO DO.
SO THAT'S WHY.
SHA (SLASH)
しゃ
THEN WE'D BETTER WORK HARDER!
SHA
しゃ
NARU'S GOTTA BECOME NUMBER ONE HERE!
SHA
しゃ
CORRECT YOUR POSTURE.

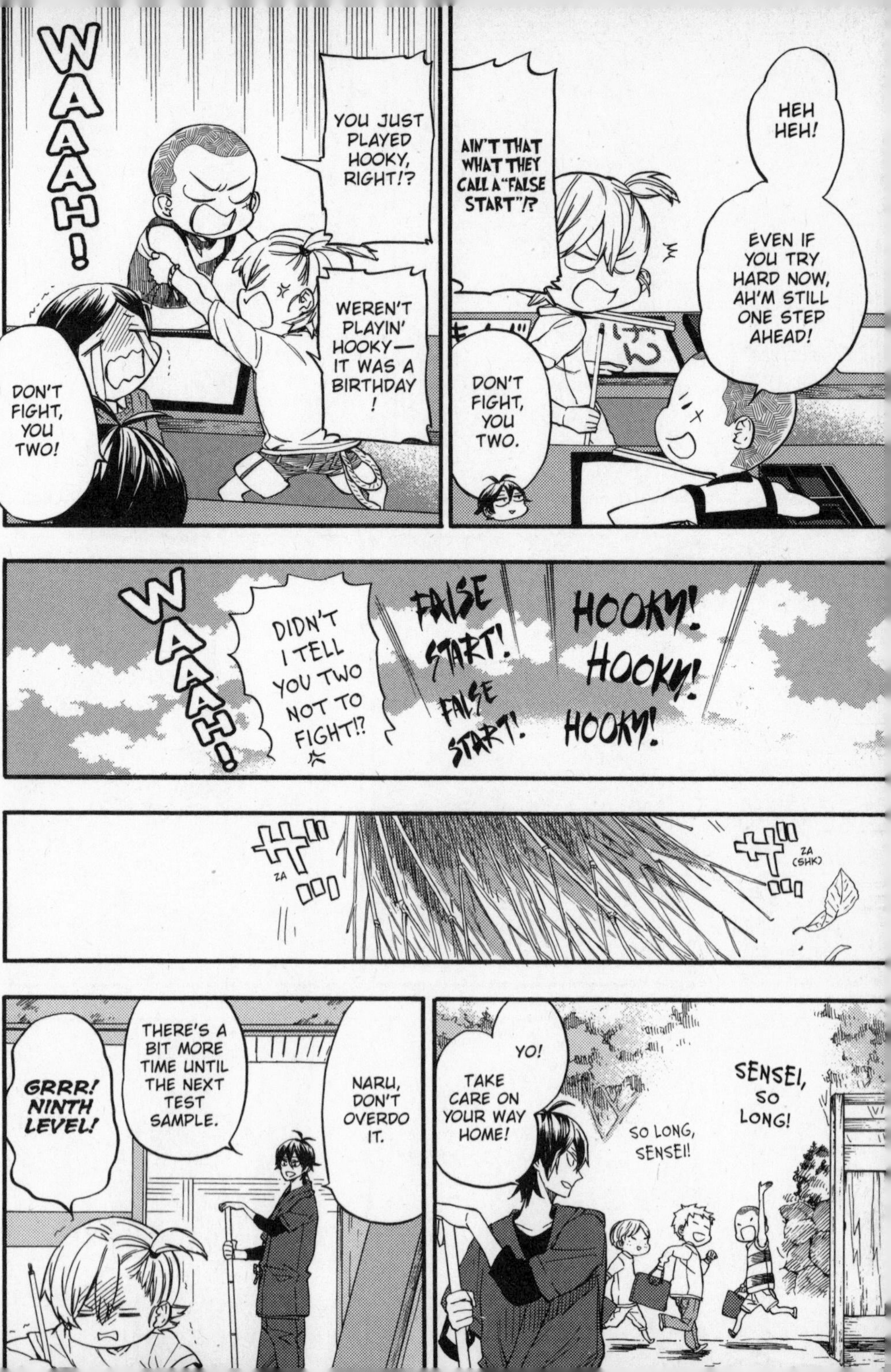
HEH HEH!
EVEN IF YOU TRY HARD NOW, AH'M STILL ONE STEP AHEAD!
AIN'T THAT WHAT THEY CALL A "FALSE START"!?
DON'T FIGHT, YOU TWO.
YOU JUST PLAYED HOOKY, RIGHT!?
WAAAAH!
WEREN'T PLAYIN' HOOKY— IT WAS A BIRTHDAY!
DON'T FIGHT, YOU TWO!
HOOKY! HOOKY! HOOKY!
FALSE START! FALSE START!
DIDN'T I TELL YOU TWO NOT TO FIGHT!?
WAAAAH!
ザッ
ZA (SHK)
ザッ
ZA
SENSEI, SO LONG!
SO LONG, SENSEI!
YO!
TAKE CARE ON YOUR WAY HOME!
NARU, DON'T OVERDO IT.
THERE'S A BIT MORE TIME UNTIL THE NEXT TEST SAMPLE.
GRRR! NINTH LEVEL!

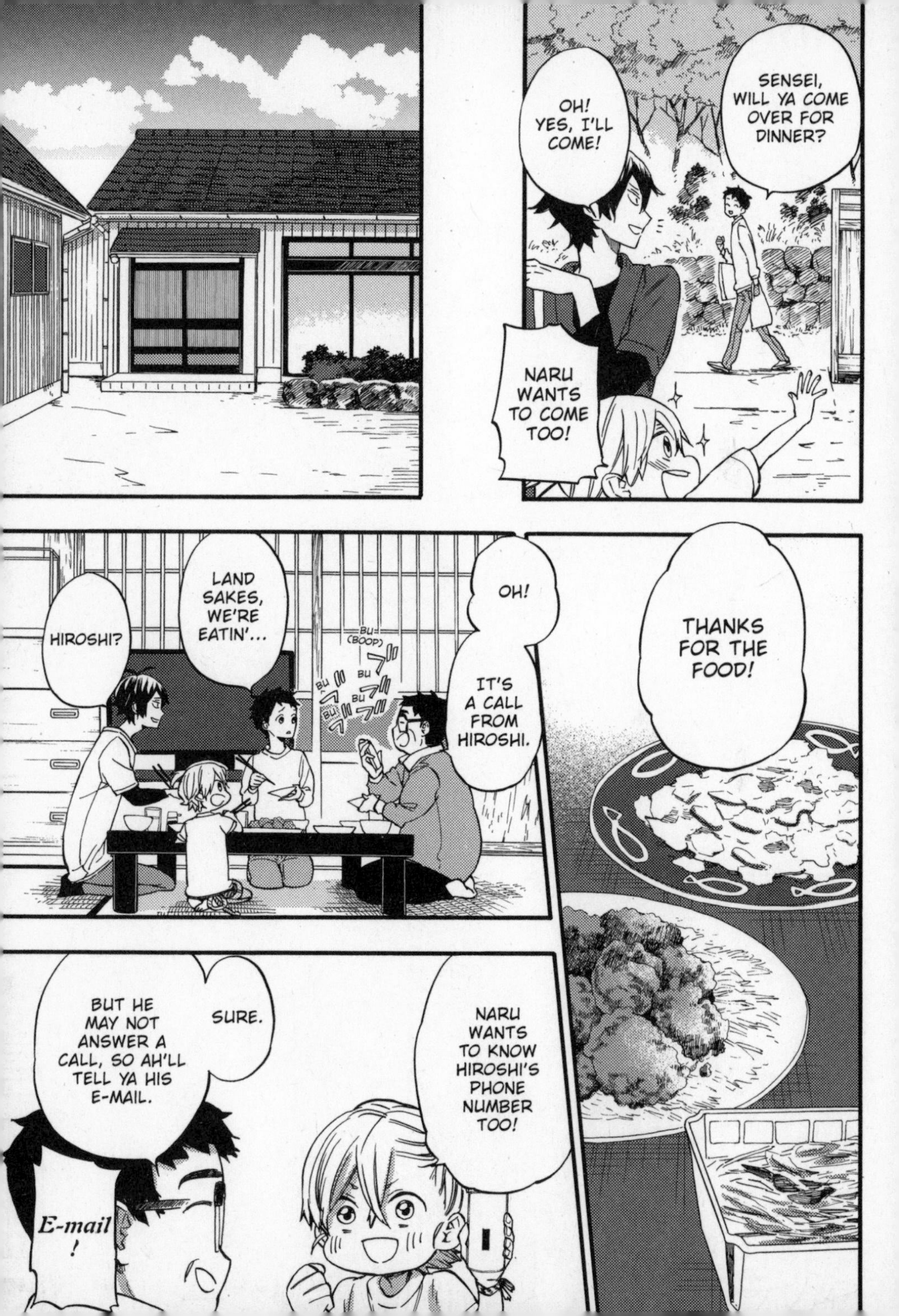
SENSEI, WILL YA COME OVER FOR DINNER?
OH! YES, I'LL COME!
NARU WANTS TO COME TOO!
THANKS FOR THE FOOD!
OH!
IT'S A CALL FROM HIROSHI.
BU BU BU BU (BOOP)
LAND SAKES, WE'RE EATIN'...
HIROSHI?
NARU WANTS TO KNOW HIROSHI'S PHONE NUMBER TOO!
SURE.
BUT HE MAY NOT ANSWER A CALL, SO AH'LL TELL YA HIS E-MAIL.
E-mail!

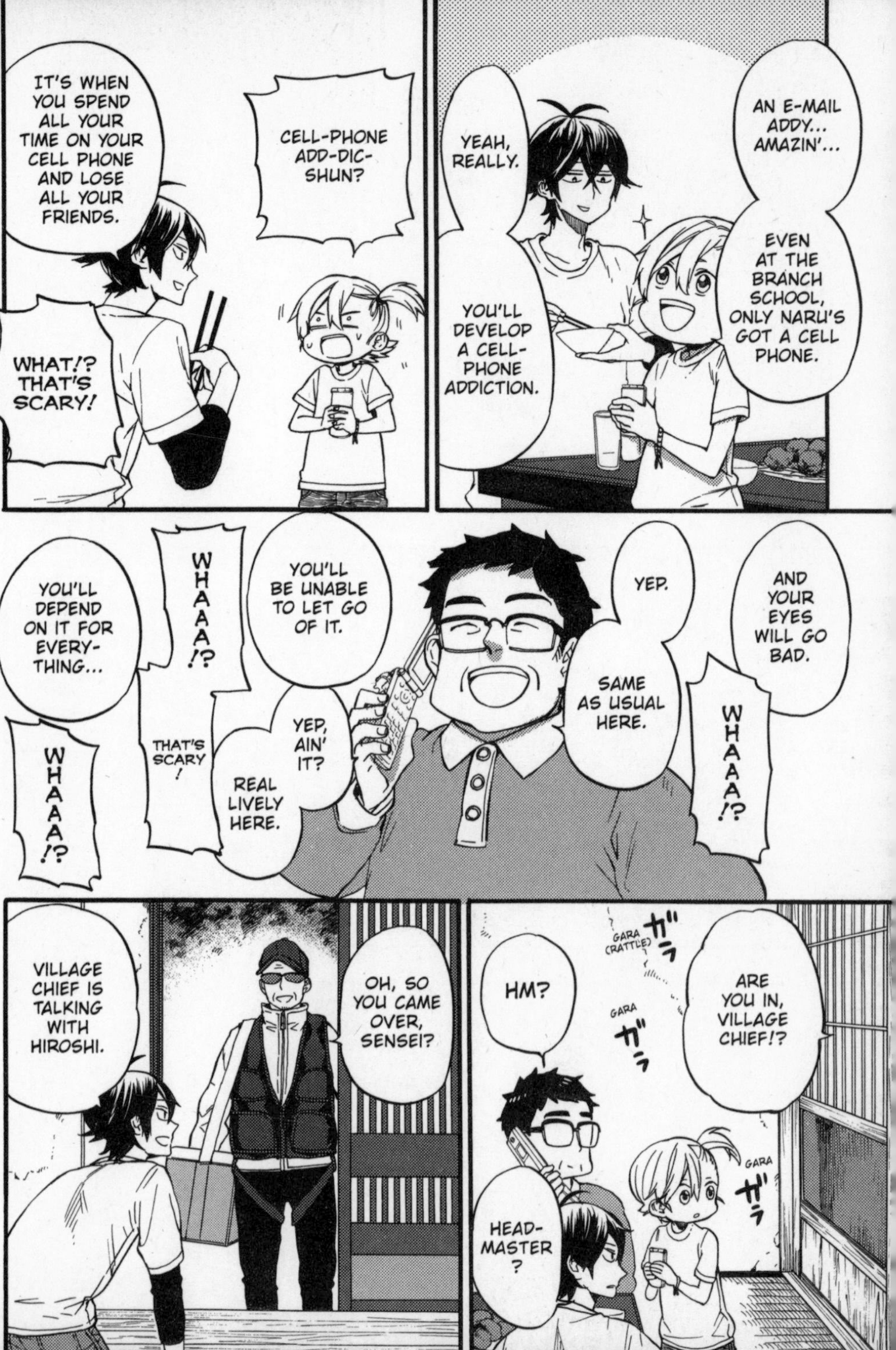
AN E-MAIL ADDY... AMAZIN'...
EVEN AT THE BRANCH SCHOOL, ONLY NARU'S GOT A CELL PHONE.
YEAH, REALLY.
YOU'LL DEVELOP A CELL-PHONE ADDICTION.
CELL-PHONE ADD-DIC-SHUN?
IT'S WHEN YOU SPEND ALL YOUR TIME ON YOUR CELL PHONE AND LOSE ALL YOUR FRIENDS.
WHAT!? THAT'S SCARY!
AND YOUR EYES WILL GO BAD.
WHAAAA!?
YEP.
SAME AS USUAL HERE.
YOU'LL BE UNABLE TO LET GO OF IT.
WHAAAA!?
YEP, AIN' IT?
REAL LIVELY HERE.
THAT'S SCARY!
YOU'LL DEPEND ON IT FOR EVERY-THING...
WHAAAA!?
GARA (RATTLE)
ARE YOU IN, VILLAGE CHIEF!?
GARA
HM?
GARA
HEAD-MASTER?
OH, SO YOU CAME OVER, SENSEI?
VILLAGE CHIEF IS TALKING WITH HIROSHI.

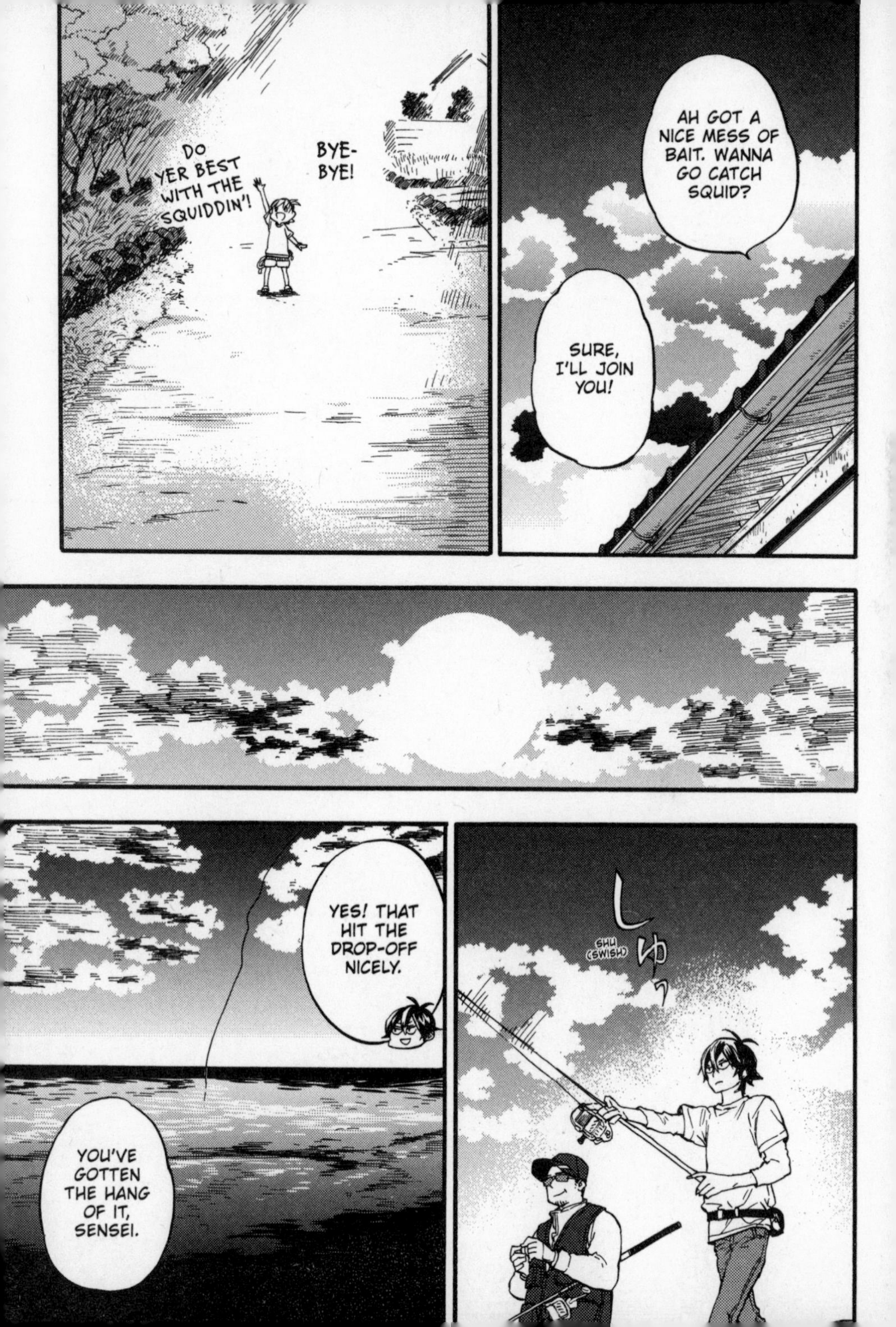
AH GOT A NICE MESS OF BAIT. WANNA GO CATCH SQUID?
SURE, I'LL JOIN YOU!
BYE-BYE!
DO YER BEST WITH THE SQUIDDIN'!
しゅっ
SHU (SWISH)
YES! THAT HIT THE DROP-OFF NICELY.
YOU'VE GOTTEN THE HANG OF IT, SENSEI.

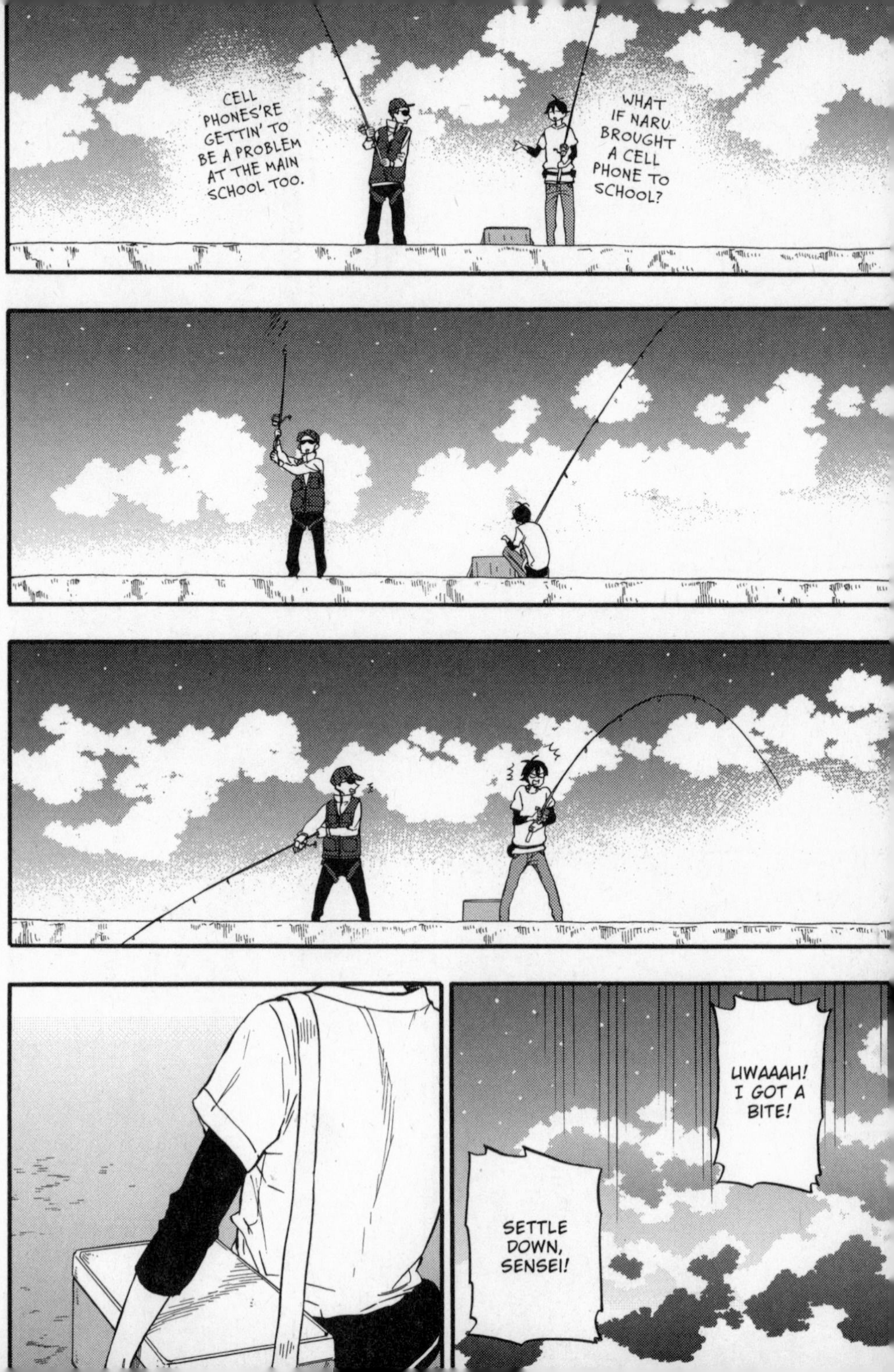
WHAT IF NARU BROUGHT A CELL PHONE TO SCHOOL?
CELL PHONES'RE GETTIN' TO BE A PROBLEM AT THE MAIN SCHOOL TOO.
UWAAAH! I GOT A BITE!
SETTLE DOWN, SENSEI!

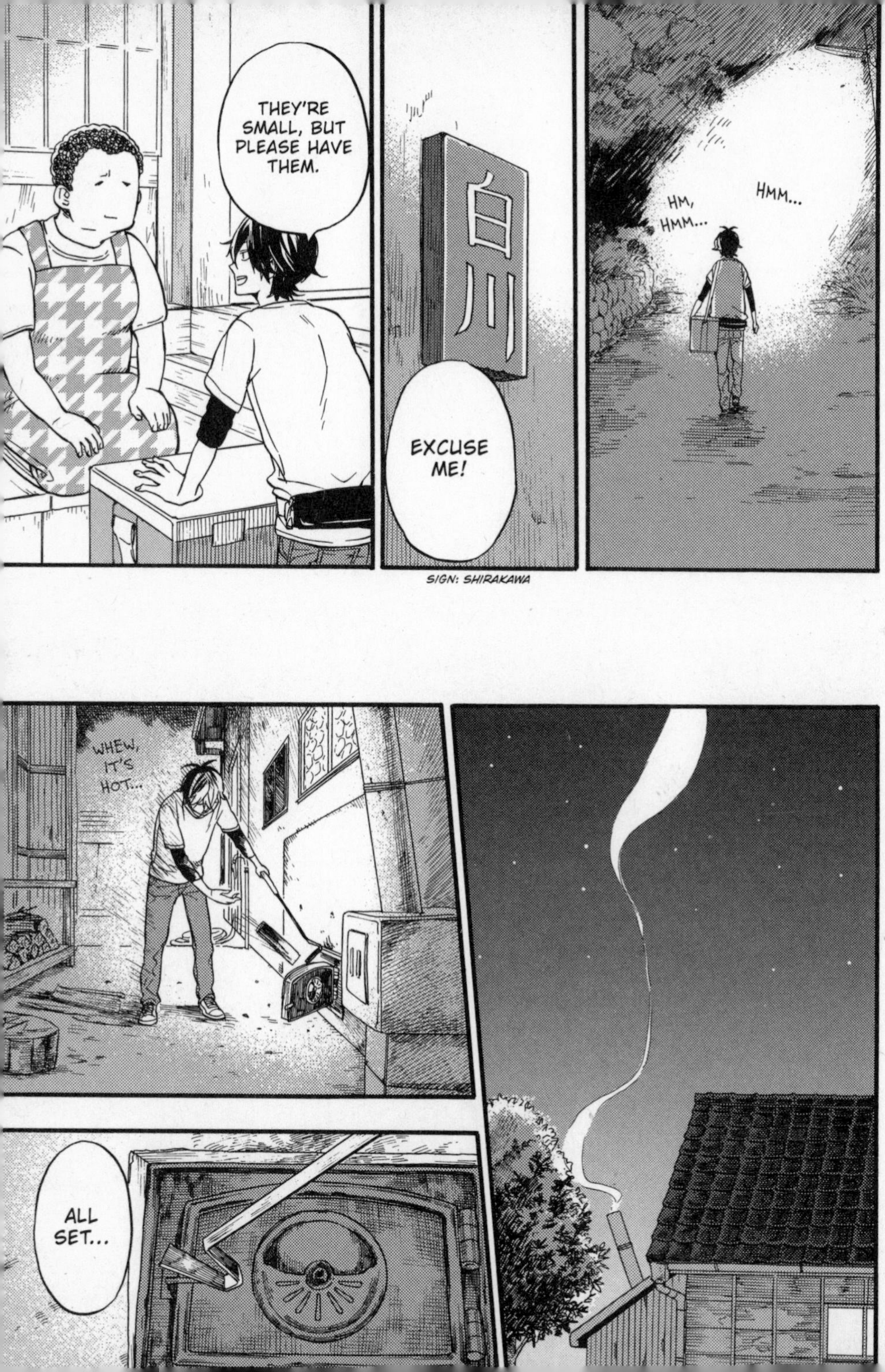
HMM...
HM, HMM...
EXCUSE ME!
SIGN: SHIRAKAWA
THEY'RE SMALL, BUT PLEASE HAVE THEM.
WHEW, IT'S HOT...
ALL SET...

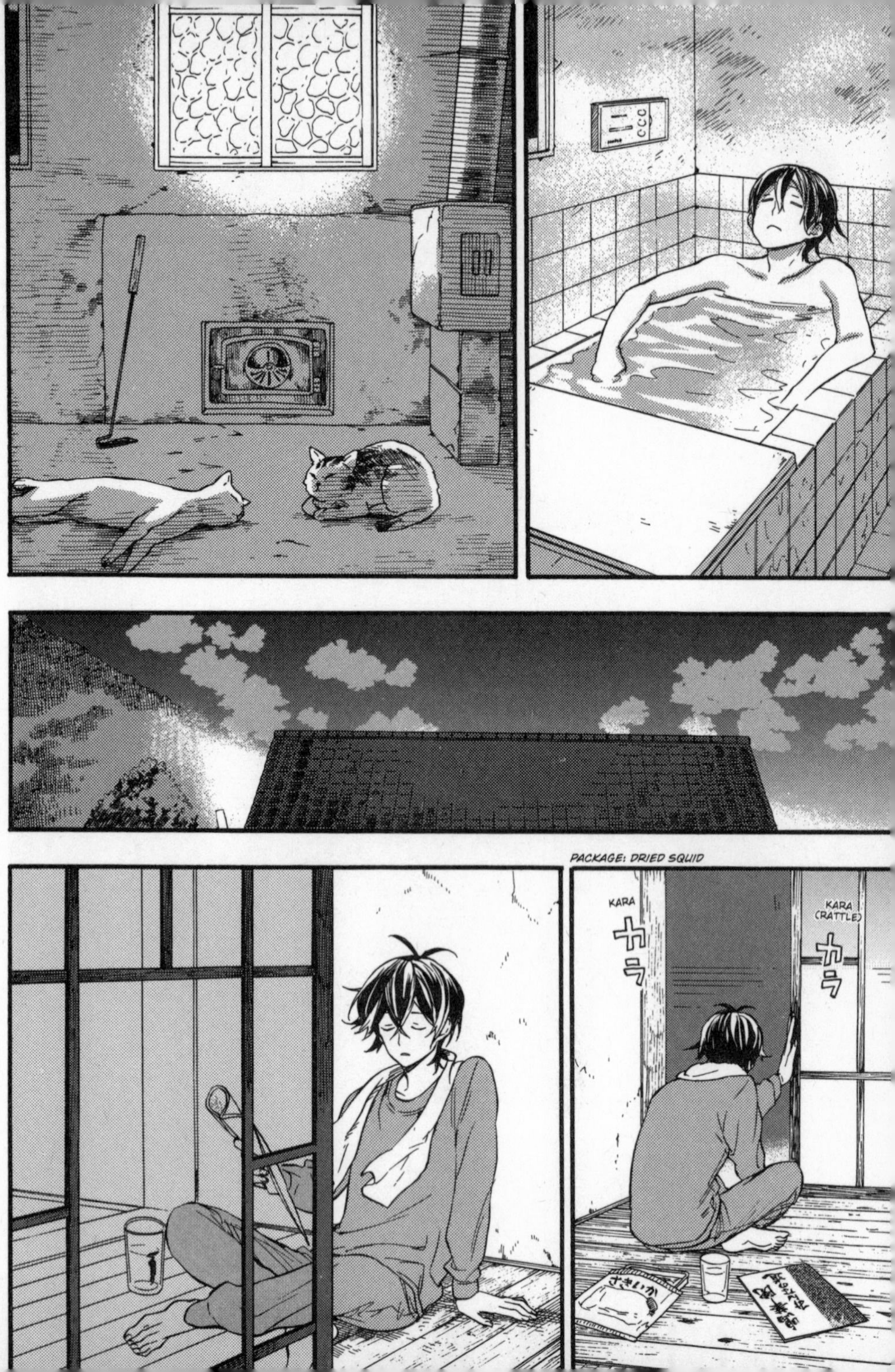
PACKAGE: DRIED SQUID
カラ
KARA (RATTLE)
カラ
KARA
さきいか

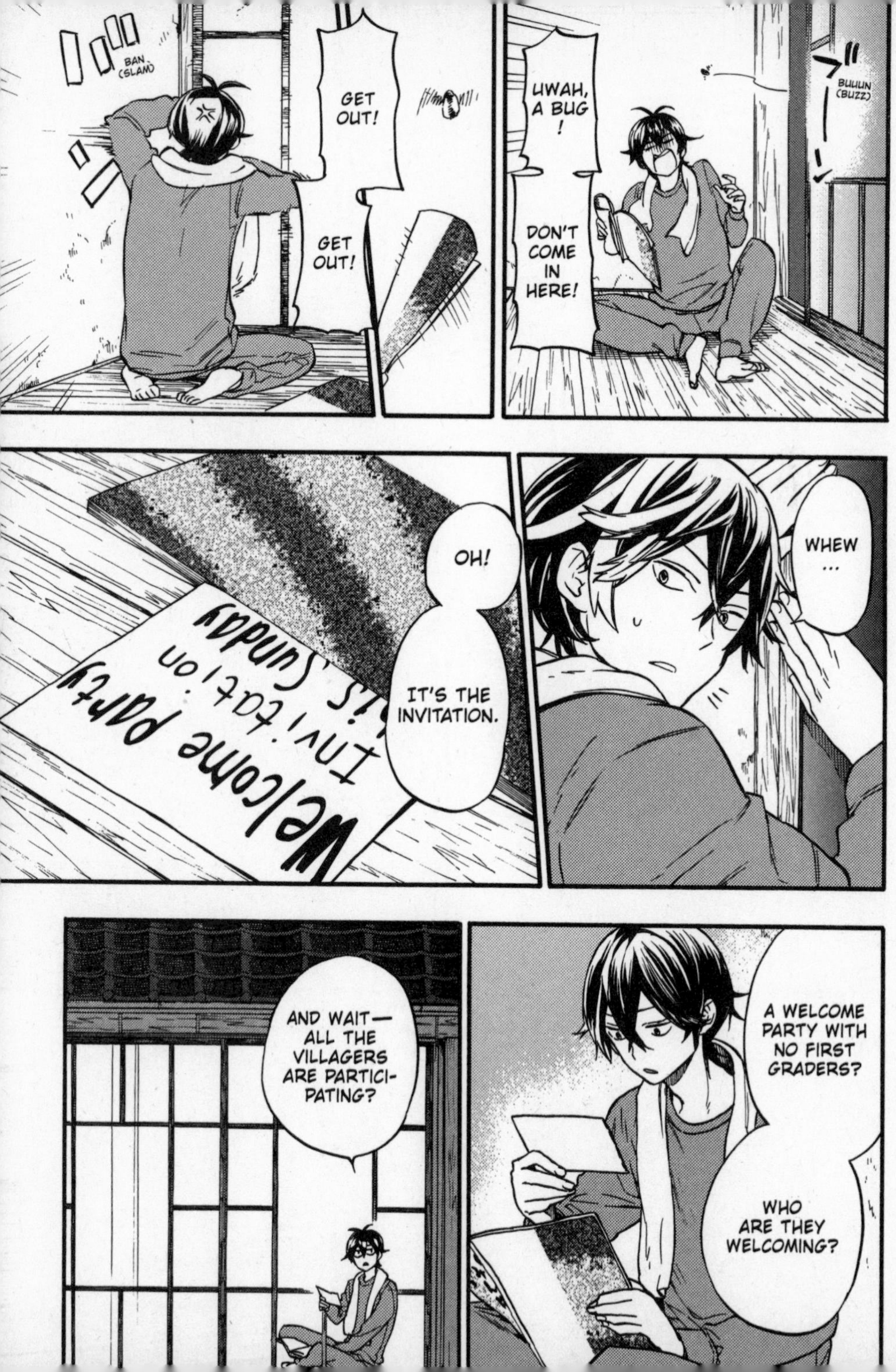
UWAH, A BUG!
DON'T COME IN HERE!
BUUUN (BUZZ)
GET OUT!
GET OUT!
BAN (SLAM)
WHEW...
OH!
IT'S THE INVITATION.
Welcome party
Invitation
A WELCOME PARTY WITH NO FIRST GRADERS?
WHO ARE THEY WELCOMING?
AND WAIT— ALL THE VILLAGERS ARE PARTICIPATING?

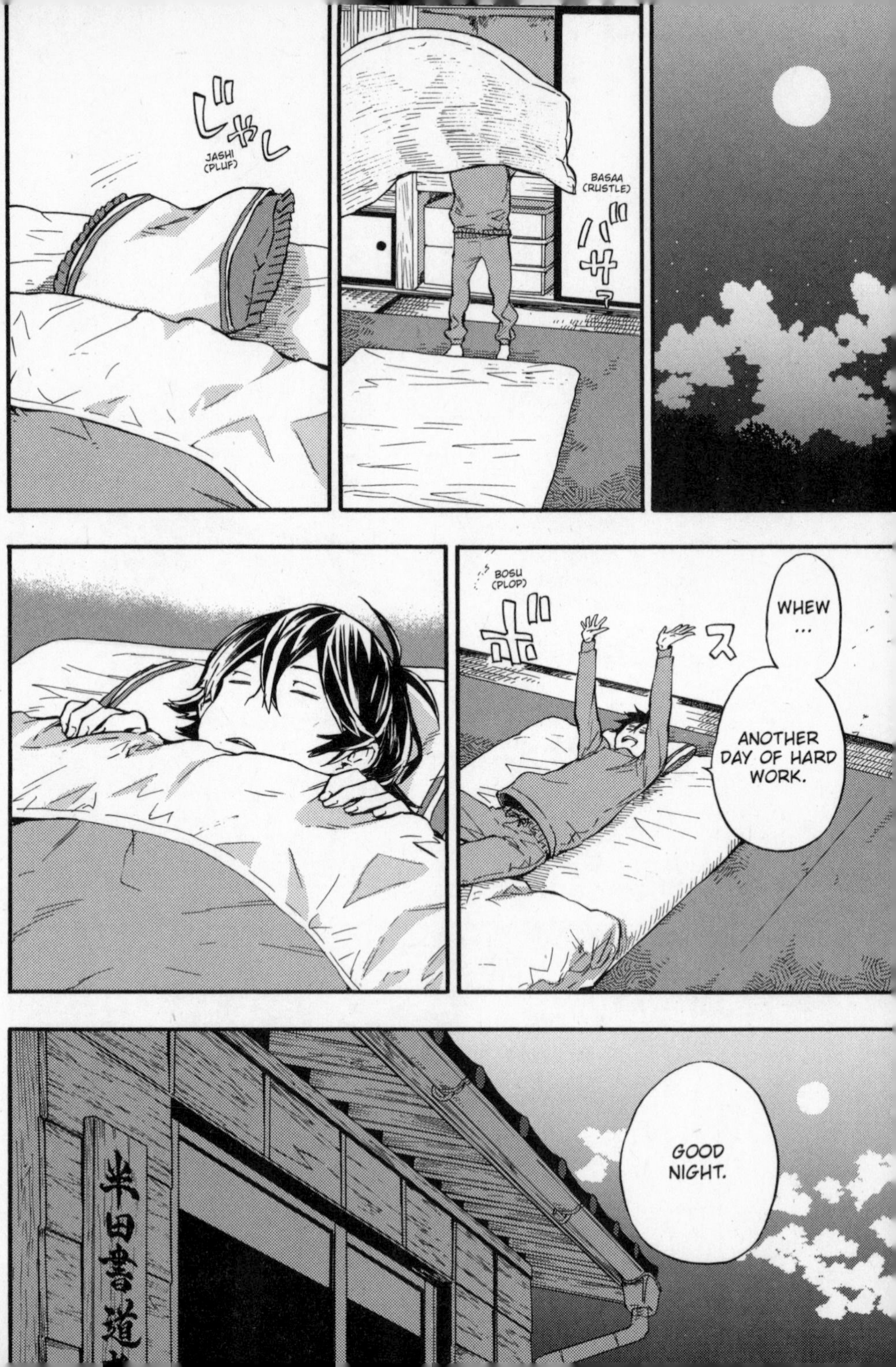
バサァ
BASAA (RUSTLE)
じゃし
JASHI (PLUF)
ボス
BOSU (PLOP)
WHEW ...
ANOTHER DAY OF HARD WORK.
GOOD NIGHT.
半田書道

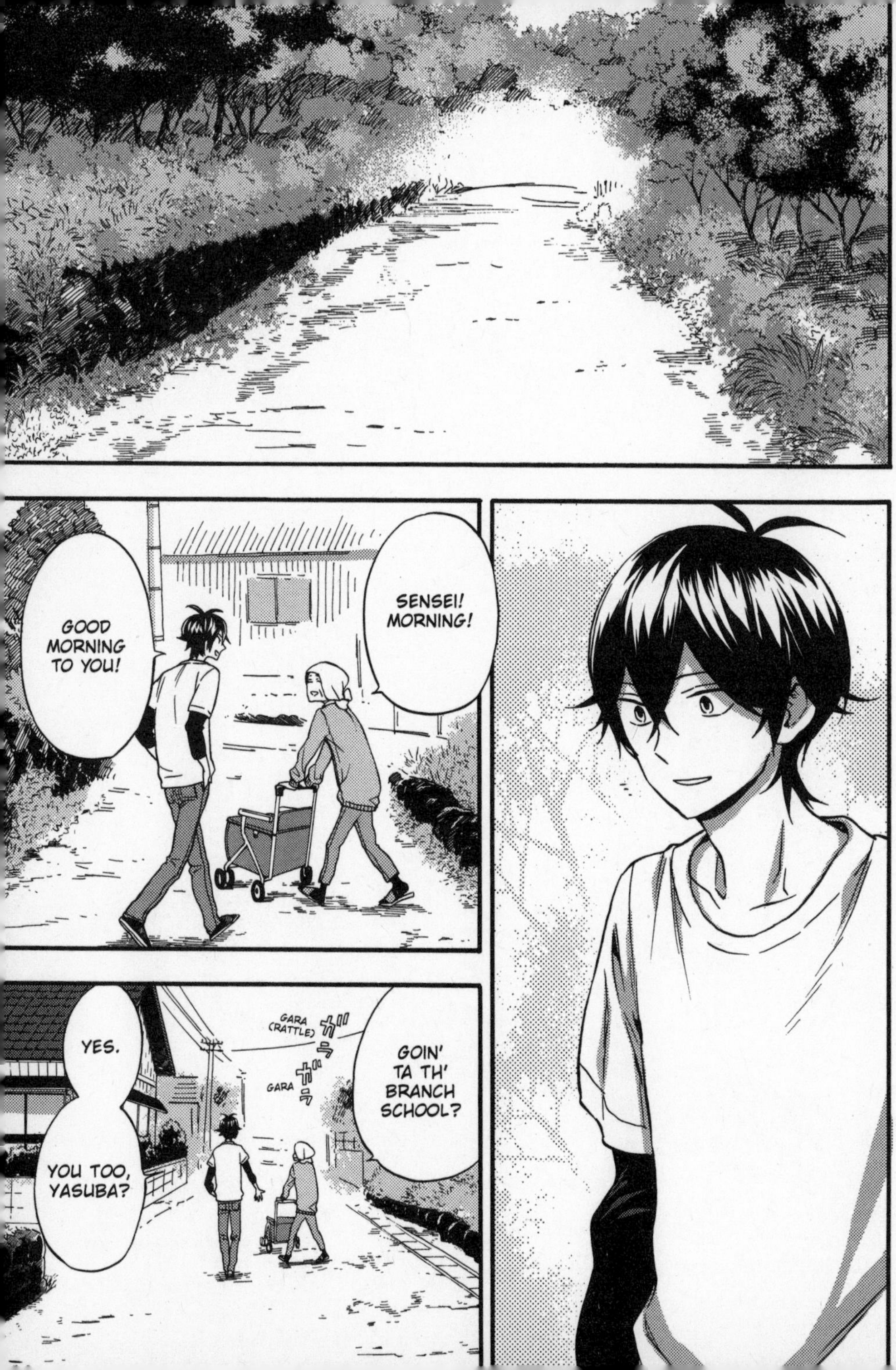
SENSEI! MORNING!
GOOD MORNING TO YOU!
GOIN' TA TH' BRANCH SCHOOL?
GARA (RATTLE) ガラ
GARA ガラ
YES.
YOU TOO, YASUBA?

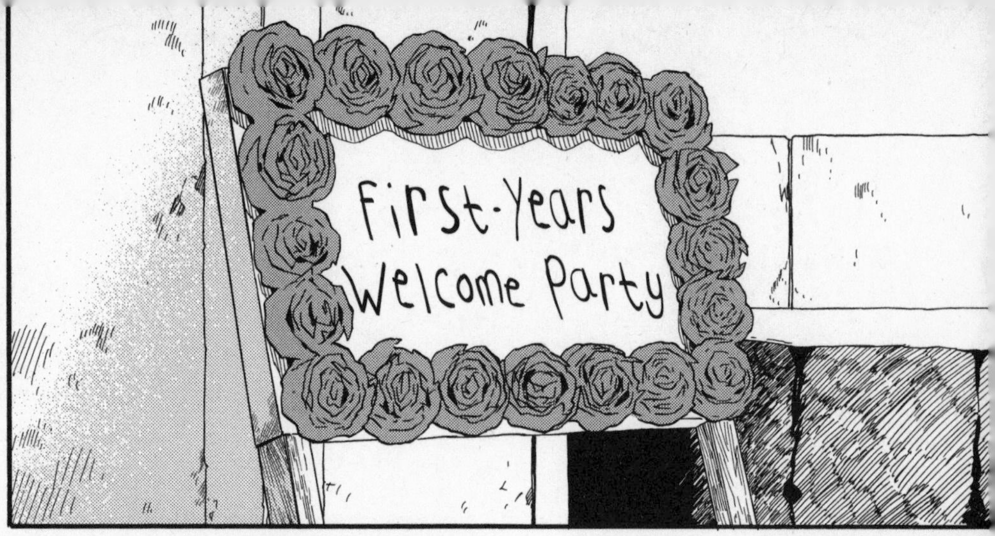
First-Years
Welcome Party

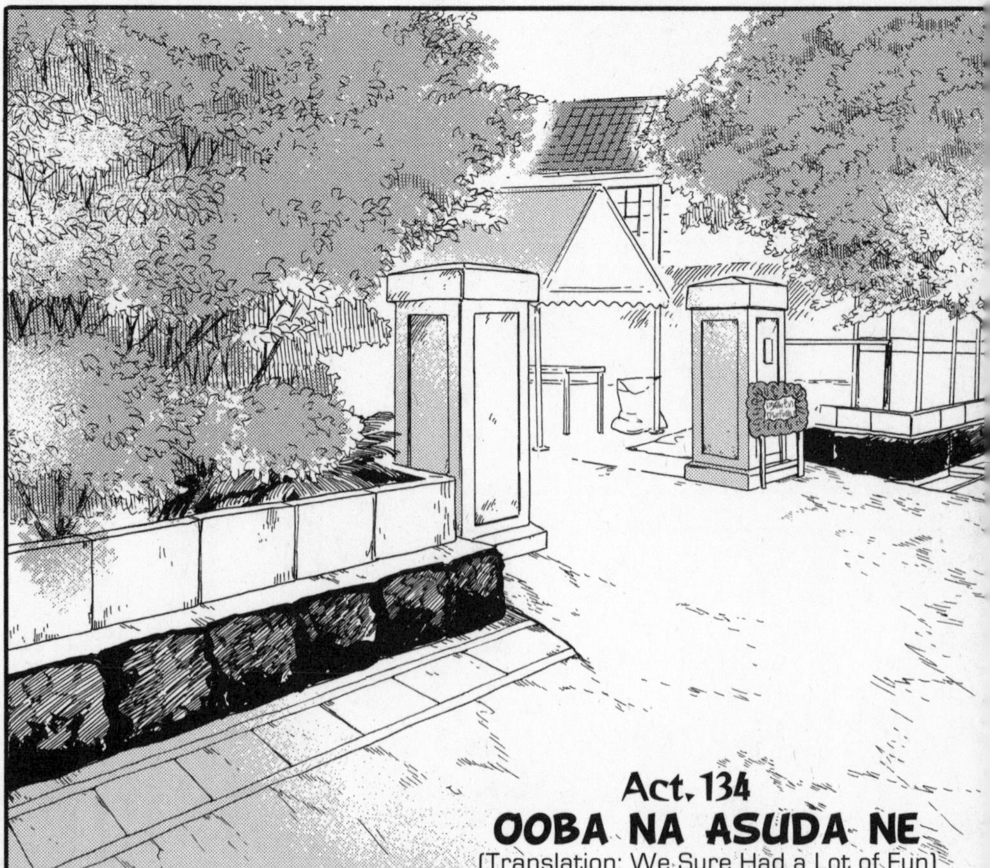

Act. 134
OOBA NA ASUDA NE
(Translation: We Sure Had a Lot of Fun)

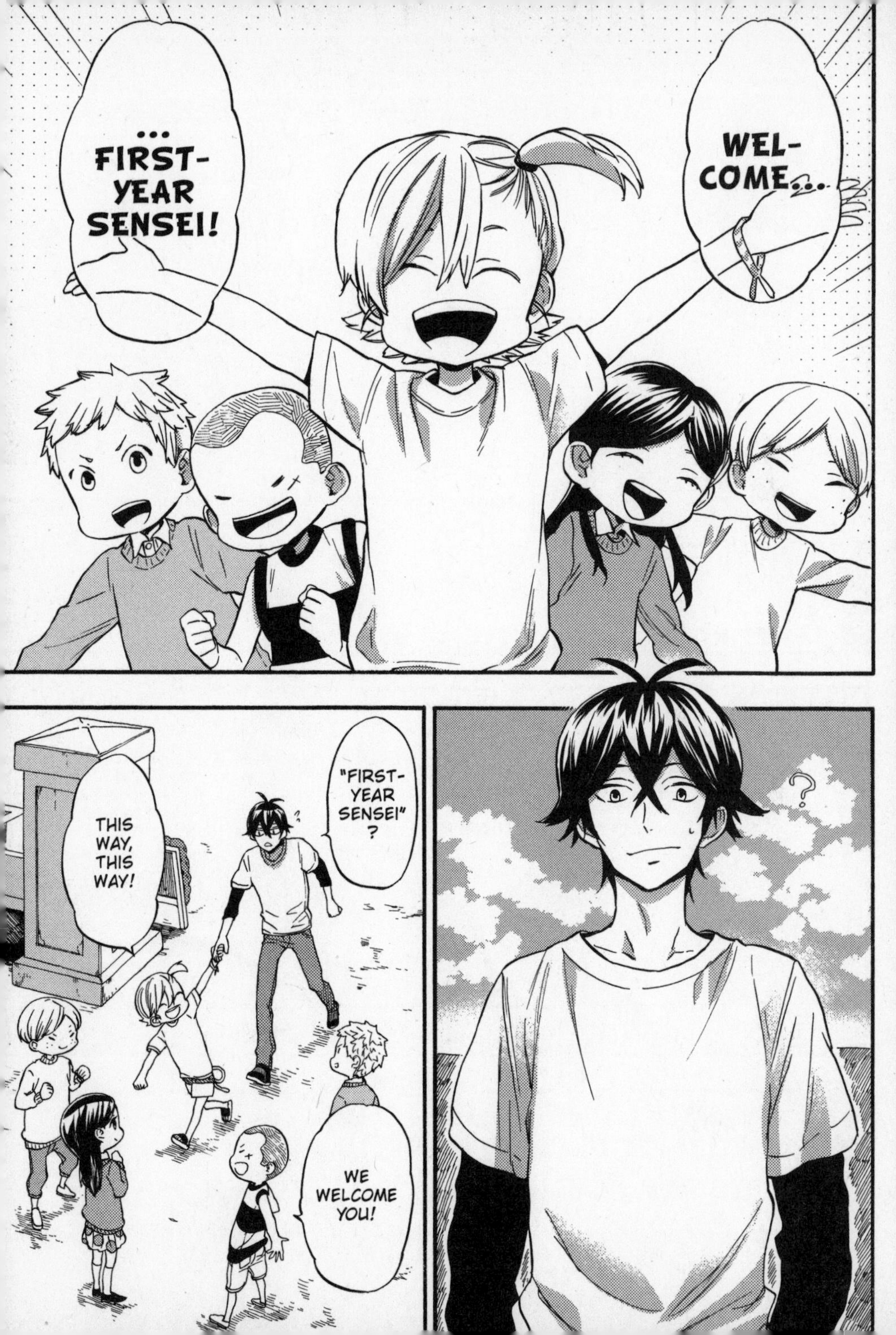
WEL-COME...
...FIRST-YEAR SENSEI!
"FIRST-YEAR SENSEI"?
THIS WAY, THIS WAY!
WE WELCOME YOU!

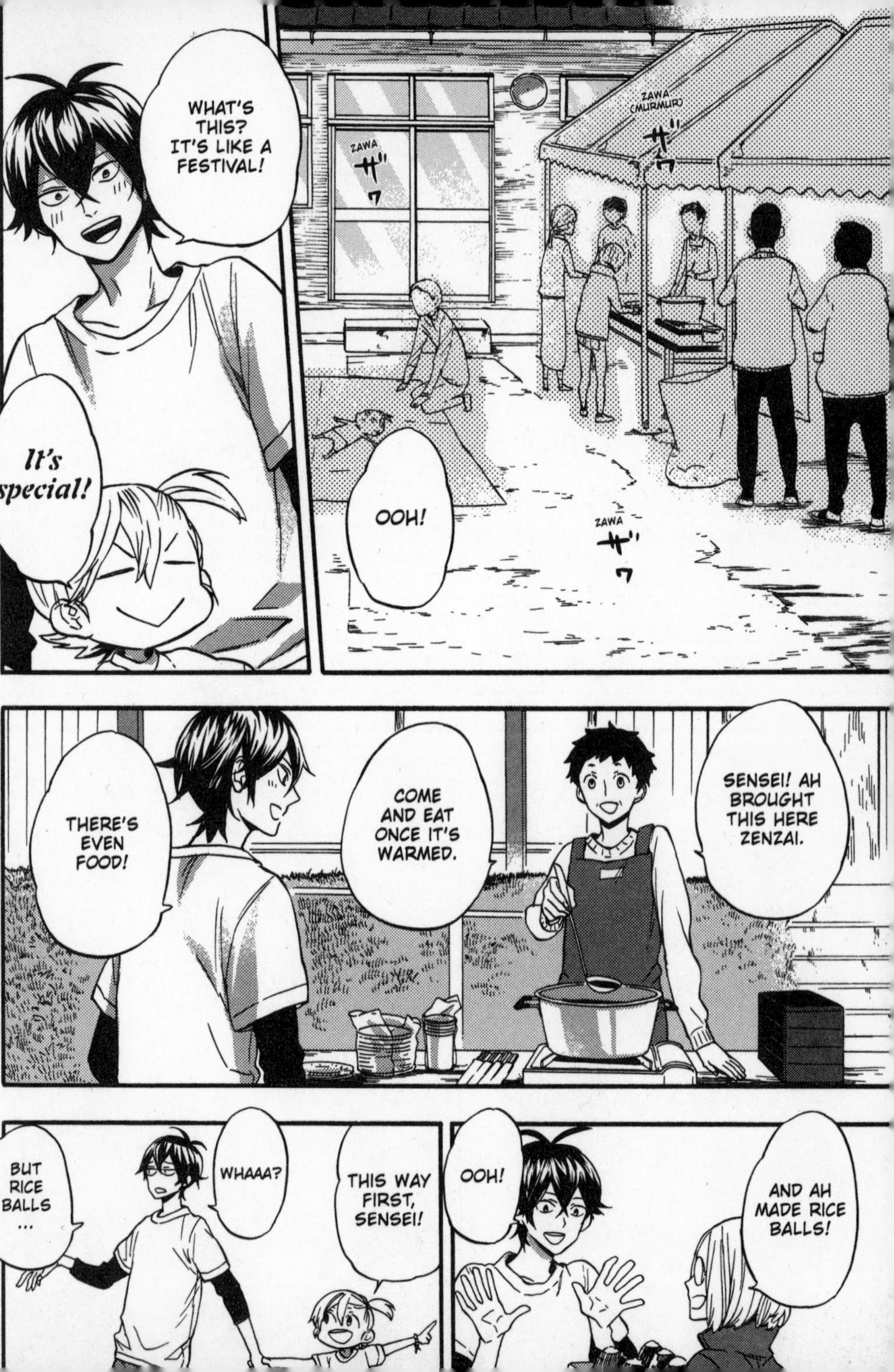
ZAWA (MURMUR)
ザワ
ZAWA
ザワ
OOH!
ZAWA
ザワ
WHAT'S THIS? IT'S LIKE A FESTIVAL!
It's special!
SENSEI! AH BROUGHT THIS HERE ZENZAI.
COME AND EAT ONCE IT'S WARMED.
THERE'S EVEN FOOD!
AND AH MADE RICE BALLS!
OOH!
THIS WAY FIRST, SENSEI!
WHAAA?
BUT RICE BALLS ...

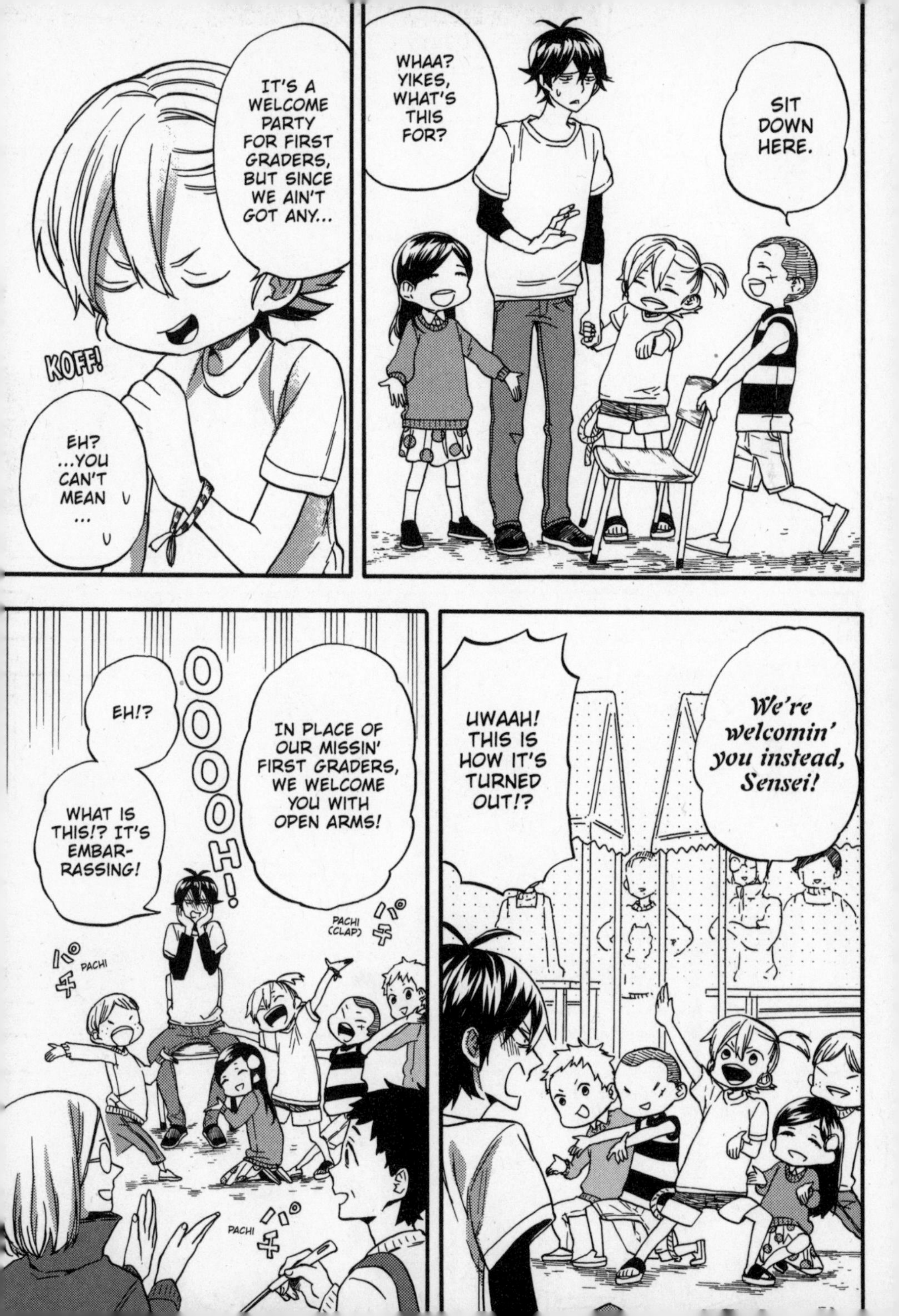
SIT DOWN HERE.
WHAA? YIKES, WHAT'S THIS FOR?
IT'S A WELCOME PARTY FOR FIRST GRADERS, BUT SINCE WE AIN'T GOT ANY...
KOFF!
EH? ...YOU CAN'T MEAN ...
We're welcomin' you instead, Sensei!
UWAAH! THIS IS HOW IT'S TURNED OUT!?
IN PLACE OF OUR MISSIN' FIRST GRADERS, WE WELCOME YOU WITH OPEN ARMS!
OOOOH!
EH!?
WHAT IS THIS!? IT'S EMBARRASSING!
PACHI (CLAP)
PACHI
PACHI

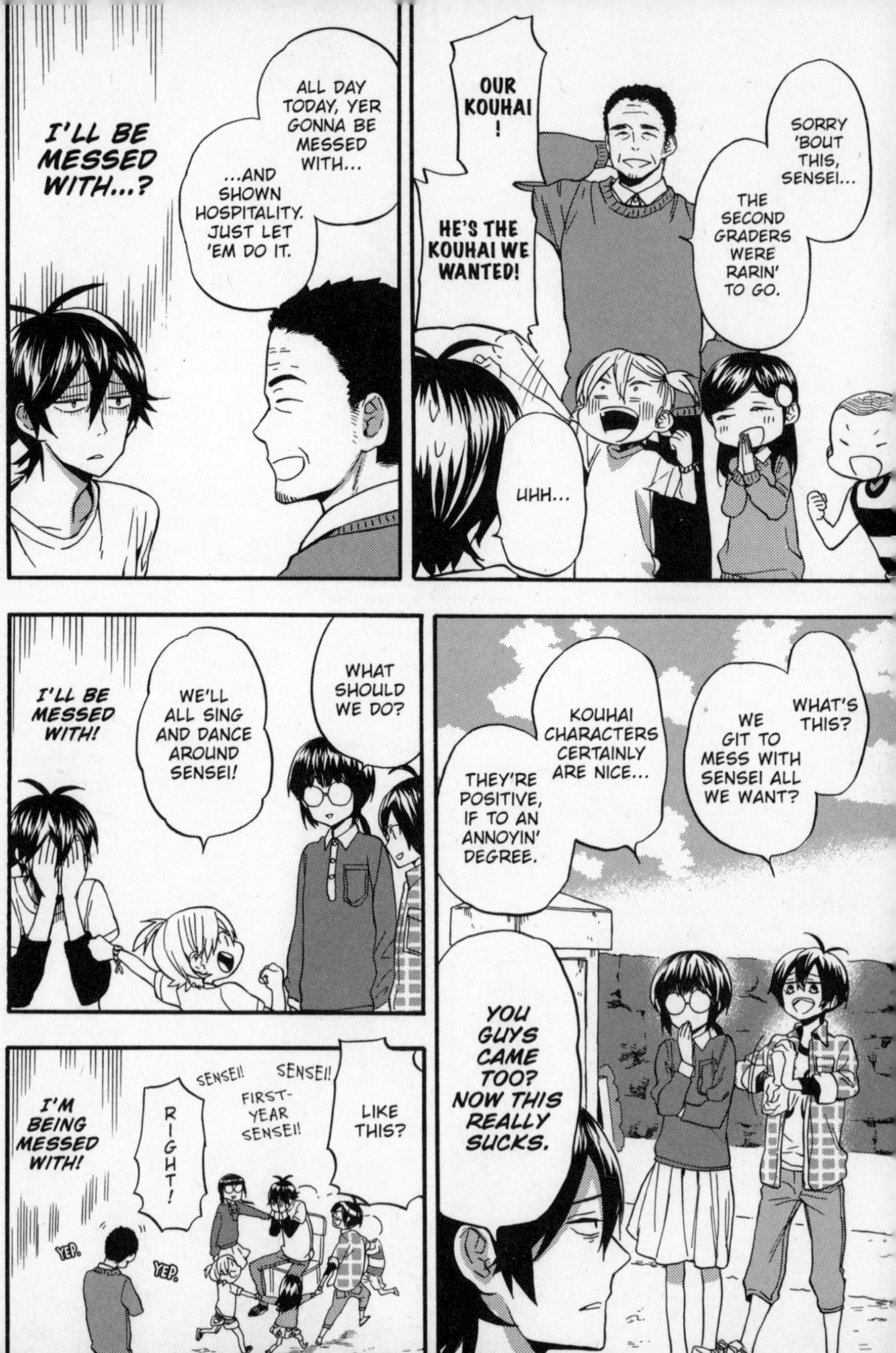
SORRY 'BOUT THIS, SENSEI...
THE SECOND GRADERS WERE RARIN' TO GO.
OUR KOUHAI!
HE'S THE KOUHAI WE WANTED!
UHH...
ALL DAY TODAY, YER GONNA BE MESSED WITH...
...AND SHOWN HOSPITALITY. JUST LET 'EM DO IT.
I'LL BE MESSED WITH...?
WHAT'S THIS?
WE GIT TO MESS WITH SENSEI ALL WE WANT?
KOUHAI CHARACTERS CERTAINLY ARE NICE...
THEY'RE POSITIVE, IF TO AN ANNOYIN' DEGREE.
YOU GUYS CAME TOO? NOW THIS REALLY SUCKS.
WHAT SHOULD WE DO?
WE'LL ALL SING AND DANCE AROUND SENSEI!
I'LL BE MESSED WITH!
LIKE THIS?
SENSEI!
SENSEI!
FIRST-YEAR SENSEI!
RIGHT!
I'M BEING MESSED WITH!
YEP.
YEP.

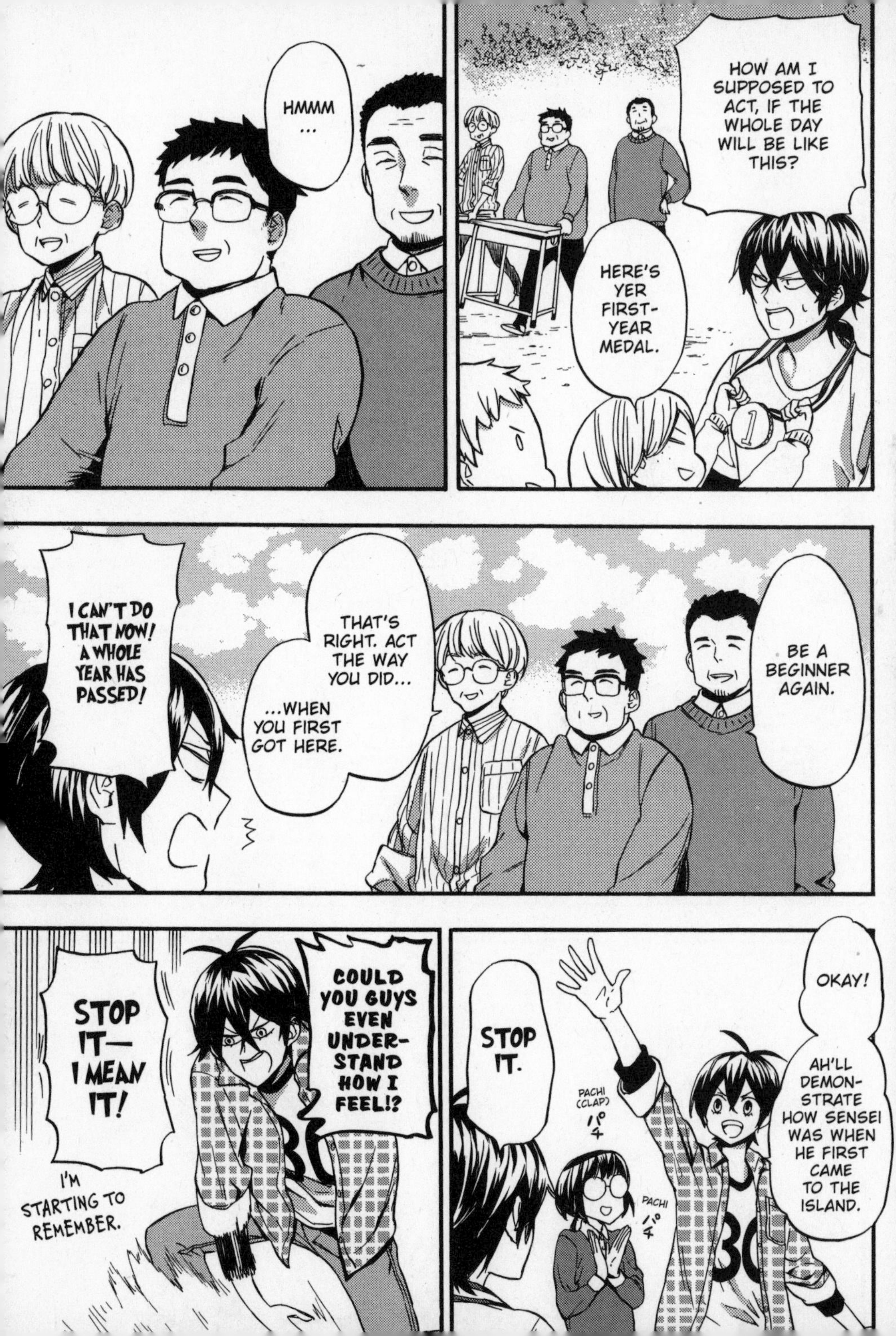
HOW AM I SUPPOSED TO ACT, IF THE WHOLE DAY WILL BE LIKE THIS?
HERE'S YER FIRST-YEAR MEDAL.
HMMM...
BE A BEGINNER AGAIN.
THAT'S RIGHT. ACT THE WAY YOU DID...
...WHEN YOU FIRST GOT HERE.
I CAN'T DO THAT NOW! A WHOLE YEAR HAS PASSED!
OKAY!
AH'LL DEMONSTRATE HOW SENSEI WAS WHEN HE FIRST CAME TO THE ISLAND.
PACHI (CLAP)
PACHI
STOP IT.
COULD YOU GUYS EVEN UNDERSTAND HOW I FEEL!?
STOP IT—I MEAN IT!
I'M STARTING TO REMEMBER.

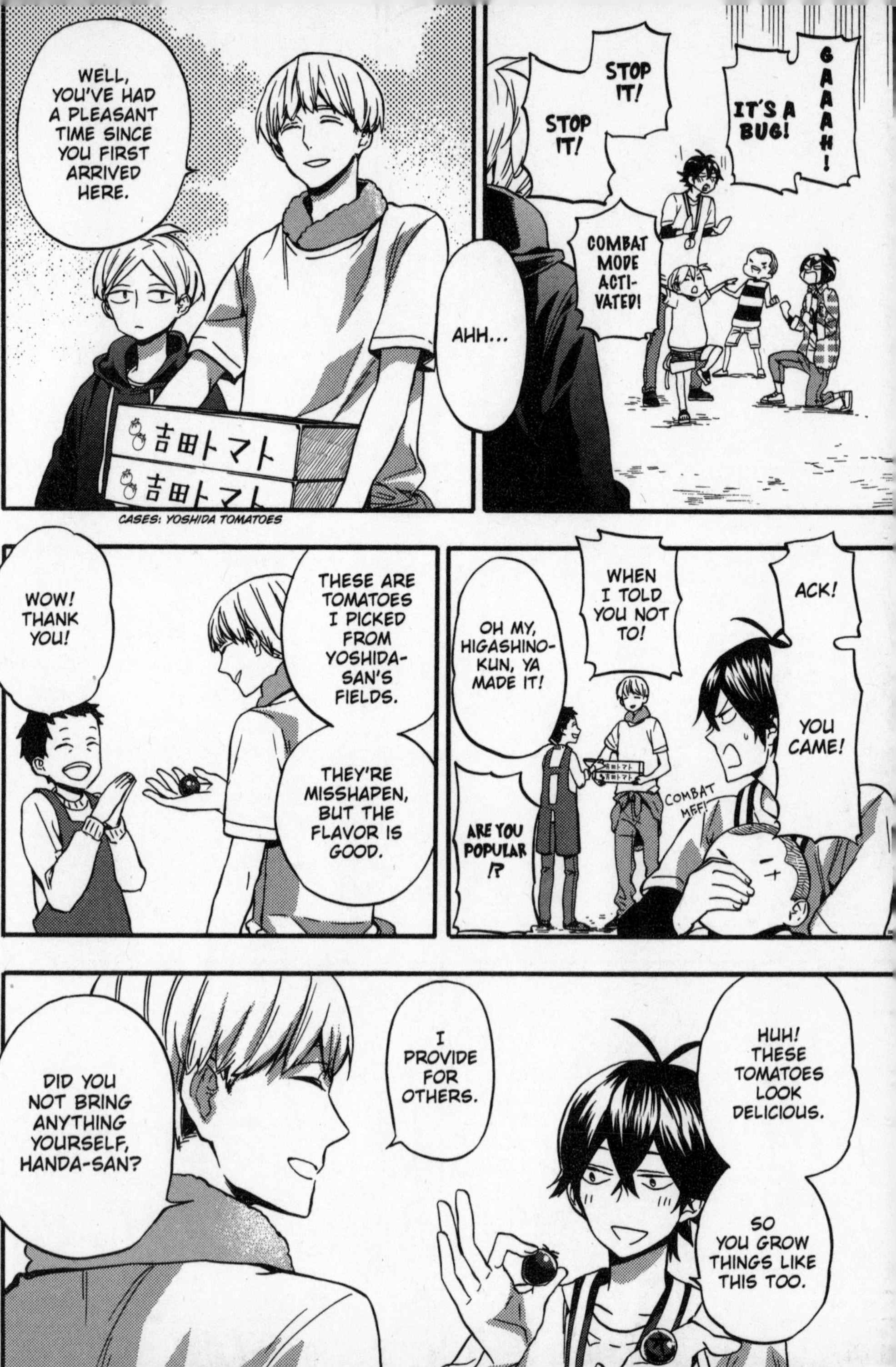
GAAAAH!
IT'S A BUG!
STOP IT!
STOP IT!
COMBAT MODE ACTIVATED!
AHH...
WELL, YOU'VE HAD A PLEASANT TIME SINCE YOU FIRST ARRIVED HERE.
吉田トマト
吉田トマト
CASES: YOSHIDA TOMATOES
ACK!
YOU CAME!
WHEN I TOLD YOU NOT TO!
COMBAT MEFF!
OH MY, HIGASHINO-KUN, YA MADE IT!
ARE YOU POPULAR!?
THESE ARE TOMATOES I PICKED FROM YOSHIDA-SAN'S FIELDS.
THEY'RE MISSHAPEN, BUT THE FLAVOR IS GOOD.
WOW! THANK YOU!
HUH! THESE TOMATOES LOOK DELICIOUS.
SO YOU GROW THINGS LIKE THIS TOO.
I PROVIDE FOR OTHERS.
DID YOU NOT BRING ANYTHING YOURSELF, HANDA-SAN?

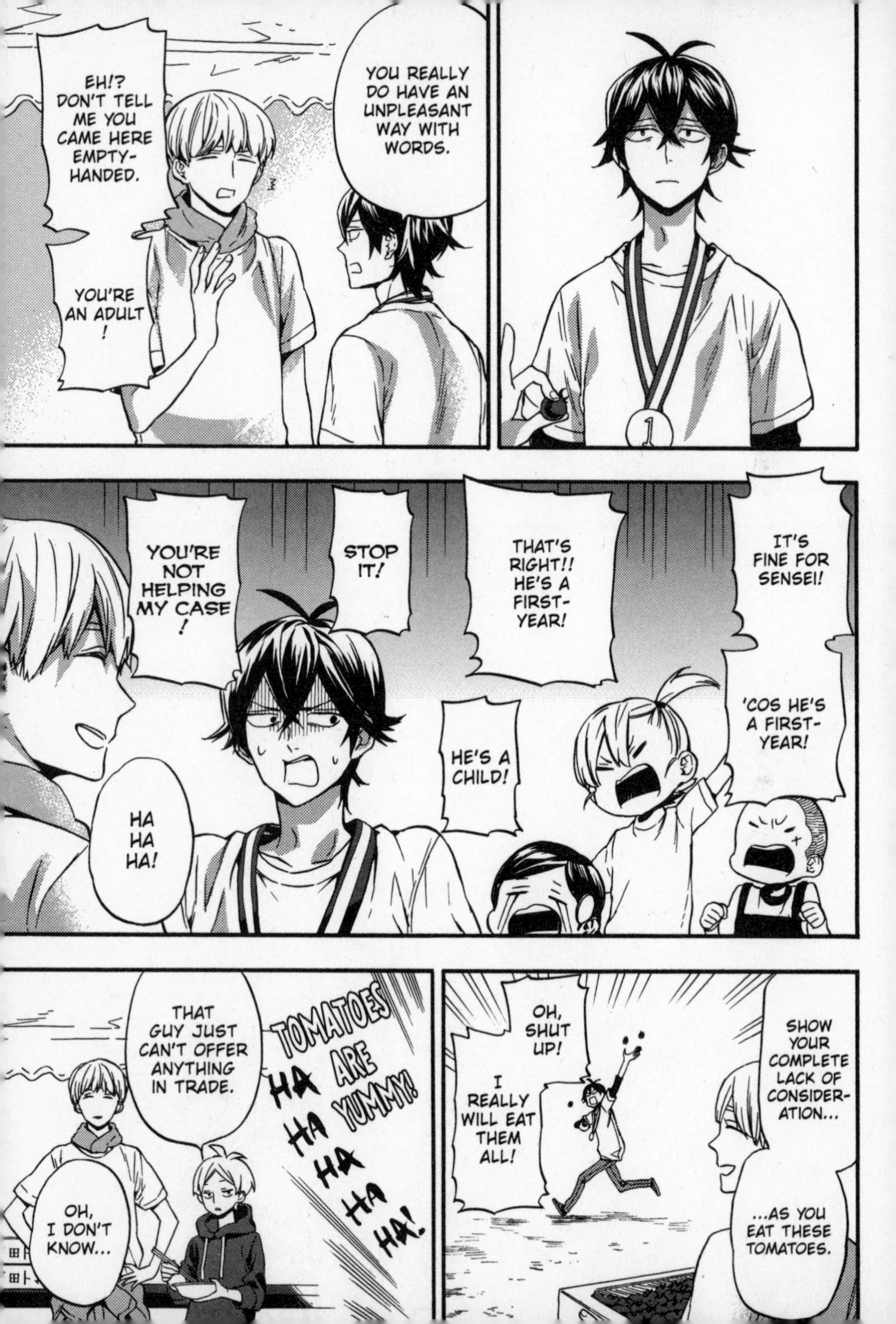
YOU REALLY DO HAVE AN UNPLEASANT WAY WITH WORDS.
EH!? DON'T TELL ME YOU CAME HERE EMPTY-HANDED.
YOU'RE AN ADULT!
IT'S FINE FOR SENSEI!
'COS HE'S A FIRST-YEAR!
THAT'S RIGHT!! HE'S A FIRST-YEAR!
HE'S A CHILD!
STOP IT!
YOU'RE NOT HELPING MY CASE!
HA HA HA!
SHOW YOUR COMPLETE LACK OF CONSIDERATION...
...AS YOU EAT THESE TOMATOES.
OH, SHUT UP!
I REALLY WILL EAT THEM ALL!
TOMATOES ARE YUMMY!
HA HA HA HA HA HA!
THAT GUY JUST CAN'T OFFER ANYTHING IN TRADE.
OH, I DON'T KNOW...

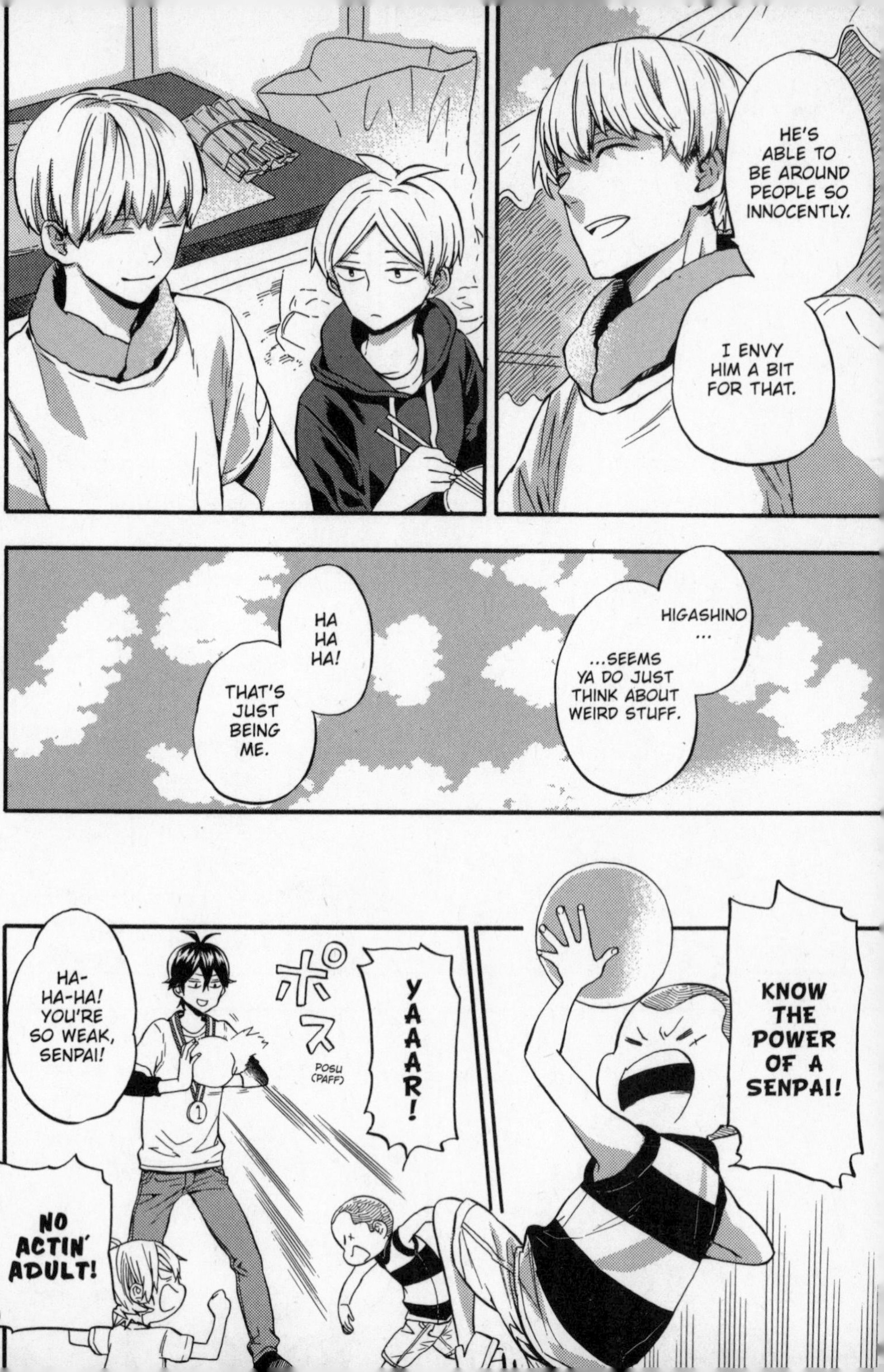
HE'S ABLE TO BE AROUND PEOPLE SO INNOCENTLY.
I ENVY HIM A BIT FOR THAT.
HIGASHINO ...
...SEEMS YA DO JUST THINK ABOUT WEIRD STUFF.
HA HA HA!
THAT'S JUST BEING ME.
KNOW THE POWER OF A SENPAI!
YAAAR!
ポス
POSU (PAFF)
HA-HA-HA! YOU'RE SO WEAK, SENPAI!
NO ACTIN' ADULT!

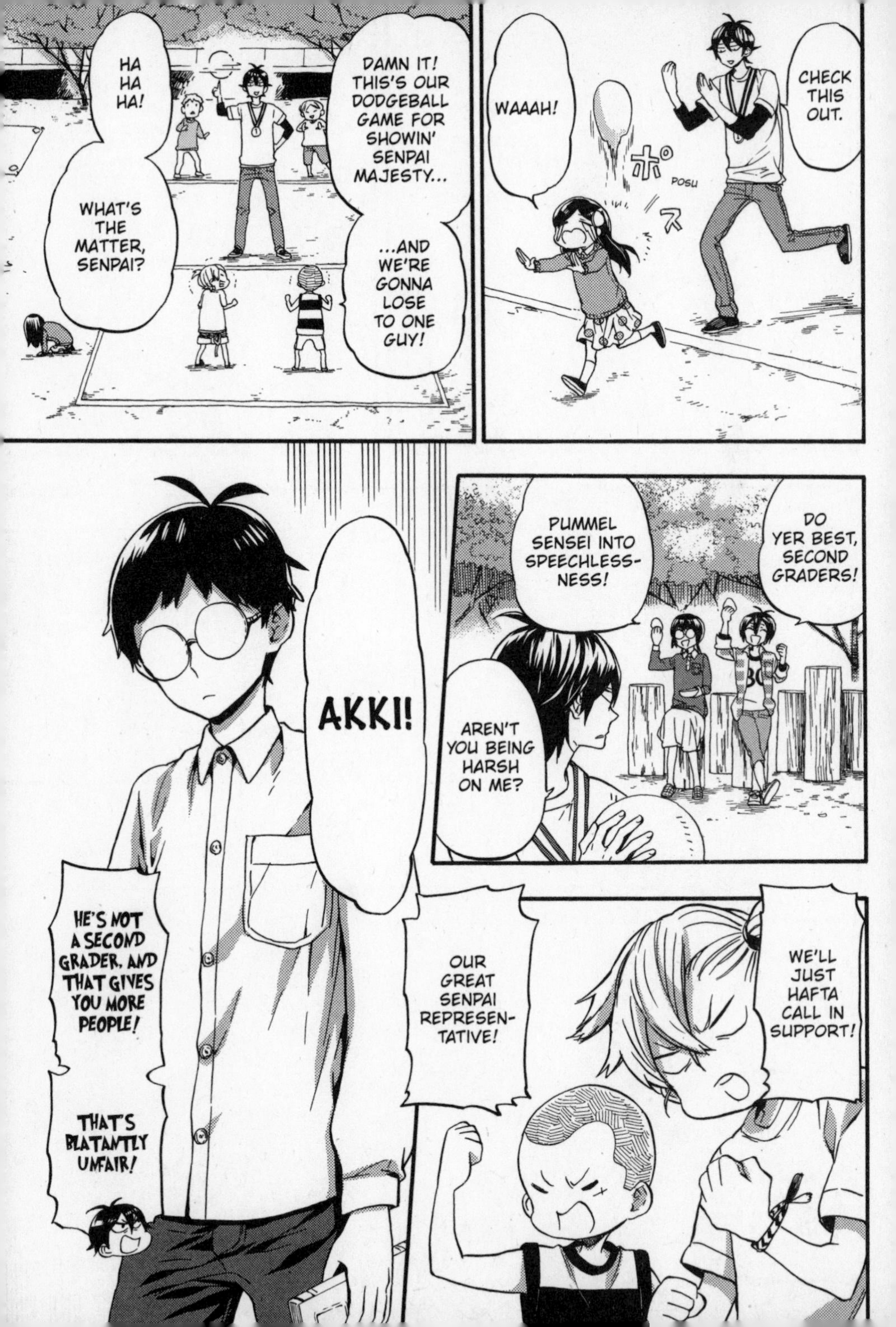
CHECK THIS OUT.
WAAAH!
ポス
POSU
DAMN IT! THIS'S OUR DODGEBALL GAME FOR SHOWIN' SENPAI MAJESTY...
...AND WE'RE GONNA LOSE TO ONE GUY!
HA HA HA!
WHAT'S THE MATTER, SENPAI?
DO YER BEST, SECOND GRADERS!
PUMMEL SENSEI INTO SPEECHLESS-NESS!
AREN'T YOU BEING HARSH ON ME?
WE'LL JUST HAFTA CALL IN SUPPORT!
OUR GREAT SENPAI REPRESEN-TATIVE!
AKKI!
HE'S NOT A SECOND GRADER, AND THAT GIVES YOU MORE PEOPLE!
THAT'S BLATANTLY UNFAIR!

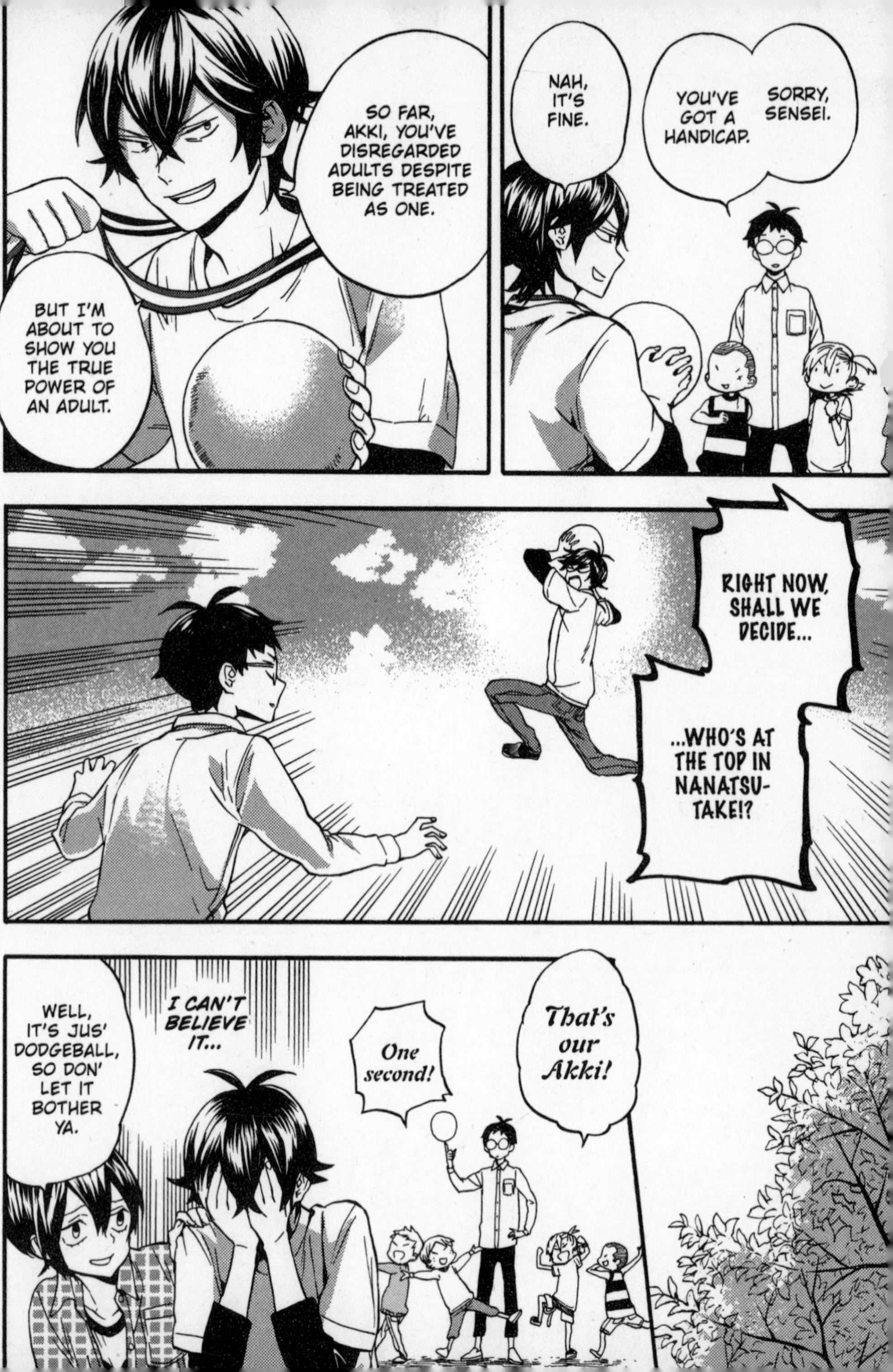
SORRY, SENSEI.
YOU'VE GOT A HANDICAP.
NAH, IT'S FINE.
SO FAR, AKKI, YOU'VE DISREGARDED ADULTS DESPITE BEING TREATED AS ONE.
BUT I'M ABOUT TO SHOW YOU THE TRUE POWER OF AN ADULT.
RIGHT NOW, SHALL WE DECIDE...
...WHO'S AT THE TOP IN NANATSU-TAKE!?
That's our Akki!
One second!
I CAN'T BELIEVE IT...
WELL, IT'S JUS' DODGEBALL, SO DON' LET IT BOTHER YA.

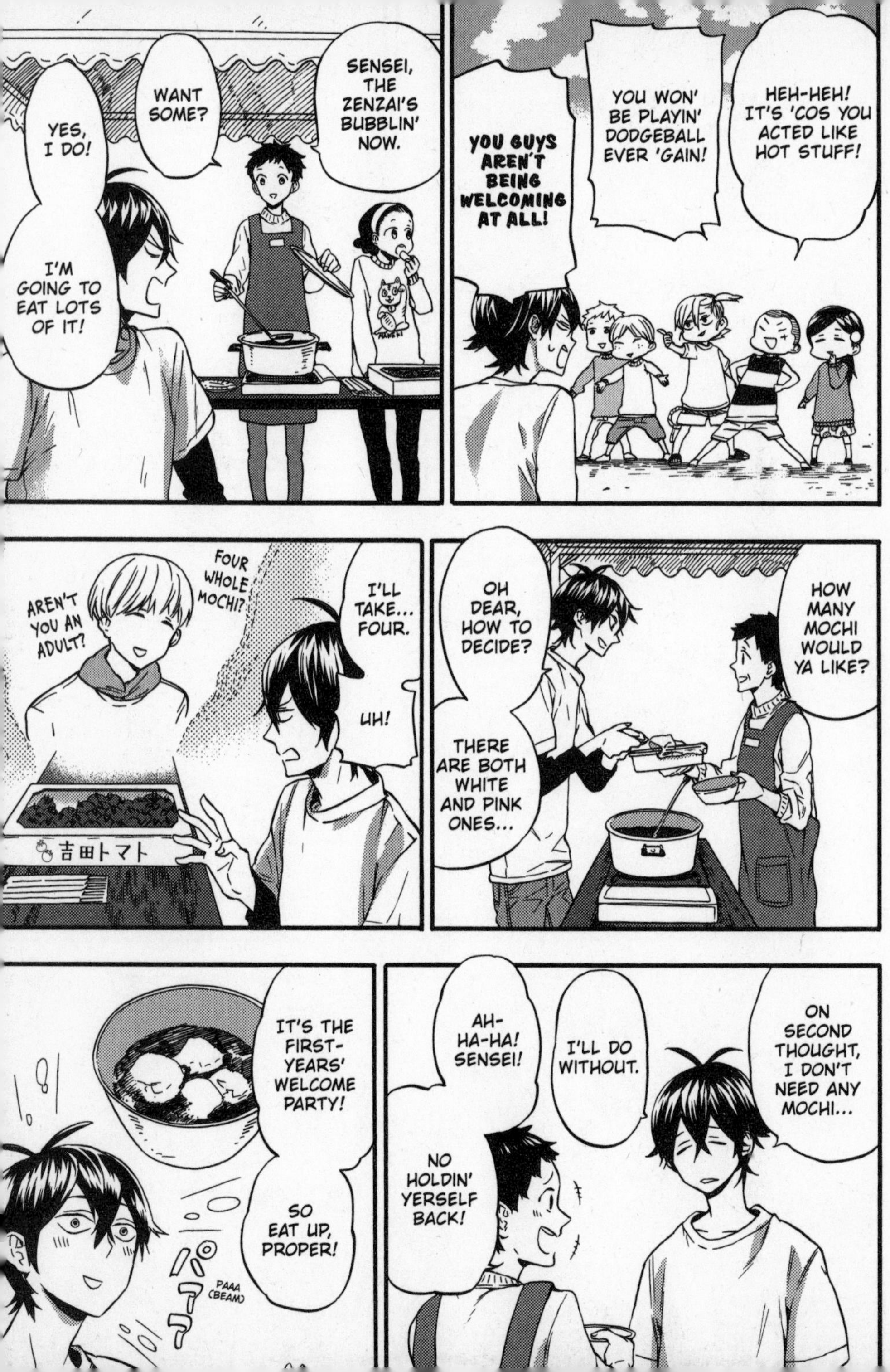
HEH-HEH! IT'S 'COS YOU ACTED LIKE HOT STUFF!
YOU WON' BE PLAYIN' DODGEBALL EVER 'GAIN!
YOU GUYS AREN'T BEING WELCOMING AT ALL!
SENSEI, THE ZENZAI'S BUBBLIN' NOW.
WANT SOME?
YES, I DO!
I'M GOING TO EAT LOTS OF IT!
HOW MANY MOCHI WOULD YA LIKE?
OH DEAR, HOW TO DECIDE?
THERE ARE BOTH WHITE AND PINK ONES...
I'LL TAKE... FOUR.
UH!
FOUR WHOLE MOCHI?
AREN'T YOU AN ADULT?
吉田トマト
ON SECOND THOUGHT, I DON'T NEED ANY MOCHI...
I'LL DO WITHOUT.
AH-HA-HA! SENSEI!
NO HOLDIN' YERSELF BACK!
IT'S THE FIRST-YEARS' WELCOME PARTY!
SO EAT UP, PROPER!
PAAA (BEAM)

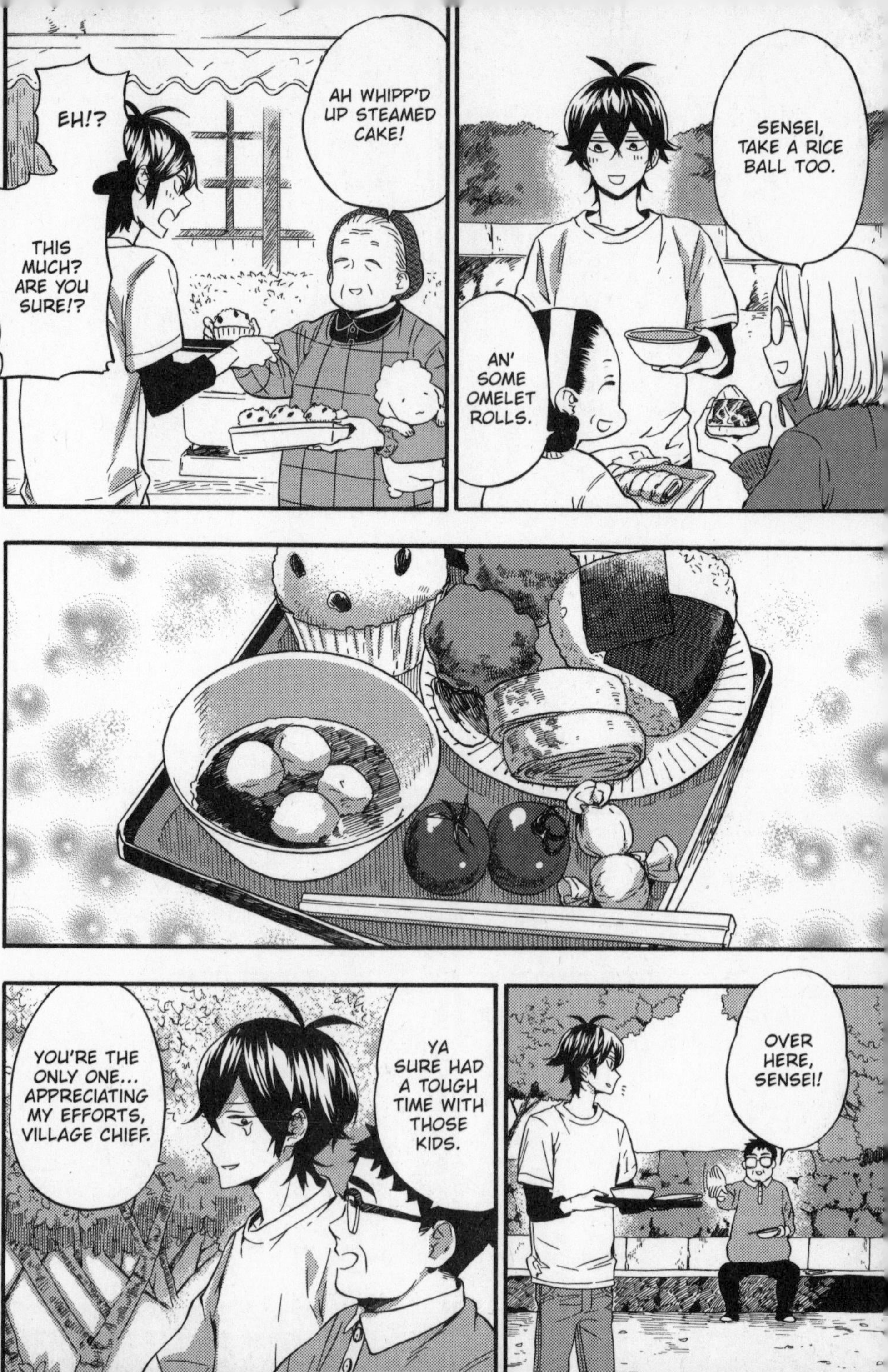
SENSEI, TAKE A RICE BALL TOO.
AN' SOME OMELET ROLLS.
AH WHIPP'D UP STEAMED CAKE!
EH!?
THIS MUCH? ARE YOU SURE!?
OVER HERE, SENSEI!
YA SURE HAD A TOUGH TIME WITH THOSE KIDS.
YOU'RE THE ONLY ONE... APPRECIATING MY EFFORTS, VILLAGE CHIEF.

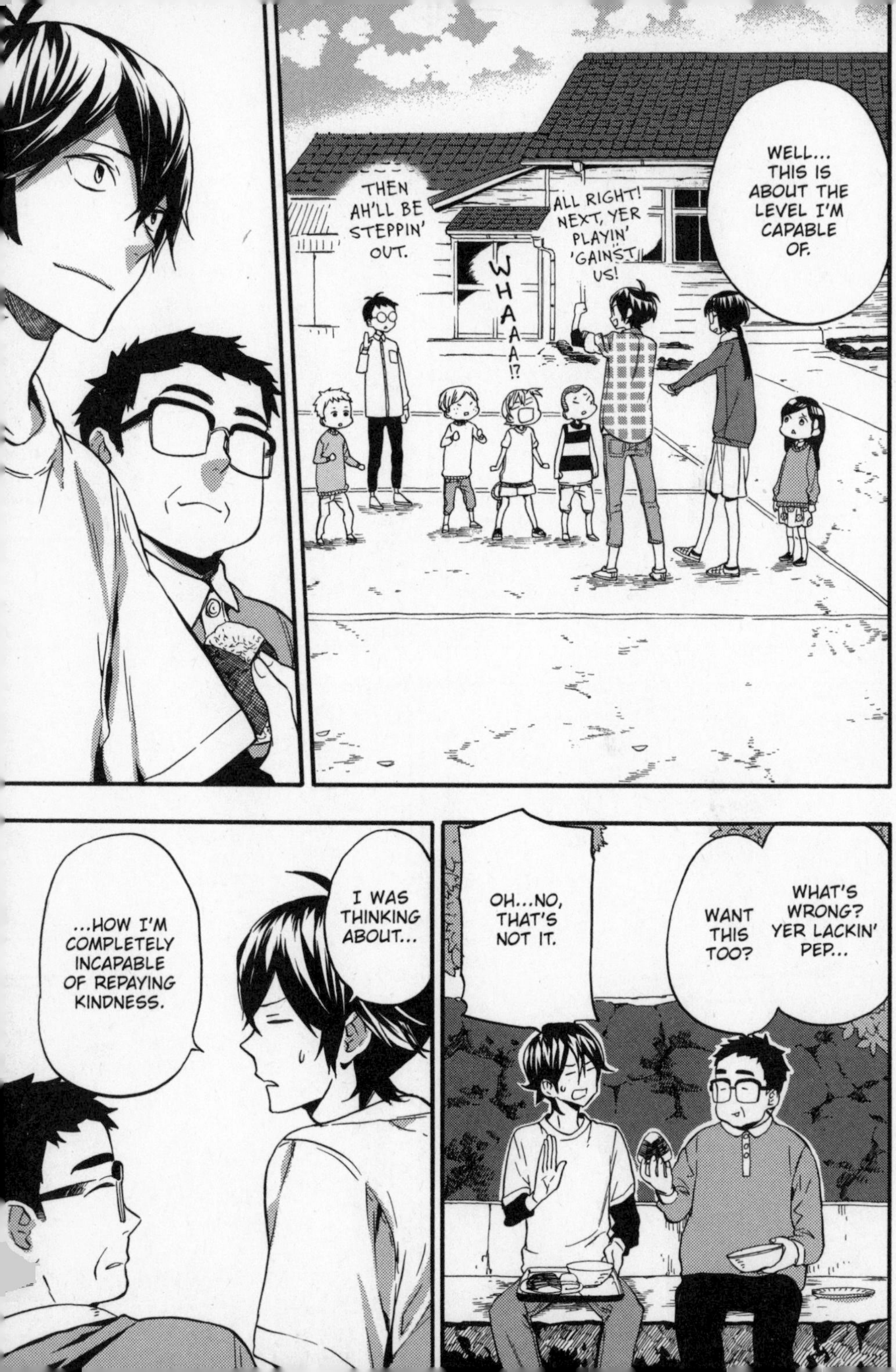
WELL... THIS IS ABOUT THE LEVEL I'M CAPABLE OF.
ALL RIGHT! NEXT, YER PLAYIN' 'GAINST US!
WHAAAA!?
THEN AH'LL BE STEPPIN' OUT.
WHAT'S WRONG? YER LACKIN' PEP...
WANT THIS TOO?
OH...NO, THAT'S NOT IT.
I WAS THINKING ABOUT...
...HOW I'M COMPLETELY INCAPABLE OF REPAYING KINDNESS.

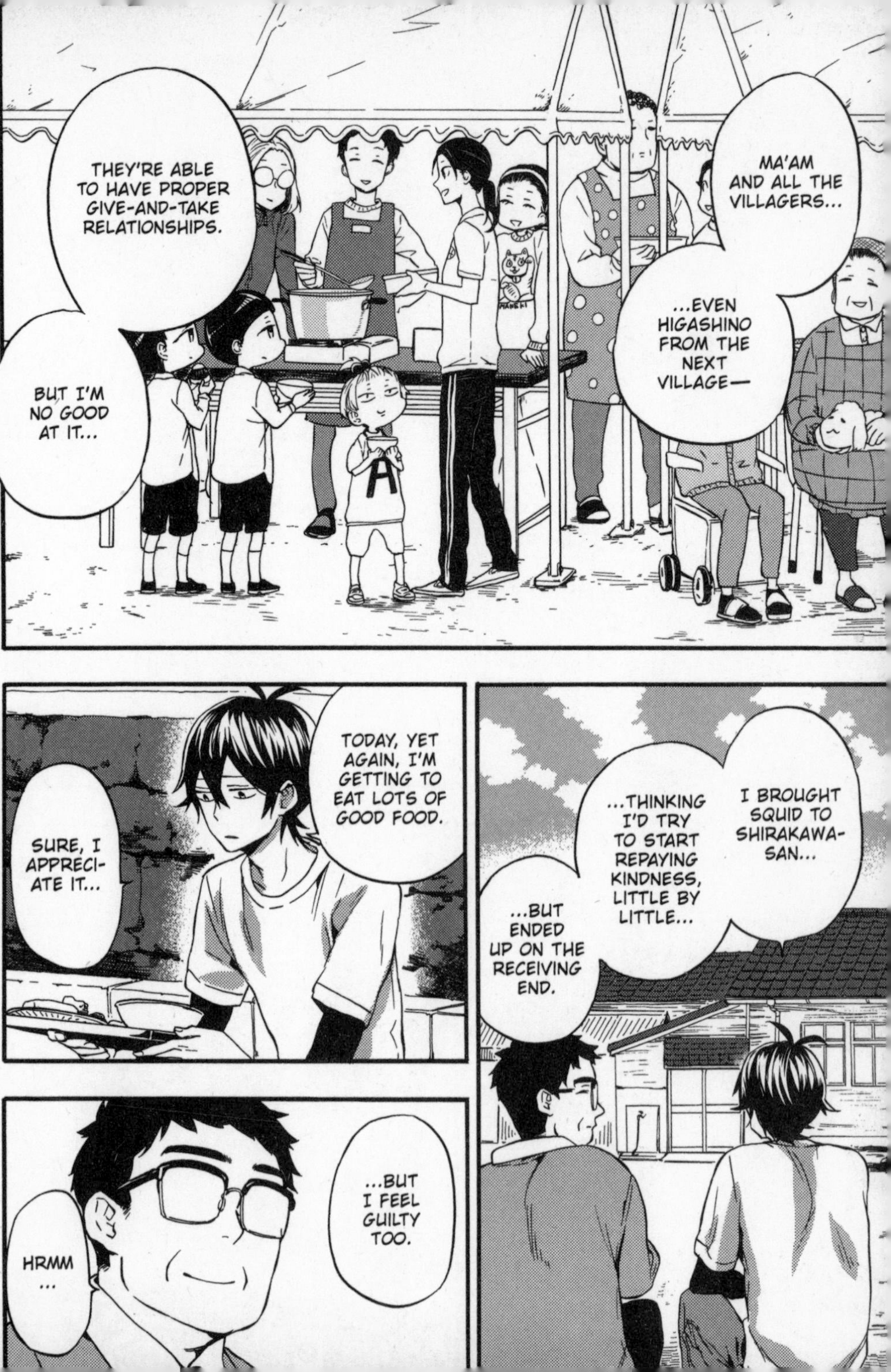
MA'AM AND ALL THE VILLAGERS...
...EVEN HIGASHINO FROM THE NEXT VILLAGE—
THEY'RE ABLE TO HAVE PROPER GIVE-AND-TAKE RELATIONSHIPS.
BUT I'M NO GOOD AT IT...
I BROUGHT SQUID TO SHIRAKAWA-SAN...
...THINKING I'D TRY TO START REPAYING KINDNESS, LITTLE BY LITTLE...
...BUT ENDED UP ON THE RECEIVING END.
TODAY, YET AGAIN, I'M GETTING TO EAT LOTS OF GOOD FOOD.
SURE, I APPRECIATE IT...
...BUT I FEEL GUILTY TOO.
HRMM ...

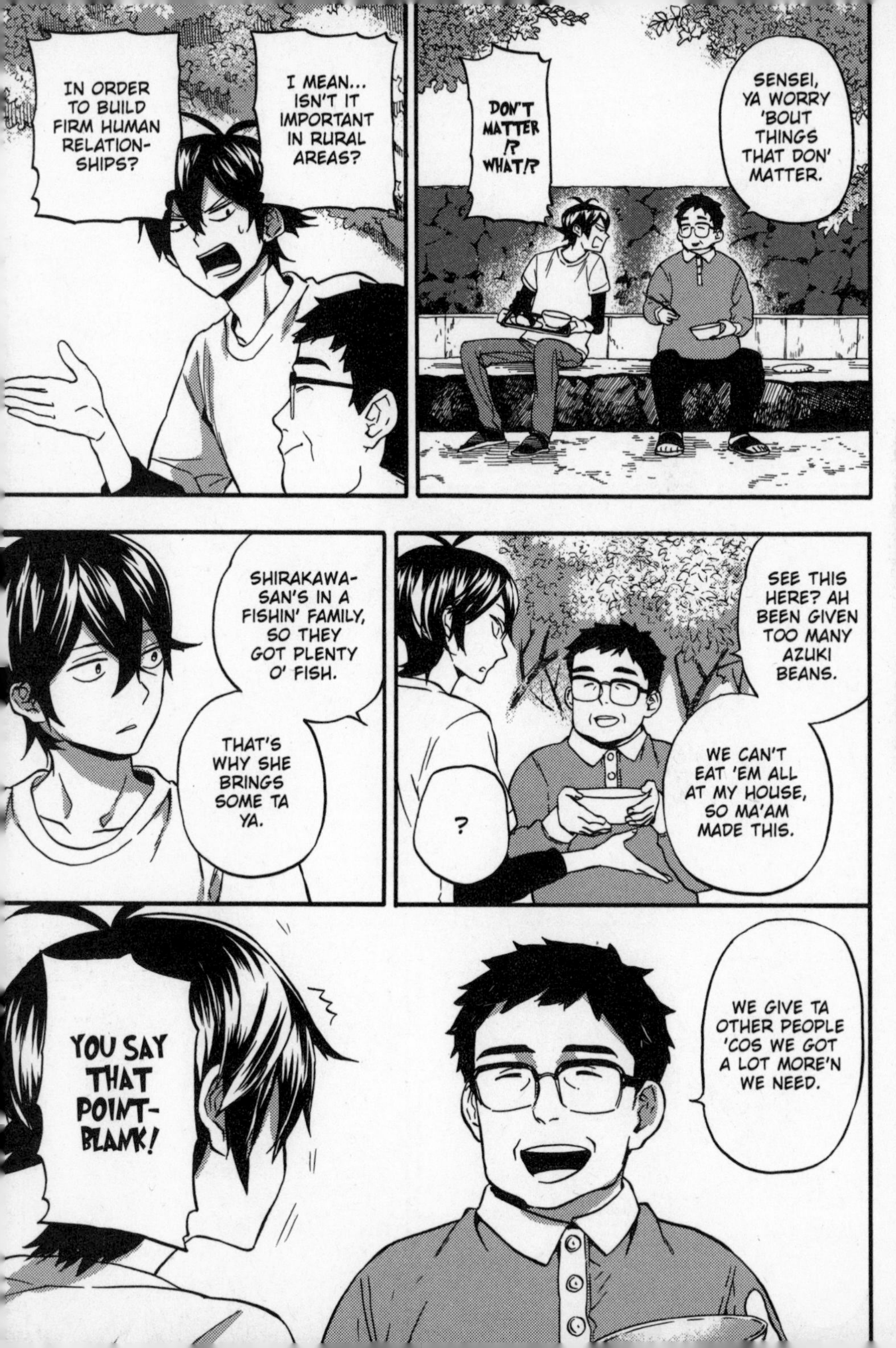
SENSEI, YA WORRY 'BOUT THINGS THAT DON' MATTER.
DON'T MATTER!? WHAT!?
I MEAN... ISN'T IT IMPORTANT IN RURAL AREAS?
IN ORDER TO BUILD FIRM HUMAN RELATIONSHIPS?
SEE THIS HERE? AH BEEN GIVEN TOO MANY AZUKI BEANS.
WE CAN'T EAT 'EM ALL AT MY HOUSE, SO MA'AM MADE THIS.
?
SHIRAKAWA-SAN'S IN A FISHIN' FAMILY, SO THEY GOT PLENTY O' FISH.
THAT'S WHY SHE BRINGS SOME TA YA.
WE GIVE TA OTHER PEOPLE 'COS WE GOT A LOT MORE'N WE NEED.
YOU SAY THAT POINT-BLANK!

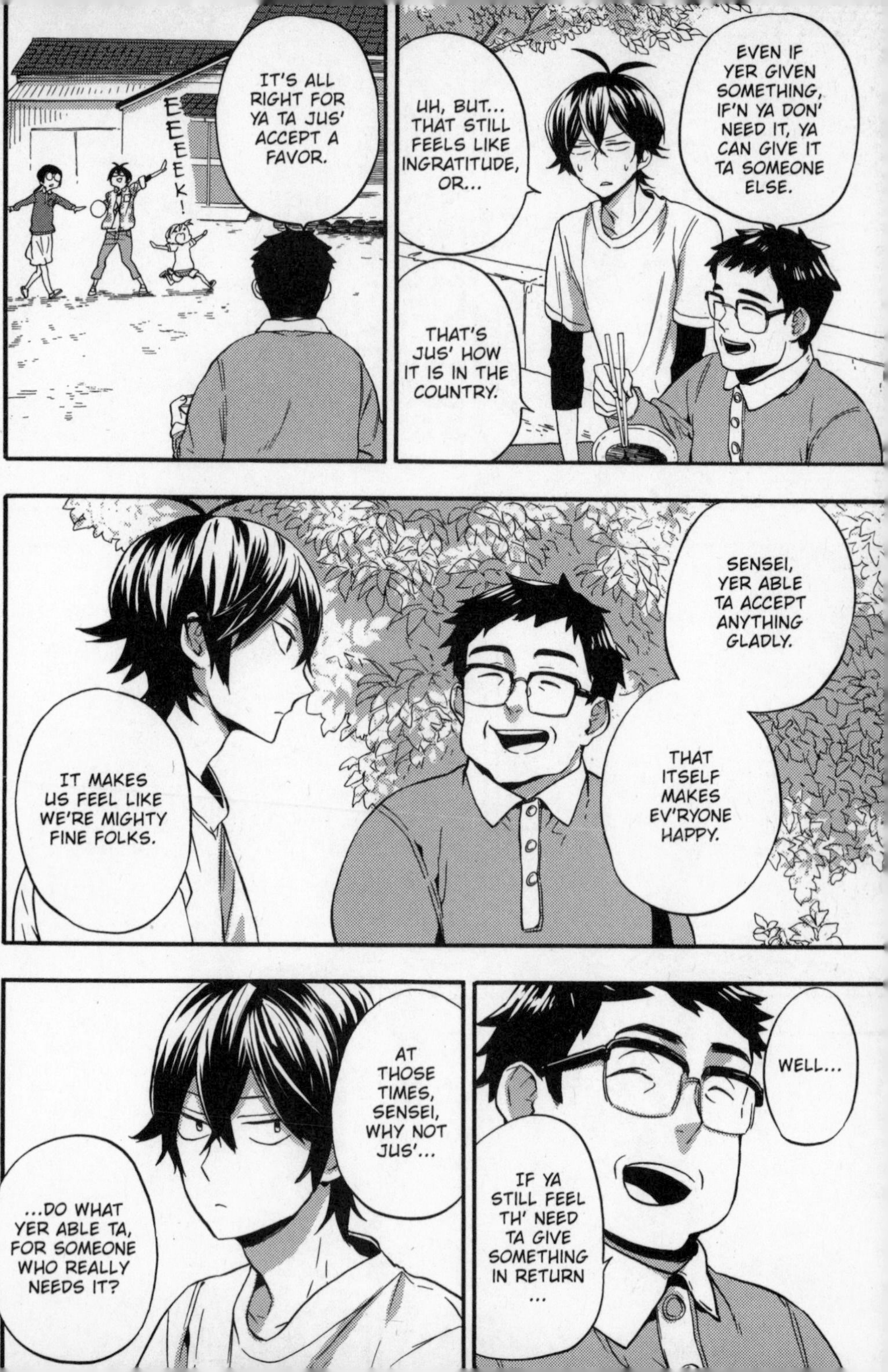
EVEN IF YER GIVEN SOMETHING, IF'N YA DON' NEED IT, YA CAN GIVE IT TA SOMEONE ELSE.
UH, BUT... THAT STILL FEELS LIKE INGRATITUDE, OR...
THAT'S JUS' HOW IT IS IN THE COUNTRY.
IT'S ALL RIGHT FOR YA TA JUS' ACCEPT A FAVOR.
EEEEEK!
SENSEI, YER ABLE TA ACCEPT ANYTHING GLADLY.
THAT ITSELF MAKES EV'RYONE HAPPY.
IT MAKES US FEEL LIKE WE'RE MIGHTY FINE FOLKS.
WELL...
IF YA STILL FEEL TH' NEED TA GIVE SOMETHING IN RETURN ...
AT THOSE TIMES, SENSEI, WHY NOT JUS'...
...DO WHAT YER ABLE TA, FOR SOMEONE WHO REALLY NEEDS IT?

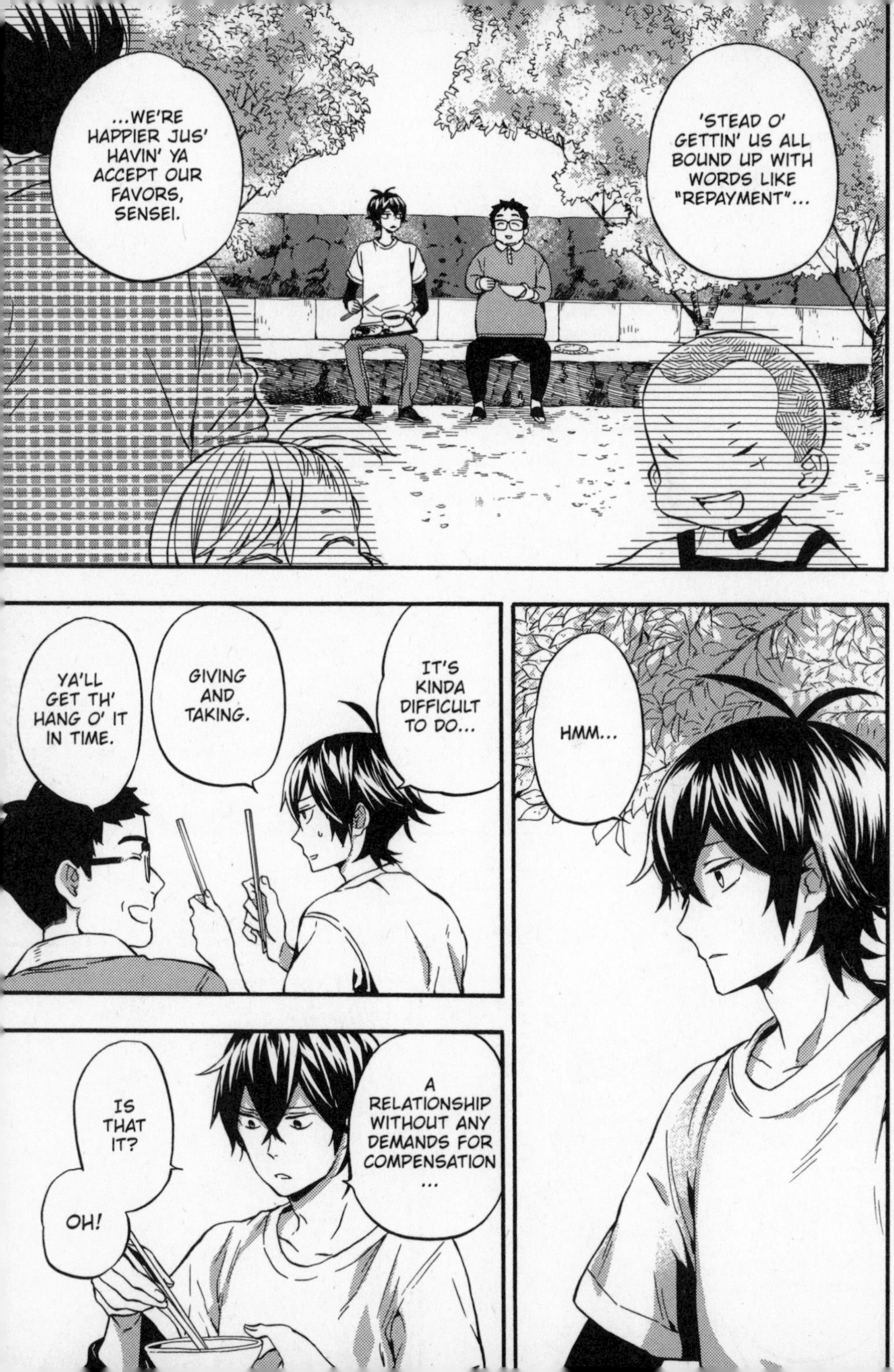
'STEAD O' GETTIN' US ALL BOUND UP WITH WORDS LIKE "REPAYMENT"...
...WE'RE HAPPIER JUS' HAVIN' YA ACCEPT OUR FAVORS, SENSEI.
HMM...
IT'S KINDA DIFFICULT TO DO...
GIVING AND TAKING.
YA'LL GET TH' HANG O' IT IN TIME.
A RELATIONSHIP WITHOUT ANY DEMANDS FOR COMPENSATION...
IS THAT IT?
OH!

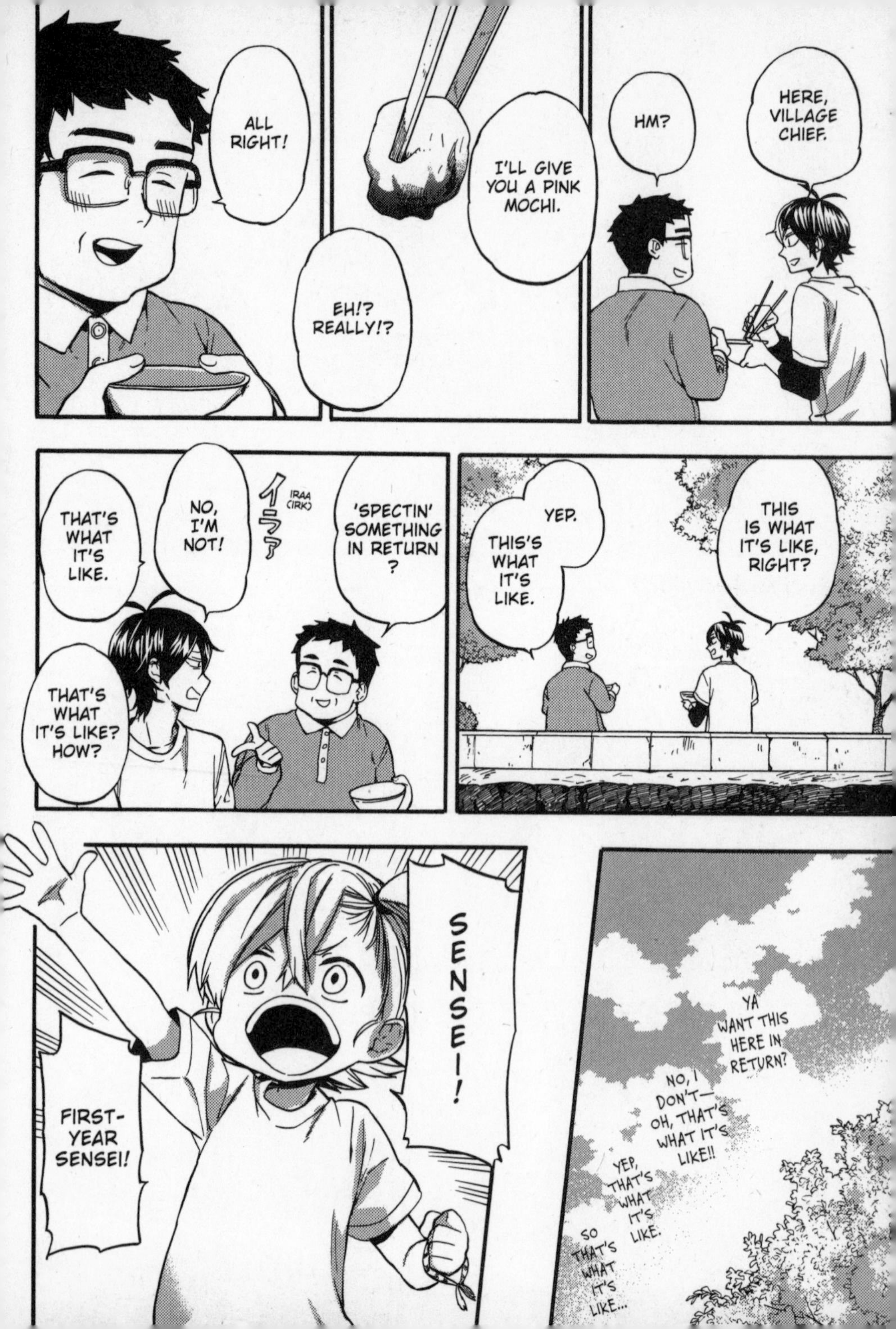
HERE, VILLAGE CHIEF.
HM?
I'LL GIVE YOU A PINK MOCHI.
EH!? REALLY!?
ALL RIGHT!
THIS IS WHAT IT'S LIKE, RIGHT?
YEP.
THIS'S WHAT IT'S LIKE.
'SPECTIN' SOMETHING IN RETURN?
イラァ IRAA (IRK)
NO, I'M NOT!
THAT'S WHAT IT'S LIKE.
THAT'S WHAT IT'S LIKE? HOW?
YA WANT THIS HERE IN RETURN?
NO, I DON'T— OH, THAT'S WHAT IT'S LIKE!!
YEP, THAT'S WHAT IT'S LIKE.
SO THAT'S WHAT IT'S LIKE...
SENSEI!
FIRST-YEAR SENSEI!

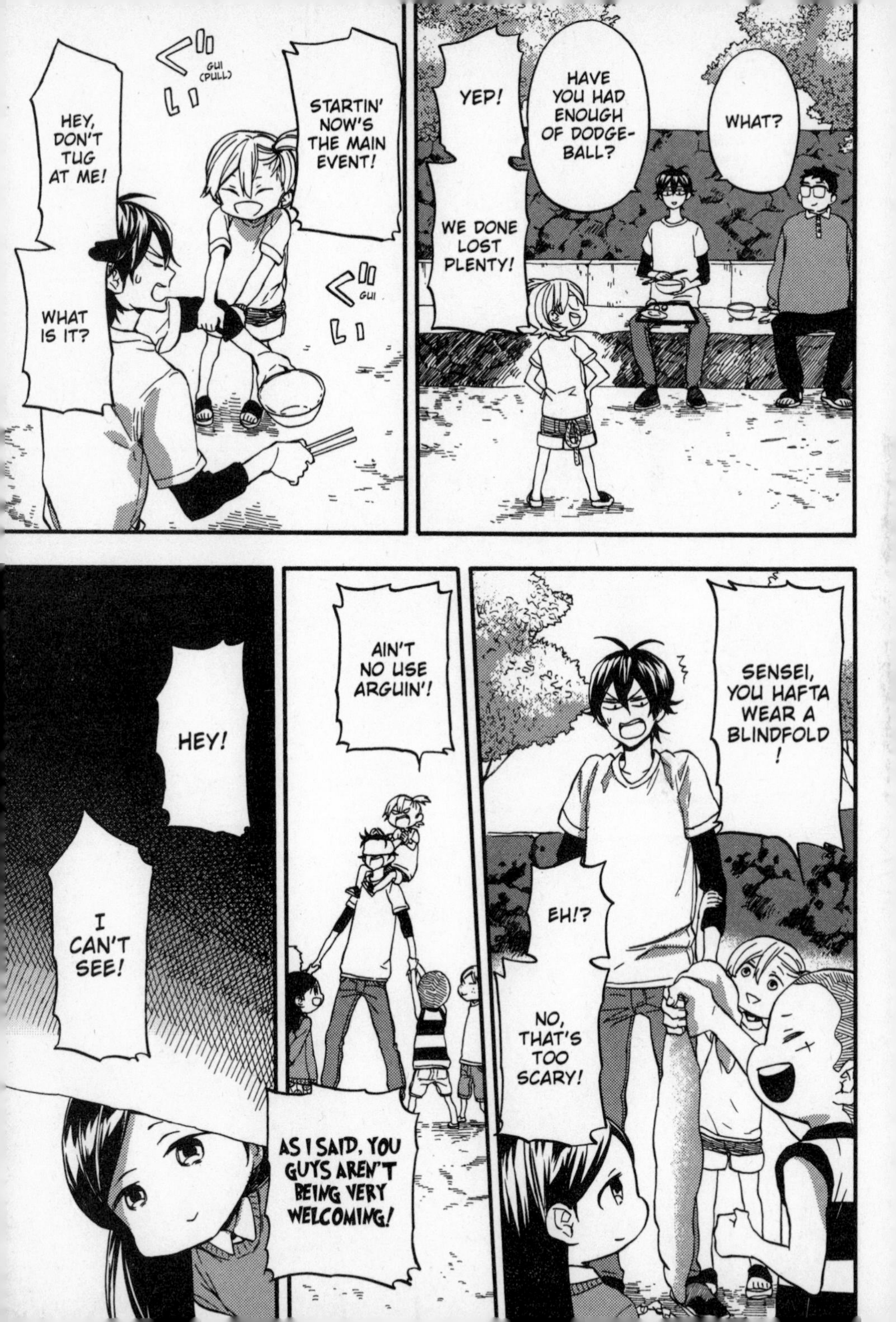
WHAT?
HAVE YOU HAD ENOUGH OF DODGE-BALL?
YEP!
WE DONE LOST PLENTY!
STARTIN' NOW'S THE MAIN EVENT!
GUI (PULL)
HEY, DON'T TUG AT ME!
GUI
WHAT IS IT?
SENSEI, YOU HAFTA WEAR A BLINDFOLD!
EH!?
NO, THAT'S TOO SCARY!
AIN'T NO USE ARGUIN'!
AS I SAID, YOU GUYS AREN'T BEING VERY WELCOMING!
HEY!
I CAN'T SEE!

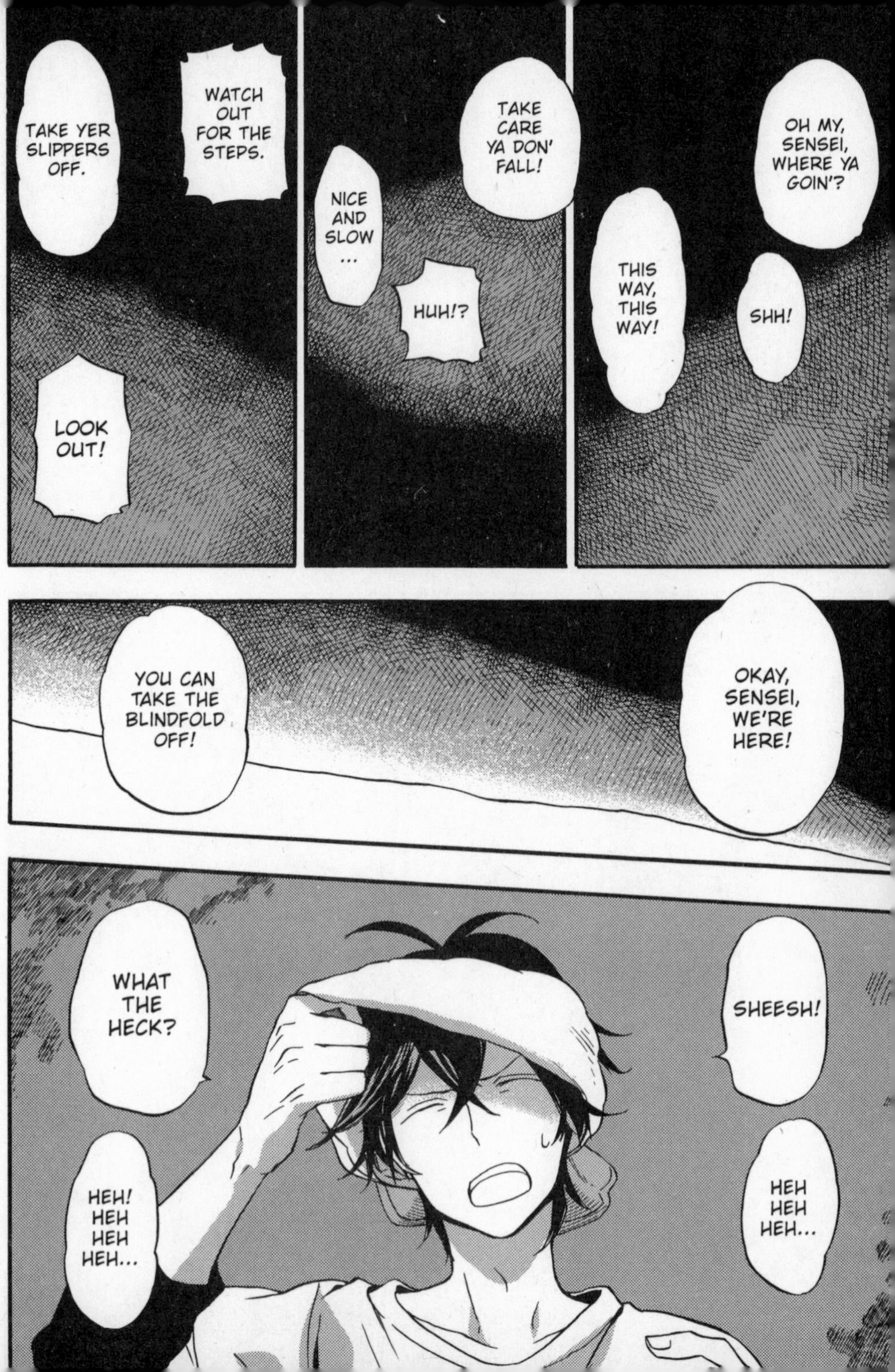
OH MY, SENSEI, WHERE YA GOIN'?
SHH!
THIS WAY, THIS WAY!
TAKE CARE YA DON' FALL!
NICE AND SLOW...
HUH!?
WATCH OUT FOR THE STEPS.
TAKE YER SLIPPERS OFF.
LOOK OUT!
OKAY, SENSEI, WE'RE HERE!
YOU CAN TAKE THE BLINDFOLD OFF!
SHEESH!
WHAT THE HECK?
HEH HEH HEH...
HEH! HEH HEH HEH...

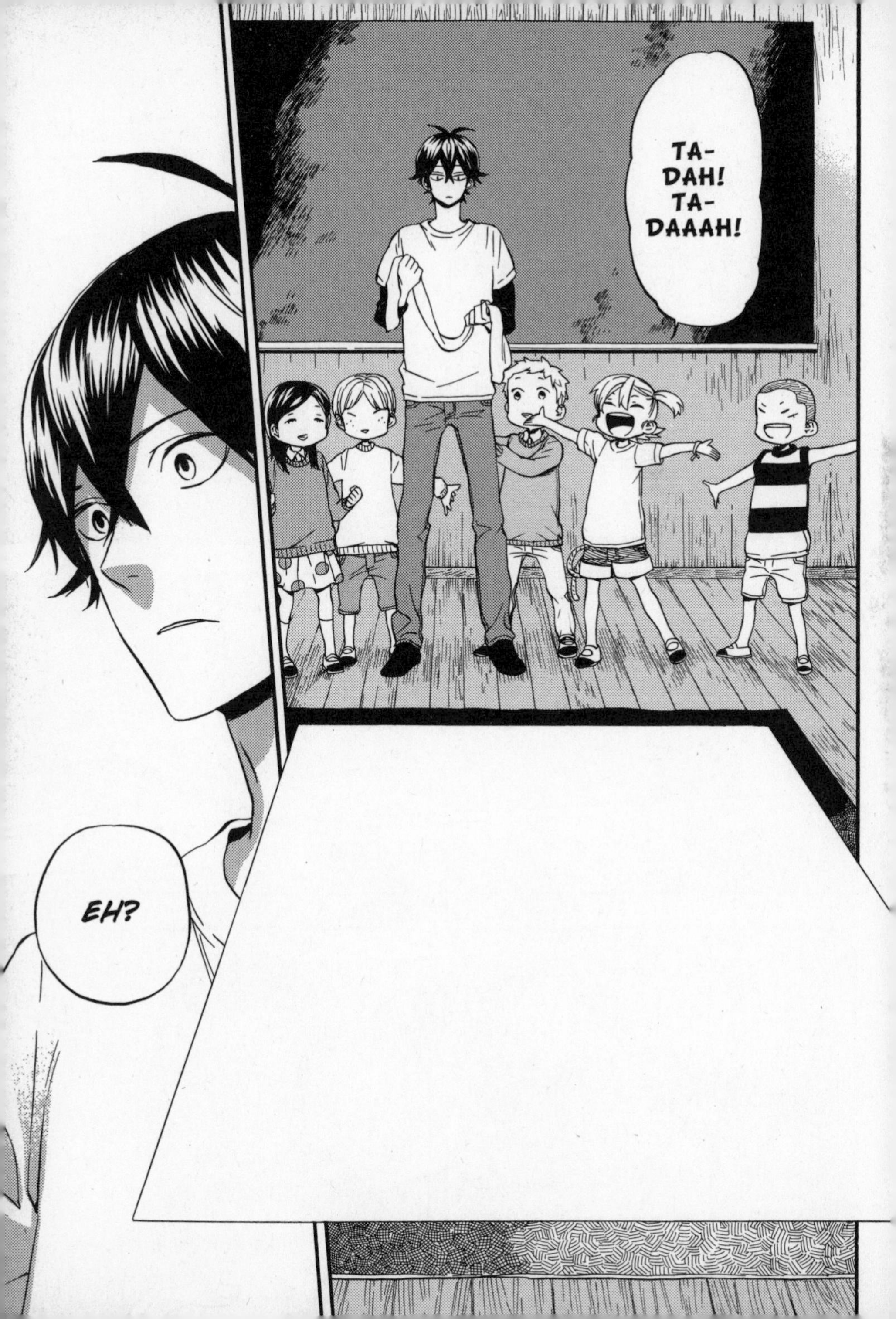
TA-DAH! TA-DAAAH!
EH?

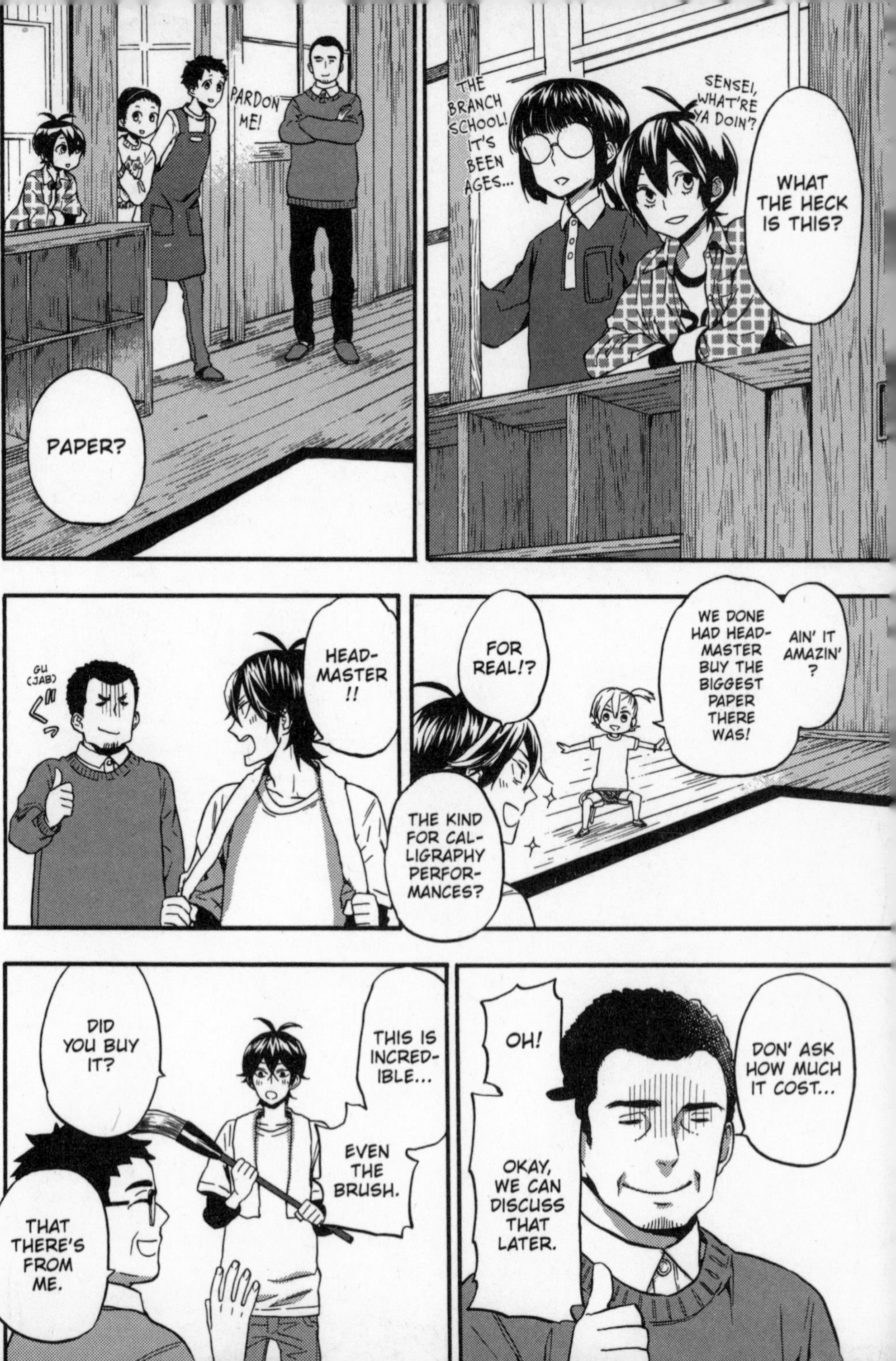
WHAT THE HECK IS THIS?
SENSEI, WHAT'RE YA DOIN'?
THE BRANCH SCHOOL! IT'S BEEN AGES...
PARDON ME!
PAPER?
AIN' IT AMAZIN'?
WE DONE HAD HEAD-MASTER BUY THE BIGGEST PAPER THERE WAS!
FOR REAL!?
THE KIND FOR CAL-LIGRAPHY PERFOR-MANCES?
HEAD-MASTER!!
GU (JAB)
DON' ASK HOW MUCH IT COST...
OH!
OKAY, WE CAN DISCUSS THAT LATER.
THIS IS INCRED-IBLE...
EVEN THE BRUSH.
DID YOU BUY IT?
THAT THERE'S FROM ME.

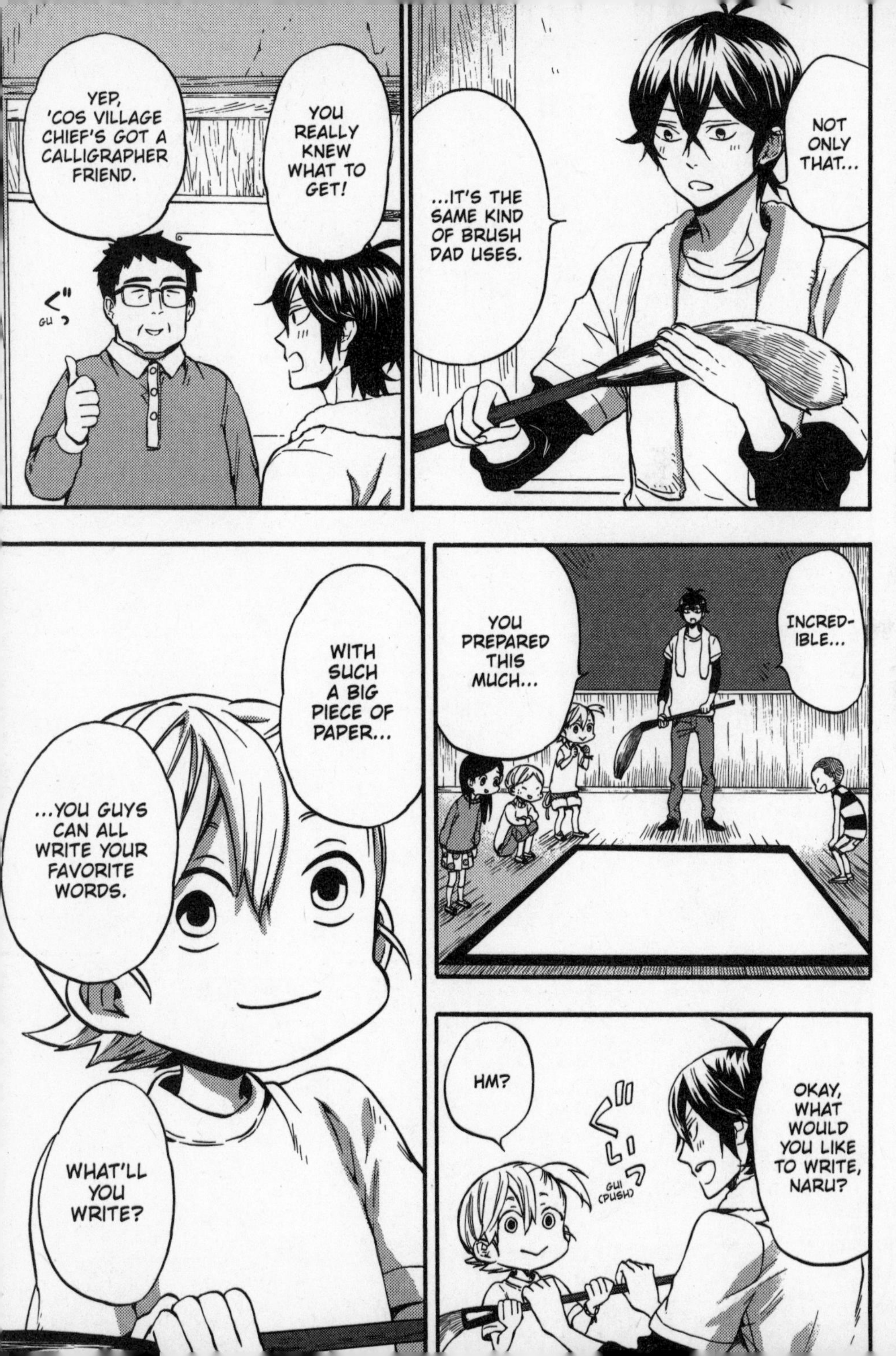
NOT ONLY THAT...
...IT'S THE SAME KIND OF BRUSH DAD USES.
YOU REALLY KNEW WHAT TO GET!
YEP, 'COS VILLAGE CHIEF'S GOT A CALLIGRAPHER FRIEND.
ぐっ
GU
INCREDIBLE...
YOU PREPARED THIS MUCH...
OKAY, WHAT WOULD YOU LIKE TO WRITE, NARU?
ぐいっ
GUI (PUSH)
HM?
WITH SUCH A BIG PIECE OF PAPER...
...YOU GUYS CAN ALL WRITE YOUR FAVORITE WORDS.
WHAT'LL YOU WRITE?

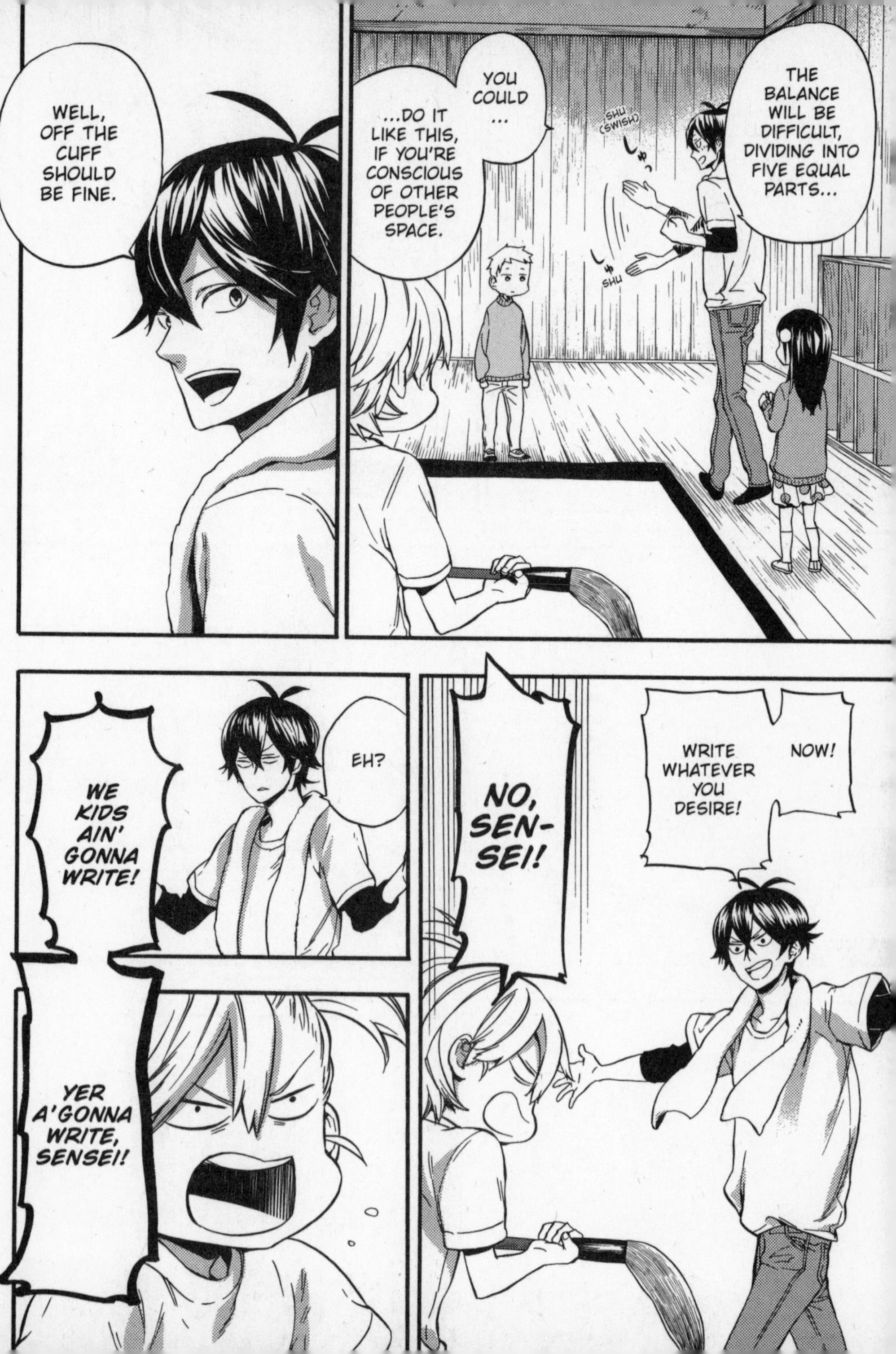
THE BALANCE WILL BE DIFFICULT, DIVIDING INTO FIVE EQUAL PARTS...
しゅっ SHU (SWISH)
YOU COULD ...
...DO IT LIKE THIS, IF YOU'RE CONSCIOUS OF OTHER PEOPLE'S SPACE.
しゅ SHU
WELL, OFF THE CUFF SHOULD BE FINE.
WRITE WHATEVER YOU DESIRE! NOW!
NO, SEN-SEI!
EH?
WE KIDS AIN' GONNA WRITE!
YER A'GONNA WRITE, SENSEI!

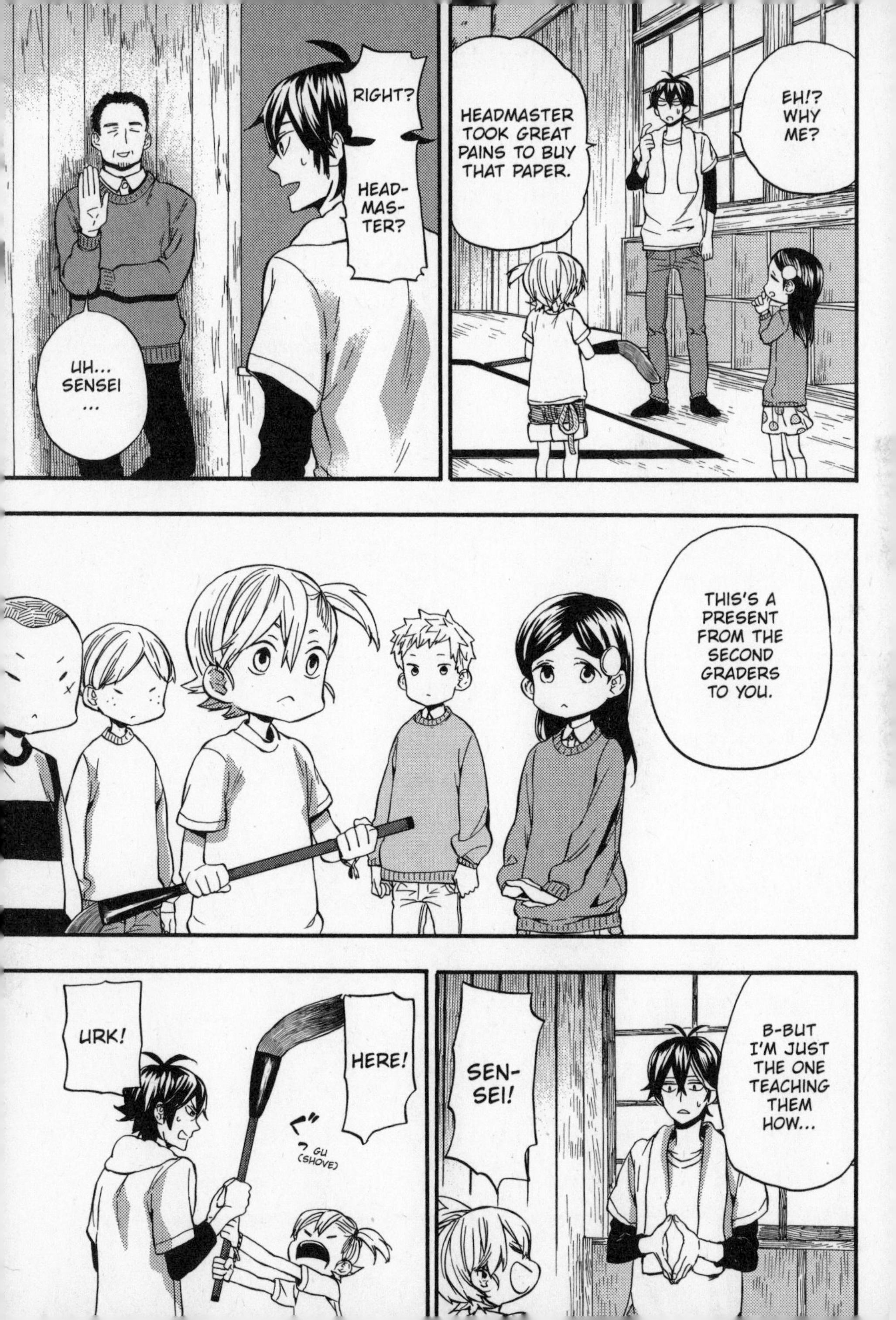
EH!? WHY ME?
HEADMASTER TOOK GREAT PAINS TO BUY THAT PAPER.
RIGHT?
HEAD-MAS-TER?
UH... SENSEI ...
THIS'S A PRESENT FROM THE SECOND GRADERS TO YOU.
B-BUT I'M JUST THE ONE TEACHING THEM HOW...
SEN-SEI!
HERE!
URK!
GU (SHOVE)

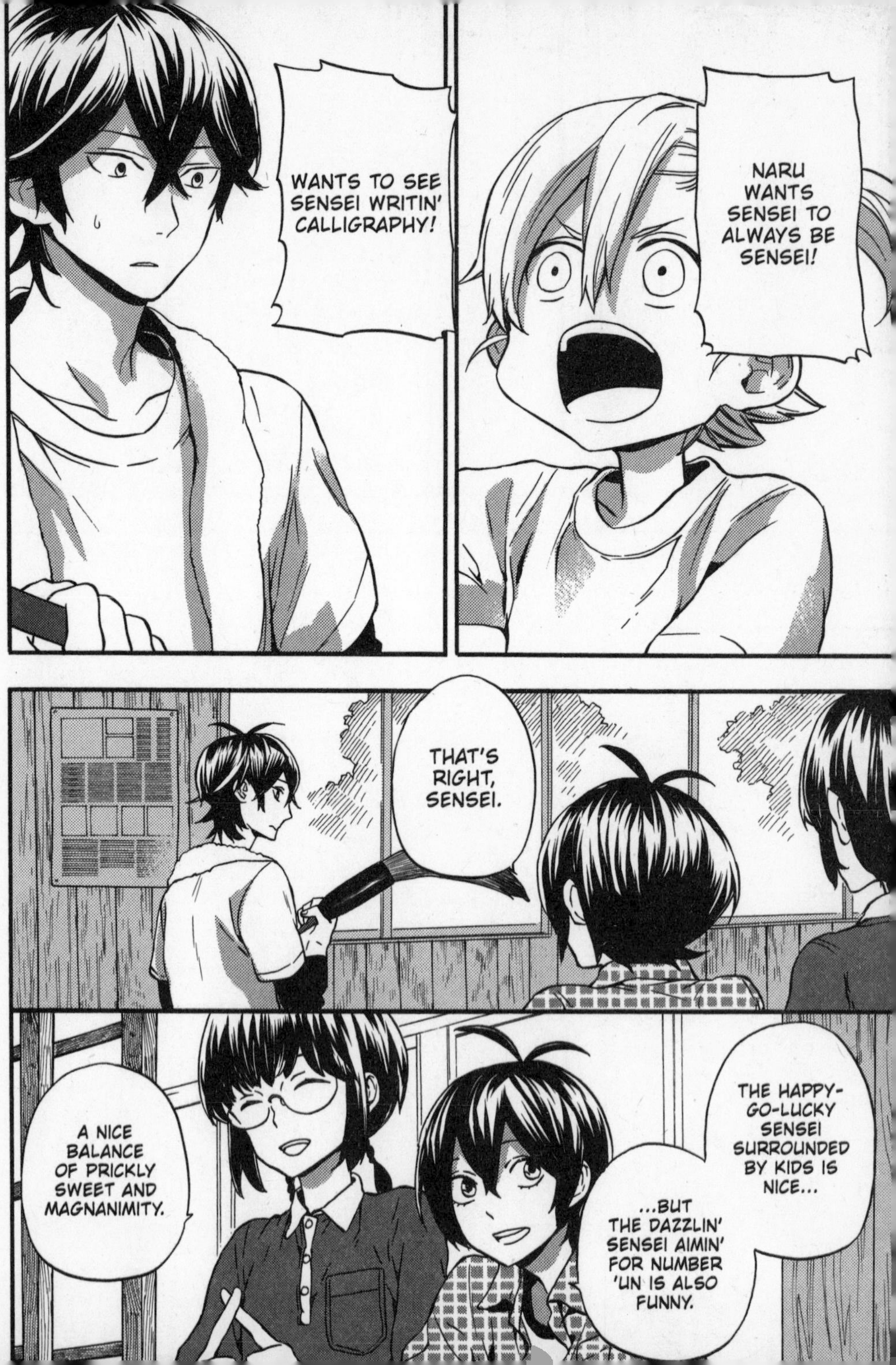
NARU WANTS SENSEI TO ALWAYS BE SENSEI!
WANTS TO SEE SENSEI WRITIN' CALLIGRAPHY!
THAT'S RIGHT, SENSEI.
THE HAPPY-GO-LUCKY SENSEI SURROUNDED BY KIDS IS NICE...
...BUT THE DAZZLIN' SENSEI AIMIN' FOR NUMBER 'UN IS ALSO FUNNY.
A NICE BALANCE OF PRICKLY SWEET AND MAGNANIMITY.

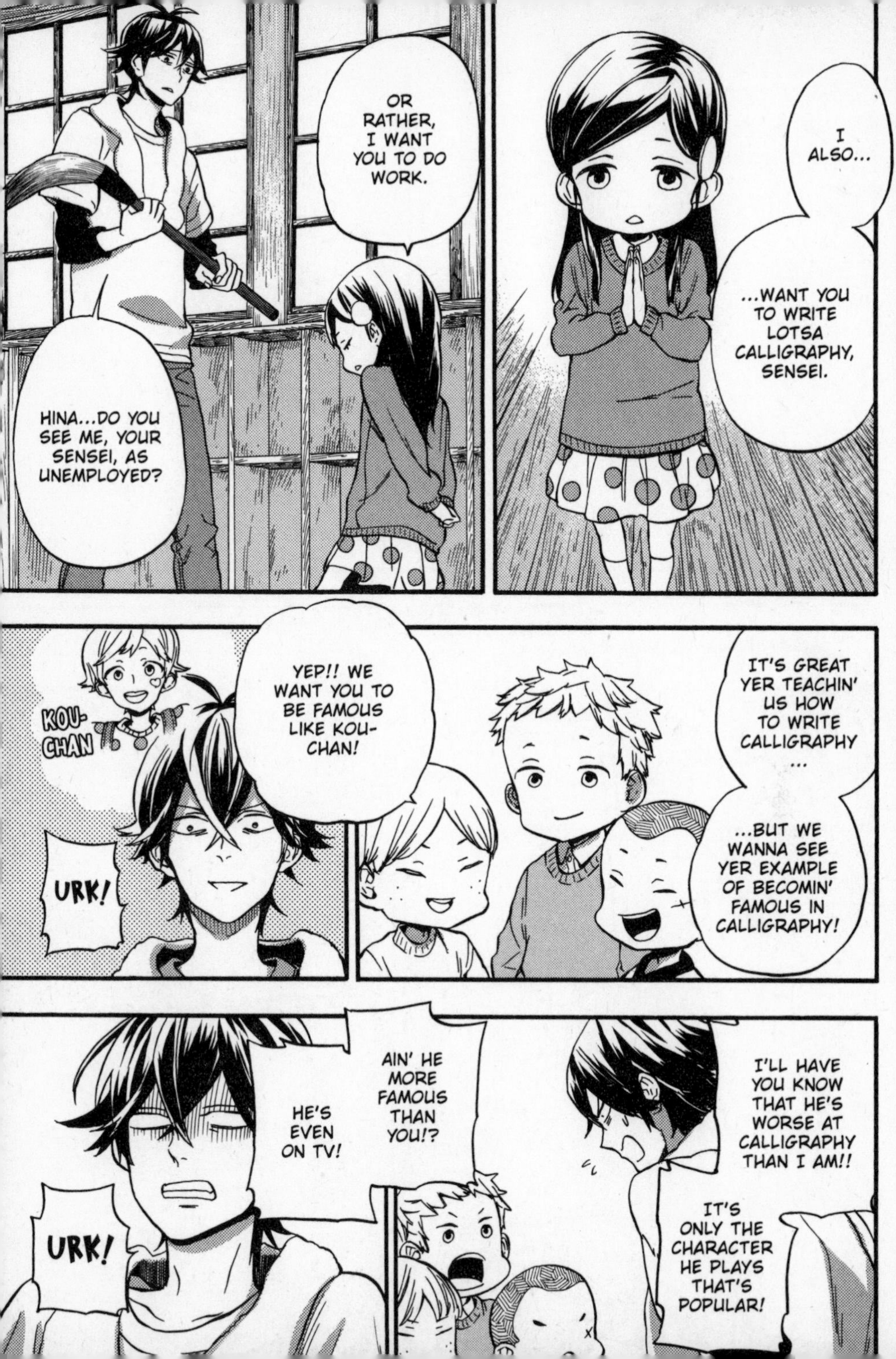
I ALSO...
...WANT YOU TO WRITE LOTSA CALLIGRAPHY, SENSEI.
OR RATHER, I WANT YOU TO DO WORK.
HINA...DO YOU SEE ME, YOUR SENSEI, AS UNEMPLOYED?
IT'S GREAT YER TEACHIN' US HOW TO WRITE CALLIGRAPHY...
...BUT WE WANNA SEE YER EXAMPLE OF BECOMIN' FAMOUS IN CALLIGRAPHY!
YEP!! WE WANT YOU TO BE FAMOUS LIKE KOU-CHAN!
KOU-CHAN
URK!
I'LL HAVE YOU KNOW THAT HE'S WORSE AT CALLIGRAPHY THAN I AM!!
IT'S ONLY THE CHARACTER HE PLAYS THAT'S POPULAR!
AIN' HE MORE FAMOUS THAN YOU!?
HE'S EVEN ON TV!
URK!

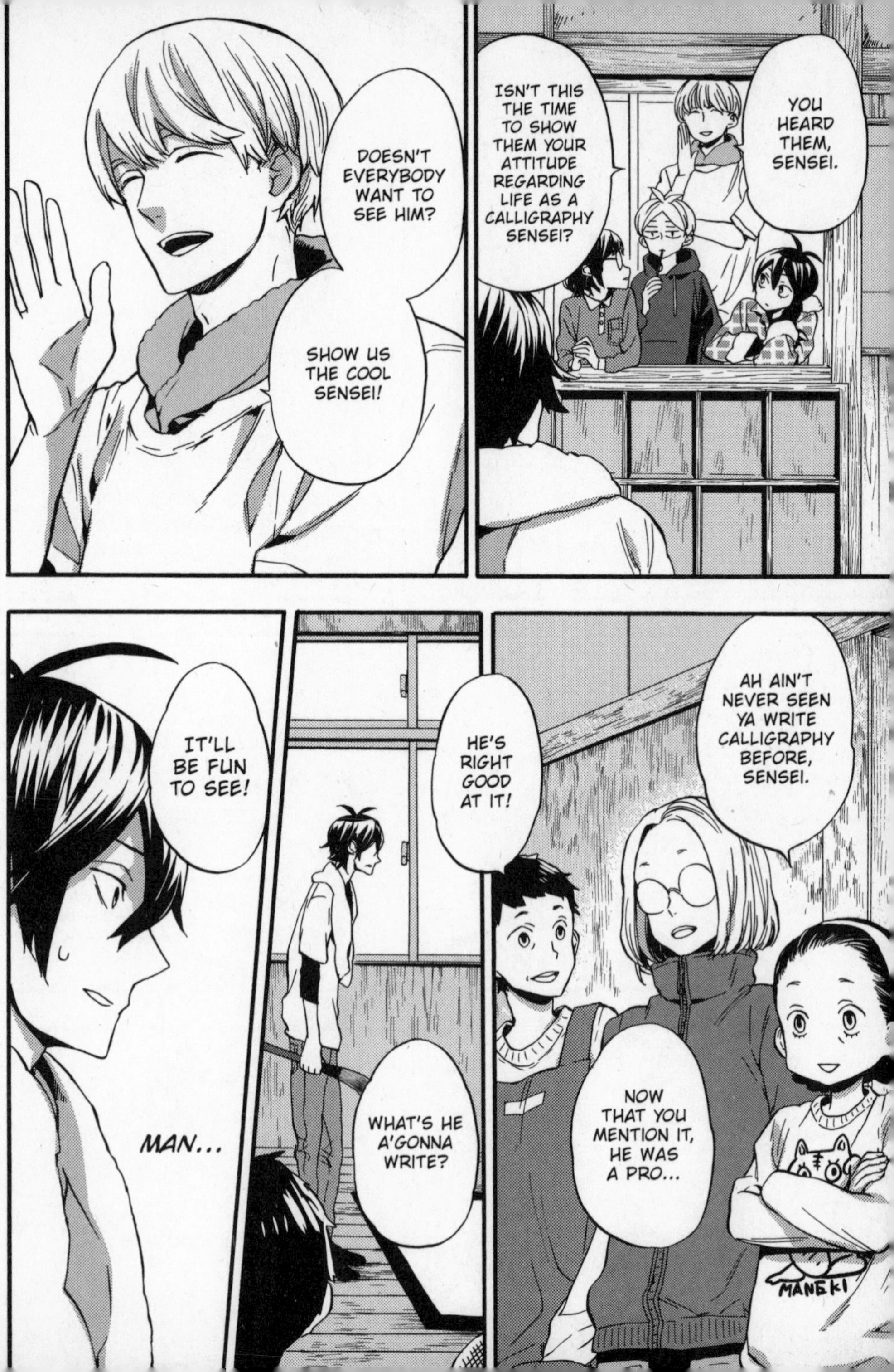
YOU HEARD THEM, SENSEI.
ISN'T THIS THE TIME TO SHOW THEM YOUR ATTITUDE REGARDING LIFE AS A CALLIGRAPHY SENSEI?
DOESN'T EVERYBODY WANT TO SEE HIM?
SHOW US THE COOL SENSEI!
AH AIN'T NEVER SEEN YA WRITE CALLIGRAPHY BEFORE, SENSEI.
HE'S RIGHT GOOD AT IT!
NOW THAT YOU MENTION IT, HE WAS A PRO...
MANEKI
WHAT'S HE A'GONNA WRITE?
IT'LL BE FUN TO SEE!
MAN...

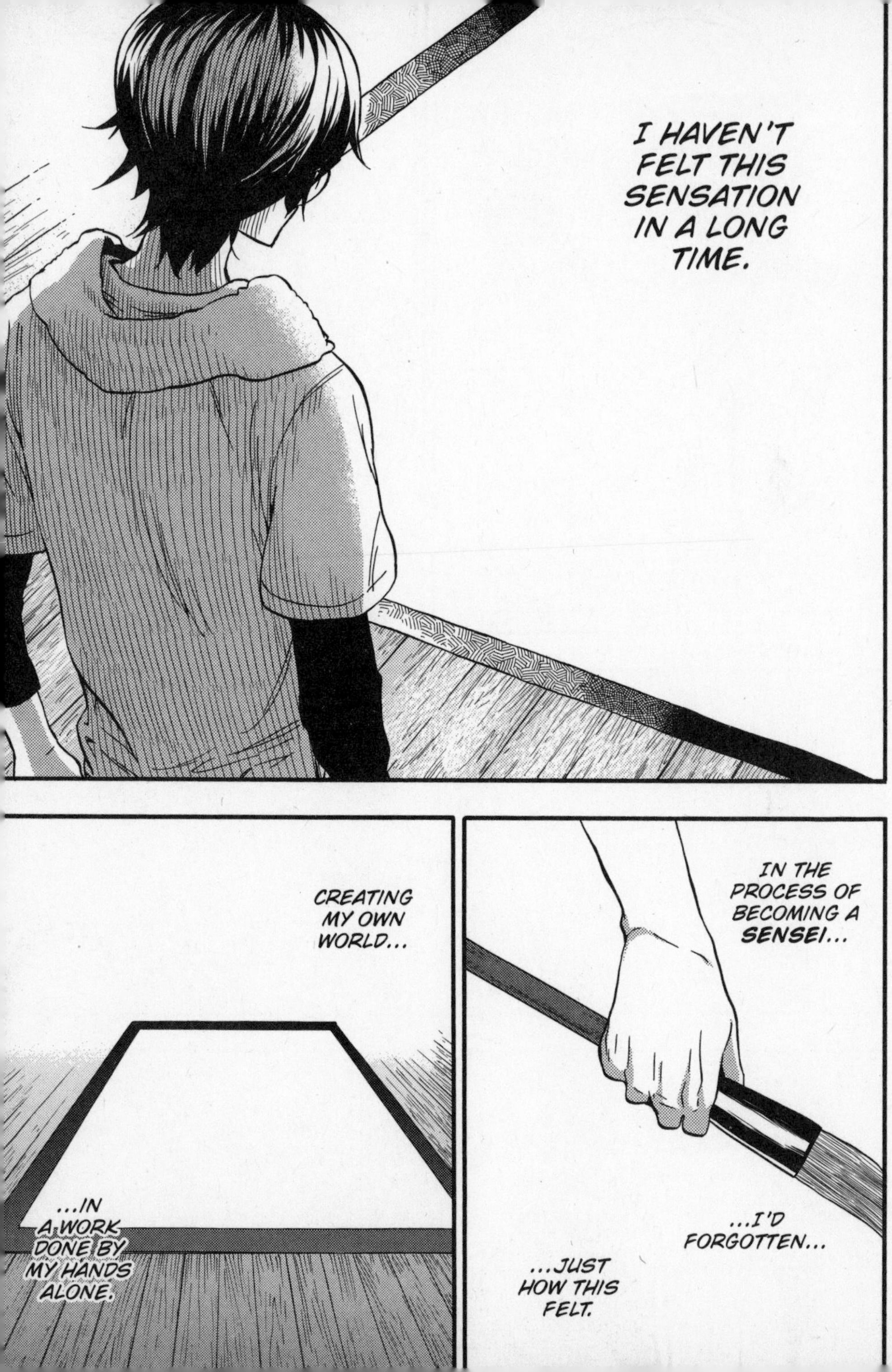
I HAVEN'T FELT THIS SENSATION IN A LONG TIME.
IN THE PROCESS OF BECOMING A **SENSEI**...
...I'D FORGOTTEN...
...JUST HOW THIS FELT.
CREATING MY OWN WORLD...
...IN A WORK DONE BY MY HANDS ALONE.

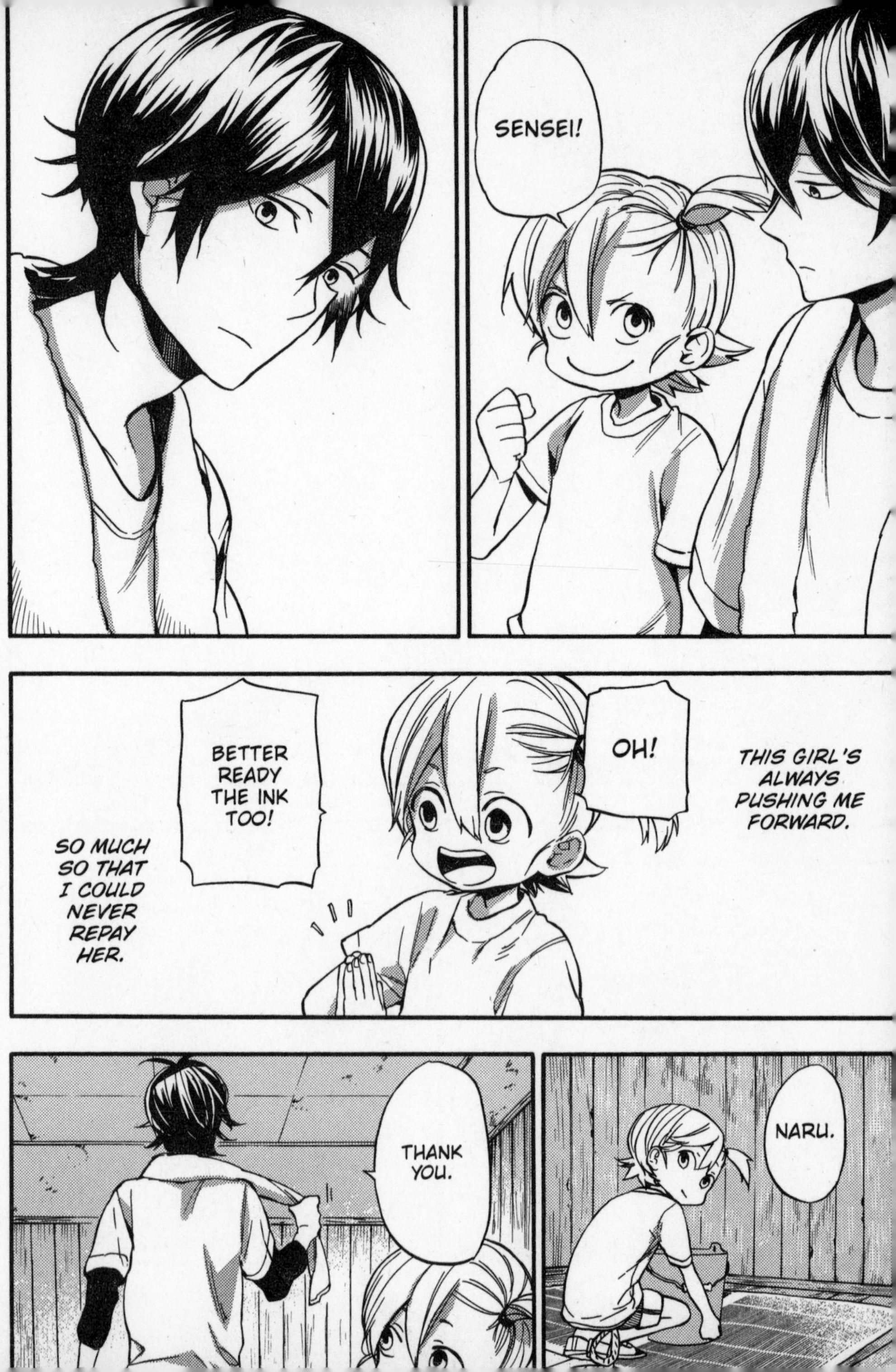
SENSEI!
THIS GIRL'S ALWAYS PUSHING ME FORWARD.
OH!
BETTER READY THE INK TOO!
SO MUCH SO THAT I COULD NEVER REPAY HER.
NARU.
THANK YOU.

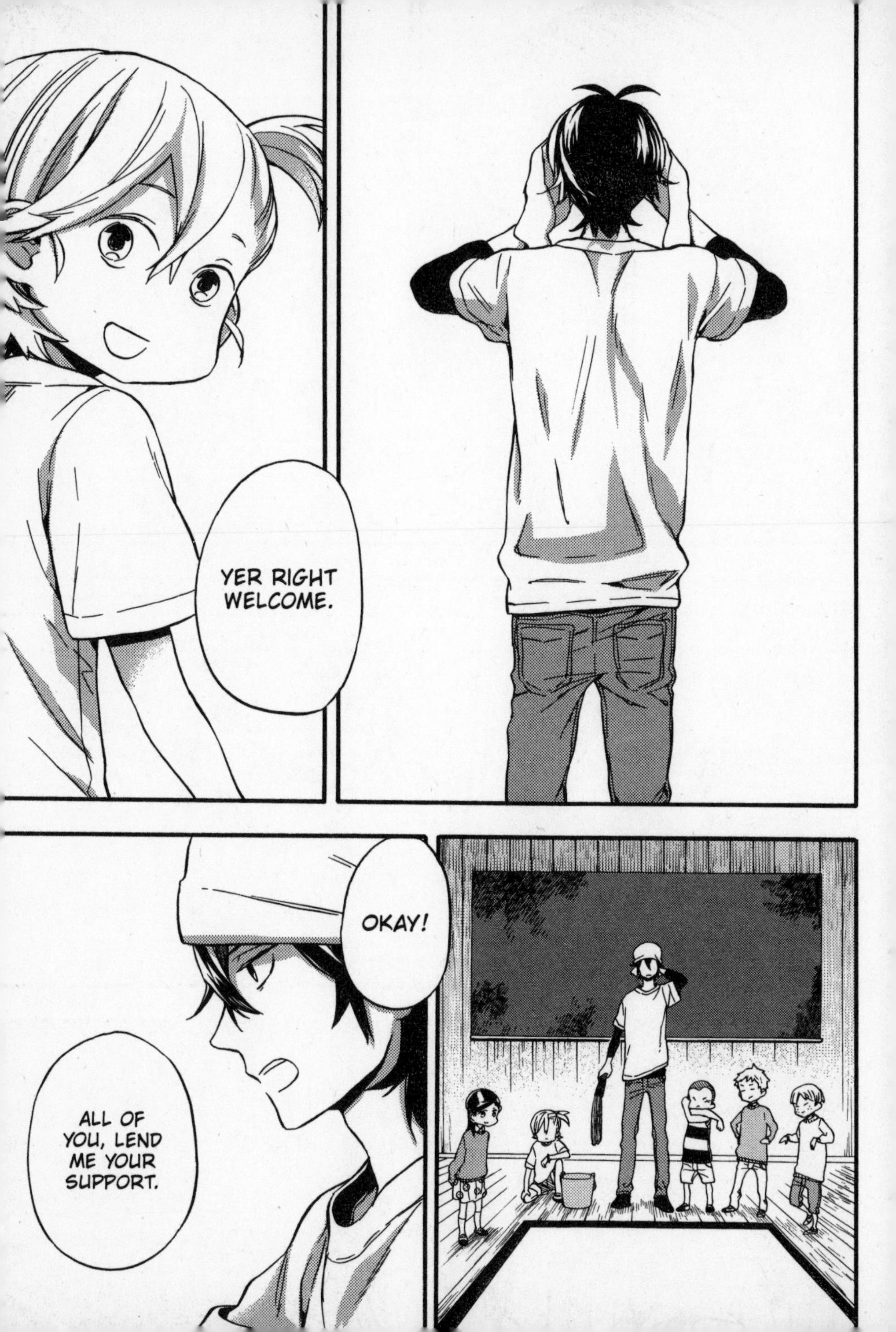
YER RIGHT WELCOME.
OKAY!
ALL OF YOU, LEND ME YOUR SUPPORT.

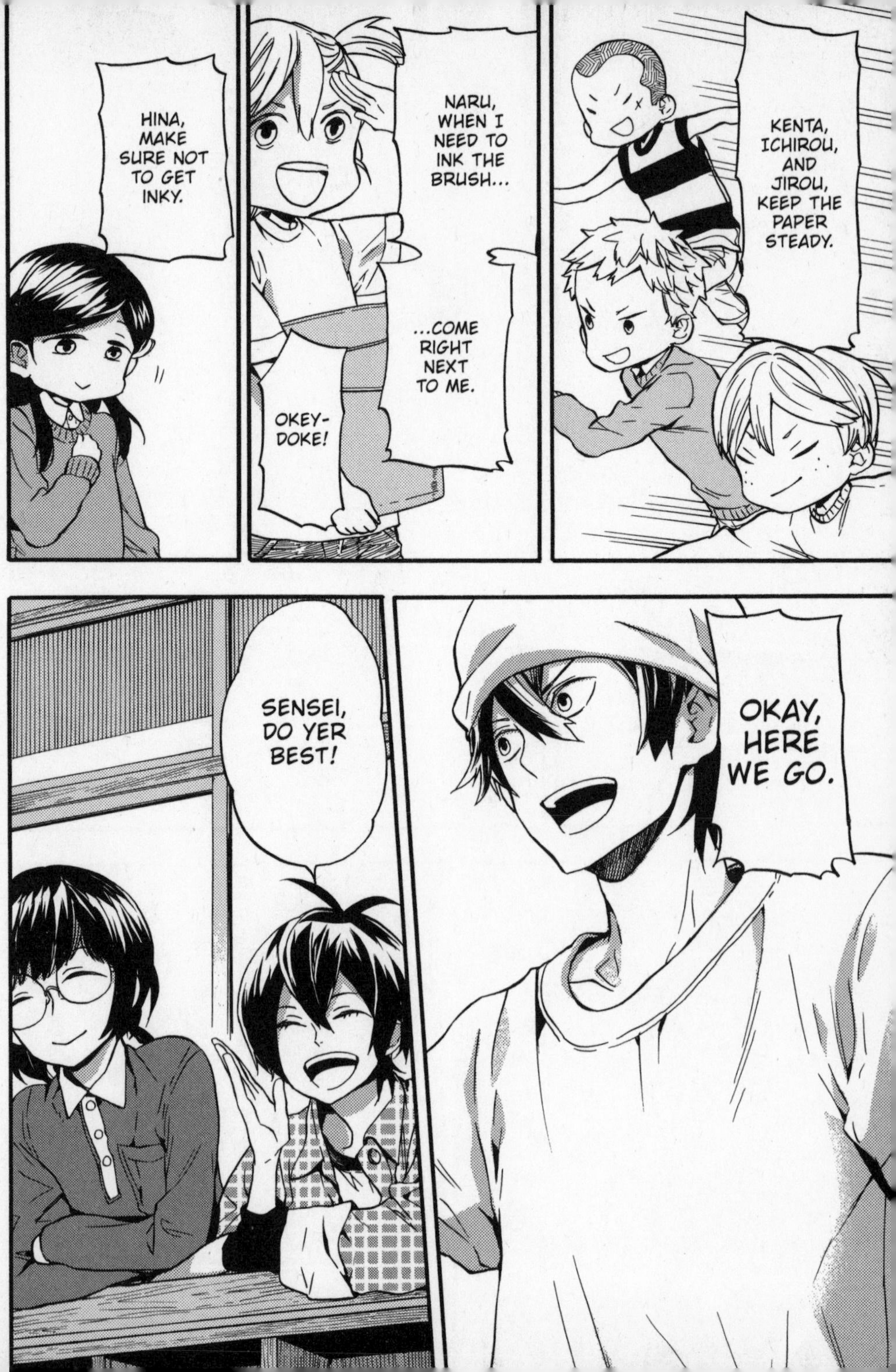
KENTA, ICHIROU, AND JIROU, KEEP THE PAPER STEADY.
NARU, WHEN I NEED TO INK THE BRUSH...
...COME RIGHT NEXT TO ME.
OKEY-DOKE!
HINA, MAKE SURE NOT TO GET INKY.
OKAY, HERE WE GO.
SENSEI, DO YER BEST!

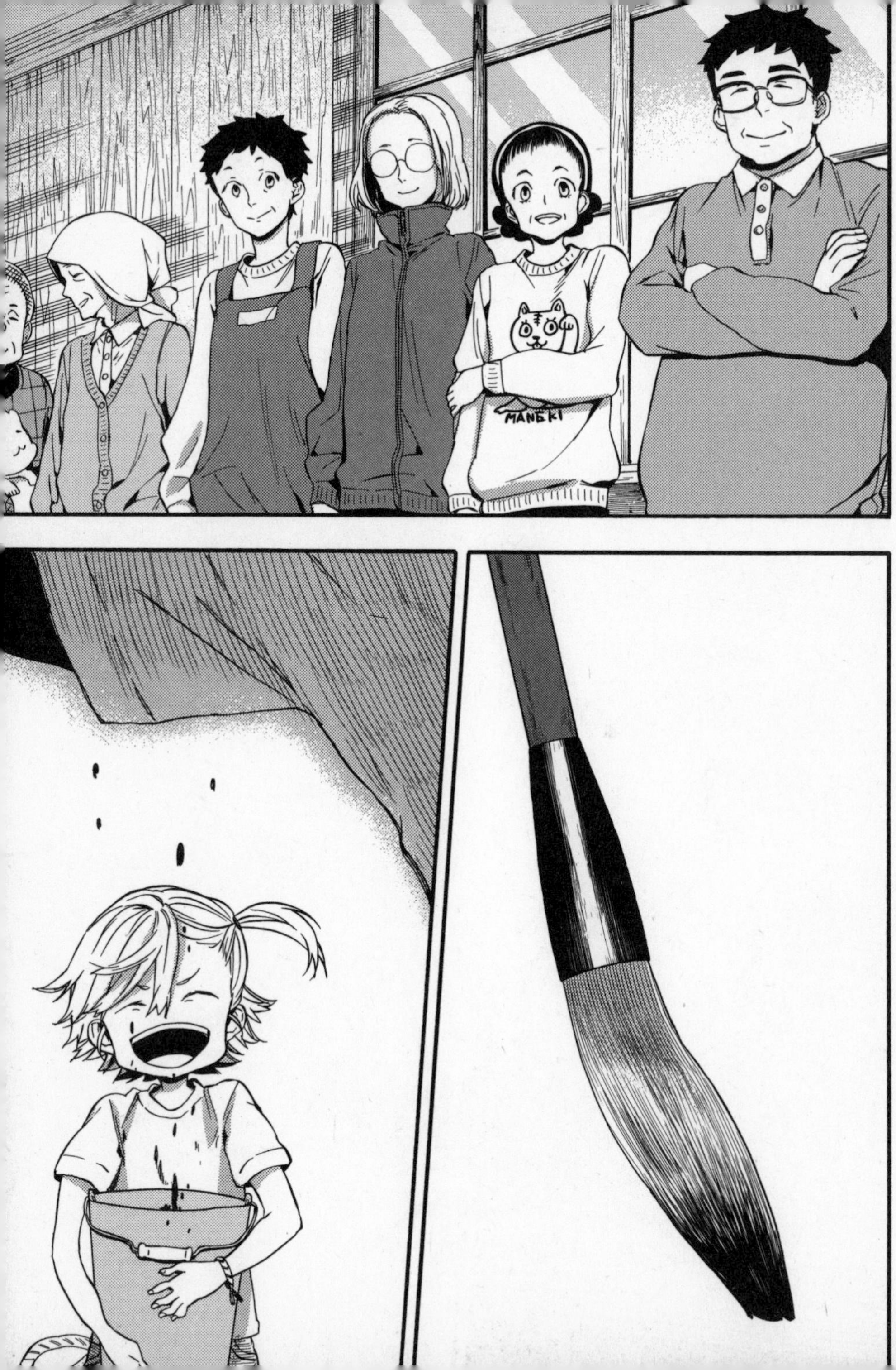
MANEKI

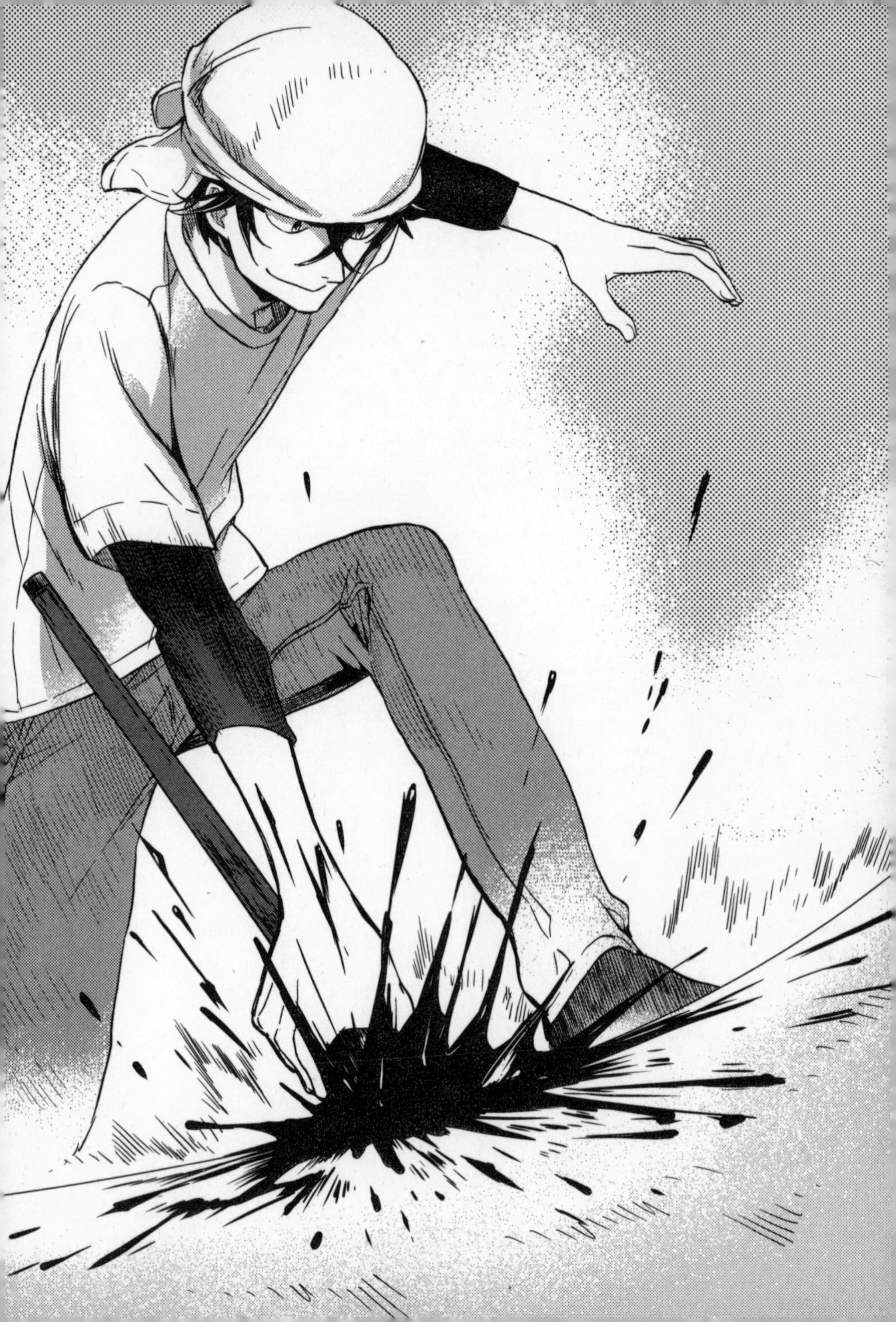

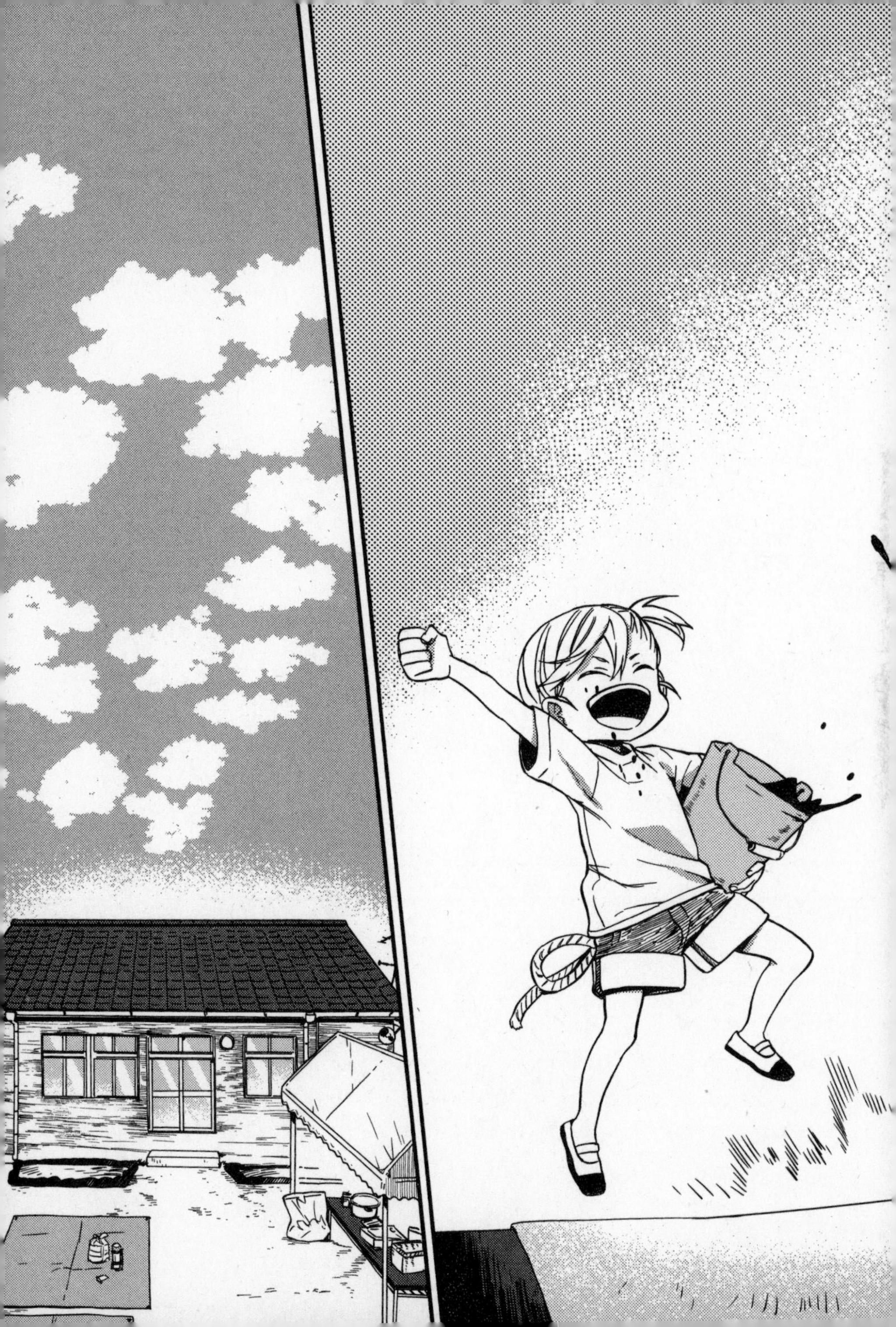

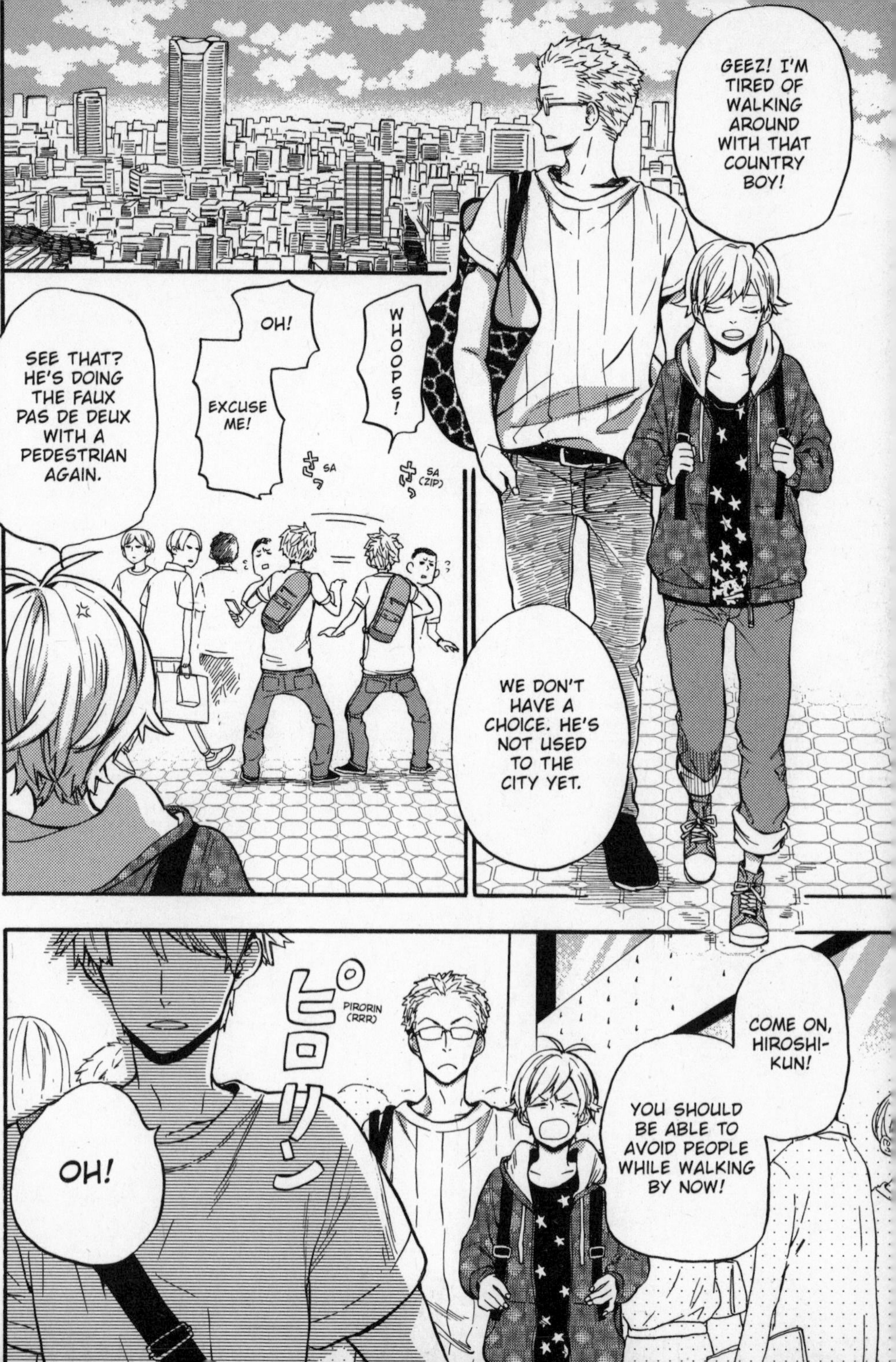
GEEZ! I'M TIRED OF WALKING AROUND WITH THAT COUNTRY BOY!
WHOOPS!
SA (ZIP)
OH!
EXCUSE ME!
SA
SEE THAT? HE'S DOING THE FAUX PAS DE DEUX WITH A PEDESTRIAN AGAIN.
WE DON'T HAVE A CHOICE. HE'S NOT USED TO THE CITY YET.
COME ON, HIROSHI-KUN!
YOU SHOULD BE ABLE TO AVOID PEOPLE WHILE WALKING BY NOW!
PIRORIN (RRR)
OH!

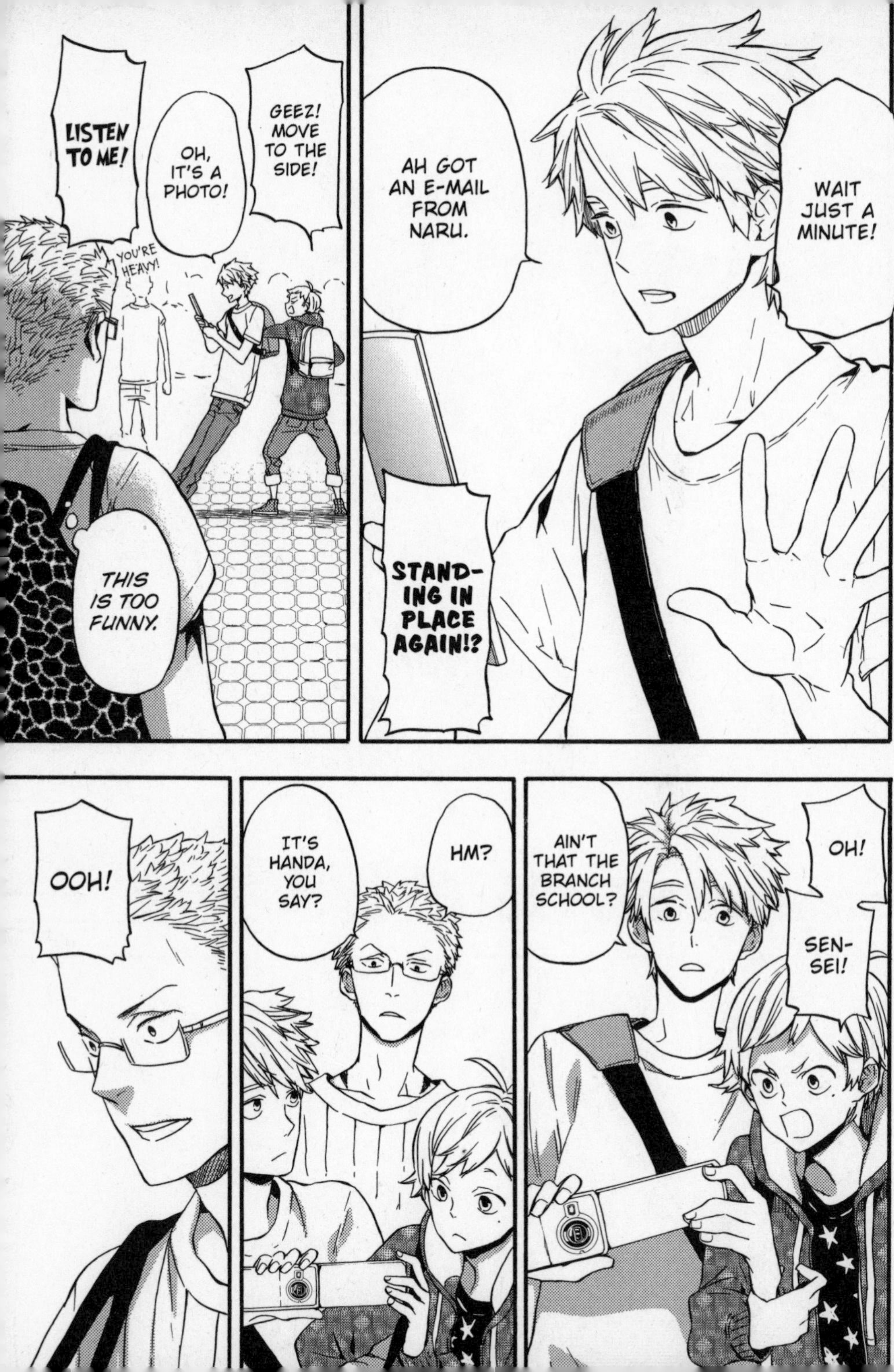
WAIT JUST A MINUTE!
AH GOT AN E-MAIL FROM NARU.
STAND-ING IN PLACE AGAIN!?
GEEZ! MOVE TO THE SIDE!
OH, IT'S A PHOTO!
LISTEN TO ME!
YOU'RE HEAVY!
THIS IS TOO FUNNY.
OH!
SEN-SEI!
AIN'T THAT THE BRANCH SCHOOL?
HM?
IT'S HANDA, YOU SAY?
OOH!

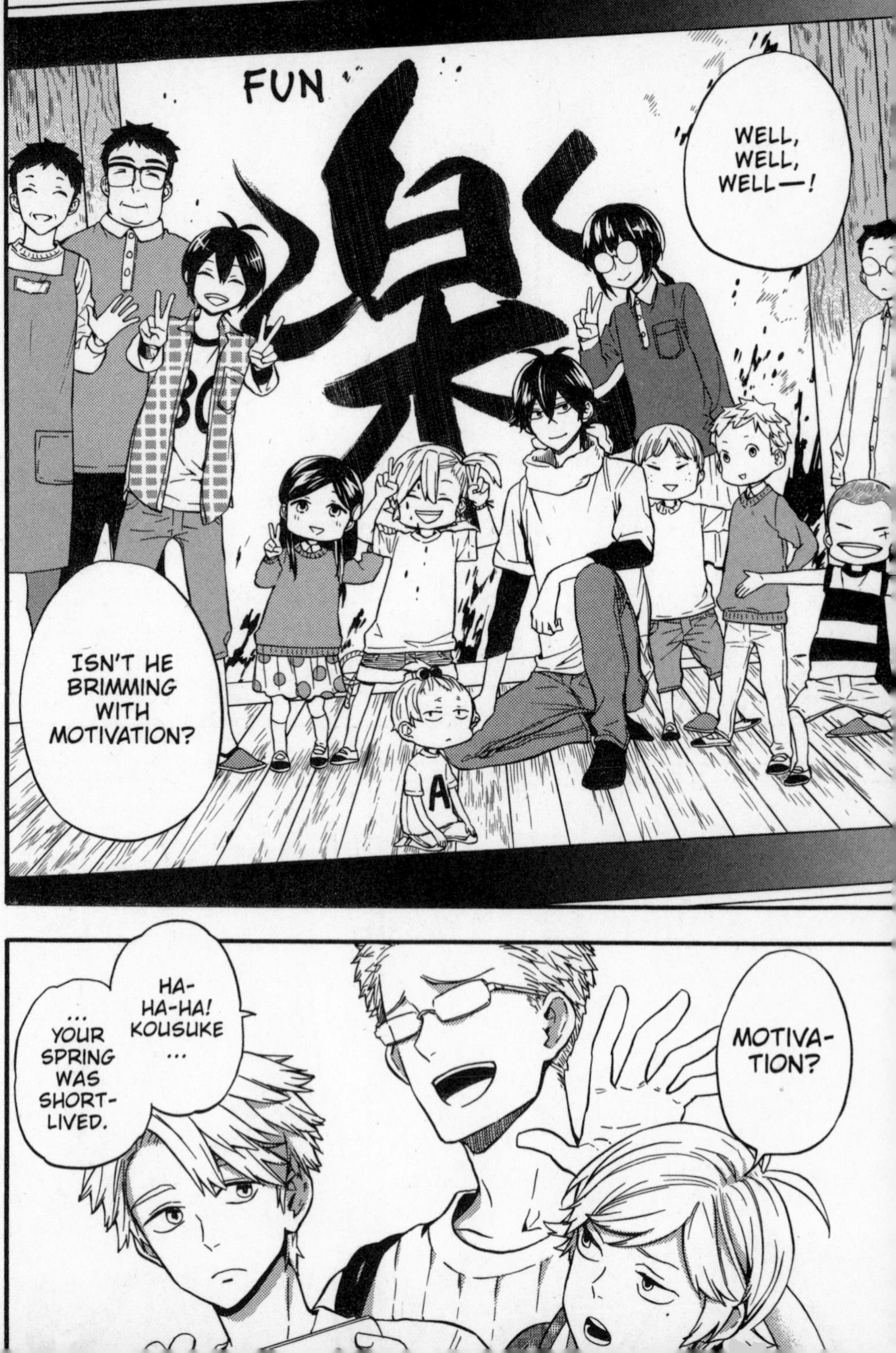
WELL, WELL, WELL—!
FUN
ISN'T HE BRIMMING WITH MOTIVATION?
MOTIVA-TION?
HA-HA-HA! KOUSUKE...
...YOUR SPRING WAS SHORT-LIVED.

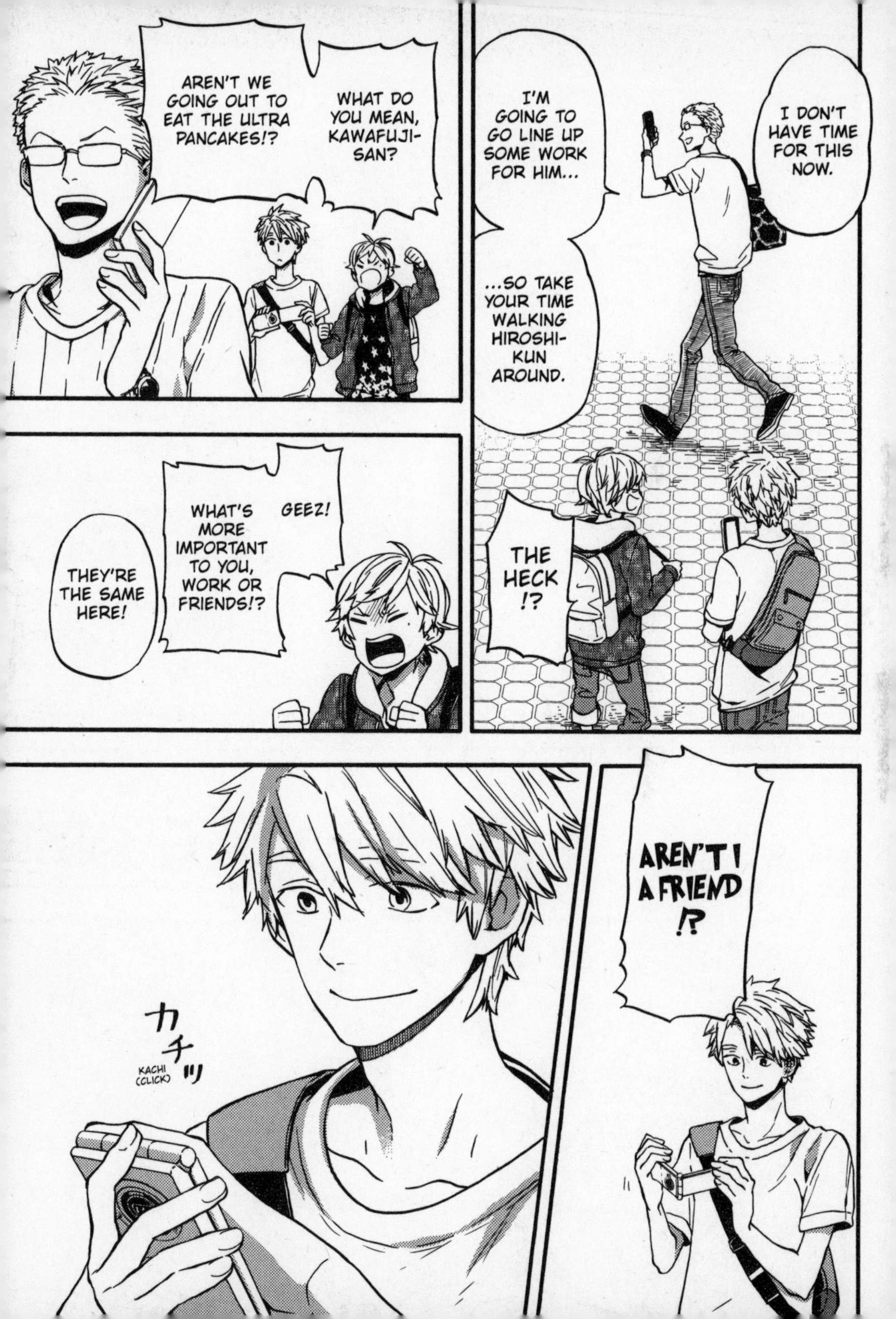
I DON'T HAVE TIME FOR THIS NOW.
I'M GOING TO GO LINE UP SOME WORK FOR HIM...
...SO TAKE YOUR TIME WALKING HIROSHI-KUN AROUND.
THE HECK!?
WHAT DO YOU MEAN, KAWAFUJI-SAN?
AREN'T WE GOING OUT TO EAT THE ULTRA PANCAKES!?
GEEZ!
WHAT'S MORE IMPORTANT TO YOU, WORK OR FRIENDS!?
THEY'RE THE SAME HERE!
AREN'T I A FRIEND!?
カチッ
KACHI (CLICK)

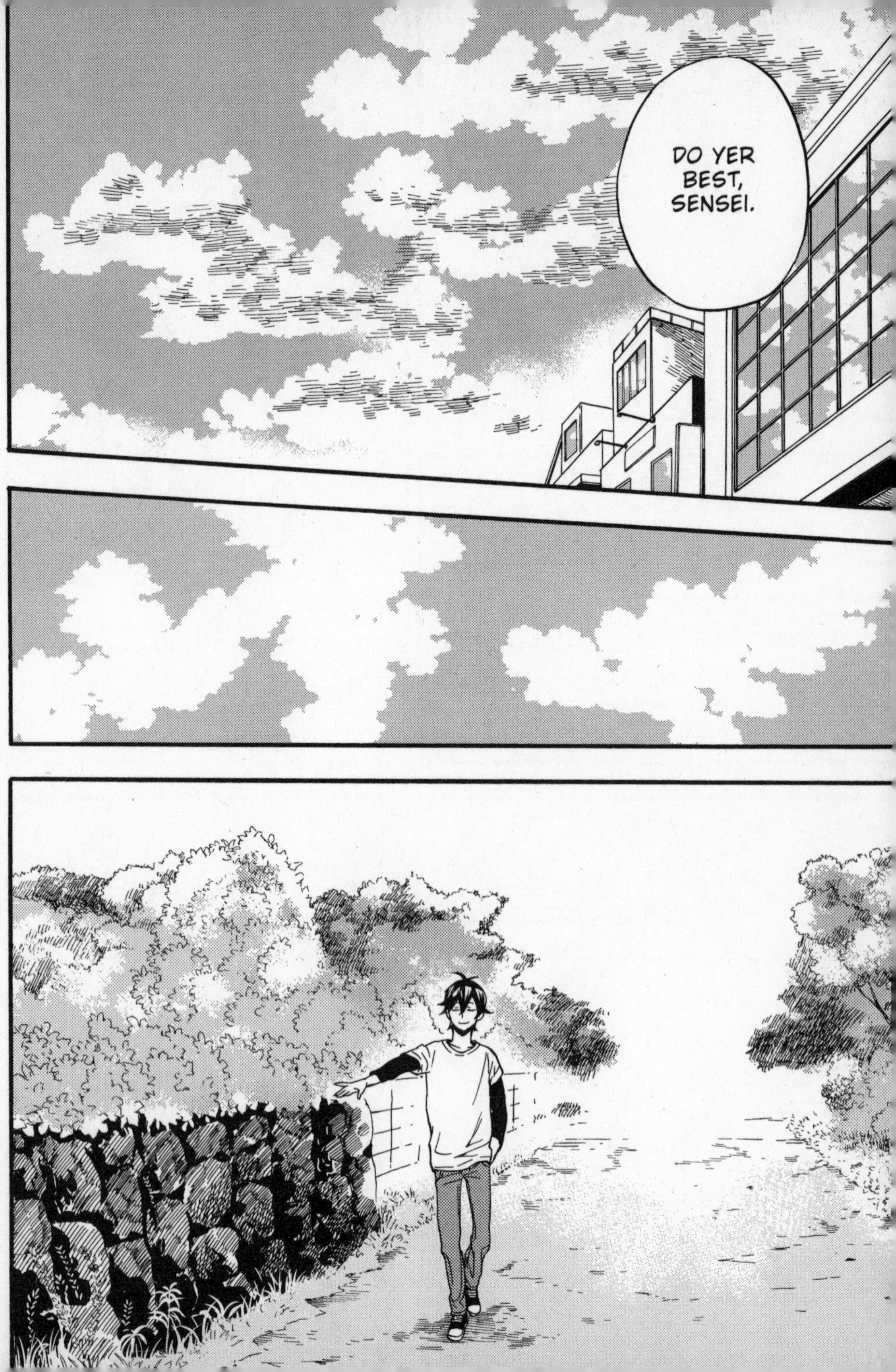
DO YER BEST, SENSEI.

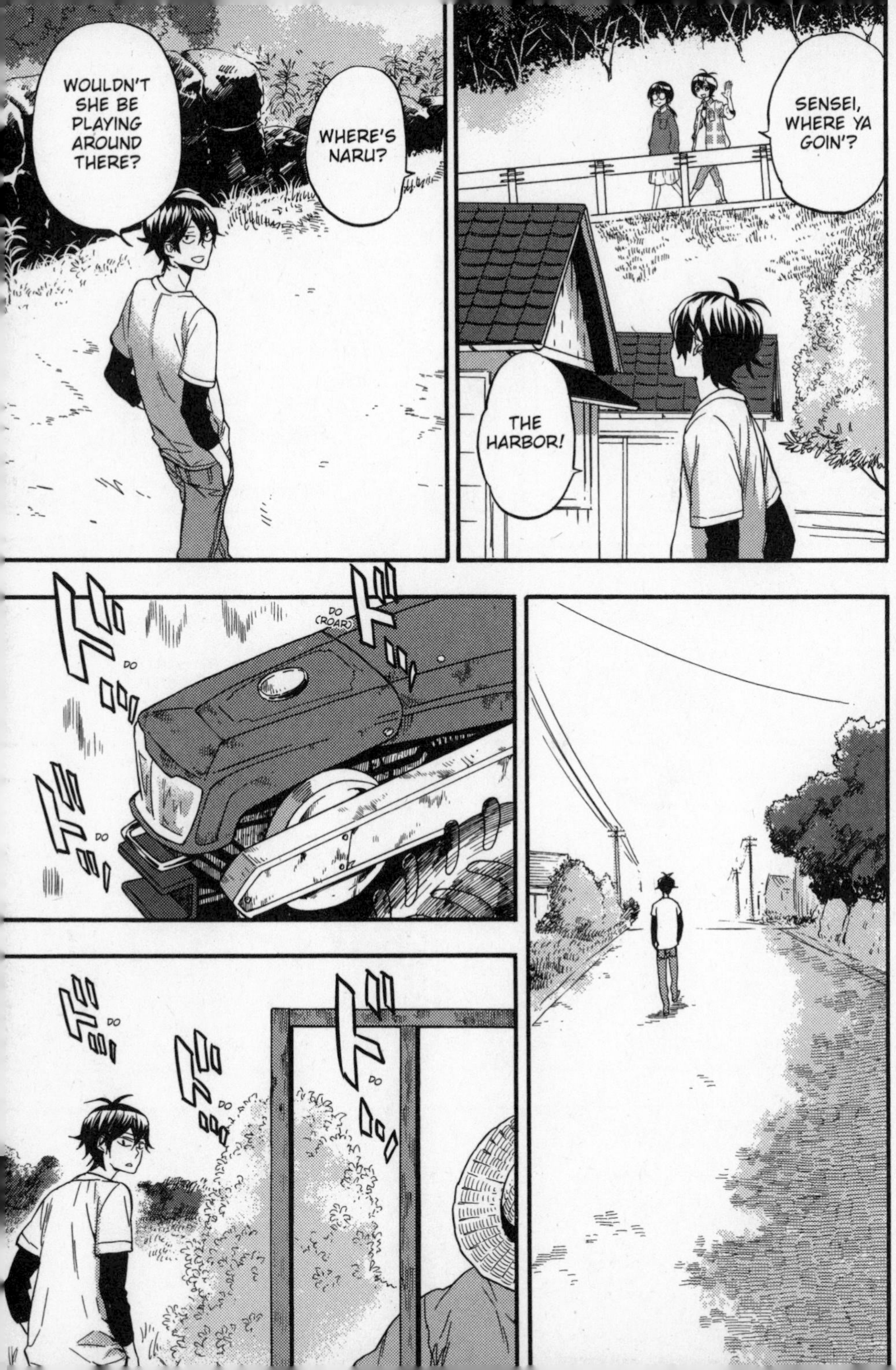
SENSEI, WHERE YA GOIN'?
THE HARBOR!
WHERE'S NARU?
WOULDN'T SHE BE PLAYING AROUND THERE?
DO (ROAR)
DO
DO
DO
DO
DO

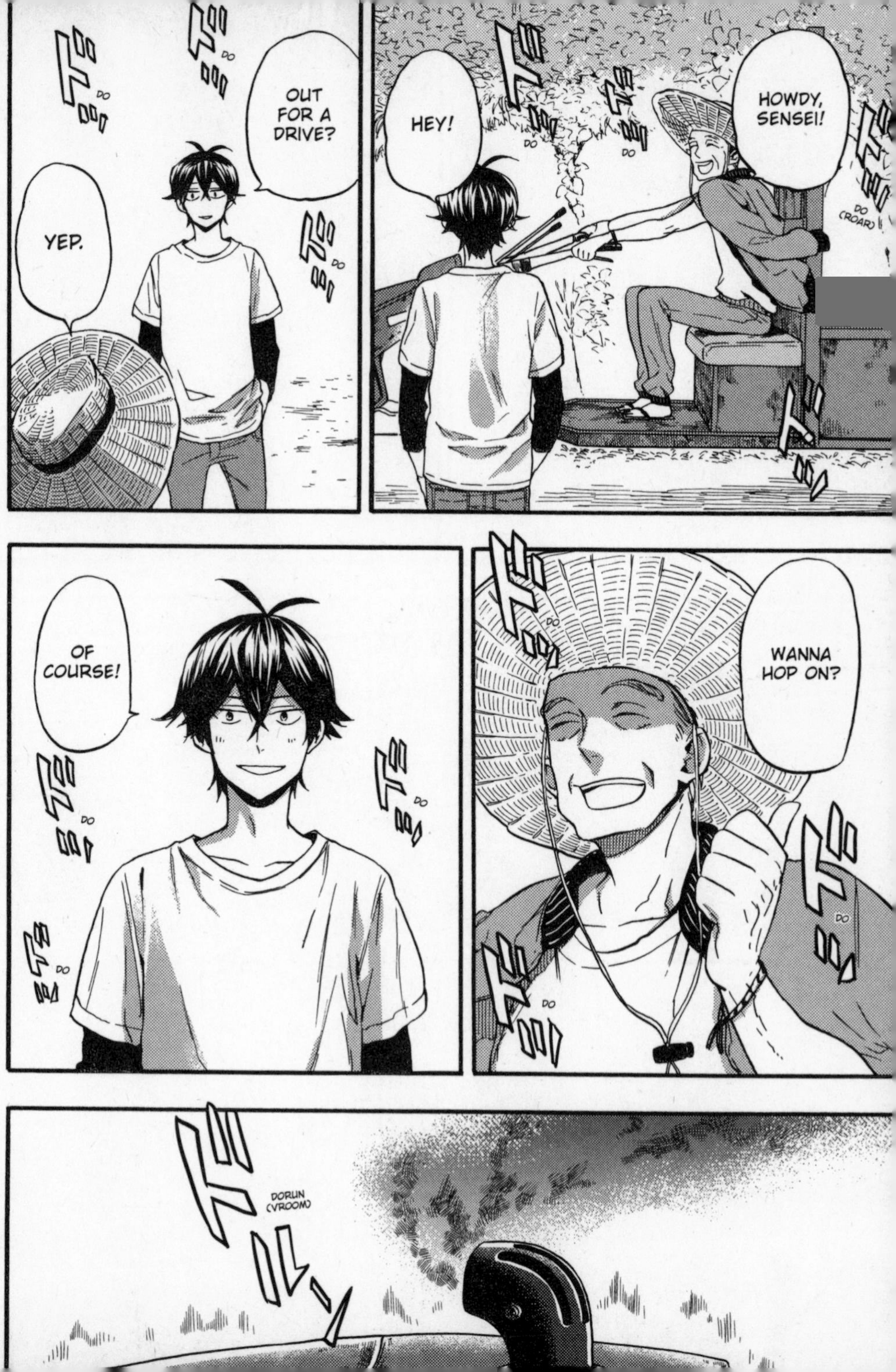
HOWDY, SENSEI!
DO (ROAR)
DO
HEY!
DO
DO
OUT FOR A DRIVE?
DO
YEP.
DO
WANNA HOP ON?
DO
DO
DO
OF COURSE!
DO
DO
DO
DORUN (VROOM)

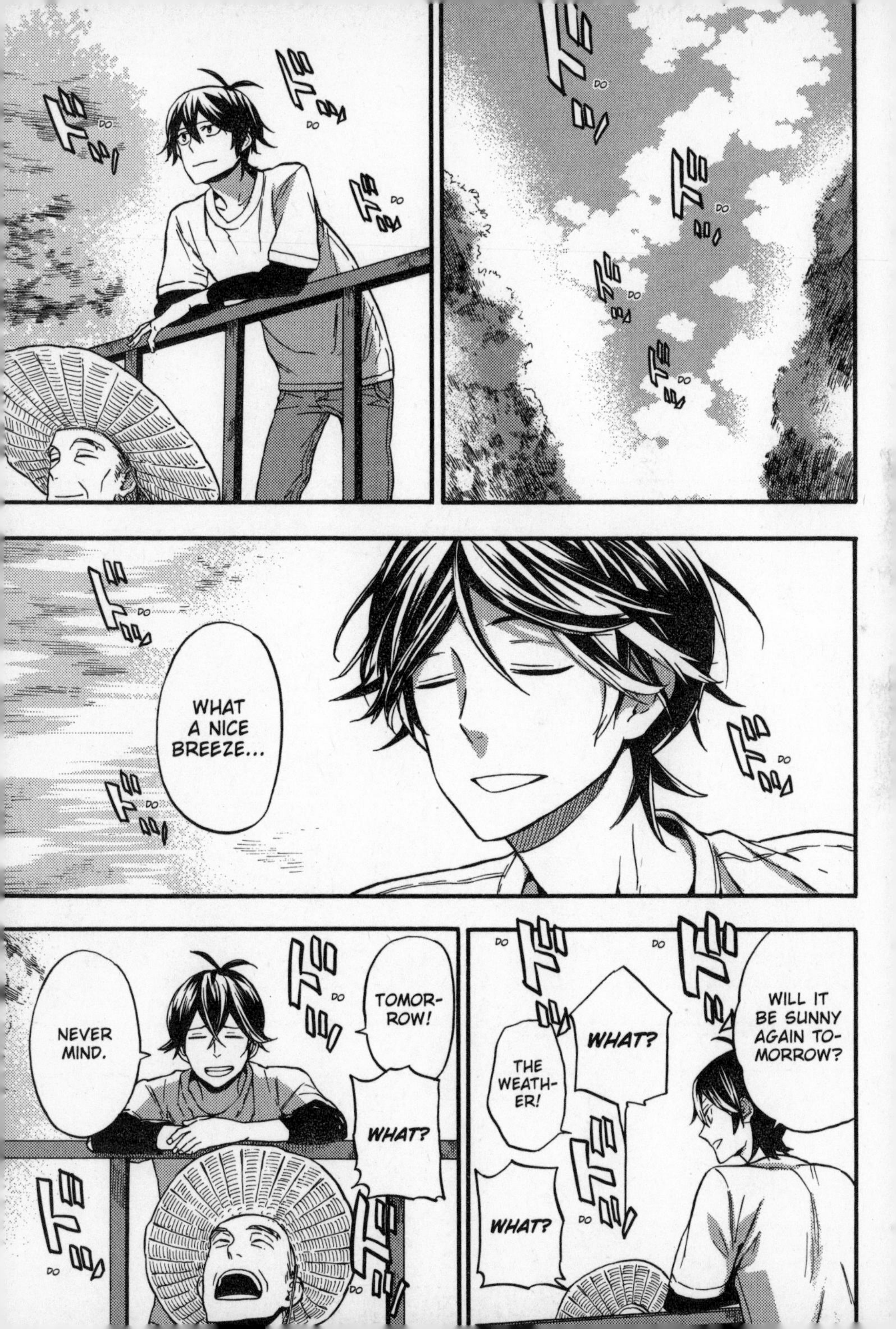
DO
DO
DO
DO
DO
DO
DO
DO
WHAT A NICE BREEZE...
DO
DO
DO
DO
WILL IT BE SUNNY AGAIN TO-MORROW?
WHAT?
THE WEATH-ER!
DO
WHAT?
DO
TOMOR-ROW!
WHAT?
NEVER MIND.
DO
DO

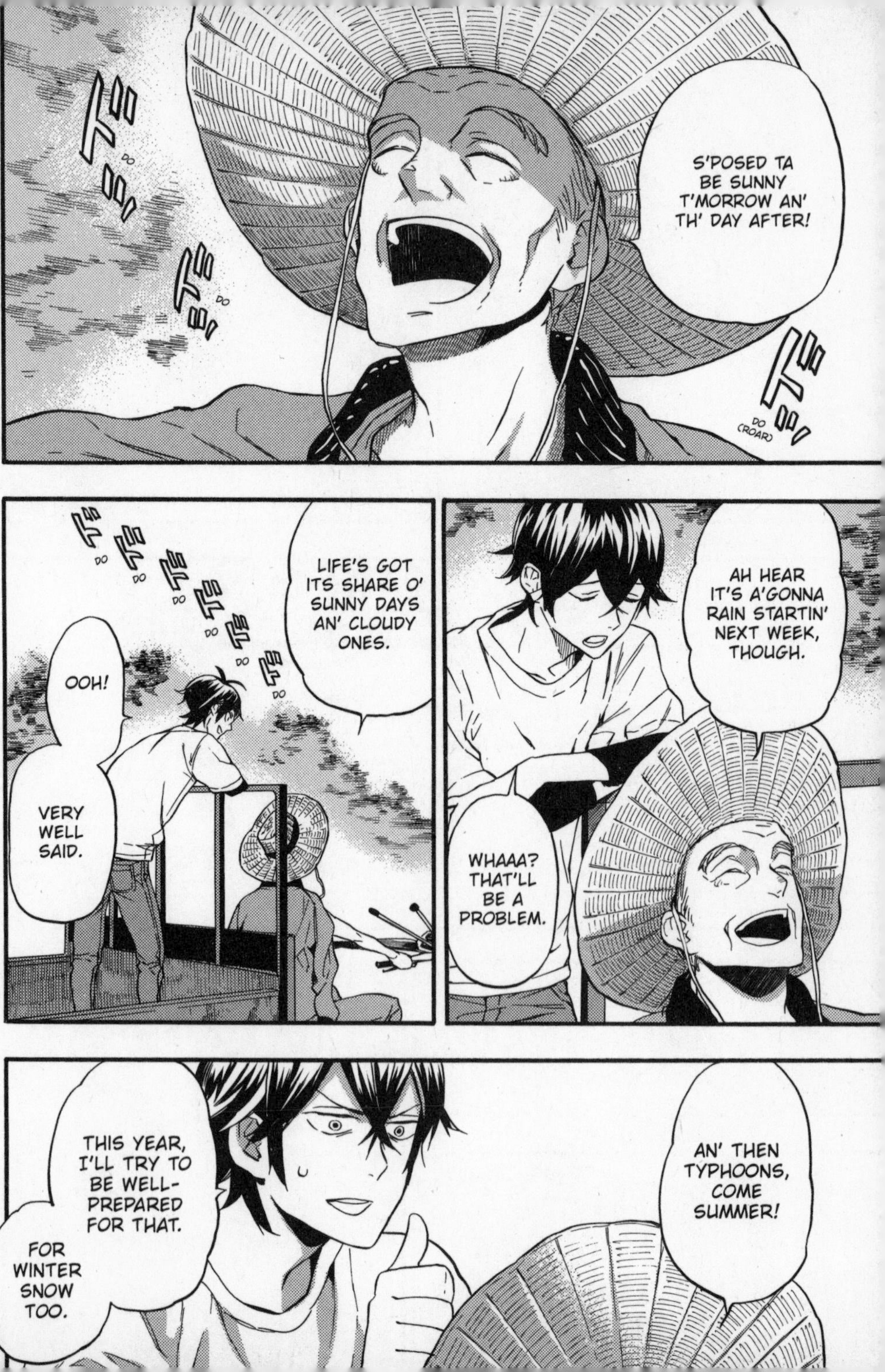
S'POSED TA BE SUNNY T'MORROW AN' TH' DAY AFTER!
ドドドドドド
DO
DO
DO (ROAR)
AH HEAR IT'S A'GONNA RAIN STARTIN' NEXT WEEK, THOUGH.
WHAAA? THAT'LL BE A PROBLEM.
LIFE'S GOT ITS SHARE O' SUNNY DAYS AN' CLOUDY ONES.
ドドドドドド
DO DO DO DO DO DO
OOH!
VERY WELL SAID.
AN' THEN TYPHOONS, COME SUMMER!
THIS YEAR, I'LL TRY TO BE WELL-PREPARED FOR THAT.
FOR WINTER SNOW TOO.

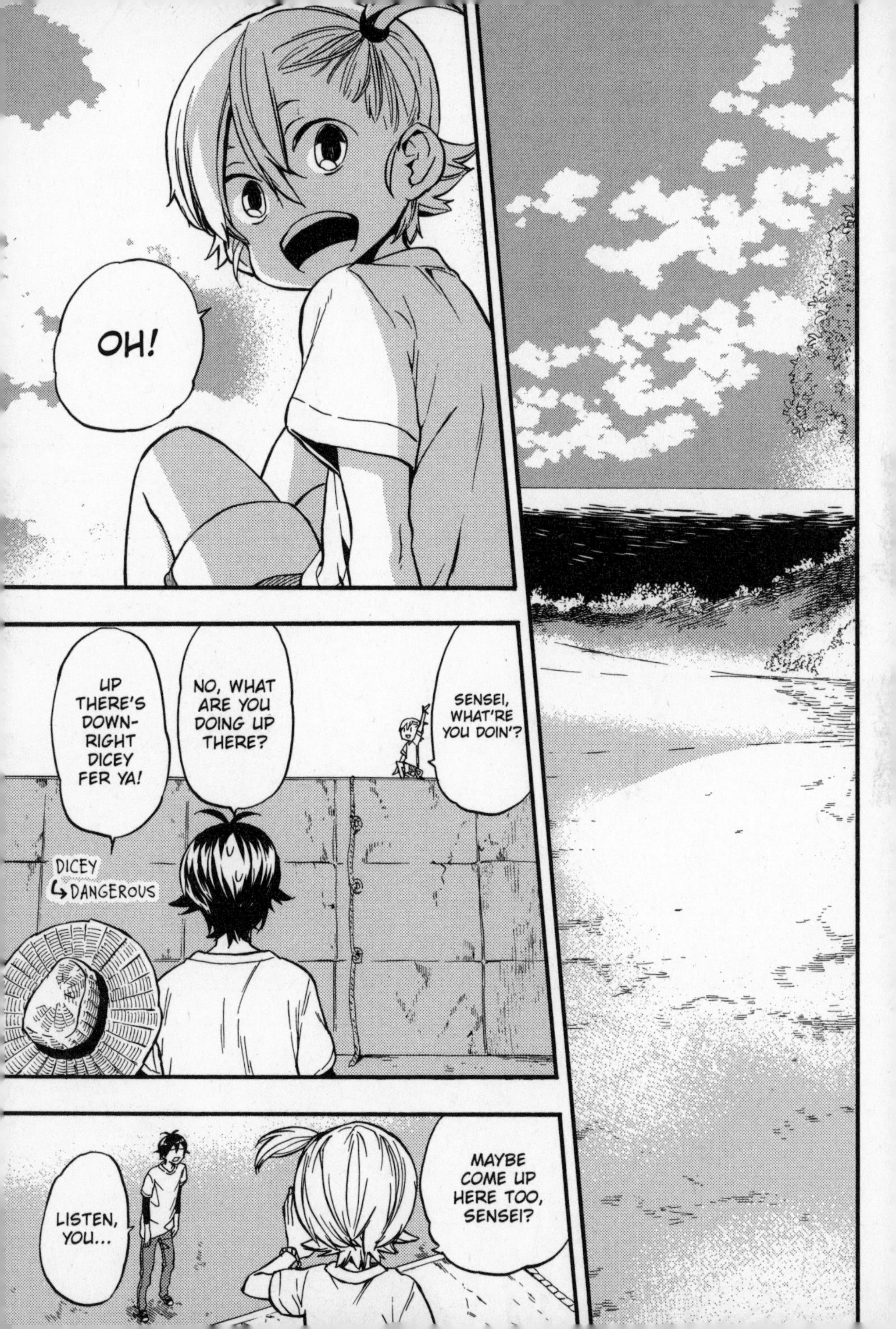
OH!
SENSEI, WHAT'RE YOU DOIN'?
NO, WHAT ARE YOU DOING UP THERE?
UP THERE'S DOWN-RIGHT DICEY FER YA!
DICEY ↳ DANGEROUS
MAYBE COME UP HERE TOO, SENSEI?
LISTEN, YOU...

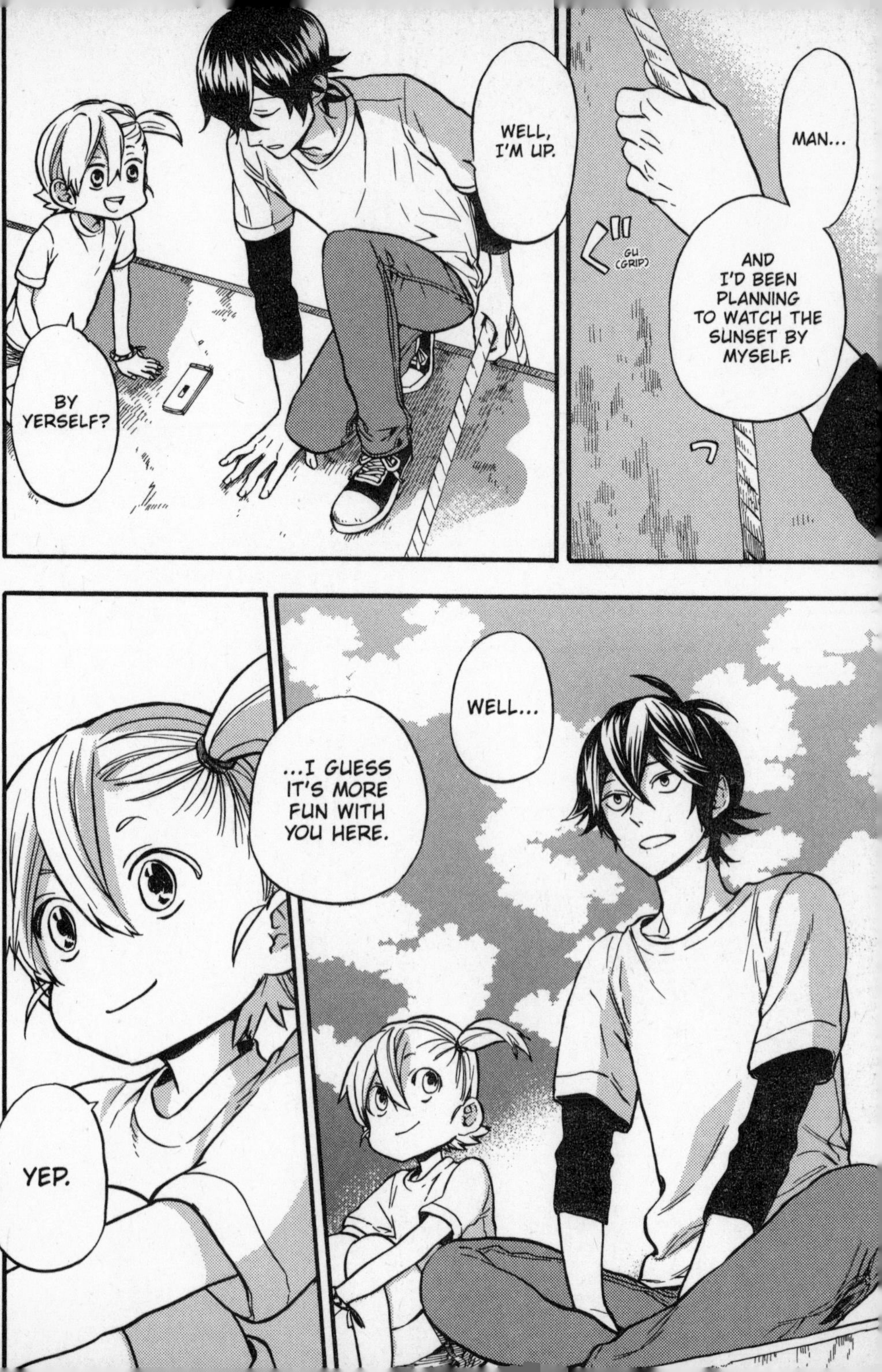
MAN...
AND I'D BEEN PLANNING TO WATCH THE SUNSET BY MYSELF.
GU (GRIP)
WELL, I'M UP.
BY YERSELF?
WELL...
...I GUESS IT'S MORE FUN WITH YOU HERE.
YEP.

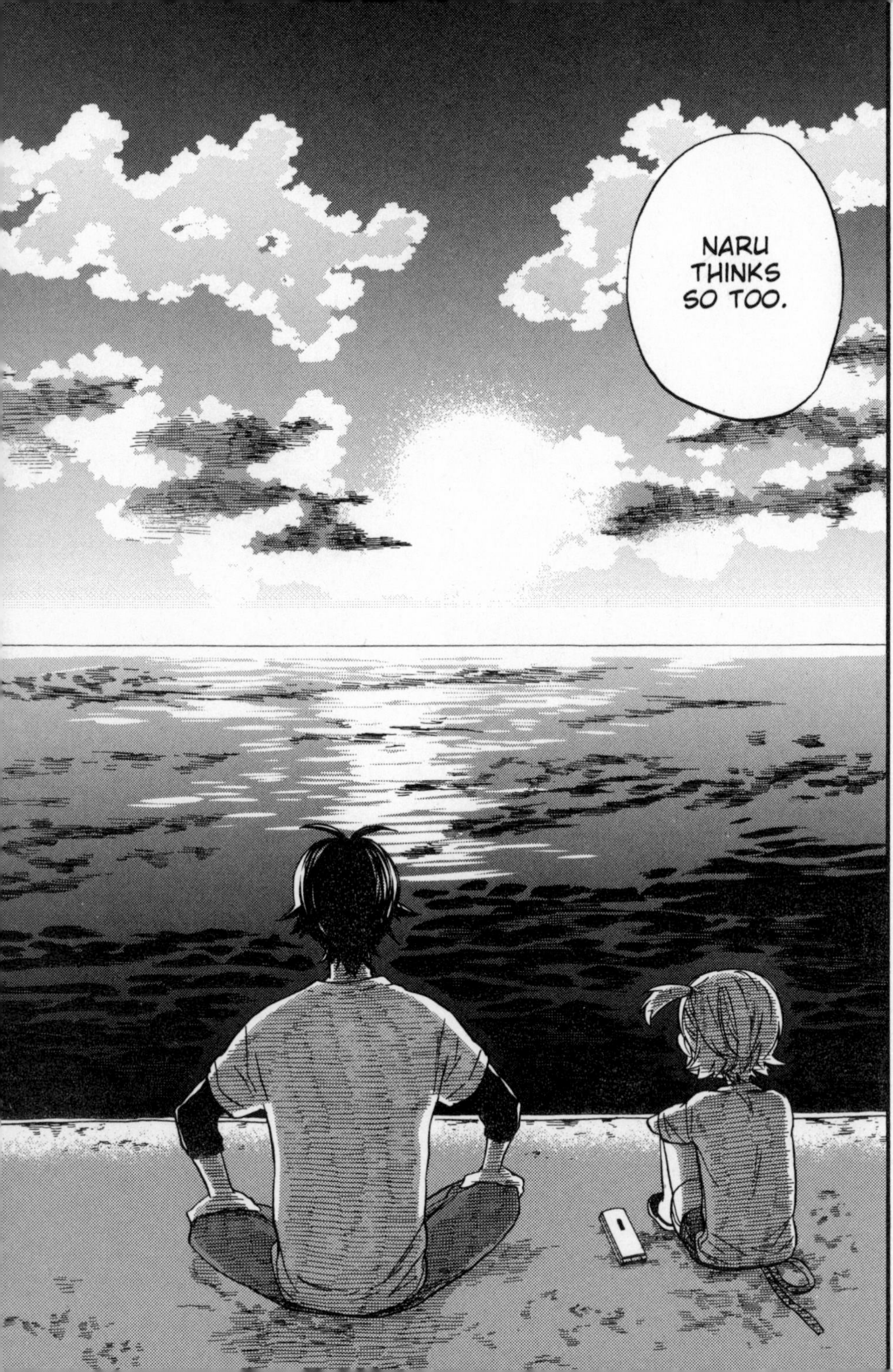
NARU THINKS SO TOO.

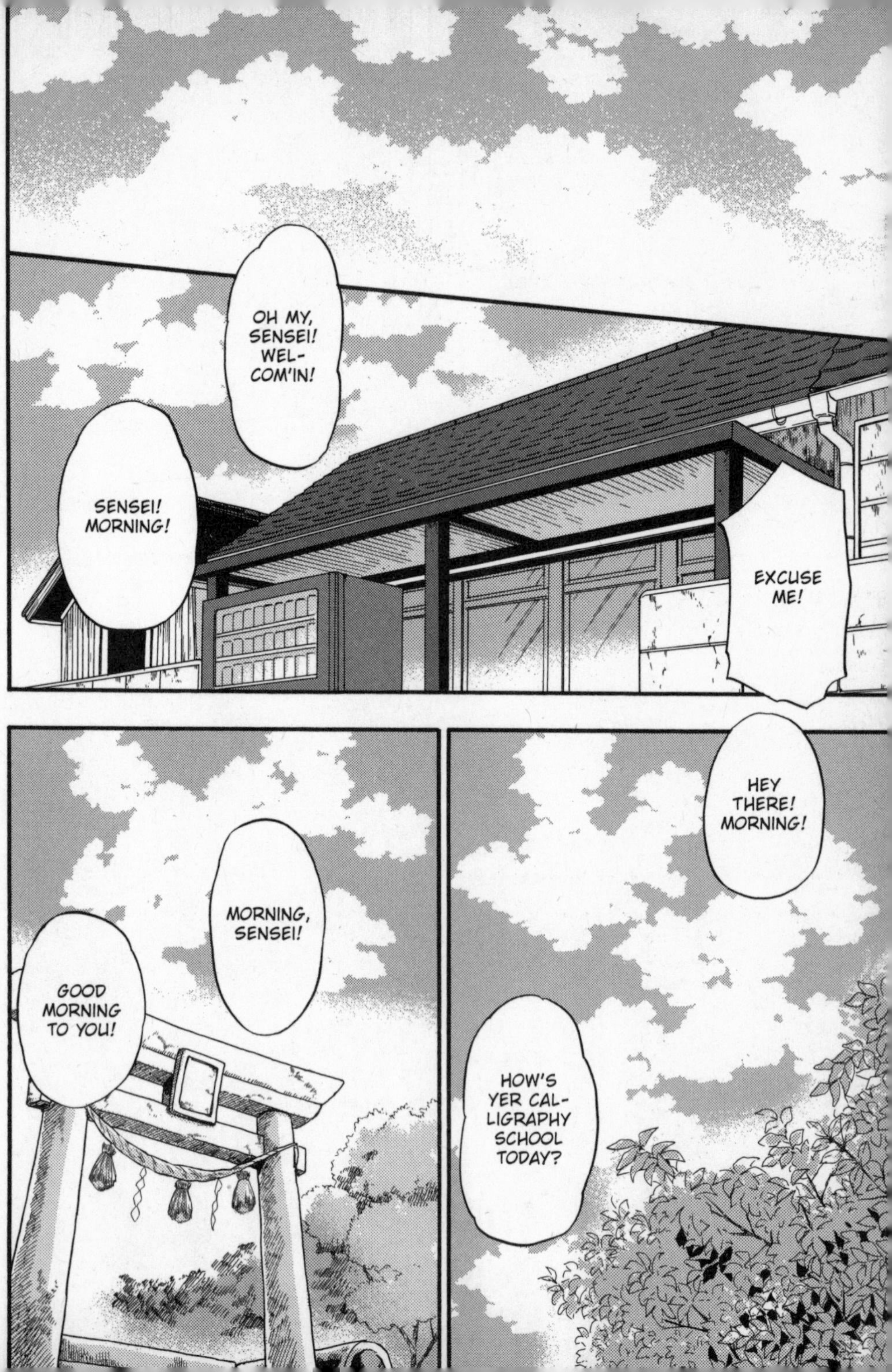
EXCUSE ME!
OH MY, SENSEI! WEL-COM'IN!
SENSEI! MORNING!
HEY THERE! MORNING!
HOW'S YER CAL-LIGRAPHY SCHOOL TODAY?
MORNING, SENSEI!
GOOD MORNING TO YOU!

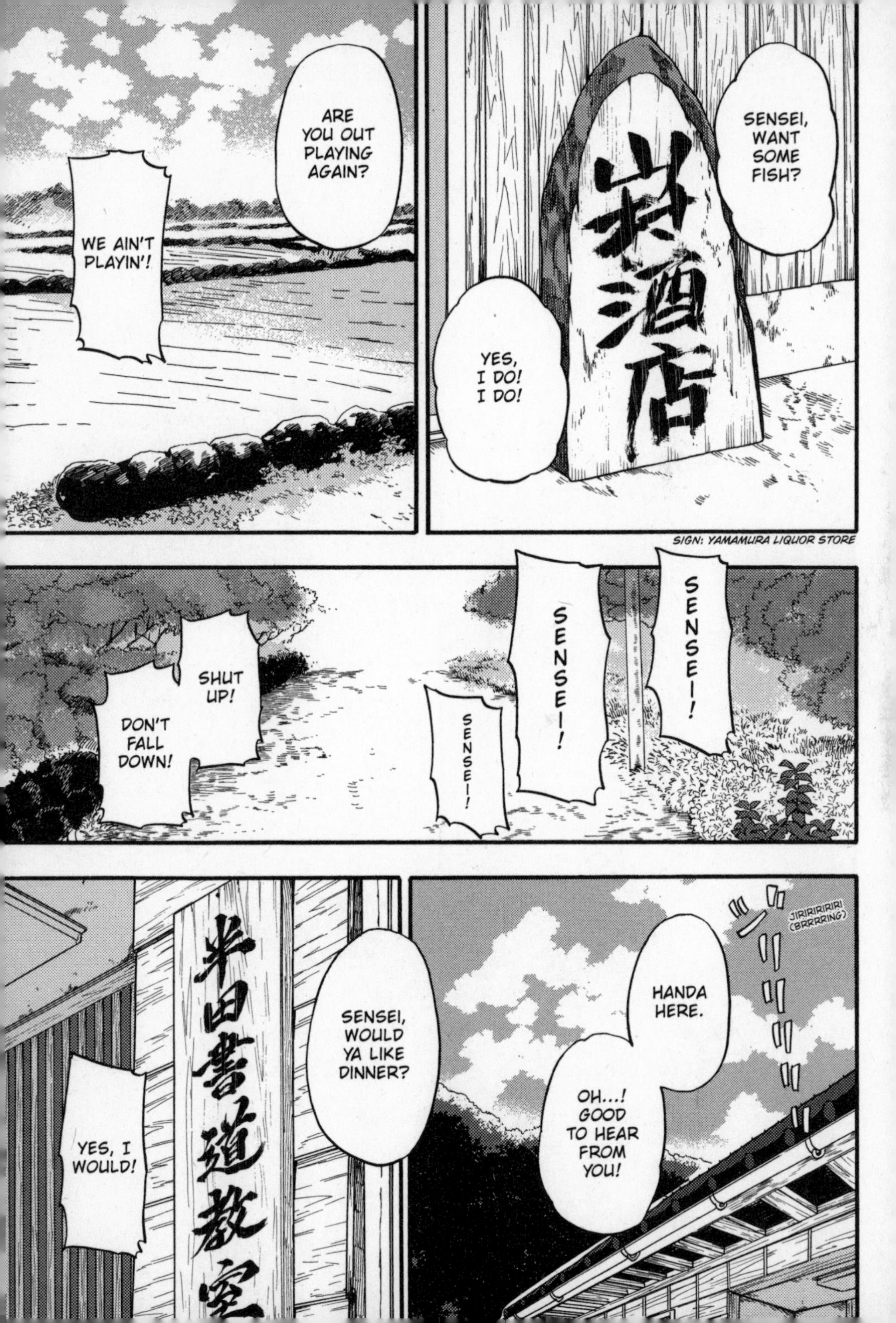
SENSEI, WANT SOME FISH?
YES, I DO! I DO!
SIGN: YAMAMURA LIQUOR STORE
ARE YOU OUT PLAYING AGAIN?
WE AIN'T PLAYIN'!
SENSEI!
SENSEI!
SENSEI!
SHUT UP!
DON'T FALL DOWN!
JIRIRIRIRI (BRRRRING)
HANDA HERE.
OH...! GOOD TO HEAR FROM YOU!
SENSEI, WOULD YA LIKE DINNER?
YES, I WOULD!

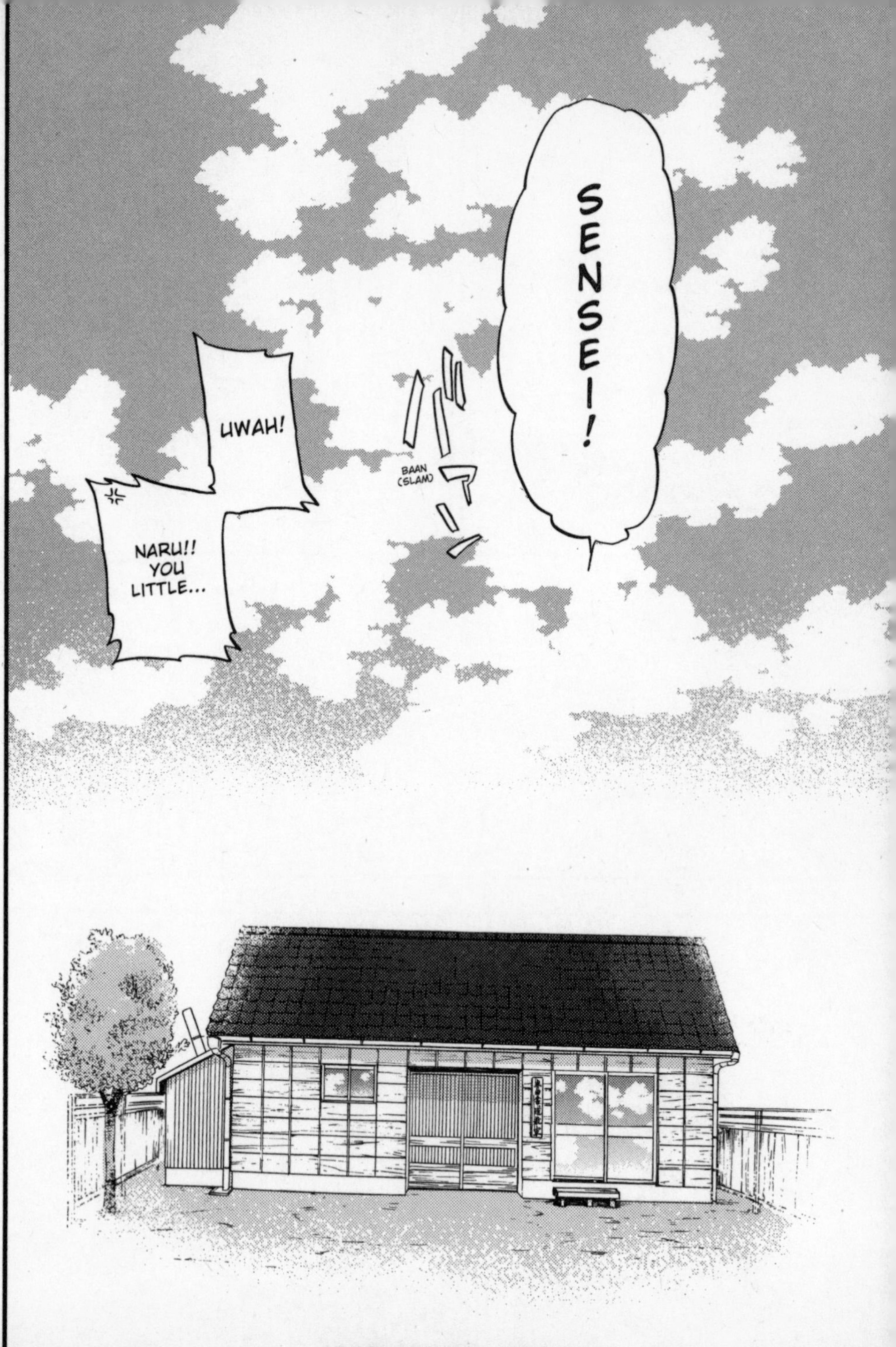
SENSEI!
BAAN (SLAM)
UWAH!
NARU!! YOU LITTLE...

BARAKAMON THE END

COMMON HONORIFICS

no honorific: Indicates familiarity or closeness; if used without permission or reason, addressing someone in this manner would constitute an insult.

-san: The Japanese equivalent of Mr./Mrs./Miss. If a situation calls for politeness, this is the fail-safe honorific.

-sama: Conveys great respect; may also indicate that the social status of the speaker is lower than that of the addressee.

-kun: Used most often when referring to boys, this indicates affection or familiarity. Occasionally used by older men among their peers, but it may also be used by anyone referring to a person of lower standing.

-chan: An affectionate honorific indicating familiarity used mostly in reference to girls; also used in reference to cute persons or animals of either gender.

-sensei: A Japanese term of respect commonly used for teachers, but can also refer to doctors, writers, and artists.

Calligraphy: Japanese calligraphy has a long history and tradition, with roots stemming from ancient China. One of the traditions carried over was the Chinese expression of the "Four Treasures," which refers to the brush, ink, paper, and inkstone used in calligraphy. Traditionally, an inkstick—solidified ink—is ground against an inkstone filled with water in order to produce ink with which to write. This time-consuming process helped to teach patience, which is important in the art of calligraphy. However, modern advances have developed a bottled liquid ink, commonly used by beginners and within the Japanese school system.

Gotou dialect: Many of the villagers, especially the elderly ones, are actually speaking the local Gotou dialect in the original Japanese. This dialect is reflected in the English translation with some of the grammar elements of older Southern American English to give it a more rustic, rural coastal feel without making it too hard to read. (It's not meant to replicate any particular American accent exactly.) This approach is similar to how dialect is made accessible in Japanese media, including *Barakamon*, because a complete dialect with all of its different vocabulary would be practically incomprehensible to most Tokyo residents.

Yen: One hundred yen is roughly equivalent to one US dollar.

PAGE 15
"No inprovement!": Naru is mispronouncing the Japanese word *kawaribae* ("change for the better") as *kawariboe*.

PAGE 24
Yuigadokuson (I Alone Am Holy): You might recognize this from Volume 4 as the name of Miwa's dad's fishing boat.

PAGE 54
"rank" and **"level"**: Japanese arts, such as calligraphy and *karate*, use two different terms to denote a person's status. The term *kyuu* is used for beginners and intermediates, who start at high *kyuu* numbers and count down as they advance to the top at *ikkyuu* ("first level"). *Dan* starts with *ichidan* ("first rank") and counts upward. It is used for those who have passed beyond all the

kyuu levels and now count as expert enough to be a pro or teacher in the art.

PAGE 62
In Shinto belief, an ***aramitama*** is the less-civilized aspect o spirit, which must be pacified by proper ritual and worship for the spirit to settle down and show its more peaceful an aspects. Though Tama also used it as part of her pen name Aramitama, in Volume 9, here it's in simple *hiragana*, witho *kanji*, and without the masculine given name, Kyouya.

Shibari-chan: The word *shibari* means "binding" or "tying in this case, it's referring to her small piece of tied-up hair.

PAGE 63
"stickin' up for me": The Japanese term Tama u *miuchihyou*, which refers to the act of voting for a perso because you have a close relationship with them.

PAGE 97
"It's candy and the lash!": The Japanese phrase *ame* means "candy and whip" and is equivalent to the Englis "carrot and stick."

PAGE 123
"streaking": *Kasure* is a lesser-known calligraphy term fo that have streaks of white showing through instead of be ink-color, produced by using a relatively dry brush.

PAGE 130
"NON." **"Why French!?"**: In the original Japanese, "NO!" prompting Miwa to say "Why English!?"

PAGE 139
A **bosun**, also known as a boatswain, supervises the deck ship to ensure the vessel itself is properly maintained.

PAGE 158
nitsuke: Fish and/or vegetables boiled in soy sauce.

PAGE 183
First-year Sensei: The original, *ichinen-sensei*, is *ichinens* grader") with the *kanji sen* inserted.

PAGE 184
Zenzai is a sweet *azuki*-bean soup which can be served co with pieces of *mochi*.

PAGE 194
"steamed cake": *Mushipan* is cake that has been steame of baked.

PAGE 227
"dicey": The dialect term Grampa used was *appai kurushik* the note explains means the same as *abunakkashii* ("dange

BARAKAMON

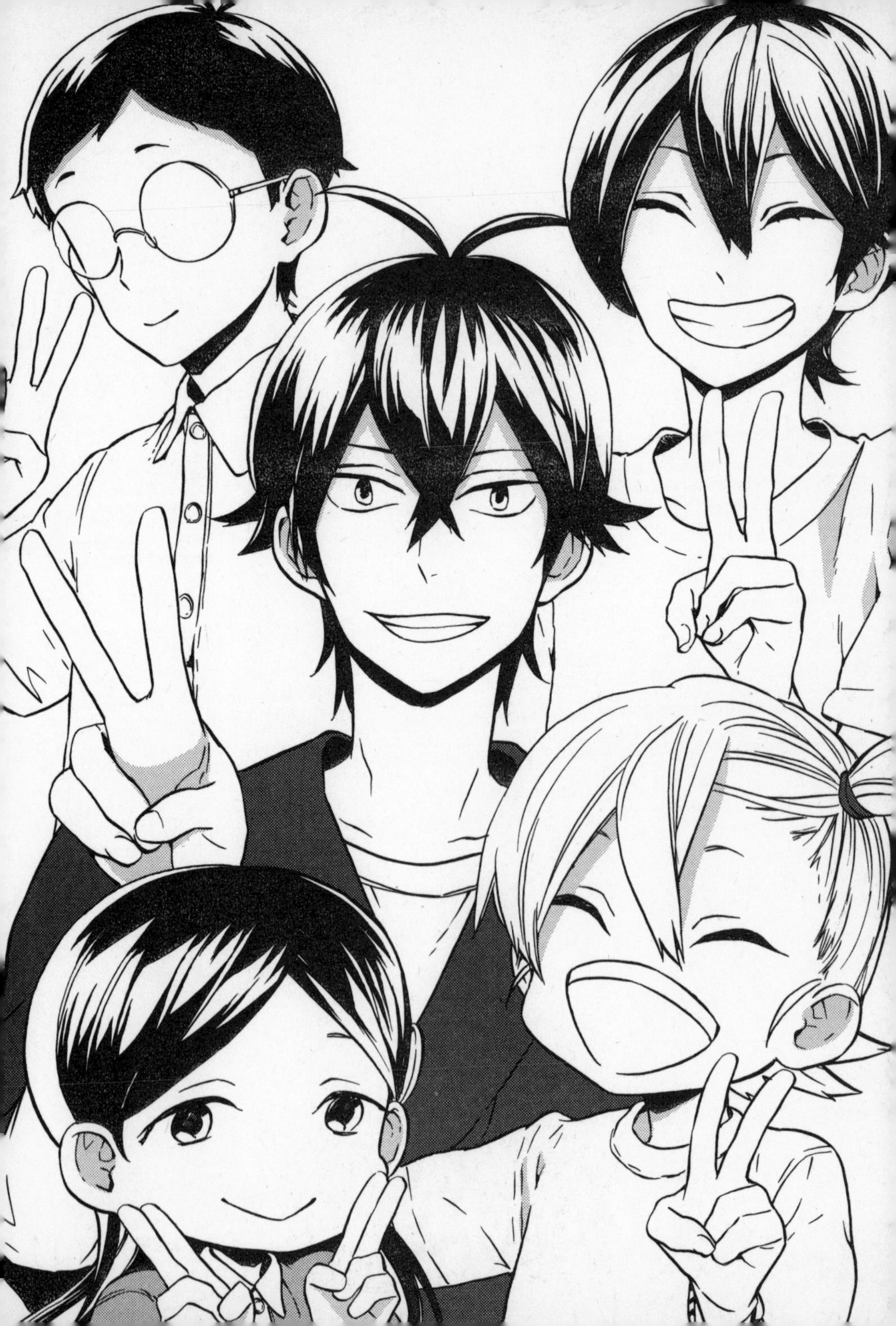

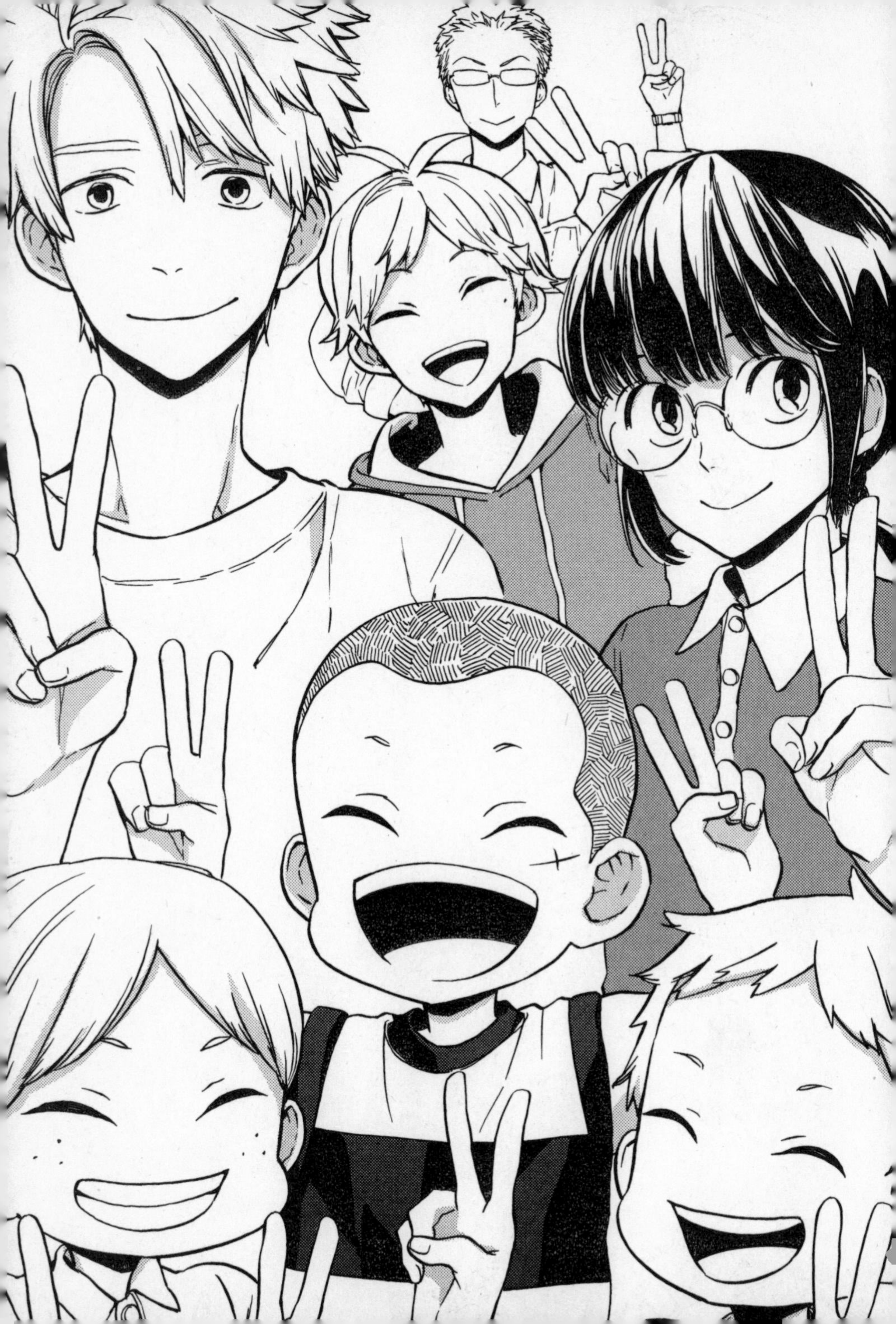

The Phantomhive family has a butler who's almost too good to be true...

...or maybe he's just too good to be human.

Black Butler

YANA TOBOSO

VOLUMES 1-23 IN STORES NOW!

Yen Press

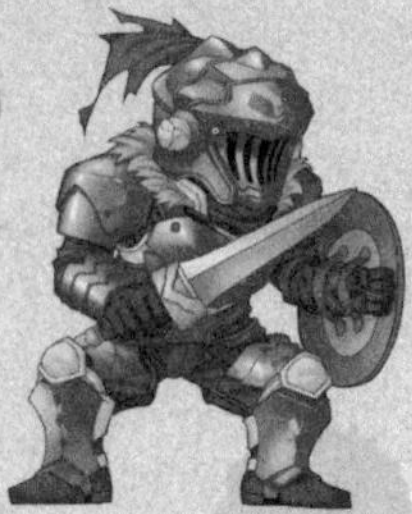

HE DOES NOT LET ANYONE ROLL THE DICE.

A young Priestess joins her first adventuring party, but blind to the dangers, they almost immediately find themselves in trouble. It's Goblin Slayer who comes to their rescue—a man who has dedicated his life to the extermination of all goblins by any means necessary. A dangerous, dirty, and thankless job, but he does it better than anyone. And when rumors of his feats begin to circulate, there's no telling who might come calling next...

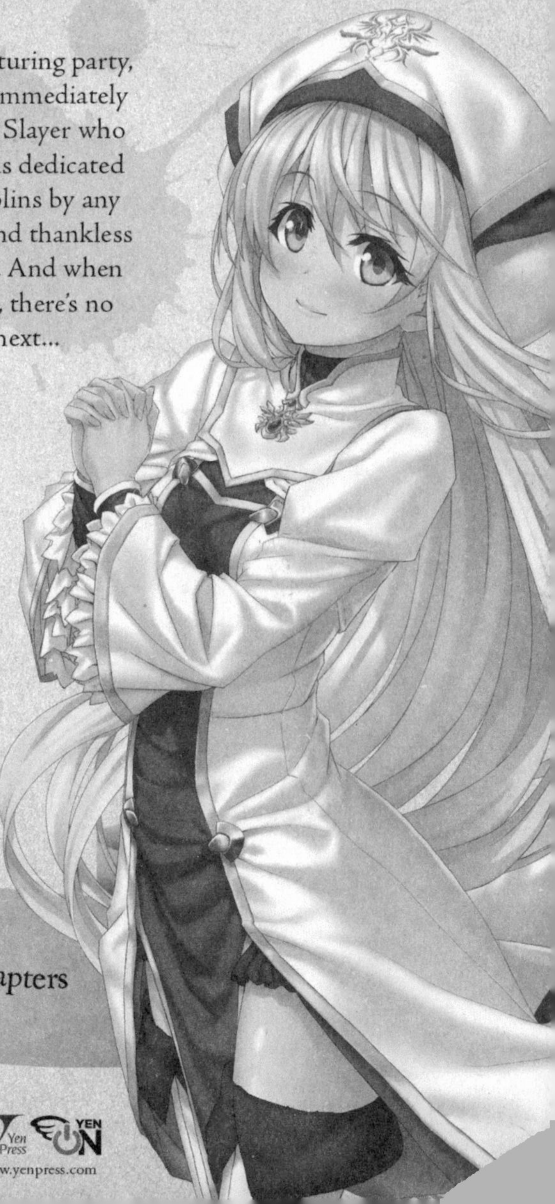

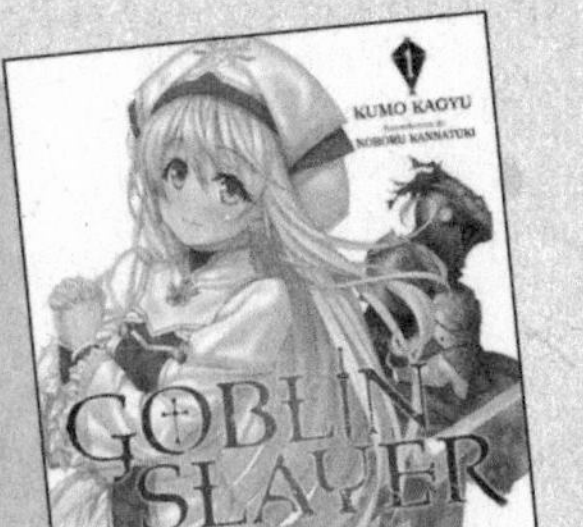
1
KUMO KAGYU
NOBORU KANNATUKI
GOBLIN SLAYER

Light Novel
V. 1-2
Available
Now!

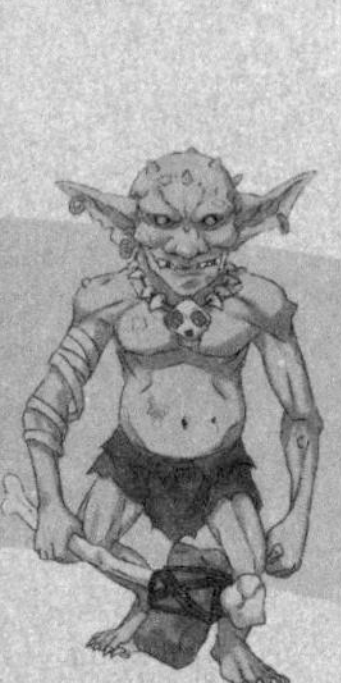

Check out the
simul-pub manga chapters
every month!

Yen Press YEN ON

www.yenpress.com

BARAKAMON 18

Satsuki Yoshino

Translation/Adaptation: Krista Shipley, Karie Shipley
Lettering: Lys Blakeslee

Barakamon Vol. 18 © 2018 Satsuki Yoshino SQUARE ENIX CO., LTD. First published in Japan in 2018 by SQUARE ENIX CO., LTD. English translation rights arranged with SQUARE ENIX CO., LTD. and Yen Press, LLC through Tuttle-Mori Agency, Inc.

English translation © 2019 by SQUARE ENIX CO., LTD.

Yen Press
150 West 30th Street, 19th Floor
New York, NY 10001

Visit us at yenpress.com
facebook.com/yenpress
twitter.com/yenpress
yenpress.tumblr.com
instagram.com/yenpress

First Yen Press Edition: August 2019

Yen Press is an imprint of Yen Press, LLC.
The Yen Press name and logo are trademarks of Yen Press, LLC.

Library of Congress Control Number: 2015296448

ISBNs: 978-1-9753-5818-1 (paperback)
978-1-9753-8428-9 (ebook)

10 9 8 7 6 5 4 3 2 1

WOR

Printed in the United States of America